# Prentice Hall LITERATURE

## PENGUIN  EDITION

# Reader's Notebook

*Grade Seven*

**PEARSON**

Upper Saddle River, New Jersey
Boston, Massachusetts
Chandler, Arizona
Glenview, Illinois

**PEARSON**

ISBN: 978-0-13-366674-8

4 5 6 7 8 9 10   V001   17 16 15 14 13 12 11 10

# ACKNOWLEDGMENTS

Grateful acknowledgment is made to the following for copyrighted material:

**Miriam Altshuler Literary Agency**
"Treasure of Lemon Brown" by Walter Dean Myers from *Boy's Life Magazine, March 1983*. Copyright © 1983, by Walter Dean Myers. Used by permission of Miriam Altshuler Literary Agency, on behalf of Walter Dean Myers.

**American National Red Cross**
"How to Recognize Venomous Snakes in North America" Copyright © 1992 by The American National Red Cross. Courtesy of the American National Red Cross. All rights reserved in all countries. Used by permission.

**Americas Magazine**
"Mongoose on the Loose" reprinted from *Americas*, a bimonthly magazine published by the General Secretariat of the Organization of American States in English and Spanish. Content may not be copied without written permission. Used by permission.

**Arte Publico Press, Inc.**
"Maestro" is used with permission from the publisher of *Borders* by Pat Mora. (Houston: Arte Publico Press—University of Houston © 1986). "Bailando" from *Chants* by Pat Mora. Used with permission from the publisher of *Chants* (Houston: Arte Publico Press—University of Houston copyright © 1985).

**Atheneum Books for Young Readers, an imprint of Simon & Schuster**
"Papa's Parrot" from *Every Living Thing* by Cynthia Rylant. Text copyright © 1985 Cynthia Rylant. Used by permission of Atheneum Books for Young Readers, an imprint of Simon & Schuster Children's Publishing Division.

**Bantam Books, a division of Random House, Inc.**
"The Eternal Frontier" from *Frontier* by Louis L'Amour, Photographs by David Muench, copyright © 1984 by Louis L'Amour Enterprises, Inc. Used by permission of Bantam Books, a division of Random House, Inc.

**Curtis Brown Ltd.**
"Two Haiku" ("O foolish ducklings..." and "After the moon sets...") first appeared in *Cricket Songs: Japanese Haiku*, published by Harcourt. Copyright © 1964 by Harry Behn. "Suzy and Leah" first published in *American Girl Magazine*. Copyright © 1993 by Jane Yolen. Used by permission of Curtis Brown, Ltd.

**Carus Publishing Company**
"The Rhythms of Rap" by Kathiann M. Kowalski from *Odyssey's March 2002 issue: Music: Why Do We Love It?* Copyright © 2002, Cobblestone Publishing, 30 Grove Street, Suite C, Peterborough, NH 03458. All rights reserved. Used by permission of Carus Publishing Company.

(Acknowledgments continue on page V71)

# CONTENTS

# CONTENTS

# CONTENTS

# CONTENTS

# UNIT 3 Nonfiction

**MODEL SELECTIONS**

## "What Makes a Rembrandt a Rembrandt?" by Richard Muhlberger

## "Life Without Gravity" by Robert Zimmerman

## "Conversational Ballgames" by Nancy Masterson Sakamoto

## "I Am a Native of North America" by Chief Dan George

## "Volar: To Fly" by Judith Ortiz Cofer

**INFORMATIONAL TEXT**

## Keeping It Quiet

# CONTENTS

## UNIT 4 Poetry

# CONTENTS

# CONTENTS

# CONTENTS

# CONTENTS

© Pearson Education

As you read your hardcover student edition of *Prentice Hall Literature* use the ***Reader's Notebook*** to guide you in learning and practicing the skills presented. In addition, many selections in your student edition are presented here in an interactive format. The notes and instruction will guide you in applying reading and literary skills and in thinking about the selection. The examples on these pages show you how to use the notes as a companion when you read.

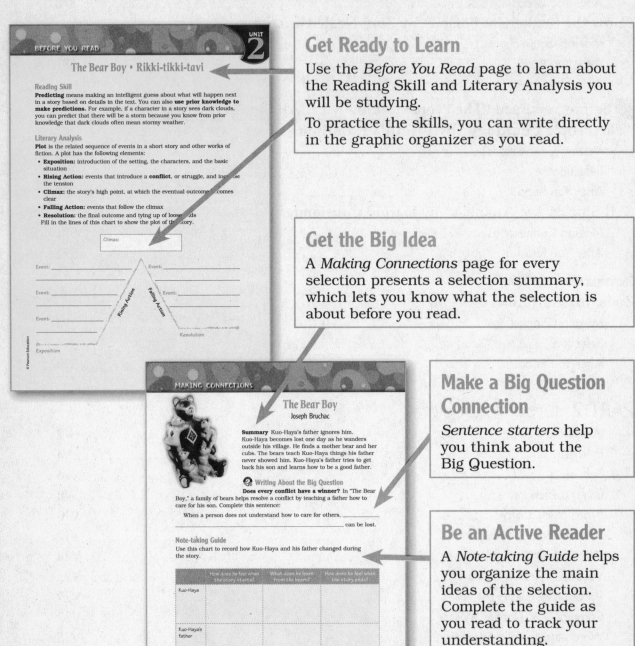

## Get Ready to Learn

Use the *Before You Read* page to learn about the Reading Skill and Literary Analysis you will be studying.

To practice the skills, you can write directly in the graphic organizer as you read.

## Get the Big Idea

A *Making Connections* page for every selection presents a selection summary, which lets you know what the selection is about before you read.

## Make a Big Question Connection

*Sentence starters* help you think about the Big Question.

## Be an Active Reader

A *Note-taking Guide* helps you organize the main ideas of the selection. Complete the guide as you read to track your understanding.

## The Bear Boy
Joseph Bruchac

Long ago, in a Pueblo village, a boy named Kuo-Haya lived with his father. But his father did not treat him well. In his heart he still mourned the death of his wife, Kuo-Haya's mother, and did not enjoy doing things with his son. He did not teach his boy how to run. He did not show him how to wrestle. He was always too busy.

As a result, Kuo-Haya was a timid boy and walked about stooped over all of the time. When the other boys raced or wrestled, Kuo-Haya slipped away. He spent much of his time alone.

Time passed, and the boy reached the age when his father should have been helping him get ready for his initiation into manhood. Still Kuo-Haya's father paid no attention at all to his son.

One day Kuo-Haya was out walking far from the village, toward the cliffs where the bears lived. Now the people of the village always knew they must stay away from these cliffs, for the bear was a very powerful animal. It was said that if someone saw a bear's tracks and followed them, he might never come back. But Kuo-Haya had never been told about this. When he came upon the tracks of a bear, Kuo-Haya followed them along an arroyo, a small canyon[1] cut by a winding stream, up into the mesas.[2] The tracks led into a little box canyon below some caves. There, he came upon some bear cubs.

When they saw Kuo-Haya, the little bears ran away. But Kuo-Haya sat down and called to them in a friendly voice.

**Vocabulary Development**
**mourned** (mawrnd) v. was very sad about
**timid** (TIM id) adj. shy
**initiation** (i ni shee AY shun) n. process by which one becomes a member of a group

1. **canyon** (KAN yuhn) n. long narrow valley between high cliffs, often with a stream flowing through it.
2. **mesas** (MAY suhz) n. plateaus (or flat-topped hills) with steep sides.

The Bear Boy 97

---

**TAKE NOTES**

**Activate Prior Knowledge**
How do you expect people and bears to interact?

**Literary Analysis**
The **plot** of a story is the series of events in the story. One element of a plot is the rising action that increases tension. Underline the sentences in the bracketed paragraph that build tension in the story.

**Stop to Reflect**
Kuo-Haya does not know that he should keep away from bear tracks. Who should have told him this?

**Reading Check**
Underline the sentence that tells why Kuo-Haya's father does not play with him.

---

## Read the Text
Text set in a wider margin provides the author's actual words.

Text set in a narrow margin provides a summary of selection events or details.

## Take Notes
Side-column questions accompany the selections that appear in the Reader's Notebooks. These questions are a built-in tutor to help you practice the skills and understand what you read.

## Mark the Text
Use write-on lines to answer questions in the side column. You may also want to use the lines for your own notes.

When you see a pencil, you should underline, circle, or mark the text as indicated.

---

### AFTER YOU READ
## The Bear Boy

1. **Compare and Contrast:** How is Kuo-Haya's life with the bears different from his life in the village?

2. **Connect:** How does seeing a bee help the father decide how to get his son back?

---

...ion based on prior knowledge that you ...se this chart.

| | Prior Knowledge | = | Prediction |
|---|---|---|---|

...events in the **plot** that increase the

---

### SUPPORT FOR WRITING AND EXTEND YOUR LEARNING

**Writing: Informative Article**
Write an **informative article** about how a mother bear raises her cubs. Use details from the story to write your article. Focus on the answers to these questions to write your article.

- How did the mother bear treat her cubs?

- What did the mother bear teach Kuo-Haya?

**Listening and Speaking: Informal Debate**
With your partner, hold an **informal debate** on the training of wild animals. In an informal debate, you and your partner exchange opinions on a topic. Choose whether you will argue for or against the training of wild animals. Write reasons why your partner should agree with your side of the argument. Use these notes during your debate.

- Write about times when animal training should be used.

- Write reasons that support your opinion.

- Write weaknesses in your position.

The Bear Boy 103

---

## Check Your Understanding
Questions after every selection help you think about the selection. You can use the write-on lines and charts to answer the questions. Then, share your ideas in class discussions.

## Go Beyond the Selection
This page provides step-by-step guidance for completing the Writing and Extend Your Learning activities presented in your student edition.

## Selections and Skills Support

The pages in your *Reader's Notebook* go with the pages in the hardcover student edition. The pages in the *Reader's Notebook* allow you to participate in class instruction and take notes on the concepts and selections.

## Before You Read

**Build Skills** Follow along in your *Reader's Notebook* as your teacher introduces the **Reading Skill** and **Literary Analysis** instruction. The graphic organizer is provided on this page so that you can take notes right in your *Reader's Notebook.*

**Preview** Use this page for the selection your teacher assigns.

- The **Summary** gives you an outline of the selection.
- Use the **Reading-Writing Connection** to understand the big idea of the selection and join in the class discussion about the ideas.
- Use the **Note-taking Guide** while you read the story. This will help you organize and remember information you will need to answer questions about the story later.

## While You Read

**Selection Text and Sidenotes** You can read the full text of one selection in each pair in your *Reader's Notebook.*

- You can write in the *Reader's Notebook.* Underline important details to help you find them later.
- Use the **Take Notes** column to jot down your reactions, ideas, and answers to questions about the text. If your assigned selection is not the one that is included in the *Reader's Notebook,* use sticky notes to make your own **Take Notes** section in the side column as you read the selection in the hardcover student edition.

## After You Read

**Apply the Skills** Use this page to answer questions about the selection directly in your *Reader's Notebook.* For example, you can complete the graphic organizer that is in the hardcover student edition by writing on the page in your *Reader's Notebook.*

**Support for Writing and Extend Your Learning** Use this page to help you jot down notes and ideas as you prepare to do one or more of the projects assigned with the selection.

**Other Features in the *Reader's Notebook*** You will also find note-taking opportunities for these features:

- Learning About the Genre
- Support for the Model Selection
- Support for Reading Informational Materials

# The Three-Century Woman

**Fiction** is writing that tells a story. The story can include some facts, be inspired by facts, or be completely made up.

## Elements of Fiction

All works of fiction share these basic elements:

- **characters**—made-up people or animals
- **plot**—a made-up series of events
- **setting**—a time and place, which can be real or made up
- **narrator**—the speaker who tells the story
- **point of view**—the narrator's relationship to the story. In **first-person point of view**, the narrator is a character in the story. In **third-person point of view**, the narrator is outside the story.
- **theme**—a message about life

| Types of Fiction | |
|---|---|
| Novel | Long work of fiction, such as *Little House on the Prairie*. A novel can have a main plot and one or more sub-plots. |
| Novella | Long work of fiction that is shorter than a novel but longer than a short story |
| Short Story | Brief work of fiction with only one main plot. |

# The Fall of the Hindenburg

Nonfiction is writing that presents facts, details, and other true information.

## Elements of Nonfiction

Nonfiction is different from fiction in these ways:

- Nonfiction contains real people, events, and ideas.
- Nonfiction works are told from the **point of view** of the author, a real person.
- Nonfiction presents facts or discusses ideas about real issues.
- Nonfiction sometimes reflects the **historical context**—the real time and place, including facts about the society and culture.

| Types of Nonfiction | |
|---|---|
| Biography | Story of someone's life told by someone else |
| Autobiography | Story of the author's life |
| Memoir | Writer's thoughts and feelings about the past |
| Letter | Communication from one person to another |
| Journal | Daily record of life and events, sometimes private |
| Diary | Daily record of life and events, usually private |
| Essay | Brief nonfiction writing about a single topic |
| Article | Brief nonfiction writing for a magazine, newspaper, or other publication |
| Informational texts | Documents such as textbooks, instructions, and applications |

# The Three-Century Woman
## Richard Peck

**Summary** Megan and her mom visit Megan's great-grandmother. Her name is Mrs. Breckenridge. She was born in 1899. By 2001, she has experienced three centuries. News people come to interview her. Mrs. Breckenridge gives the reporters some great stories about her past. The stories are not true.

## Note-taking Guide

Use this story map to record the elements of fiction in the story.

| | |
|---|---|
| Characters | Mom, Megan, Great-grandmother Breckenridge, and news people |
| Setting | |
| Narrator | |
| Events of the Plot | • Mom and Megan go to Whispering Oaks on New Year's Day.<br>•<br>•<br>•<br>• |
| Ending | |

# The Three-Century Woman
## Richard Peck

"I guess if you live long enough," my mom said to Aunt Gloria, "you get your fifteen minutes of fame."

Mom was on the car phone to Aunt Gloria. The minute Mom rolls out of the garage, she's on her car phone. It's state-of-the-art and better than her car.

We were heading for Whispering Oaks to see my great-grandmother Breckenridge, who's lived there since I was a little girl. They call it an Elder Care Facility. Needless to say, I hated going.

The reason for Great-grandmother's fame is that she was born in 1899. Now it's January 2001. If you're one of those people who claim the new century begins in 2001, not 2000, even you have to agree that Great-grandmother Breckenridge has lived in three centuries. This is her claim to fame.

We waited for a light to change along by Northbrook Mall, and I gazed <u>fondly</u> over at it. Except for the Multiplex,[1] it was closed because of New Year's Day. I have a <u>severe</u>[2] mall habit. But I'm fourteen, and the mall is the place without homework. Aunt Gloria's voice filled the car.

"If you take my advice," she told Mom, "you'll keep those Whispering Oaks people from letting the media in to interview Grandma. Interview her my foot! Honestly. She doesn't know where she is, let alone how many centuries she's lived in. The poor old soul. Leave her in peace. She's already got one foot in the—"

"Gloria, your trouble is you have no sense of history." Mom gunned across the <u>intersection</u>. "You got a C in history."

"I was sick a lot that year," Aunt Gloria said.

---

**Vocabulary Development**

**fondly** (FAHND lee) *adv.* showing kindness and love

**intersection** (IN ter sek shuhn) *n.* a place where two or more roads cross

---

1. **Multiplex** *n.* a movie theater with a large number of screens for showing different films.

2. **severe** (suh VIR) *adj.* very bad or serious.

**Activate Prior Knowledge**

Think about an older person who tells stories about the past. How do you feel about the stories?

_____

_____

_____

_____

_____

_____

**Fiction**

The **setting** of a story is where and when it takes place. Circle the sentence in the bracketed paragraph that tells where the characters are going.

**Fiction**

What have you learned about Great-grandmother Breckenridge so far? List three facts about her.

_____

_____

_____

_____

_____

### Fiction

In **first-person point of view**, the narrator uses words such as *I*, *me*, *my*, and *mine* and *we*, *us*, *our*, and *ours*. Circle the words in the first bracketed paragraph that show **first-person point of view.**

### Fiction

Read the second bracketed passage. What problem does Mom have with the news reporters?

_____

_____

### Reading Check ✎

Megan, her mom, and her aunt find people in Great-grandma's wing of the house. Underline the words that tell who these people are.

"Sick of history," Mom mumbled.

"I heard that," Aunt Gloria said.

They bickered on, but I tuned them out. Then when we turned in at Whispering Pines, a sound truck from IBC-TV was blocking the drive.

"Good grief," Mom murmured. "TV."

"I told you," Aunt Gloria said, but Mom switched her off. She parked in a frozen rut.

"I'll wait in the car," I said. "I have homework."

"Get out of the car," Mom said.

If you get so old you have to be put away, Whispering Oaks isn't that bad. It smells all right, and a Christmas tree glittered in the lobby. A real tree. On the other hand, you have to push a red button to unlock the front door. I guess it's to keep the inmates from escaping, though Great-grandmother Breckenridge wasn't going anywhere and hadn't for twenty years.

When we got to her wing, the hall was full of camera crews and a woman from the suburban newspaper with a notepad.

Mom sighed. It was like that first day of school when you think you'll be okay until the teachers learn your name. Stepping over a cable, we stopped at Great-grandma's door, and they were on to us.

"Who are you people to Mrs. Breckenridge?" the newspaperwoman said. "I want names."

These people were seriously pushy. And the TV guy was wearing more makeup than Mom. It dawned on me that they couldn't get into Great-grandma's room without her permission. Mom turned on them.

"Listen, you're not going to be interviewing my grandmother," she said in a quiet bark. "I'll be glad to tell you anything you want to know about her, but you're not going in there. She's got nothing to say, and . . . she needs a lot of rest."

"Is it Alzheimer's?"[3] the newswoman asked. "Because we're thinking Alzheimer's."

"Think what you want," Mom said. "But this is as far as you get. And you people with the camera and the light, you're not going in there either. You'd scare her to death, and then I'd sue the pants off you."

---

3. **Alzheimer's** (AHLTS hy muhrz) *n.* a progressive disease in which brain cells degenerate, leading to severe dementia.

They pulled back.

But a voice came wavering out of Great-grandma's room. Quite an eerie, echoing voice.

"Let them in!" the voice said.

It had to be Great-grandma Breckenridge. Her roommate had died. "Good grief," Mom muttered, and the press surged forward.

Mom and I went in first, and our eyes popped. Great-grandma was usually flat out in the bed, dozing, with her teeth in a glass and a book in her hand. Today she was bright-eyed and propped up. She wore a fuzzy pink bed jacket. A matching bow was stuck in what remained of her hair.

"Oh, for pity's sake," Mom said. "They've got her done up like a Barbie doll."

Great-grandma peered from the bed at Mom. "And who are you?" she asked.

"I'm Ann," Mom said carefully. "This is Megan," she said, meaning me.

"That's right," Great-grandma said. "At least you know who you are. Plenty around this place don't."

The guy with the camera on his shoulder barged in. The other guy turned on a blinding light.

Great-grandma blinked. In the glare we noticed she wore a trace of lipstick. The TV <u>anchor</u> elbowed the woman reporter aside and stuck a mike in Great-grandma's face. Her claw hand came out from under the covers and tapped it.

"Is this thing on?" she inquired.

"Yes, ma'am," the TV anchor said in his broadcasting voice. "Don't you worry about all this modern technology. We don't understand half of it ourselves." He gave her his big, five-thirty news smile and settled on the edge of the bed. There was room for him. She was tiny.

"We're here to congratulate you for having lived in three centuries—for being a Three-Century Woman! A great achievement!"

Great-grandma waved a casual claw. "Nothing to it," she said. "You sure this mike's on? Let's do this in one take."

**Vocabulary Development**

**anchor** (ANG ker) *n.* news reporter

**Stop to Reflect**

Earlier, Aunt Gloria said that Great-grandma Breckenridge "doesn't know where she is. . . . She's already got one foot in the—". Read the first bracketed paragraph. Do you think Aunt Gloria is correct? Explain.

_____

_____

_____

**Fiction**

A **short story** has one main plot, or series of events. Read the second bracketed section. Tell what is happening in the plot now.

_____

_____

_____

**Reading Check** ✏️

What does Great-grandma think about having reporters interview her? Circle the words that show her opinion.

## Fiction

A **character** is a made-up person or animal. You can learn about characters from details in the story. Read the first bracketed paragraph. What can you tell about Megan's mom?

_____

_____

_____

_____

_____

## Fiction

Read the second bracketed paragraph. Is Great-grandma enjoying the interview? How do you know?

_____

_____

_____

_____

_____

_____

## Reading Check

What major event in history does Great-grandma say she lived through? Circle it.

The cameraman snorted and moved in for a closer shot. Mom stood still as a statue, wondering what was going to come out of Great-grandma's mouth next.

"Mrs. Breckenridge," the anchor said, "to what do you attribute[4] your long life?"

"I was only married once," Great-grandma said. "And he died young."

The anchor stared. "Ah. And anything else?"

"Yes. I don't look back. I live in the present."

The camera panned around the room. This was all the present she had, and it didn't look like much.

"You live for the present," the anchor said, looking for an angle, "even now?"

Great-grandma nodded. "Something's always happening. Last night I fell off the bed pan."

Mom groaned.

The cameraman pulled in for a tighter shot. The anchor seemed to search his mind. You could tell he thought he was a great interviewer, though he had no sense of humor. A tiny smile played around Great-grandma's wrinkled lips.

"But you've lived through amazing times, Mrs. Breckenridge. And you never think back about them?"

Great-grandma stroked her chin and considered. "You mean you want to hear something interesting? Like how I lived through the San Francisco earthquake—the big one of oh-six?"[5]

Beside me, Mom stirred. We were crowded over by the dead lady's bed. "You survived the 1906 San Francisco earthquake?" the anchor said.

Great-grandma gazed at the ceiling, lost in thought.

"I'd have been about seven years old. My folks and I were staying at that big hotel. You know the one. I slept in a cot at the foot of their bed. In the middle of the night, that room gave a shake, and the chiffonier walked right across the floor. You know what a chiffonier is?"

"A chest of drawers?" the anchor said.

"Close enough," Great-grandma said. "And the pictures flapped on the walls. We had to walk down

4. **attribute** (uh TRIB yoot) v. think of as caused by.

5. **oh-six** 1906, the year a large earthquake hit San Francisco.

twelve flights because the <u>elevators</u> didn't work. When we got outside, the streets were ankle-deep in broken glass. You never saw such a mess in your life."

Mom <u>nudged</u> me and hissed: "She's never been to San Francisco. She's never been west of Denver. I've heard her say so."

"Incredible!" the anchor said.

"Truth's stranger than fiction," Great-grandma said, smoothing her sheet.

"And you never think back about it?"

Great-grandma shrugged her little fuzzy pink shoulders. "I've been through too much. I don't have time to remember it all. I was on the Hindenburg when it blew up, you know."

Mom moaned, and the cameraman was practically standing on his head for a close-up.

"The Hindenburg!"

"That big gas thing the Germans built to fly over the Atlantic Ocean. It was called a zeppelin.[6] Biggest thing you ever saw—five city blocks long. It was in May of 1937, before your time. You wouldn't remember. My husband and I were coming back from Europe. No, wait a minute."

Great-grandma cocked her head and <u>pondered</u> for the camera.

"My husband was dead by then. It was some other man. Anyway, the two of us were coming back on the Hindenburg. It was smooth as silk. You didn't know you were moving. When we flew in over New York, they stopped the ball game at Yankee Stadium to see us passing overhead."

Great-grandma paused, caught up in the memories.

"And then the Hindenburg exploded," the anchor said, prompting her.

## Vocabulary Development

**elevators** (EL uh vay terz) *n.* machines for moving people between different levels of a building

**nudged** (NUDJD) *v.* pushed gently

**pondered** (PAHN derd) *v.* thought about deeply; meditated

6. **zeppelin** (ZEP uh lin) *n.* a large, cigar-shaped airship with separate compartments filled with gas; used from 1900 to 1937.

---

## TAKE NOTES

### Fiction

Read the first bracketed passage. Mom is not enjoying Great-grandma's stories, but the cameraman is. Circle the sentence that shows these two characters' feelings.

### Stop to Reflect

Read the first bracketed passage. What does "standing on his head" mean?

_____

_____

_____

### Fiction

People often feel nervous in front of television cameras. Read the second bracketed passage. How does Great-grandma Breckenridge feel in front of the camera?

_____

_____

### Reading Check

Great-grandma names a second major event in history that she lived through. Circle it.

**Stop to Reflect**

Read the bracketed passage. What do Mom's words tell you about Great-grandma's stories?

_____

_____

_____

**Fiction**

The **theme** is a message about life. State a **theme** in this story about older people.

_____

_____

_____

_____

**Stop to Reflect**

Does Great-grandma think the future will be positive or negative? Give one example to support your answer.

_____

_____

_____

_____

_____

_____

She nodded. "We had no complaints about the trip till then. The luggage was all stacked, and we were coming in at Lakehurst, New Jersey. I was wearing my beige coat—beige or off-white, I forget. Then whoosh! The gondola[7] heated up like an oven, and people peeled out of the windows. We hit the ground and bounced. When we hit again, the door fell off, and I walked out and kept going. When they caught up to me in the parking lot, they wanted to put me in the hospital. I looked down and thought I was wearing a lace dress. The fire had about burned up my coat. And I lost a shoe."

"Fantastic!" the anchor breathed. "What detail!" Behind him the woman reporter was scribbling away on her pad.

"Never," Mom muttered. "Never in her life."

"Ma'am, you are living history!" the anchor said. "In your sensational span of years you've survived two great disasters!"

"Three." Great-grandma patted the bow on her head. "I told you I'd been married."

"And before we leave this <u>venerable</u> lady," the anchor said, flashing a smile for the camera, "we'll ask Mrs. Breckenridge if she has any predictions for this new twenty-first century ahead of us here in the Dawn of the <u>Millennium</u>."

"Three or four predictions," Great-grandma said, and paused again, stretching out her airtime. "Number one, taxes will be higher. Number two, it's going to be harder to find a place to park. And number three, a whole lot of people are going to live as long as I have, so get ready for us."

"And with those wise words," the anchor said, easing off the bed, "we leave Mrs. B—"

**Vocabulary Development**

**venerable** (VEN uhr uh buhl) *adj.* worthy of respect or reverence by reason of age

**Millennium** (muh LEN ee uhm) *n.* the year 2000 or, some people say, the year 2001

7. **gondola** (GAHN duh luh) *n.* a cabin attached to the underside of an airship to hold the motors, instruments, passengers, and so on.

"And one more prediction," she said. "TV's on the way out. Your network ratings are already in the basement. It's all web-sites now. Son, I predict you'll be looking for work."

And that was it. The light went dead. The anchor, looking shaken, followed his crew out the door. When TV's done with you, they're done with you. "Is that a wrap?" Great-grandma asked.

But now the woman from the <u>suburban</u> paper was moving in on her. "Just a few more questions, Mrs. Breckenridge."

"Where you from?" Great-grandma blinked pink-eyed at her.

"The Glenview Weekly Shopper."

"You bring a still photographer with you?" Great-grandma asked.

"Well, no."

"And you never learned shorthand[8] either, did you?"

"Well, no."

"Honey, I only deal with professionals. There's the door."

So then it was just Mom and Great-grandma and I in the room. Mom planted a hand on her hip. "Grandma. Number one, you've never been to San Francisco. And number two, you never saw one of those zeppelin things."

Great-grandma shrugged. "No, but I can read." She nodded to the pile of books on her nightstand with her <u>spectacles</u> folded on top. "You can pick up all that stuff in books."

"And number three," Mom said, "Your husband didn't die young. I can remember Grandpa Breckenridge."

"It was that TV dude in the five-hundred-dollar suit who set me off," Great-grandma said. "He dyes his

Vocabulary Development

**suburban** (suh BER buhn) *adj.* relating to a place where large groups of people live outside of a larger city

**spectacles** (SPEK tuh kuhlz) *n.* an older word for glasses

8. **shorthand** (SHAWRT hand) *n.* a system of speed writing using symbols to represent letters, words, and phrases.

---

## TAKE NOTES

### Stop to Reflect

The first bracketed passage helps show Grandma's strength of character. How does the passage tell you that she is in control here?

_____

_____

_____

_____

### Fiction

Is "The Three-Century Woman" a novel or a short story? How do you know?

_____

_____

_____

### Reading Check

Great-grandma did not experience the San Francisco earthquake or ride on the Hindenburg. How did she know so many details about them? Circle the sentences that give the answer.

## Fiction

Read the bracketed paragraph. The **theme** is a lesson about life. What lesson about older people does Great-grandma explain?

_____

_____

_____

## Stop to Reflect

How does Megan feel about her great-grandma? Support your answer with one example from the text.

_____

_____

_____

hair, did you notice? He made me mad, and it put my nose out of joint. He didn't notice I'm still here. He thought I was nothing but my memories. So I gave him some."

Now Mom and I stood beside her bed.

"I'll tell you something else," Great-grandma said. "And it's no lie."

We waited, holding our breath to hear. Great-grandma Breckenridge was pointing her little old bent finger right at me. "You, Megan," she said. "Once upon a time, I was your age. How scary is that?"

Then she hunched up her little pink shoulders and winked at me. She grinned and I grinned. She was just this little withered-up leaf of a lady in the bed. But I felt like giving her a kiss on her little wrinkled cheek, so I did.

"I'll come and see you more often," I told her.

"Call first," she said. "I might be busy." Then she dozed.

---

Reader's Response: What did you like best about this story? Tell why.

_____

_____

_____

_____

_____

_____

**Vocabulary Development**

**dozed** (DOHZD) _v._ napped, slept for a short time

# The Fall of the Hindenburg

## Michael Morrison

**Summary** The Hindenburg was a German airship. This giant, hydrogen-filled balloon was once the fastest way for the rich to cross the Atlantic. It burst into flames in 1937, just as it was about to land in New Jersey. Thirty-five of the ninety-seven people aboard died. No one knows for sure what caused the fire. It may have been the varnish on the fabric.

## Note-taking Guide

Use this chart to record important facts and details from the article.

| What |
| --- |
| the Hindenburg |
| **When** |
| May 6, 1937 |
| **Where** |
| |
| **What Happened** |
| • burst into flames as it was being pulled down |
| • |
| • |
| **Why** |
| |

## Activate Prior Knowledge

List two things you learned about the Hindenburg in "The Three-Century Woman."

_____

_____

_____

## Nonfiction

With what real event does this nonfiction work deal?

_____

What real person is discussed in this nonfiction work?

_____

_____

## Nonfiction

There are many kinds of nonfiction, including **biographies, diaries**, and **articles**. Explain why this work of nonfiction is classified as an **article**.

_____

_____

## Reading Check ✎

Where did the journey of the Hindenburg begin? Circle the city and country.

---

# The Fall of the Hindenburg
## Michael Morrison

On May 6, 1937, the German <u>airship</u> Hindenburg burst into flames 200 feet over its intended landing spot at New Jersey's Lakehurst Naval Air Station. Thirty-five people on board were killed (13 passengers and 22 crewmen), along with one crewman on the ground.

### 803 Feet Long and 242 Tons

The giant flying vessel measured 803.8 feet in length and weighed approximately 242 tons. Its mostly metal frame was filled with hydrogen. It came complete with sleeping quarters, a library, dining room, and a magnificent lounge, but still managed a top speed of just over 80 miles per hour. The zeppelin had just crossed the Atlantic Ocean after taking off from Frankfurt, Germany $2^{1}/_{2}$ days prior on its first transatlantic voyage of the season. Thirty-six passengers and a crew of 61 were on board.

### Disaster Strikes

As it reached its final destination in New Jersey, it hovered over its landing spot and was beginning to be pulled down to the ground by landing lines by over 200 crewmen when disaster struck. A burst of flame started just forward of the upper fin, then blossomed into an <u>inferno</u> that engulfed the Hindenburg's tail.

### "Oh, the Humanity!"

Many jumped from the burning craft, landed on the soft sand of the naval base below, and lived to tell about it; others weren't so lucky. Herb Morrison, a reporter for WLS Radio in Chicago, happened to be covering the event and cried out the now famous words, "Oh, the Humanity!" The majestic ship turned into a ball of flames on the ground in only 34 seconds.

**Vocabulary Development**
**airship** (ER ship) *n.* a machine that uses a gas-filled balloon to fly
**inferno** (in FER noh) *n.* a very large, hot fire

## Unknown Cause

The cause of the disaster is still uncertain. At the time, many thought the ship had been hit by lightning. Many still believe that the highly flammable hydrogen was the cause. Some Germans even cried foul play, suspecting sabotage intended to <u>sully</u> the reputation of the Nazi regime. NASA research, however, has shown that the highly <u>combustible</u> <u>varnish</u> treating the fabric on the outside of the vessel most likely caused the tragedy.

Reader's Response: Imagine that you saw the Hindenburg burst into flames. Write two or three sentences that you might have written in your diary on that day.

_____

_____

_____

_____

_____

_____

© Pearson Education

### Vocabulary Development

**sully** (SUHL ee) *v.* to make dirty or unclean

**combustible** (kuhm BUS tuh buhl) *adj.* easy to burn

**varnish** (VAHR nish) *n.* a clear liquid painted onto objects to protect them

**Nonfiction**

**Historical context** is the real time and place for an event. When the Hindenburg was destroyed, which nation or group was becoming an enemy of the United States?

_____

_____

**Stop to Reflect**

Why is the Hindenburg so famous?

_____

_____

_____

# Fiction and Nonfiction

1. **Respond:** Would you want someone like Great-grandmother Breckenridge as a friend? Why or why not?

   _____

   _____

2. **Interpret:** Describe Great-grandma Breckenridge and the message she teaches in the story. Use this chart. In the first column, write two things Grandma says or does in response to the news people. In the second column, tell what each reply or action shows about Great-grandma's character and her ideas about herself. In the last column, explain the theme or message that these ideas convey.

| Her Comments | Her Character | Message/Theme |
|---|---|---|
|  |  |  |

3. **Fiction:** How can you tell that "The Three-Century Woman" is a work of **fiction**?

   _____

   _____

4. **Nonfiction:** How does the fictional account of the Hindenburg differ from the **nonfiction** article?

   _____

   _____

   _____

## Oral Report

- Richard Peck's other fiction includes many novels for both adults and young adults. He says that in fiction, "you can go anywhere and be anybody." He also believes that his experience as a junior high school teacher helped make him a writer. He decided that he wanted to write for the students he taught. In many cases, his novels teach about life. They help show young adult readers about problems they face and people they meet.

**What I learned from Peck's writing:**

_____

_____

_____

_____

- Search the Internet. Use search terms such as "Richard Peck" and "interview." Choose reliable sites from your list of hits. Reliable sites include sites that end in *.gov, .edu,* or *.org.*

**What I learned from my own Internet research about Peck:**

_____

_____

_____

_____

- Watch the video interview with Richard Peck. List something you learned in the interview that you did not learn in your research.

_____

_____

_____

_____

# Papa's Parrot • mk

## Reading Skill

**Context**, the words and phrases surrounding a word, can help you understand a word you do not know. When you come across an unfamiliar word, **use context clues to unlock the meaning**. Look for a word or words that might mean the same thing as or have the opposite meaning of the unfamiliar word. In addition, you may find definitions, examples, or descriptions of the unfamiliar word.

As you read, use context clues to find possible meanings for unfamiliar words. Check the words in a dictionary after you read.

## Literary Analysis

**Narrative writing** is any type of writing that tells a story. The act or process of telling a story is called **narration**.

- A narrative is usually told in chronological order—the order in which events occurred in time.
- A narrative may be fiction, nonfiction, or poetry.

Use this graphic organizer to record events from the story.

| Sequence of Events |
|---|
| Beginning |
| Middle |
| End |

# Papa's Parrot
## Cynthia Rylant

**Summary** Harry Tillian is now in junior high. He does not visit his father's store as often as he used to. Mr. Tillian buys a talking parrot for the store. One day, Mr. Tillian gets sick and must go to the hospital. The parrot helps Harry realize that Mr. Tillian misses Harry.

## Writing About the Big Question

**What is the best way to find the truth?** In "Papa's Parrot," the truth about a father's feelings toward his son comes out in an unexpected way. Complete this sentence:

Sometimes we can discover the truth by _____.

## Note-taking Guide

Use this chart to list the order of events in the story.

| Before Harry Starts Junior High | After Harry Starts Junior High | After Harry's Father Gets Sick |
| --- | --- | --- |
| • Harry visits his father's store often. | • Harry stops going to his father's store. | |
| _____ | _____ | _____ |
| _____ | _____ | _____ |

## Activate Prior Knowledge

Think about a time when your feelings about someone close to you changed. What caused your feelings to change?

_____

_____

## Reading Skill

Read the underlined sentences. The word *company* can mean either "a place of business" or "people with whom you enjoy spending time." Circle the correct meaning of *company* in this story. Now, circle the **context clues** that helped you find the meaning.

## Literary Analysis

**Narratives** tell stories. Read the bracketed paragraph. What details about Harry and his friends make this story seem true?

_____

_____

_____

_____

# Papa's Parrot

## Cynthia Rylant

Though his father was fat and merely owned a candy and nut shop, Harry Tillian liked his papa. Harry stopped liking candy and nuts when he was around seven, but, in spite of this, he and Mr. Tillian had remained friends and were still friends the year Harry turned twelve.

For years, after school, Harry had always stopped in to see his father at work. Many of Harry's friends stopped there, too, to spend a few cents choosing penny candy from the giant bins or to sample Mr. Tillian's latest batch of roasted peanuts. Mr. Tillian looked forward to seeing his son and his son's friends every day. He liked the company.

When Harry entered junior high school, though, he didn't come by the candy and nut shop as often. Nor did his friends. They were older and they had more spending money. They went to a burger place. They played video games. They shopped for records.[1] None of them were much interested in candy and nuts anymore.

A new group of children came to Mr. Tillian's shop now. But not Harry Tillian and his friends.

The year Harry turned twelve was also the year Mr. Tillian got a parrot. He went to a pet store one day and bought one for more money than he could really afford. He brought the parrot to his shop, set its cage near the sign for maple clusters,[2] and named it Rocky.

Harry thought this was the strangest thing his father had ever done, and he told him so, but Mr. Tillian just ignored him.

Rocky was good company for Mr. Tillian. When business was slow, Mr. Tillian would turn on a small color television he had sitting in a corner, and he and Rocky would watch the soap operas. Rocky liked to

**Vocabulary Development**

**ignored** (ig NAWRD) *v.* paid no attention to

1. **records** (REK erdz) *n.* thin grooved discs on which music is recorded and played on a phonograph, or record player.

2. **maple clusters** *n.* a candy made with chocolate and maple sugar.

scream when the romantic music came on, and Mr. Tillian would yell at him to shut up, but they seemed to enjoy themselves.

The more Mr. Tillian grew to like his parrot, and the more he talked to it instead of to people, the more embarrassed Harry became. Harry would stroll past the shop, on his way somewhere else, and he'd take a quick look inside to see what his dad was doing. Mr. Tillian was always talking to the bird. So Harry kept walking.

At home things were different. Harry and his father joked with each other at the dinner table as they always had—Mr. Tillian teasing Harry about his smelly socks; Harry teasing Mr. Tillian about his blubbery stomach. At home things seemed all right.

But one day, Mr. Tillian became ill. He had been at work, unpacking boxes of caramels, when he had grabbed his chest and fallen over on top of the candy. A customer had found him, and he was taken to the hospital in an ambulance.

Mr. Tillian couldn't leave the hospital. He lay in bed, tubes in his arms, and he worried about his shop. New shipments of candy and nuts would be arriving. Rocky would be hungry. Who would take care of things?

Harry said he would. Harry told his father that he would go to the store every day after school and unpack boxes. He would sort out all the candy and nuts. He would even feed Rocky.

So, the next morning, while Mr. Tillian lay in his hospital bed, Harry took the shop key to school with him. After school he left his friends and walked to the empty shop alone. In all the days of his life, Harry had never seen the shop closed after school. Harry didn't even remember what the CLOSED sign looked like. The key stuck in the lock three times, and inside he had to search all the walls for the light switch.

The shop was as his father had left it. Even the caramels were still spilled on the floor. Harry bent down and picked them up one by one, dropping them back in the boxes. The bird in its cage watched him silently.

Vocabulary Development
**blubbery** (BLUB er ee) *adj.* fat, overweight

---

## TAKE NOTES

**Stop to Reflect**

Why do you think Harry and Mr. Tillian's relationship at home was different from their relationship after school at the store?

_____

_____

_____

**Reading Skill**

Read the bracketed paragraph. What context clues help you understand the meaning of *teasing*?

_____

_____

**Literary Analysis**

In most **narrative writing**, the events are told in the order in which they happened. How has Harry's relationship with his father changed from the beginning to the middle of this story?

_____

_____

**Reading Check**

Circle the three tasks that Harry does at the store.

## Literary Analysis

**Narrative writing** usually tells events in the order in which they happened. Harry is busy putting candies in their bins. Why is it important to the story that Harry forgot about Rocky until Rocky spoke?

_____

_____

_____

## Stop to Reflect

A writer often reveals a character's personality by what others say to or about a character. This is called **indirect characterization**. List two examples of indirect characterization in the bracketed passage. Explain how they are characteristics of Harry.

_____

_____

_____

_____

_____

_____

## Reading Check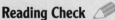

How does Harry react when Rocky says "Hello!"? Circle the correct answer.

---

Harry opened the new boxes his father hadn't gotten to. Peppermints. Jawbreakers. Toffee creams. Strawberry kisses. Harry traveled from bin to bin, putting the candies where they belonged.

"Hello!"

Harry jumped, spilling a box of jawbreakers.

"Hello, Rocky!"

Harry stared at the parrot. He had forgotten it was there. The bird had been so quiet, and Harry had been thinking only of the candy.

"Hello," Harry said.

"Hello, Rocky!" answered the parrot.

Harry walked slowly over to the cage. The parrot's food cup was empty. Its water was dirty. The bottom of the cage was a mess.

Harry carried the cage into the back room.

"Hello, Rocky!"

"Is that all you can say, you dumb bird?" Harry mumbled. The bird said nothing else.

Harry cleaned the bottom of the cage, refilled the food and water cups, and then put the cage back in its place and resumed sorting the candy.

"Where's Harry?"

Harry looked up.

"Where's Harry?"

Harry stared at the parrot.

"Where's Harry?"

Chills ran down Harry's back. What could the bird mean? It was something from "The Twilight Zone."[2]

"Where's Harry?"

Harry swallowed and said, "I'm here. I'm here, you stupid bird."

"You stupid bird!" said the parrot.

Well, at least he's got one thing straight, thought Harry.

"Miss him! Miss him! Where's Harry? You stupid bird!"

---

**Vocabulary Development**

**mumbled** (MUM buhld) *v.* said too quietly or not clearly enough to be understood

**resumed** (ri ZOOMD) *v.* began again; continued

---

2. "The Twilight Zone" science-fiction television series from the 1960s.

Harry stood with a handful of peppermints.

"What?" he asked.

"Where's Harry?" said the parrot.

"I'm here, you stupid bird! I'm here!" Harry yelled. He threw the peppermints at the cage, and the bird screamed and clung to its perch.

Harry sobbed, "I'm here." The tears were coming. Harry leaned over the glass counter.

"Papa." Harry buried his face in his arms.

"Where's Harry?" repeated the bird.

Harry sighed and wiped his face on his sleeve. He watched the parrot. He understood now: someone had been saying, for a long time, "Where's Harry? Miss him."

Harry finished his unpacking and then swept the floor of the shop. He checked the <u>furnace</u> so the bird wouldn't get cold. Then he left to go visit his papa.

---

Reader's Response: Do you think Harry will change the way he thinks about and acts toward his father? Explain.

_____

_____

_____

_____

_____

_____

**Literary Analysis**

Read the bracketed text.

**Narrative writing** tells a story, often in a familiar way. How do you know the story is ending?

_____

_____

_____

**Stop to Reflect**

Should Harry tell his father about what happened with Rocky at the store? Explain.

_____

_____

_____

**Reading Check** ✎

Where does Harry go after he finishes his work at the store? Circle the answer.

---

**Vocabulary Development**

**furnace** (FER nis) *n.* a machine used to heat buildings

# Papa's Parrot

1. **Infer:** Why have Harry and his friends stopped visiting Harry's father?

_____

_____

2. **Cause and Effect:** Why does Mr. Tillian buy Rocky?

_____

_____

3. **Reading Skill:** The chart below contains sentences from the story. Use **context clues** to find the meaning of each italicized word. First, write the context clues from each sentence in the middle column. Then, write the possible meaning of the italicized word in the right column.

| Sentences from Story | Context Clues | Possible Meaning |
|---|---|---|
| Harry would *stroll* past the pet shop on his way somewhere else. . . . Mr. Tillian was always talking to the bird. So Harry kept walking. | _____  _____  _____ | _____  _____  _____ |
| He checked the *furnace* so the bird wouldn't get cold. | _____  _____ | _____  _____ |

## Writing: Brief Essay

Write a **brief essay** in which you compare and contrast Harry's behavior before and after he enters junior high school.

- What causes Harry to change his behavior toward his father?

  _____

  _____

- What similarities are there between Harry's behavior at the beginning of the story and what Harry will probably do at the end of the story?

  _____

  _____

Use these notes to help you write your essay.

## Listening and Speaking: Dramatic Reading

With a partner, decide who will read the narration, who will read Harry's lines, and who will read Rocky's lines. Then, answer the questions about the parts you will perform in the **dramatic reading**.

- What actions does my character perform?

  _____

  _____

- When should I speak loudly and when softly?

  _____

  _____

- In which lines should I show strong emotion?

  _____

  _____

- Which words should I stress for effect?

  _____

# mk
## Jean Fritz

**Summary** Jean Fritz describes her early life as an MK, or missionary kid. She does not feel like a real American because she was born in China. Fritz and her parents move home to America when she is 12. She longs to feel at home in America.

## ❓ Writing About the Big Question

**What is the best way to find the truth?**
In "mk," the story is a true account from Fritz's childhood. Complete this sentence:

Sometimes we believe in things that are not true because it helps us

_____.

## Note-taking Guide
Describe Jean's character in "mk." Use this chart.

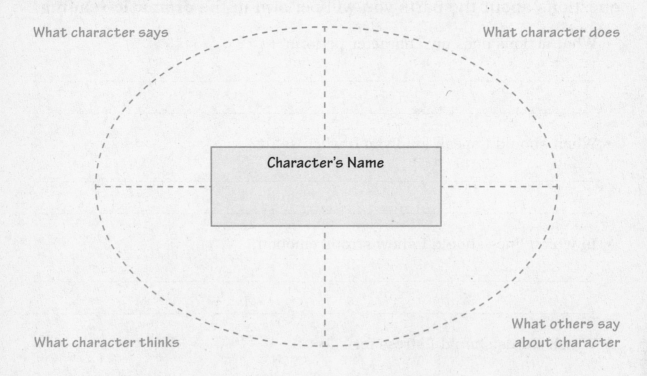

What character says

What character does

Character's Name

What character thinks

What others say about character

# mk

1. **Infer:** Does the American school in Shanghai live up to Jean's expectations? Why or why not?

_____

_____

_____

2. **Interpret:** Why do you think Jean relates to the main character, Priscilla Alden, in her favorite book?

_____

_____

_____

3. **Reading Skill:** The chart below contains sentences from the story. Use **context clues** to find the meaning of the italicized word. First, write the context clues from the sentences in the middle column. Then, write the possible meaning of the italicized word in the right column.

| Sentences from Story | Context Clues | Possible Meaning |
|---|---|---|
| "I always felt a tingling when I saw the American flag flying over the American consulate. Surely it would be more than a tingling now; surely it would *overwhelm* me." | _____ _____ _____ _____ | _____ _____ _____ |

4. **Literary Analysis:** Identify the main reason that "mk" is classified as a **narrative**.

_____

_____

## Writing: Brief Essay

Write a **brief essay** in which you compare and contrast Jean's feelings about America before and after she arrives in the United States. Answer the following questions to get started.

- How did Jean Fritz feel about America when she lived in China? List three adjectives that describe her feelings.

  _____

  _____

- What did it mean to her to live in America?

  _____

  _____

## Listening and Speaking: Dramatic Reading

Decide which passage you will present as a **dramatic reading**. Then, answer the following questions to help you prepare.

- What actions does my character perform?

  _____

  _____

- When should I speak loudly and when softly?

  _____

  _____

- In which lines should I show strong emotion?

  _____

  _____

- Which words should I stress for effect?

  _____

  _____

# from An American Childhood • The Luckiest Time of All

## Reading Skill

**Context clues** are the examples, descriptions, and other details in the text around an unfamiliar or unusual word or expression. When you come across an unfamiliar word, use context clues to figure out what the word probably means. Then, **reread and read ahead to confirm the meaning**. Use this chart to help you use context clues as you read.

| Unfamiliar Word in Context |
| --- |
|  |

| Word's Function in Sentence |
| --- |
|  |

| Meaning of Word |
| --- |
|  |

## Literary Analysis

**Point of view** is the perspective from which a narrative is told. Point of view affects the kinds of details revealed to the reader.

- **First-person point of view:** The narrator is a character who participates in the action of the story and uses the first person pronouns *I* and *me*. The narrator can reveal only his or her own observations, thoughts, and feelings.

- **Third-person point of view:** The narrator is not a character in the story. He or she uses third-person pronouns such as *he, she*, and *they* to refer to the characters. The narrator may know and reveal the observations, thoughts, and feelings of more than one character.

# from An American Childhood
## Annie Dillard

**Summary** Seven-year old Dillard and her friends throw snowballs at passing cars. They are surprised when one driver gets out of the car and chases them for several blocks. The experience strengthens Dillard's belief that people should throw themselves into an activity with all their energy.

## Writing About the Big Question

**What is the best way to find the truth?** In the excerpt from *An American Childhood*, a young man chases the narrator and her friends through the streets of their neighborhood. Complete this sentence:

Being challenged when we do not expect it gives us insight about _____

_____ because _____.

## Note-taking Guide

Use this chart to record details about the events of the story.

Climax: ·

Event: Dillard and her friends hit the Buick with snowballs.

Event: _____

Event: _____

Rising Action

Falling Action

Resolution

Exposition
Dillard and her friends are throwing snowballs at cars.

Conflict: _____

# from An American Childhood

## Annie Dillard

Some boys taught me to play football. This was fine sport. You thought up a new strategy for every play and whispered it to the others. You went out for a pass, fooling everyone. Best, you got to throw yourself mightily at someone's running legs. Either you brought him down or you hit the ground flat out on your chin, with your arms empty before you. It was all or nothing. If you hesitated in fear, you would miss and get hurt: you would take a hard fall while the kid got away, or you would get kicked in the face while the kid got away. But if you flung yourself wholeheartedly at the back of his knees—if you gathered and joined body and soul and pointed them diving fearlessly—then you likely wouldn't get hurt, and you'd stop the ball. Your fate, and your team's score, depended on your concentration and courage. Nothing girls did could compare with it.

Boys welcomed me at baseball, too, for I had, through enthusiastic practice, what was weirdly known as a boy's arm. In winter, in the snow, there was neither baseball nor football, so the boys and I threw snowballs at passing cars. I got in trouble throwing snowballs, and have seldom been happier since.

On one weekday morning after Christmas, six inches of new snow had just fallen. We were standing up to our boot tops in snow on a front yard on trafficked Reynolds Street, waiting for cars. The cars traveled Reynolds Street slowly and evenly; they were targets all but wrapped in red ribbons, cream puffs. We couldn't miss.

I was seven; the boys were eight, nine, and ten. The oldest two Fahey boys were there—Mikey and Peter—polite blond boys who lived near me on Lloyd Street, and who already had four brothers and sisters. My parents approved Mikey and Peter Fahey. Chickie McBride was there, a tough kid, and Billy

© Pearson Education

### Vocabulary Development

**strategy** (STRAT uh jee) *n.* set of plans used to gain success or achieve a goal

**concentration** (kahn suhn TRAY shuhn) *n.* ability to think carefully

---

### Activate Prior Knowledge

Tell about a time when you have thrown yourself completely into an activity.

_____

_____

_____

_____

_____

### Literary Analysis

**Point of view** is the perspective from which a story is told. In **first-person point of view**, the author tells the story from his or her own perspective and participates in it. Underline the sentence in the bracketed paragraph that shows that this story is told from the first-person point of view.

### Reading Check

Why are Dillard and the boys waiting for cars? Circle the answer.

## Reading Skill

**Context clues** are the surrounding examples and descriptions in the text that help you figure out the meaning of an unfamiliar first word. Which words in the first bracketed passage provide a clue to the meaning of *embarked*?

_____

_____

What does *embarked* mean?

_____

_____

## Literary Analysis

Circle the word in the second bracketed passage that shows **first-person point of view**.

## Reading Check

Underline the sentences that tell what makes this particular snowball-throwing episode different from all the others.

Paul and Mackie Kean too, from across Reynolds, where the boys grew up dark and furious, grew up skinny, knowing, and skilled. We had all drifted from our houses that morning looking for action, and had found it here on Reynolds Street.

It was cloudy but cold. The cars' tires laid behind them on the snowy street a complex trail of beige chunks like crenellated castle walls.[1] I had stepped on some earlier; they squeaked. We could have wished for more traffic. When a car came, we all popped it one. In the intervals between cars we reverted to the natural solitude of children.

I started making an iceball—a perfect iceball, from perfectly white snow, perfectly spherical, and squeezed perfectly translucent so no snow remained all the way through. (The Fahey boys and I considered it unfair actually to throw an iceball at somebody, but it had been known to happen.)

I had just embarked on the iceball project when we heard tire chains come clanking from afar. A black Buick was moving toward us down the street. We all spread out, banged together some regular snowballs, took aim, and, when the Buick drew nigh, fired.

A soft snowball hit the driver's windshield right before the driver's face. It made a smashed star with a hump in the middle.

Often, of course, we hit our target, but this time, the only time in all of life, the car pulled over and stopped. Its wide black door opened; a man got out of it, running. He didn't even close the car door.

He ran after us, and we ran away from him, up the snowy Reynolds sidewalk. At the corner, I looked back; <u>incredibly</u>, he was still after us. He was in city clothes: a suit and tie, street shoes. Any normal adult would have quit, having sprung us into flight and made his point. This man was gaining on us. He was a thin man, all action. All of a sudden, we were running for our lives.

© Pearson Education

**Vocabulary Development**

**incredibly** (in KRED un blee) *adv.* in a way that is hard to believe

1. **like crenellated** (KREN uhl ayt id) **castle walls** in rows of squares like the notches along the top of castle walls.

Wordless, we split up. We were on our turf; we could lose ourselves in the neighborhood backyards, everyone for himself. I paused and considered. Everyone had vanished except Mikey Fahey, who was just rounding the corner of a yellow brick house. Poor Mikey, I trailed him. The driver of the Buick sensibly picked the two of us to follow. The man apparently had all day.

He chased Mikey and me around the yellow house and up a backyard path we knew by heart: under a low tree, up a bank, through a hedge, down some snowy steps, and across the grocery store's delivery driveway. We smashed through a gap in another hedge, entered a scruffy backyard and ran around its back porch and tight between houses to Edgerton Avenue; we ran across Edgerton to an alley and up our own sliding woodpile to the Halls' front yard; he kept coming. We ran up Lloyd Street and wound through mazy backyards toward the steep hilltop at Willard and Lang.

He chased us silently, block after block. He chased us silently over picket fences, through thorny hedges, between houses, around garbage cans, and across streets. Every time I glanced back, choking for breath, I expected he would have quit. He must have been as breathless as we were. His jacket strained over his body. It was an immense discovery, pounding into my hot head with every sliding, joyous step, that this ordinary adult evidently knew what I thought only children who trained at football knew: that you have to fling yourself at what you're doing, you have to point yourself, forget yourself, aim, dive.

Mikey and I had nowhere to go, in our own neighborhood or out of it, but away from this man who was chasing us. He impelled us forward; we compelled him to follow our route. The air was cold; every breath tore my throat. We kept running, block after block; we kept improvising, backyard after

### Vocabulary Development

**impelled** (im PELD) *v.* made to feel strongly that one must do something

**compelled** (kuhm PELD) *v.* forced

**improvising** (IM pruh vyz ing) *v.* making up or inventing on the spur of the moment

**Literary Analysis**

Why are the man's thoughts not told in this narrative?

_____

_____

**Stop to Reflect**

What important fact does the man chasing them know?

_____

_____

_____

**Reading Skill**

Draw a box around a word on this page that is unfamiliar to you. Then, circle the **context clues** that help you figure out the meaning of that word.

**Reading Check**

Whom does the man pick to follow? Underline the sentences with the answer.

## Literary Analysis

Underline the sentence in the first bracketed paragraph that tells how Dillard felt after being caught. Is this the reaction you expected? Explain.

_____

_____

_____

## Reading Skill

Draw a box around the word *redundant*. Circle the words that state the meaning of *redundant* in the second bracketed passage.

## Reading Check

Why is the author disappointed when the chase ends? Underline one reason in the story.

backyard, running a frantic course and choosing it simultaneously, failing always to find small places or hard places to slow him down, and discovering always, exhilarated, dismayed, that only bare speed could save us—for he would never give up, this man—and we were losing speed.

He chased us through the backyard labyrinths of ten blocks before he caught us by our jackets. He caught us and we all stopped.

We three stood staggering, half blinded, coughing, in an obscure hilltop backyard: a man in his twenties, a boy, a girl. He had released our jackets, our pursuer, our captor, our hero: he knew we weren't going anywhere. We all played by the rules. Mikey and I unzipped our jackets. I pulled off my sopping mittens. Our tracks multiplied in the backyard's new snow. We had been breaking new snow all morning. We didn't look at each other. I was cherishing my excitement. The man's lower pants legs were wet; his cuffs were full of snow, and there was a prow of snow beneath them on his shoes and socks. Some trees bordered the little flat backyard, some messy winter trees. There was no one around: a clearing in a grove, and we the only players.

It was a long time before he could speak. I had some difficulty at first recalling why we were there. My lips felt swollen; I couldn't see out of the sides of my eyes; I kept coughing.

"You stupid kids," he began perfunctorily.

We listened perfunctorily indeed, if we listened at all, for the chewing out was redundant, a mere formality, and beside the point. The point was that he had chased us passionately without giving up, and so he had caught us. Now he came down to earth. I wanted the glory to last forever.

But how could the glory have lasted forever? We could have run through every backyard in North America until we got to Panama. But when he trapped us at the lip of the Panama Canal, what precisely could he have done to prolong the drama of the chase and cap its glory? I brooded about this for

### Vocabulary Development

**perfunctorily** (per FUHNGK tuh ri lee) *adj.* without enthusiasm; routinely

the next few years. He could only have fried Mikey Fahey and me in boiling oil, say, or dismembered us piecemeal, or staked us to anthills. None of which I really wanted, and none of which any adult was likely to do, even in the spirit of fun. He could only chew us out there in the Panamanian jungle, after months or years of exalting pursuit. He could only begin, "You stupid kids," and continue in his ordinary Pittsburgh accent with his normal <u>righteous</u> anger and the usual common sense.

If in that snowy backyard the driver of the black Buick had cut off our heads, Mikey's and mine, I would have died happy, for nothing has required so much of me since as being chased all over Pittsburgh in the middle of winter—running terrified, exhausted—by this sainted, skinny, furious red-headed man who wished to have a word with us. I don't know how he found his way back to his car.

Reader's Response: Would you want the young Annie Dillard as a friend? Why or why not?

_____

_____

_____

_____

_____

_____

© Pearson Education

**Vocabulary Development**

**righteous** (RY chuhs) *adj.* angry because a situation is not right or fair

**Reading Check**

What does the man from the black Buick look like? Underline the answer.

**Stop to Reflect**

Why does Dillard say in the bracketed passage that she "would have died happy"?

_____

_____

_____

_____

_____

_____

**TAKE NOTES**

# from An American Childhood

1. **Interpret:** Why does Dillard call the man who chased her "our hero"?

   _____

   _____

2. **Reading Skill:** Read these lines from the narrative: *"You stupid kids,"
   he began perfunctorily. We listened perfunctorily indeed, if we listened
   at all, for the chewing out was redundant, a mere formality, and beside
   the point.* What **context clues** suggest a possible meaning for the word
   *perfunctorily*?

   _____

   _____

3. **Reading Skill:** What is a possible meaning for *perfunctorily*?

   _____

   _____

4. **Literary Analysis:** Use the chart below to give two examples from the
   story in which the narrator shares her thoughts or feelings about a
   situation.

   | Situation | Thoughts or Feelings |
   |-----------|----------------------|
   |           |                      |

## Writing: Description Using Hyperbole

**Hyperbole** is exaggeration for effect. Annie Dillard describes what the driver could have done to them: "He could only have fried Mikey Fahey and me in boiling oil, . . ." This example tells you how frightened the kids were. Write a description that uses hyperbole.

- State a situation, such as being very happy.

  _____

- Think of an exaggeration for this situation. For example, you might say *He was so happy, he was dancing on the clouds.*

  _____

  _____

- Write two more sentences to expand your description.

  _____

  _____

## Research and Technology: Biographical Report

Use the following chart to record information about Annie Dillard. Use this information in your **biographical report**.

| Major Life Events | Major Events from Writing Career |
|---|---|
|  |  |
|  |  |

# The Luckiest Time of All
## Lucille Clifton

**Summary** Elzie Pickens tells her great-granddaughter Tee a story. The story is about the time Elzie tosses her lucky stone at a dancing dog. The stone hits the dog on the nose. The angry dog begins to chase Elzie. Tee thinks that the stone was unlucky. The stone turns out to be lucky after all.

 ## Writing About the Big Question

**What is the best way to find the truth?** In "The Luckiest Time of All," a girl meets her future husband when he rescues her by capturing the dog that is chasing her. Complete this sentence:

When we believe something is lucky, we feel _____.

## Note-taking Guide
Use this chart to help you understand the relationship of events in the story.

| Cause | Effect/Cause | Effect/Cause |
|-------|--------------|--------------|
|       |              |              |

| Effect/Cause | Effect/Cause | Effect |
|--------------|--------------|--------|
|              |              |        |

# The Luckiest Time of All

1. **Infer:** What can you tell about Elzie as a young woman from the second paragraph of the story?

   _____

2. **Analyze:** How does Elzie know that Mr. Pickens is a good man?

   _____

3. **Reading Skill:** Read these sentences from the story:

   _Well, he lit out after me, poor thing. He lit out after me and I flew! Round and round the Silas Green we run . . . but now that dancin dog was a runnin dog._

   What is a possible meaning for _lit out_?

   _____

4. **Reading Skill:** What context clues help you figure out the meaning of _lit out_ in the passage?

   _____

5. **Literary Analysis:** Give two examples in which Elzie tells what she thinks or feels about a situation. Use this chart to write your examples.

| Situation | Thoughts or Feelings |
| --- | --- |
|  |  |

## Writing: Description Using Hyperbole

**Hyperbole** is exaggeration for effect. Ms. Elzie uses hyperbole to describe Mr. Pickens: "the finest fast running hero in the bottoms of Virginia." Use hyperbole to complete the following sentences. For example, you might say *She was the prettiest girl in the state.*

- She had hair as yellow as _____.

- The tree was as tall as _____.

- He was the smartest boy _____.

- That is the fastest horse _____.

## Research and Technology: Biographical Report

Research and write a short **biographical report** on Lucille Clifton. For online research, go to www.poets.org. You can also input "Lucille Clifton" at www.google.com. Brainstorm other possible places to find information.

_____

_____

_____

_____

_____

_____

_____

_____

_____

_____

# Reference Materials

## About Reference Materials

Reference materials provide many kinds of information. These references can help you find facts and details:

- atlases
- almanacs
- encyclopedias
- Internet resources

An **atlas** is a book containing maps of places in the world. **Maps** provide information about the geography, population, and economy of various places. Maps have one or more of these features:

- **legend** or **key:** explains map symbols
- **scale:** shows the relationship between the size of a map and the actual size of the place that the map represents
- **compass rose:** shows directions (north, south, east, west)

## Reading Skill

Reference materials contain **visual aids** and **text features** that organize details and highlight important information. To **locate information,** follow these steps:

1. Decide what **type of information** you need.

2. Select a reference. Atlases, maps, and almanacs provide facts. Encyclopedias and Internet resources provide more details.

3. Skim the reference. To **skim a text,** look through it quickly to learn what type of information it contains. Look at visual aids, such as photographs, maps and charts. Read text features, such as headings, subheadings, captions, and highlighted vocabulary. Look for **keywords** that relate to the information you need.

| Features in Atlases |
|---|
| • headings |
| • bold print |
| • map keys or legends |
| • captions for graphs |

# EAST ASIA

## China, Mongolia, Taiwan

China is the world's third-largest country and its most populous—over one billion people live there. Under its communist government, which came to power in 1949, China has became a major industrial nation, but most of its people still live and work on the land as they have for thousands of years. Taiwan also has a booming economy and exports its products around the world. Mongolia is a vast, remote country with a small population, many of whom are nomads.

**Features:**

- maps that give an overview of geographic locations
- articles that provide information about places shown in maps
- legends, or keys, that explain symbols and colors used in maps
- reference material for a general audience

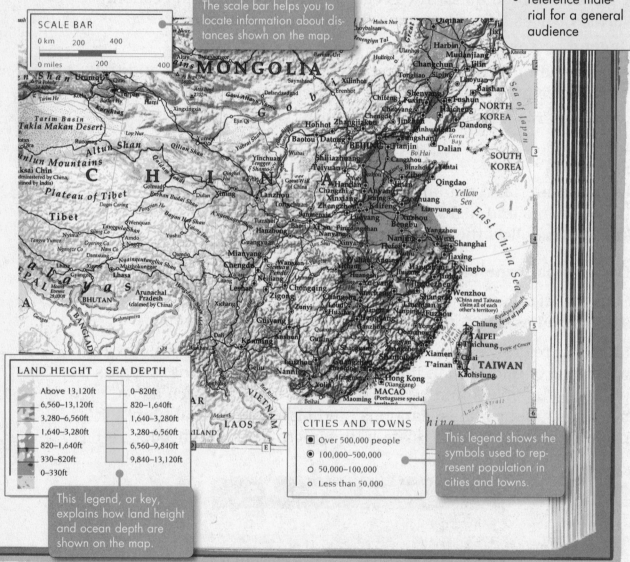

The scale bar helps you to locate information about distances shown on the map.

This legend shows the symbols used to represent population in cities and towns.

This legend, or key, explains how land height and ocean depth are shown on the map.

**SCALE BAR**

| LAND HEIGHT | SEA DEPTH |
|---|---|
| Above 13,120ft | 0–820ft |
| 6,560–13,120ft | 820–1,640ft |
| 3,280–6,560ft | 1,640–3,280ft |
| 1,640–3,280ft | 3,280–6,560ft |
| 820–1,640ft | 6,560–9,840ft |
| 330–820ft | 9,840–13,120ft |
| 0–330ft | |

**CITIES AND TOWNS**

- ■ Over 500,000 people
- ◉ 100,000–500,000
- ○ 50,000–100,000
- ○ Less than 50,000

## Population

Most of China's people live in the eastern part of the country, where climate, landscape and soils are most favorable. Urban areas there house more than 250 million people, but almost 75% of the population lives in villages and farms the land. Taiwan's lowlands are very densely populated. In Mongolia, about 50% of the people live in the countryside.

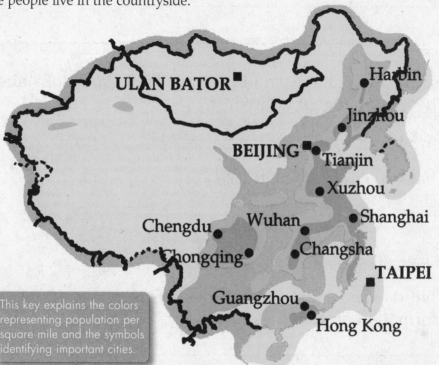

This key explains the colors representing population per square mile and the symbols identifying important cities.

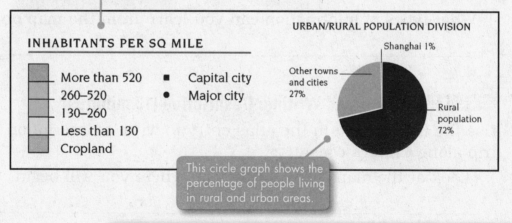

### INHABITANTS PER SQ MILE

- More than 520
- 260–520
- 130–260
- Less than 130
- Cropland

- ■ Capital city
- ● Major city

### URBAN/RURAL POPULATION DIVISION

Shanghai 1%

Other towns and cities 27%

Rural population 72%

This circle graph shows the percentage of people living in rural and urban areas.

**What is the best way to find the truth?**

If you were trying to find the truth about life in East Asia, in what ways would this atlas entry be useful?

# Thinking About the Reference Material

1. Why do you think most of China's people live in the eastern part of the country?

_____

_____

2. Use the map and legend to answer these questions about Shanghai: Where is Shanghai located?

_____

What two cities are near it?

_____

**Reading Skill**

3. What do the heading and subheading on page 40 tell you about the information on that page?

_____

4. What types of information can you learn from the map on page 41?

_____

**WRITE ABOUT IT**  **Timed Writing: Description (15 minutes)**

Use the information in the atlas entry to write a description of a boat trip along China's coast.

• Look at the maps. Choose the city where you will begin.

_____

• List five cities that you will visit on your trip.

_____

• Use the scale bar to find out how many miles your trip will cover.

_____

# All Summer in a Day • Suzy and Leah

## Reading Skill

Fiction writers may write for a variety of **purposes**. They may wish to entertain, to teach, or to reflect on experiences. **Recognizing details that indicate the author's purpose** can give you a rich understanding of a text. As you read, use this chart to note details from the story that fit the different possible purposes of the author.

| Entertain |
| --- |
|  |

| Teach |
| --- |
|  |

| Reflect |
| --- |
|  |

## Literary Analysis

The **setting** of a story is the time and place of the action. In this example, the details in italics help establish the story's setting:

As *night fell*, the hungry raccoons roamed the *forest* for food.

- In some stories, setting is just a backdrop; the same story events could take place in a completely different setting.

- In other stories, setting is very important; it develops a specific atmosphere or mood in the story. The setting may even relate directly to the story's central conflict or problem.

# All Summer in a Day
## Ray Bradbury

**Summary** This story takes place on the planet Venus. It never stops raining there. Margot is the only child in her class who has ever seen the sun. One day, the sun comes out for the first time in seven years. Margot's classmates play a terrible trick that makes her miss playing in the sunshine.

## Writing About the Big Question

**What is the best way to find the truth?** In "All Summer in a Day," a girl living on another planet longs for the thing she misses the most about living on Earth. These days, living in space is more real than ever. Complete this sentence:

When we have evidence that something exists, but others don't believe us,

we can _____.

## Note-taking Guide

Use this chart to record how Margot's classmates feel about her in the story.

| What Happens | What Is the Result? |
|---|---|
| 1. Margot tells about the sun. | 1. Other students seem unbelieving. |
| 2. | 2. |
| 3. | 3. |
| 4. | 4. |

# All Summer in a Day

1. **Infer:** Why do the children reject Margot's description of the sun?

   _____

2. **Draw Conclusions:** Why do the children go along with the prank that is played on Margot?

   _____

   _____

3. **Reading Skill:** In your own words, what was the author's main **purpose** in writing this story?

   _____

   _____

4. **Literary Analysis:** How does the **setting** of the story affect the events that occur?

   _____

   _____

5. **Literary Analysis:** Using this chart, give two examples from the story to show how **setting** affects a character's mood.

| Setting | Character's Mood |
|---|---|
| _____ | _____ |
| _____ | _____ |

## Writing: News Report

Write a **news report** showing the events of the story.

- Look at a few news stories to see how they are written. Notice how the first paragraph summarizes the story. Note how other paragraphs add details.

- Use this chart to record the main idea and the details of the story.

- Include descriptive phrases and active verbs in your news report.

| Main Idea |
|---|
|  |
| Details |
|  |

## Listening and Speaking: Discussion

Prepare for a class **discussion**. Think about the story and what you learned from it. Review the events of the story and answer these questions.

- What do the children's words and actions tell about them?

  _____

  _____

- What lesson can you learn from how the children behave toward Margot?

  _____

  _____

- What lesson can you learn from how the children feel at the end of the story?

  _____

# Suzy and Leah
## Jane Yolen

**Summary** The story is told through diary entries written by Suzy and Leah. Leah is new to America. She lives in a refugee camp. Leah goes to Suzy's school. Suzy must help Leah learn English. The girls dislike each other. Each girl judges the other. Then, something happens that helps them get to know each other.

###  Writing About the Big Question

**What is the best way to find the truth?** In "Suzy and Leah," the characters and story are based on real events in history. Complete this sentence:

When we have insight about someone's life, we can _____

_____.

### Note-taking Guide

Use this chart to record details about how Suzy and Leah feel toward each other.

|  | At the Beginning | At the End |
|---|---|---|
| What does Leah say about Suzy? |  |  |
| What does Suzy say about Leah? |  |  |

# Suzy and Leah
## Jane Yolen

Many people keep diaries. Do you know anyone who keeps a diary? Who?

_____

_____

Have you heard of any famous people who kept diaries? Explain.

_____

_____

**Literary Analysis**

A story's **setting** is the time and place of the action. Underline the details in Suzy's first diary entry that help tell the story's setting.

**Reading Check** 🖉

What does Suzy take with her to the camp? Underline the answer in the text.

August 5, 1944

Dear Diary,

Today I walked past that place, the one that was in the newspaper, the one all the kids have been talking about. Gosh, is it ugly! A line of rickety wooden buildings just like in the army. And a fence lots higher than my head. With barbed wire[1] on top. How can anyone—even a refugee—live there?

I took two candy bars along, just like everyone said I should. When I held them up, all those kids just swarmed over to the fence, grabbing. Like in a zoo. Except for this one girl, with two dark braids and bangs nearly covering her eyes. She was just standing to one side, staring at me. It was so creepy. After a minute I looked away. When I looked back, she was gone. I mean gone. Disappeared as if she'd never been.

Suzy

August 5, 1944

My dear Mutti,[2]

I have but a single piece of paper to write on. And a broken pencil. But I will write small so I can tell all. I address it to you, Mutti, though you are gone from me forever. I write in English, to learn better, because I want to make myself be understood.

Today another girl came. With more sweets. A girl with yellow hair and a false smile. Yonni and Zipporah and Ruth, my friends, all grabbed for the sweets. Like wild animals. Like . . . like prisoners. But we are not wild animals. And we are no longer prisoners. Even though we are still penned in.

**Vocabulary Development**

**rickety** (RIK uht ee) *adj.* likely to break if used
**refugee** (REF yoo jee) *n.* person who flees home or country to seek shelter from war or cruelty

1. **barbed wire** twisted wire with sharp points all along it, used for fences and barriers.
2. **Mutti** (MOO tee) German equivalent of "Mommy."

I stared at the yellow-haired girl until she was forced to look down. Then I walked away. When I turned to look back, she was gone. Disappeared. As if she had never been.

Leah

September 2, 1944

Dear Diary,

I brought the refugee kids oranges today. Can you believe it—they didn't know you're supposed to peel oranges first. One boy tried to eat one like an apple. He made an awful face, but then he ate it anyway. I showed them how to peel oranges with the second one. After I stopped laughing.

Mom says they are going to be coming to school. Of course they'll have to be cleaned up first. Ugh. My hand still feels itchy from where one little boy grabbed it in his. I wonder if he had bugs.

Suzy

September 2, 1944

My dear Mutti,

Today we got cereal in a box. At first I did not know what it was. Before the war we ate such lovely porridge with milk straight from our cows. And eggs fresh from the hen's nest, though you know how I hated that nasty old chicken. How often she pecked me! In the German camp, it was potato soup—with onions when we were lucky, without either onion or potato when we were not. And after, when I was running from the Nazis, it was stale brown bread, if we could find any. But cereal in a box—that is something.

I will not take a sweet from that yellow-haired girl, though. She laughed at Yonni. I will not take another orange fruit.

Leah

© Pearson Education

**Vocabulary Development**

**porridge** (PAWR ij) *n.* soft food made of cereal boiled in water or milk

---

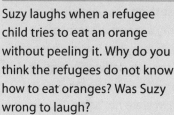

**Stop to Reflect**

Suzy laughs when a refugee child tries to eat an orange without peeling it. Why do you think the refugees do not know how to eat oranges? Was Suzy wrong to laugh?

_____

_____

_____

_____

**Reading Skill**

Authors put details in their stories for a purpose. The underlined details give us information about Leah's life before the war. What do you think was the **author's purpose** for putting these details in the story?

_____

_____

_____

**Literary Analysis**

What **setting** was Leah used to before the war?

_____

_____

© Pearson Education

## Literary Analysis

A **setting** can help create a story's mood or atmosphere. Leah says that "no place is safe for us." Underline the details that show why the places she has been were not safe.

## Stop to Reflect

Leah tells us that one of the refugees, a little boy named Avi, will not speak at all. Why did Avi stop speaking?

_____

_____

_____

## Reading Skill

Leah says, "There is barbed wire still between us and the world." For what **purpose** does the author include this **detail**?

_____

_____

_____

September 5, 1944

Dear Diary,

So how are those refugee kids going to learn? Our teachers teach in English. This is America, after all.

I wouldn't want to be one of them. Imagine going to school and not being able to speak English or understand anything that's going on. I can't imagine anything worse.

Suzy

September 5, 1944

My dear Mutti,

The adults of the Americans say we are safe now. And so we must go to their school. But I say no place is safe for us. Did not the Germans say that we were safe in their camps? And there you and baby Natan were killed.

And how could we learn in this American school anyway? I have a little English. But Ruth and Zipporah and the others, though they speak Yiddish[3] and Russian and German, they have no English at all. None beyond *thank you* and *please* and *more sweets*. And then there is little Avi. How could he go to this school? He will speak nothing at all. He stopped speaking, they say, when he was hidden away in a cupboard by his grandmother who was taken by the Nazis after she swore there was no child in the house. And he was almost three days in that cupboard without food, without water, without words to comfort him. Is English a safer language than German?

There is barbed wire still between us and the world.

Leah

September 14, 1944

Dear Diary,

At least the refugee kids are wearing better clothes now. And they all have shoes. Some of them still had those stripy pajamas[4] on when they arrived in America.

---

3. **Yiddish** (YID ish) *n.* language spoken by eastern European Jews and their descendants. It is written with Hebrew letters and contains words from Hebrew, German, Russian, and Polish.

4. **stripy pajamas** striped outfits worn by prisoners in work camps.

The girls all wore dresses to their first day at school, though. They even had hair bows, gifts from the teachers. Of course I recognized my old blue pinafore.[5] The girl with the dark braids had it on, and Mom hadn't even told me she was giving it away. I wouldn't have minded so much if she had only asked. It doesn't fit me anymore, anyway.

The girl in my old pinafore was the only one without a name tag, so all day long no one knew her name.

Suzy

September 14, 1944

My dear Mutti,

I put on the blue dress for our first day. It fit me well. The color reminded me of your eyes and the blue skies over our farm before the smoke from the burning darkened it. Zipporah braided my hair, but I had no mirror until we got to the school and they showed us the toilets. They call it a bathroom, but there is no bath in it at all, which is strange. I have never been in a school with boys before.

They have placed us all in low grades. Because of our English. I do not care. This way I do not have to see the girl with the yellow hair who smiles so falsely at me.

But they made us wear tags with our names printed on them. That made me afraid. What next? Yellow stars?[6] I tore mine off and threw it behind a bush before we went in.

Leah

September 16, 1944

Dear Diary,

Mr. Forest has assigned each of us to a refugee to help them with their English. He gave me the girl with the dark braids, the one without the name tag, the one in my pinafore. Gee, she's as prickly as a

## TAKE NOTES

### Reading Skill

Read the bracketed passage. In it, Suzy realizes that Leah is wearing her old dress. What author's **purpose** does this **detail** indicate?

_____

_____

_____

### Literary Analysis

How is Leah's **setting** strange to her?

_____

_____

_____

### Reading Check ✏

What gift do the teachers give the new girls at school? Circle the answer in the text.

5. **pinafore** (PIN uh fawr) *n.* sleeveless garment worn over a dress, often over a blouse.

6. **yellow stars** Jews were forced to wear fabric stars during the Holocaust to distinguish them from other people.

© Pearson Education

### Reading Skill

Read the bracketed passage. Authors have a **purpose** for making characters act a certain way. What does Leah call Suzy?

_____

What is the **author's purpose** for having Leah refer to Suzy in this way?

_____

_____

_____

### Stop to Reflect

Suzy calls Leah a grouch. Is she? Explain why or why not.

_____

_____

_____

_____

### Reading Check

Both Suzy and Leah wish things would happen. Underline the sentences in which the two girls make wishes.

porcupine. I asked if I could have a different kid. He said I was the best English student and she already spoke the best English. He wants her to learn as fast as possible so she can help the others. As if she would, Miss Porcupine.

Her name is Leah. I wish she would wear another dress.

Suzy

September 16, 1944

My dear Mutti,

Now I have a real notebook and a pen. I am writing to you at school now. I cannot take the notebook back to the shelter. Someone there will surely borrow it. I will instead keep it here. In the little cupboard each one of us has been given.

I wish I had another dress. I wish I had a different student helping me and not the yellow-haired girl.

Leah

September 20, 1944

Dear Diary,

Can't she ever smile, that Leah? I've brought her candy bars and apples from home. I tried to give her a handkerchief with a yellow flower on it. She wouldn't take any of them.

Her whole name is Leah Shoshana Hershkowitz. At least, that's the way she writes it. When she says it, it sounds all different, low and growly. I laughed when I tried to say it, but she wouldn't laugh with me. What a grouch.

And yesterday, when I took her English paper to correct it, she shrank back against her chair as if I was going to hit her or something. Honestly!

Mom says I should invite her home for dinner soon. We'll have to get her a special pass for that. But I don't know if I want her to come. It's not like she's any fun at all. I wish Mr. Forest would let me trade.

Suzy

### Vocabulary Development

**porcupine** (PAWR kyoo pyn) *n.* small animal covered with long, needle-shaped quills

**grouch** (growch) *n.* person who complains a great deal

September 20, 1944

My dear Mutti,

The girl with the yellow hair is called Suzy Ann McCarthy. It is a silly name. It means nothing. I asked her who she was named for, and she said, "For a book my mom liked." A book! <u>I am named after my great-grandmother on my mother's side, who was an important woman in our village. I am proud to carry on her name.</u>

This Suzy brings many sweets. But I must call them candies now. And a handkerchief. She expects me to be grateful. But how can I be grateful? She treats me like a pet, a pet she does not really like or trust. She wants to feed me like an animal behind bars.

If I write all this down, I will not hold so much anger. I have much anger. And terror besides. *Terror.* It is a new word for me, but an old feeling. One day soon this Suzy and her people will stop being nice to us. They will remember we are not just refugees but Jews, and they will turn on us. Just as the Germans did. Of this I am sure.

Leah


September 30, 1944

Dear Diary,

Leah's English is very good now. But she still never smiles. Especially she never smiles at me. It's like she has a <u>permanent</u> frown and permanent frown lines between her eyes. It makes her look much older than anyone in our class. Like a little old lady.

I wonder if she eats enough. She won't take the candy bars. And she saves the school lunch in her napkin, hiding it away in her pocket. She thinks no one sees her do it, but I do. Does she eat it later? I'm sure they get dinner at the shelter. Mom says they do. Mom also says we have to eat everything on our plates. Sometimes when we're having dinner I think of Leah Shoshana Hershkowitz.

Suzy

**Vocabulary Development**

**permanent** (PER muh nuhnt) *adj.* lasting for all time

**Literary Analysis**

A **setting** can be very important to the characters in a story. Read the underlined sentences. What do they tell you about how Leah feels about her village?

_____

_____

_____

**Reading Skill**

Read the bracketed paragraph. What do you think was the **author's purpose** for writing this paragraph?

_____

_____

_____

**Literary Analysis**

Even details about food can tell you about **settings.** Underline the details that tell you what Suzy's home and the shelter where Leah lives are like.

One of the author's **purposes** in writing this story is to show the differences between Suzy and Leah. How do the details help show these differences? Underline details in Suzy's diary entry that show how different Leah is from Suzy.

## Literary Analysis

**Setting** has an effect on characters. How does Suzy's house affect Leah?

_____

_____

_____

_____

_____

## Reading Check

Leah does not always eat her food. Underline the sentences in which she tells you what she does with the food she saves.

September 30, 1944

My dear Mutti,

Avi loves the food I bring home from school. What does he know? It is not even kosher.[7] Sometimes they serve ham. But I do not tell Avi. He needs all the food he can get. He is a growing boy.

I, too, am growing fast. Soon I will not fit into the blue dress. I have no other.

Leah

October 9, 1944

Dear Diary,

They skipped Leah up to our grade, her English has gotten so good. Except for some words, like victory, which she pronounces "wick-toe-ree." I try not to laugh, but sometimes I just can't help it!

Leah knows a lot about the world and nothing about America. She thinks New York is right next to Chicago, for goodness sakes! She can't dance at all. She doesn't know the words to any of the top songs. And she's so stuck up, she only talks in class to answer questions. The other refugees aren't like that at all. Why is it only my refugee who's so mean?

Suzy

October 9, 1944

My dear Mutti,

I think of you all the time. I went to Suzy's house because Mr. Forest said they had gone to a great deal of trouble to get a pass for me. I did not want to go so much, my stomach hurt the whole time I was there.

Suzy's Mutti was nice, all pink and gold. She wore a dress with pink roses all over it and it reminded me of your dress, the blue one with the asters. You were wearing it when we were put on the train. And the last time I saw you at the camp with Natan. Oh, Mutti. I had to steel my heart against Suzy's mother. If I love her, I will forget you. And that I must never do.

**Vocabulary Development**

**asters** (AS terz) _n._ flowers

7. **kosher** (KOH sher) _adj._ fit to eat according to the Jewish laws of diet.

I brought back food from her house, though, for Avi. I could not eat it myself. You would like the way Avi grows bigger and stronger. And he talks now, but only to me. He says, "More, Leah, please." And he says "light" for the sun. Sometimes when I am really lonely I call him Natan, but only at night after he has fallen asleep.

Leah

October 10, 1944

Dear Diary,

Leah was not in school today. When I asked her friend Zipporah, she shrugged. "She is ill in her stomach," she said. "What did she eat at your house?"

I didn't answer "Nothing," though that would have been true. She hid it all in a handkerchief Mom gave her. Mom said, "She eats like a bird. How does she stay alive?"

Suzy

October 11, 1944

Dear Diary,

They've asked me to gather Leah's things from school and bring them to the hospital. She had to have her <u>appendix</u> out and nearly died. She almost didn't tell them she was sick until too late. Why did she do that? I would have been screaming my head off with the pain.

Mom says we have to visit, that I'm Leah's American best friend. Hah! We're going to bring several of my old dresses, but not my green one with the white trim. I don't want her to have it. Even if it doesn't fit me anymore.

Suzy

October 12, 1944

Dear Diary,

I did a terrible thing. I read Leah's diary. I'd kill anyone who did that to me!

© Pearson Education

**Reading Skill**

Read the underlined sentence. What is the **author's purpose** for including this detail?

_____

_____

_____

_____

_____

**Stop to Reflect**

Suzy does not understand why Leah didn't tell anyone that she was sick and in pain. Think about all that Leah has said about herself. Why do you think she didn't tell?

_____

_____

_____

_____

_____

**Reading Check**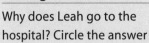

Why does Leah go to the hospital? Circle the answer in the text.

**Vocabulary Development**

**appendix** (uh PEN diks) *n.* body organ that has no known use

### Reading Skill

One of the author's **purposes** for writing this story is to teach readers about World War II. Read the bracketed paragraph. Underline the facts about World War II that this diary entry teaches you.

### Literary Analysis

**Setting** can be part of a story's central conflict or problem. Suzy learns a great deal about Germany during the war from reading Leah's diary. How important is this setting? Is it part of the story's central conflict?

_____

_____

_____

_____

### Stop to Reflect

Leah gets very sick and nearly dies. How does Avi help her?

_____

_____

What makes his action so important?

_____

_____

_____

_____

At first it made no sense. Who were Mutti and Natan, and why were they killed? What were the yellow stars? What does kosher mean? And the way she talked about me made me furious. Who did she think she was, little Miss Porcupine? All I did was bring candy and fruit and try to make those poor refugee kids feel at home.

Then, when I asked Mom some questions, carefully, so she wouldn't guess I had read Leah's diary, she explained. She said the Nazis killed people, mothers and children as well as men. In places called concentration camps. And that all the Jews—people who weren't Christians like us—had to wear yellow stars on their clothes so they could be spotted blocks and blocks away. It was so awful I could hardly believe it, but Mom said it was true.

How was I supposed to know all that? How can Leah stand any of us? How could she live with all that pain?

Suzy

October 12, 1944

My dear Mutti,

Suzy and her mother came to see me in the hospital. They brought me my notebook so now I can write again.

I was so frightened about being sick. I did not tell anyone for a long time, even though it hurt so much. In the German camp, if you were sick and could not do your work, they did not let you live.

But in the middle of the night, I had so much fever, a doctor was sent for. Little Avi found me. He ran to one of the guards. He spoke out loud for the first time. He said, "Please, for Leah. Do not let her go into the dark."

The doctor tells me I nearly died, but they saved me. They have given me much medicines and soon I will eat the food and they will be sure it is kosher, too. And I am alive. This I can hardly believe. Alive!

Then Suzy came with her Mutti, saying, "I am sorry. I am so sorry. I did not know. I did not understand." Suzy did a bad thing. She read my notebook. But it helped her understand. And then, instead of making an apology, she did a strange thing. She took a red book with a lock out of her pocket and gave it to me. "Read this," she said. "And when you are out of the hospital, I have a green dress with white trim I want you to have. It will be just perfect with your eyes."

I do not know what this trim may be. But I like the idea of a green dress. And I have a new word now, as well. It is this: *diary*.

A new word. A new land. And—it is just possible— a new friend.

Leah

---

**Reader's Response:** Suzy welcomes Leah into her home and shares her clothes and her diary. If you met someone from another culture, what would you share with him or her?

_____

_____

_____

_____

_____

**Reading Skill**

What do you think is the **author's purpose** for having young people tell this story?

_____

_____

_____

**Reading Check**

What new word has Leah learned? Underline the answer in the text.

# Suzy and Leah

1. **Analyze:** What do Suzy's reactions to Leah tell you about Suzy?

   _____

   _____

2. **Analyze:** What do Leah's reactions to Suzy tell you about Leah?

   _____

   _____

3. **Reading Skill:** Identify one of the **author's purposes** for writing this story.

   _____

4. **Literary Analysis:** Write examples from the story that show how **setting** affects a character's mood. Use this chart.

| Setting | Character's Mood |
|---------|------------------|
|         |                  |
|         |                  |

## Writing: News Report

Write a **news report** that tells about the refugee camp in which Leah is living. Answer the following questions to get started.

- Who is the audience for your report? Are your readers adults, students, or children?

  _____

- What is the main idea that you wish to tell about Leah's camp?

  _____

  _____

- The first paragraph of a news report usually summarizes the story. Write a summary of the news report. Include the main idea.

  _____

  _____

  _____

## Listening and Speaking: Discussion

Answer the following questions in order to prepare for a discussion about what you learned from reading "Suzy and Leah."

- What did you know about the Holocaust before you read the story?

  _____

- What did you learn from the story?

  _____

- Did the character's ages change what you thought about the event? Explain.

  _____

- What question or questions do you still have about the Holocaust?

  _____

# My First Free Summer • from Angela's Ashes

## Reading Skill

The **author's purpose** is the reason that he or she writes a work. **Use background information** to help you figure out the author's purpose for writing a nonfiction work. Background information is information that you already know about an author and a topic.

Use this chart to help you determine the author's purpose as you read.

| What I Know About the Author | What I Know About the Topic |
|---|---|

| Author's Purpose |
|---|

## Literary Analysis

Some literary works are based on real events and real people. The **historical context** is the real time and place of an event. Knowing the historical context of a work can help you understand the action. It can also help you understand why characters act and think as they do.

# My First Free Summer
## Julia Alvarez

**Summary** Julia Alvarez had to go to summer school each year. One summer she did not have to go to school. She was excited about having a free summer. Events in the Dominican Republic soon taught her that the word *freedom* has a bigger meaning.

 ## Writing About the Big Question

**What is the best way to find the truth?** In "My First Free Summer," a young girl and her family flee their country when the father's involvement in an underground rebellion puts them in danger. Complete this sentence:

When we evaluate what is best for us, we must sometimes consider

_____.

## Note-taking Guide

Use this plot diagram to list the important events in "My First Free Summer."

Climax: Julia's English improves. She does not have to go to summer school!

Event:_____

_____

Event: _____

Rising Action

Falling Action

Event:_____

_____

Resolution
Julia's family arrives safely in America.

Exposition
Julia has to study English.

Conflict:

## Activate Prior Knowledge

Summer means the freedom of vacation for many students. Describe your summer vacations. What was your happiest summer experience?

_____

_____

What was your biggest summer disappointment?

_____

_____

## Literary Analysis

The **historical context** of a literary work is the events that are happening in the world when it takes place. Read the first bracketed paragraph. Underline the sentence that tells you the most about this work's historical context.

## Reading Check ✐

Julia, the narrator, does not know that "the dictator was bad." What does Julia know about the dictator? Circle the answers in the text.

# My First Free Summer
## Julia Alvarez

I never had summer—I had summer school. First grade, summer school. Second grade, summer school. Thirdgradesummerschoolfourthgradesummerschool. In fifth grade, I <u>vowed</u> I would get interested in fractions, the presidents of the United States, Mesopotamia; I would learn my English.

That was the problem. English. My mother had decided to send her children to the American school so we could learn the language of the nation that would soon be liberating us. For thirty years, the Dominican Republic had endured a bloody and <u>repressive</u> dictatorship. From my father, who was involved in an underground plot, my mother knew that los américanos[1] had promised to help bring democracy to the island.

"You have to learn your English!" Mami kept scolding me.

"But why?" I'd ask. I didn't know about my father's activities. I didn't know the <u>dictator</u> was bad. All I knew was that my friends who were attending Dominican schools were often on holiday to honor the dictator's birthday, the dictator's saint day, the day the dictator became the dictator, the day the dictator's oldest son was born, and so on. They marched in parades and visited the palace and had their picture in the paper.

Meanwhile, I had to learn about the pilgrims with their funny witch hats, about the 50 states and where they were on the map, about Dick and Jane[2] and their tame little pets, Puff and Spot, about freedom and liberty and justice for all—while being imprisoned

**Vocabulary Development**

**vowed** (vowd) *v.* promised solemnly

**repressive** (ri PRES iv) *adj.* cruel and harsh

**dictator** (DIK tayt er) *n.* leader of a country who controls everything and usually rules by fear

1. **los américanos** (LOHS ah me ree KAH nohs) *n.* Spanish for "the Americans."
2. **Dick and Jane** characters in a reading book commonly used by students in the 1950s.

in a hot classroom with a picture of a man wearing a silly wig hanging above the blackboard. And all of this learning I had to do in that impossibly difficult, rocks-in-your-mouth language of English!

Somehow, I managed to scrape by. Every June, when my prospects looked iffy, Mami and I met with the principal. I squirmed in my seat while they arranged for my special summer lessons.

"She is going to work extra hard. Aren't you, young lady?" the principal would quiz me at the end of our session.

My mother's eye on me, I'd murmur, "Yeah."

"Yes, what?" Mami coached.

"Yes." I sighed. "Sir."

It's a wonder that I just wasn't thrown out, which was what I secretly hoped for. But there were extenuating circumstances, the grounds on which the American school stood had been donated by my grandfather. In fact, it had been my grandmother who had encouraged Carol Morgan to start her school. The bulk of the student body was made up of the sons and daughters of American <u>diplomats</u> and business people, but a few Dominicans—most of them friends or members of my family—were allowed to attend.

"You should be grateful!" Mami scolded on the way home from our meeting. "Not every girl is lucky enough to go to the Carol Morgan School!"

In fifth grade, I straightened out. "Yes, ma'am!" I learned to say brightly. "Yes, sir!" To wave my hand in sword-wielding swoops so I could get called on with the right answer. What had changed me? Gratitude? A realization of my luckiness? No, sir! The thought of a fun summer? Yes, ma'am! I wanted to run with the pack of cousins and friends in the common yard that connected all our properties. To play on the trampoline and go off to la playa[3] and get brown as a berry. I wanted to be free. Maybe American principles had finally sunk in!

**Reading Skill**

Julia makes fun of summer classes at the American school. What is the **author's purpose** in the bracketed paragraph?

_____

_____

_____

**Literary Analysis**

The **historical context** of a work can help you understand how people in it act. How does going to the Carol Morgan School make Julia different from other Dominicans?

_____

_____

_____

**Reading Check**

Who encouraged Carol Morgan to start the school? Circle the answer in the text.

---

**Vocabulary Development**

**diplomats** (DIP luh mats) *n.* government representatives who work with other nations

3. **la playa** (lah PLAH yah) *n.* the beach.

The **historical context** can be very important in a true story. Events in the Dominican Republic in 1960 shape the plot of this true story. Underline the sentence that says what event made the United States advise Americans to return home.

### Stop to Reflect

How does Julia like her first summer without summer school? Which details in the text tell you how she feels?

_____

_____

_____

### Reading Skill

Read the underlined sentence. Use **background information** about Julia and her mother to explain the look Julia's mother gives her.

_____

_____

_____

_____

The summer of 1960 began in <u>bliss</u>: I did not have to go to summer school! *Attitude much improved. Her English progressing nicely. Attentive and cooperative in classroom.* I grinned as Mami read off the note that accompanied my report card of Bs.

But the yard replete with cousins and friends that I had dreamed about all year was deserted. Family members were leaving for the United States, using whatever connections they could drum up. The plot had unraveled. Every day there were massive arrests. The United States had closed its embassy and was advising Americans to return home.

My own parents were terrified. Every night black Volks-wagens blocked our driveway and stayed there until morning. "Secret police," my older sister whispered.

"Why are they secret if they're the police?" I asked.

"Shut up!" my sister hissed. "Do you want to get us all killed?"

Day after day, I kicked a <u>deflated</u> beach ball around the empty yard, feeling as if I'd been tricked into good behavior by whomever God put in charge of the lives of 10-year-olds. I was bored. Even summer school would have been better than this!

One day toward the end of the summer, my mother <u>summoned</u> my sisters and me. She wore that too-bright smile she sometimes pasted on her terrified face.

"Good news, girls! Our papers and tickets came! We're leaving for the United States!"

Our mouths dropped. We hadn't been told we were going on a trip anywhere, no less to some place so far away.

I was the first to speak up, "But why?"

<u>My mother flashed me the same look she used to give me when I'd ask why I had to learn English.</u>

---

**Vocabulary Development**

**bliss** (blis) *n.* perfect happiness

**deflated** (di FLAYT id) *adj.* smaller and softer because the air inside has leaked out

**summoned** (SUM uhnd) *v.* called together

I was about to tell her that I didn't want to go to the United States, where summer school had been invented and everyone spoke English. But my mother lifted a hand for silence. "We're leaving in a few hours. I want you all to go get ready! I'll be in to pack soon." The <u>desperate</u> look in her eyes did not allow for contradiction. We raced off, wondering how to fit the contents of our Dominican lives into four small suitcases.

Our flight was scheduled for that afternoon, but the airplane did not appear. The terminal lined with soldiers <u>wielding</u> machine guns, checking papers, escorting passengers into a small interrogation room. Not everyone returned.

"It's a trap," I heard my mother whisper to my father.

This had happened before, a cat-and-mouse game the dictator liked to play. Pretend that he was letting someone go, and then at the last minute, their family and friends conveniently gathered together—wham! The secret police would haul the whole clan away.

Of course, I didn't know that this was what my parents were dreading. But as the hours ticked away, and afternoon turned into evening and evening into night and night into midnight with no plane in sight, a light came on in my head. If the light could be translated into words, instead, they would say: Freedom and liberty and justice for all . . . I knew that ours was not a trip, but an escape. We had to get to the United States.

The rest of that night is a blur. It is one, then two the next morning. A plane lands, lights flashing. We are walking on the runway, climbing up the stairs into the cabin. An American lady wearing a cap welcomes us. We sit down, ready to depart. But suddenly, soldiers come on board. They go seat by seat, looking at our faces. Finally, they leave, the door closes, and with a powerful roar we lift off and I fall asleep.

**Vocabulary Development**

**desperate** (DES prit) *adj.* serious or dangerous
**wielding** (WEELD ing) *v.* holding

---

## TAKE NOTES

**Reading Skill**

The author says that "Not everyone returned" from the airport's interrogation room. What could be the **author's purpose** for not explaining what happened to these people?

_____

_____

_____

**Literary Analysis** 🔍

The **historical context** can help shape the plot in a work of nonfiction. Read the bracketed paragraph. How does the information about events in the Dominican Republic help build the action?

_____

_____

_____

**Reading Check**

What does Julia finally realize about going to the United States? Circle the answer in the text.

## Reading Skill

**Background information** about the author and her topic can help you understand the **author's purpose** for writing a work. Think about what you already know about Julia. Why does she act the way she does in the bracketed paragraphs?

_____

_____

_____

What does this scene tell you about the **author's purpose** for writing this story?

_____

_____

_____

## Reading Check

What does the American official say to Julia and her sisters that lets Julia know that she can enter the United States? Underline the sentence in the text.

Next morning, we are standing inside a large, echoing hall as a stern American official reviews our documents. What if he doesn't let us in? What if we have to go back? I am holding my breath. My parents' terror has become mine.

He checks our faces against the passport pictures. When he is done, he asks, "You girls ready for school?" I swear he is looking at me.

"Yes, sir!" I speak up.

The man laughs. He stamps our papers and hands them to my father. Then wonderfully, a smile spreads across his face. "Welcome to the United States," he says, waving us in.

**Reader's Response:** Julia's description of the airport is tense and frightening. Were you surprised by the Alvarez family's experience at the airport? Explain you answer.

_____

_____

_____

_____

# My First Free Summer

1. **Compare and Contrast:** How does the American school differ from the other schools on the island?

   _____

   _____

2. **Connect:** How does Alvarez change her behavior in the fifth grade?

   _____

   _____

3. **Reading Skill:** What is the **author's purpose** for writing this essay?

   _____

   _____

4. **Literary Analysis:** Give an example from the story that shows how the **historical context** of the Dominican Republic affects Alvarez's actions in "My First Free Summer." Use this chart.

| Historical Context | Author's Actions |
|---|---|
| Dictatorship | 1. Goes to the American school |
| | 2. |

## Writing: Letter

Write a **letter** to the young Julia Alvarez, describing what it is like to go to school in the United States. Answer the following questions to help you write your letter.

- How are schools in the United States different from the schools that Julia Alvarez is used to? List at least two differences.

  _____

  _____

- What might Alvarez like best about American schools?

  _____

- What might Alvarez like least about American schools?

  _____

## Listening and Speaking: Interview

Complete the following outline to prepare for your **interview**.

- Questions to ask at the interview:

  1. _____

  2. _____

- Follow-up questions based on your subject's responses to your questions:

  1. _____

  2. _____

  Conclusions to draw from the interview:

  1. _____

  2. _____

# from Angela's Ashes
### Frank McCourt

**Summary** A young boy is sick in an empty hospital room. He begins to talk secretly with the girl in the next room. She reads him poetry and sends him a book. Before long, the nurses discover their friendship and move the boy upstairs. The girl dies before the two can ever see each other.

## ? Writing About the Big Question

**What is the best way to find the truth?** In this excerpt from *Angela's Ashes*, a young boy discovers the joy of language while recovering from a serious illness. Complete this sentence:

A difficult experience can increase our awareness of _____

_____ because _____.

## Note-taking Guide

Use this chart to record details about the people in McCourt's story.

| Character | Details from the story |
| --- | --- |
| Frank | He has typhoid. He wants to recite "The Highwayman" for Patricia. |
| Patricia | |
| Seamus | |
| Sister Rita | |

# from Angela's Ashes

1. **Analyze:** Why does Frank want to memorize "The Highwayman" and read it back to Patricia?

   _____

2. **Compare and Contrast:** Describe how Seamus and Sister Rita are alike and different.

   _____

   _____

   _____

3. **Reading Skill:** What is the **author's purpose** for writing this story?

   _____

   _____

4. **Literary Analysis:** Show how events, or **historical context,** in the story affected Frank McCourt's life.

| Historical Context | McCourt's Life |
| --- | --- |
| Unclean conditions long ago in Ireland | Ill with typhoid; in a hospital away from his family |
| | |

## Writing: Letter of Proposal

A **letter of proposal** explains an action or idea to a business leader. Write a letter of proposal that Frank McCourt might have written to a book publisher. Answer these questions as though you were Frank McCourt.

- Why should the book be published?

  _____

  _____

- Who will be interested in reading this book?

  _____

  _____

- How might this book inspire a reader?

  _____

  _____

Use your answers to help you finish your letter.

## Listening and Speaking: Interview

Conduct an **interview** with an older person to learn about how people lived in an earlier time. Answer the following questions to get started.

- Whom will you interview?

  _____

- What were important historical events during this person's life?

  _____

  _____

- What questions do you have about these historical events?

  _____

  _____

# Applications

## About Applications

An **application** is a form that gives information about you. Groups and organizations use this information to make decisions. You may fill out an application to do one of the following:

- apply for a job
- open a bank account
- apply for admission to a school
- get a library card
- get a driver's license
- join a club or sports team

Before you fill out an application, read the directions carefully. Make sure you know the following:

- when and where to turn in the application
- whether extra materials are required
- what information is needed in the application

## Reading Skill

The **purpose** of an application is to gather information about a person. Applicants should pay attention to the **structure** of an application in order to provide the correct information.

Read an application carefully before filling it out. Check the headings, subheadings, and other labels to find out what information you need to provide. Make sure that you write information in the correct section or space. Then, gather any additional material or documents that you need to provide with the application.

---

### Structural Features of Applications

- **introduction:** provides a description of the open position and an explanation of the application process
- **headings:** show where to find categories of information
- **directions:** explain how to fill out the application
- **rows and columns:** allow applicants to provide information in an organized format

# The Flat Rock Playhouse

The Flat Rock Playhouse has grown in recent years from a traditional summer theater to a regional powerhouse. It boasts one of the largest Resident Contract Agreements with Actors' Equity Association, the union of actors and stage managers, in the southern region. Flat Rock Playhouse unites its seasonal talent pool with its year-round administrative and artistic staff, 70% of whom were formerly apprentices and interns. The Playhouse proudly trains and educates to nurture its own future.

**Do you have a reputable Equity Apprenticeship in your background?** Outside an education setting what steps have you taken to build a career? **Have you begun professional networking?** • How are you going to make the contacts necessary to get the job? • Do you have **acting professionals** on your reference list? • What do you know about marketing yourself in the theater business? Do you have a professionally photographed head shot? • Do you have a means to continually **update** your resume? • Do you know **how to find an agent?** • Do you know how to get call backs at a cattle-call audition? • Would you feel comfortable in a **professional** environment? • Are you ready to join a union? • **Are you a triple-threat talent?**

## Cultural Understanding

The Flat Rock Playhouse is located in North Carolina. A group of performers began the Flat Rock Playhouse in 1952. In 1961, it became The State Theatre of North Carolina.

## Vocabulary Builder

Pronouns such as *you, he, she, they, them,* and *it* are often used in place of a noun. A pronoun stands for or refers to the noun it replaces. Read the first paragraph. Underline the pronouns. What noun does the pronoun *It* stand for at the beginning of the second sentence?

_____

_____

## Vocabulary Builder

**Job Terms** *Professional networking* means "the practice of meeting other people involved in the same kind of work in order to share information and support one another." A *reference list* is a list of people who know you and will recommend you for a job. A *résumé* (REZ oo may) is a short written description of your education and work experience. A *cattle-call audition* is an audition, or chance to perform, in which hundreds of actors compete for a certain number of roles. A *union* is an organization formed by workers to protect their rights.

### Vocabulary Builder

**Parts of Speech** *Contact* can be a verb meaning "write or telephone someone." It can also be a noun meaning "communication with a person or organization." Circle *contact* when it is used as a noun in the paragraph. Draw a box around *contact* when it is used as a verb.

### Comprehension Builder

In what two ways can applicants audition for the Vagabond School of the Drama at Flat Rock Playhouse?

_____

_____

### Text Structure

What type of information is required in the first bracketed section of the application?

_____

What type of information is required in the second bracketed section?

_____

What type of information is required in the third bracketed section?

_____

We will be attending SETC (Southeastern Theatre Conference) in March and will be happy to contact all serious applicants who have already **initiated** contact regarding their audition numbers. Applicants can, of course, call and set up personal auditions at the Playhouse if they are not attending SETC. However, if one's schedule or geographic distance from the Playhouse makes a personal audition impossible, one may send a videotaped audition consisting of[1] two monologues[2] and if applicable examples of singing and dance work. Also to **expedite** our selection and registration process, be sure to include two reference letters with the return correspondence. An application form and descriptive material about the program are subject to change due to[3] variations in the talents and needs of each student class. Please complete and return the application at your earliest **convenience** if you wish to be considered among this year's candidates.

---

**Everyday Words**

**initiated** (i NI shee ayt id) *v.* began doing something; arranged for something important to start, such as an official process

**expedite** (EKS pi dyt) *v.* make a process or action happen more quickly

**convenience** (kuhn VEE nee uhns) *n.* a suitable or agreeable time

---

1. **consisting of** being formed from two or more things or people
2. **monologues** (MAHN uh lahgz) *n.* long speeches made by one person
3. **due to** *prep.* because of

# Apprentice Application Form for the Vagabond School of the Drama

**TO ENROLL:** PLEASE **PRINT** THIS FORM, COMPLETE IT, AND RETURN IT WITH A HEADSHOT OR SNAP SHOT, as well as any other information you deem necessary. Videotapes are welcome. Auditions and/or interviews by the Executive Director or his appointee are required.

| Student Name | Social Security |
|---|---|

| Address |
|---|

| City | State | Zip |
|---|---|---|

| Home Phone | Work Phone | E-mail |
|---|---|---|

| Age | Date of Birth / / | Weight | Height | Hair Color |
|---|---|---|---|---|

**Instruction**

| Song | Dance | Instruments |
|---|---|---|

| Theater Training |
|---|

| Parent/Guardian Name |
|---|

| Address |
|---|

| City | State | Zip |
|---|---|---|

| Home Phone | Work Phone | E-mail |
|---|---|---|

**Please provide a character reference**

| Name |
|---|

| Address |
|---|

| City | State | Zip |
|---|---|---|

| Home Phone | Work Phone | E-mail |
|---|---|---|

The Vagabond School of the Drama, Inc. is a not-for-profit educational institution that admits students of any race, creed, sex, nationality, or ethnic origin.

# Thinking About the Application

1. Why do you think this application provides more space for the applicant's previous instruction in song, dance, and instrument than for the applicant's name?

   _____

2. Explain two advantages of becoming a member of the Vagabond School of the Drama for people looking for a career in acting.

   _____

   _____

**TALK ABOUT IT** Reading Skill

3. What does the first part of the application, beginning "TO ENROLL," contain?

   _____

4. Which part of the application specifically seeks to determine the applicant's experience?

   _____

**WRITE ABOUT IT** Timed Writing: Summary **(20 minutes)**

Answer these questions to help you write your summary about the Vagabond School of the Drama.

- What is the school's mission or purpose?

  _____

- What is its history?

  _____

- Where is the school located?

  _____

# The Treasure of Lemon Brown

All short stories have these elements:

**Characters**—people or animals who take part in the action
  **Motivation** is the reason or reasons that people act as they do.

**Characterization**—the way a writer reveals the characters
* In **direct characterization**, the writer tells about the character.
* In **indirect characterization**, the writer shows the character through the character's words and actions.

**Theme**—the central message in a story
  A **universal theme** is a message about life that appears in many cultures and time periods. Examples of universal themes are:
* Hard work always pays off in the end.
* Old age brings wisdom.

**Plot**—the sequence of events, or things that happen, in a story
  These five parts make up a plot:
* **Exposition**—an introduction or beginning of a story. The exposition tells the characters and the setting (time and place).
* **Rising action**—the **conflict** (or main problem) of a story and the first events
* **Climax**—the turning point of the story
* **Falling action**—events after the climax that show that the conflict is solved or lessened
* **Resolution**—the ending of a story

## Literary Devices in Fiction

**Literary devices** are tools that writers use to make their stories more interesting, more lifelike, or more entertaining.

| Literary Device | Definition | Example |
|---|---|---|
| **Foreshadowing** | clues to what will happen later | Before the day was over, Priya would learn the meaning of fear. |
| **Flashback** | a switch from the present time to the story to a scene in the past | As he waited for the mail, Jason remembered the last time he had seen Carla. |
| **Irony** | surprising, interesting, or amusing contradictions | A character who gives up all hope of ever paying her bills suddenly becomes a millionaire. |
| **Dialect** | form of a language that people speak in a certain region or group | People in Texas or the Southwest might say "Howdy, ma'am." |

# The Treasure of Lemon Brown
## Walter Dean Myers

**Summary** Fourteen-year-old Greg should study. Instead, he remembers how angry his father was with him two nights ago. Greg walks into an empty building. He hears the sound of breathing. It turns out to be Lemon Brown, a homeless man. Greg learns from Lemon that something that connects a parent and a child is a treasure.

## Note-taking Guide
Use this chart to record details about the events of the story.

Climax:

Event: _____

_____

Event: _____

Event: Greg meets Lemon Brown

Event: _____

Event: Greg enters the empty
building

_____

Rising Action

Falling Action

Setting: an empty building
at night;
Characters: Greg, his
father, Lemon Brown

Resolution

Conflict:

Exposition

### Activate Prior Knowledge

Tell about a time when you learned something from an older person. Describe your experience.

_____

_____

_____

_____

_____

### Short Story

A **flashback** is a switch from the present time of the story to a scene from the past. Underline the names of the characters who are in the flashback in the bracketed passage. Tell what they are talking about.

_____

_____

_____

### Short Story

How might Greg and his father's relationship be related to a **theme** of the story?

_____

_____

_____

_____

# The Treasure of Lemon Brown
## Walter Dean Myers

The dark sky, filled with angry, swirling clouds, reflected Greg Ridley's mood as he sat on the stoop of his building. His father's voice came to him again, first reading the letter the principal had sent to the house, then lecturing endlessly about his poor efforts in math.

"I had to leave school when I was thirteen," his father had said, "that's a year younger than you are now. If I'd had half the chances that you have, I'd . . ."

Greg had sat in the small, pale green kitchen listening, knowing the lecture would end with his father saying he couldn't play ball with the Scorpions. He had asked his father the week before, and his father had said it depended on his next report card. It wasn't often the Scorpions took on new players, especially fourteen-year-olds, and this was a chance of a lifetime for Greg. He hadn't been allowed to play high school ball, which he had really wanted to do, but playing for the Community Center team was the next best thing. Report cards were due in a week, and Greg had been hoping for the best. But the principal had ended the suspense early when she sent that letter saying Greg would probably fail math if he didn't spend more time studying.

"And you want to play *basketball*?" His father's brows knitted over deep brown eyes. "That must be some kind of a joke. Now you just get into your room and hit those books[1]."

That had been two nights before. His father's words, like the distant thunder that now echoed through the streets of Harlem, still rumbled softly in his ears.

It was beginning to cool. Gusts of wind made bits of paper dance between the parked cars. There was a flash of nearby lightning, and soon large drops of

---

**Vocabulary Development**

**lecturing** (LEK cher ing) *v.* talking or scolding for a long time about a certain subject

**suspense** (suh SPENS) *n.* not knowing how an event or action will turn out and feeling uncertain

---

1. **"hit those books"** *v.* study.

rain splashed onto his jeans. He stood to go upstairs, thought of the lecture that probably awaited him if he did anything except shut himself in his room with his math book, and started walking down the street instead. Down the block there was an old tenement[2] that had been abandoned for some months. Some of the guys had held an <u>impromptu</u> checker tournament there the week before, and Greg had noticed that the door, once boarded over, had been slightly <u>ajar</u>.

Pulling his collar up as high as he could, he checked for traffic and made a dash across the street. He reached the house just as another flash of lightning changed the night to day for an instant, then returned the graffiti-scarred building to the grim shadows. He vaulted over the outer stairs and pushed <u>tentatively</u> on the door. It was open, and he let himself in.

The inside of the building was dark except for the dim light that filtered through the dirty windows from the streetlamps. There was a room a few feet from the door, and from where he stood at the entrance, Greg could see a squarish patch of light on the floor. He entered the room, frowning at the musty smell. It was a large room that might have been someone's parlor at one time. Squinting, Greg could see an old table on its side against one wall, what looked like a pile of rags or a torn mattress in the corner, and a couch, with one side broken, in front of the window.

He went to the couch. The side that wasn't broken was comfortable enough, though a little creaky. From the spot he could see the blinking neon sign over the bodega[3] on the corner. He sat awhile, watching the sign blink first green then red, allowing his mind to drift to the Scorpions, then to his father. His father had been a postal worker for all Greg's life, and was

## TAKE NOTES

### Stop to Reflect

Circle details in the bracketed passage that tell about the building Greg enters. Then, tell whether you would enter it, and why or why not.

_____

_____

_____

_____

### Short Story

The **exposition** of a story introduces the characters and setting, including the time and place. List details of the exposition below.

**Characters:** _____

**Time:** _____

**Place:** _____

### Reading Check

Why does Greg prefer going to the tenement instead of home? Underline the sentence that tells the reason.

---

**Vocabulary Development**

**impromptu** (im PRAHMP too) *adj.* unscheduled; unplanned

**ajar** (uh JAHR) *adj.* slightly open

**tentatively** (TEN tuh tiv lee) *adv.* hesitantly; with uncertainty

---

2. **tenement** (TEN uh muhnt) *n.* old, run-down apartment house.

3. **bodega** (boh DAY gah) *n.* small grocery store serving a Latino neighborhood.

**Foreshadowing** is clues about what will happen later. Read the clues in the first bracketed passage. Predict what might happen later.

_____

_____

_____

_____

**Short Story**

**Dialect** is a form of language that people speak in a certain region or group. One clue that the words in a sentence are in dialect is that they contain a double negative. Underline the two words in the second bracketed paragraph that form the double negative.

**Stop to Reflect**

Is a razor that could "cut a week into nine days" sharp or not? Explain.

_____

_____

_____

_____

_____

proud of it, often telling Greg how hard he had worked to pass the test. Greg had heard the story too many times to be interested now.

For a moment Greg thought he heard something that sounded like a scraping against the wall. He listened carefully, but it was gone.

Outside the wind had picked up, sending the rain against the window with a force that shook the glass in its frame. A car passed, its tires hissing over the wet street and its red taillights glowing in the darkness.

Greg thought he heard the noise again. His stomach tightened as he held himself still and listened <u>intently</u>. There weren't any more scraping noises, but he was sure he had heard something in the darkness—something breathing!

He tried to figure out just where the breathing was coming from; he knew it was in the room with him. Slowly he stood, <u>tensing</u>. As he turned, a flash of lightning lit up the room, frightening him with its sudden brilliance. He saw nothing, just the overturned table, the pile of rags and an old newspaper on the floor. Could he have been imagining the sounds? He continued listening, but heard nothing and thought that it might have just been rats. Still, he thought, as soon as the rain let up he would leave. He went to the window and was about to look when he heard a voice behind him.

"Don't try nothin' 'cause I got a razor here sharp enough to cut a week into nine days!"

Greg, except for an involuntary tremor[4] in his knees, stood stock still.[5] The voice was high and brittle, like dry twigs being broken, surely not one he had ever heard before. There was a shuffling sound as the person who had been speaking moved a step closer. Greg turned, holding his breath, his eyes straining to see in the dark room.

**Vocabulary Development**

**intently** (in TENT lee) *adv.* with purpose or concentration

**tensing** (TENS ing) *v.* becoming stiff or uptight, often from fear or being nervous

4. **involuntary** (in VAHL uhn ter ee) **tremor** (TREM er) *n.* automatic trembling or shaking.

5. **stock still** not moving at all.

The upper part of the figure before him was still in darkness. The lower half was in the dim rectangle of light that fell unevenly from the window. There were two feet, in cracked, dirty shoes from which rose legs that were wrapped in rags.

"Who are you?" Greg hardly recognized his own voice.

"I'm Lemon Brown," came the answer. "Who're you?"

"Greg Ridley."

"What you doing here?" The figure shuffled forward again, and Greg took a small step backward.

"It's raining," Greg said.

"I can see that," the figure said.

The person who called himself Lemon Brown peered forward, and Greg could see him clearly. He was an old man. His black, heavily wrinkled face was surrounded by a halo of crinkly white hair and whiskers that seemed to separate his head from the layers of dirty coats piled on his smallish frame. His pants were bagged to the knee, where they were met with rags that went down to the old shoes. The rags were held on with strings, and there was a rope around his middle. Greg relaxed. He had seen the man before, picking through the trash on the corner and pulling clothes out of a Salvation Army box. There was no sign of the razor that could "cut a week into nine days."

"What are you doing here?" Greg asked.

"This is where I'm staying," Lemon Brown said. "What you here for?"

"Told you it was raining out," Greg said, leaning against the back of the couch until he felt it give slightly.

"Ain't you got no home?"

"I got a home," Greg answered.

"You ain't one of them bad boys looking for my treasure, is you?" Lemon Brown cocked his head to one side and <u>squinted</u> one eye. "Because I told you I got me a razor."

"I'm not looking for your treasure," Greg answered, smiling. "If you have one."

© Pearson Education

**Vocabulary Development**

**squinted** (SKWINT id) *v.* looked at something with one's eyes partly closed to see it better

**TAKE NOTES**

**Short Story**

**Characterization** is the way the writer reveals the characters. Underline details of Lemon's characterization in the bracketed passage. These include his words and actions. Then tell whether the writer is using direct or indirect characterization.

_____

_____

_____

_____

_____

_____

**Stop to Reflect**

Who do you think Lemon Brown is? Why do you think that?

_____

_____

_____

_____

_____

**Reading Check**

Where had Greg seen Lemon Brown before? Circle your answer.

Lemon Brown's **dialect** sometimes results in sentences without verbs or verb parts. Insert the correct verb in the underlined sentence. Then tell what Lemon Brown means by this sentence.

_____

_____

_____

_____

**Stop to Reflect**

An **irony** is a surprising twist or contradiction. What is ironic about the way Lemon Brown first appeared to Greg and how he appears to him now?

_____

_____

_____

_____

**Reading Check**

Underline the sentence that tells why Lemon Brown was called Sweet Lemon Brown.

"What you mean, if I have one," Lemon Brown said. "Every man got a treasure. You don't know that, you must be a fool!"

"Sure," Greg said as he sat on the sofa and put one leg over the back. "What do you have, gold coins?"

"Don't worry none about what I got," Lemon Brown said. "You know who I am?"

"You told me your name was orange or lemon or something like that."

"Lemon Brown," the old man said, pulling back his shoulders as he did so, "they used to call me Sweet Lemon Brown."

"Sweet Lemon?" Greg asked.

"Yessir. Sweet Lemon Brown. They used to say I sung the blues so sweet that if I sang at a funeral, the dead would <u>commence</u> to rocking with the beat. Used to travel all over Mississippi and as far as Monroe, Louisiana, and east on over to Macon, Georgia. You mean you ain't never heard of Sweet Lemon Brown?"

"Afraid not," Greg said. "What . . . what happened to you?"

"Hard times, boy. <u>Hard times always after a poor man.</u> One day I got tired, sat down to rest a spell and felt a tap on my shoulder. Hard times caught up with me."

"Sorry about that."

"What you doing here? How come you didn't go on home when the rain come? Rain don't bother you young folks none."

"Just didn't." Greg looked away.

"I used to have a knotty-headed boy just like you." Lemon Brown had half walked, half shuffled back to the corner and sat down against the wall. "Had them big eyes like you got, I used to call them moon eyes. Look into them moon eyes and see anything you want."

"How come you gave up singing the blues?" Greg asked.

"Didn't give it up," Lemon Brown said. "You don't give up the blues; they give you up. After a while you do good for yourself, and it ain't nothing but foolishness singing about how hard you got it. Ain't that right?"

**Vocabulary Development**
**commence** (kuh MENS) *v.* begin

"I guess so."

"What's that noise?" Lemon Brown asked, suddenly sitting upright.

Greg listened, and he heard a noise outside.

He looked at Lemon Brown and saw the old man pointing toward the window.

Greg went to the window and saw three men, neighborhood thugs, on the stoop. One was carrying a length of pipe. Greg looked back toward Lemon Brown, who moved quietly across the room to the window. The old man looked out, then beckoned frantically for Greg to follow him. For a moment Greg couldn't move. Then he found himself following Lemon Brown into the hallway and up darkened stairs. Greg followed as closely as he could. They reached the top of the stairs, and Greg felt Lemon Brown's hand first lying on his shoulder, then probing down his arm until he finally took Greg's hand into his own as they crouched in the darkness.

"They's bad men," Lemon Brown whispered. His breath was warm against Greg's skin.

"Hey! Rag man!" A voice called. "We know you in here. What you got up under them rags? You got any money?"

Silence.

"We don't want to have to come in and hurt you, old man, but we don't mind if we have to."

Lemon Brown squeezed Greg's hand in his own hard, gnarled fist.

There was a banging downstairs and a light as the men entered. They banged around noisily, calling for the rag man.

"We heard you talking about your treasure." The voice was slurred. "We just want to see it, that's all."

"You sure he's here?" One voice seemed to come from the room with the sofa.

"Yeah, he stays here every night."

"There's another room over there; I'm going to take a look. You got that flashlight?"

## TAKE NOTES

### Reading Check

Why do the bad men come to find Lemon Brown? Underline the sentence that tells their reason.

### Short Story

The **rising action** of a story includes the events that lead up to the climax. What is happening in the bracketed passage?

_____

_____

_____

_____

### Short Story

In the underlined sentence, why does Lemon Brown squeeze Greg's hand? What might this situation have to do with a **theme** of the story?

_____

_____

_____

_____

---

**Vocabulary Development**

**probing** (PROHB ing) *v.* looking or searching for something

**gnarled** (nahrld) *adj.* rough and bent out of shape, twisted

## Short Story

The author uses **direct characterization** to show what the bad men are like. Underline an example of direct characterization of the bad men in the bracketed passage. Tell what it shows about them.

_____

_____

_____

_____

## Stop to Reflect

What do you think the men are planning to do with Lemon Brown's treasure?

_____

_____

_____

_____

## Reading Check ✎

Lemon Brown acts bravely. Underline the sentence that tells what he does.

_____

_____

_____

"Yeah, here, take the pipe too."

Greg opened his mouth to quiet the sound of his breath as he sucked it in uneasily. A beam of light hit the wall a few feet opposite him, then went out.

"Ain't nobody in that room," a voice said. "You think he gone or something?"

"I don't know," came the answer. "All I know is that I heard him talking about some kind of treasure. You know they found that shopping bag lady with that money in her bags."

"Yeah. You think he's upstairs?"

"Hey, old man, are you up there?"

Silence.

"Watch my back, I'm going up."

There was a footstep on the stairs, and the beam from the flashlight danced crazily along the peeling wallpaper. Greg held his breath. There was another step and a loud crashing noise as the man banged the pipe against the wooden banister.[6]

Greg could feel his temples throb as the man slowly neared them. Greg thought about the pipe, wondering what he would do when the man reached them—what he *could* do.

Then Lemon Brown released his hand and moved toward the top of the stairs. Greg looked around and saw stairs going up to the next floor. He tried waving to Lemon Brown, hoping the old man would see him in the dim light and follow him to the next floor. Maybe, Greg thought, the man wouldn't follow them up there. Suddenly, though, Lemon Brown stood at the top of the stairs, both arms raised high above his head.

"There he is!" A voice cried from below.

"Throw down your money, old man, so I won't have to bash your head in!"

Lemon Brown didn't move. Greg felt himself near panic. The steps came closer, and still Lemon Brown didn't move. He was an eerie sight, a bundle of rags standing at the top of the stairs, his shadow on the wall looming over him. Maybe, the thought came to Greg, the scene could be even eerier.

**Vocabulary Development**

**temples** (TEM puhlz) *n.* flattened parts of the sides of the forehead

**eerie** (EE ree) *adj.* strange, scary

6. **banister** (BAN uhs ter) *n.* railing along a staircase.v

Greg wet his lips, put his hands to his mouth and tried to make a sound. Nothing came out. He swallowed hard, wet his lips once more and howled as evenly as he could.

"What's that?"

As Greg howled, the light moved away from Lemon Brown, but not before Greg saw him hurl his body down the stairs at the men who had come to take his treasure. There was a crashing noise, and then footsteps. A rush of warm air came in as the downstairs door opened, then there was only an <u>ominous</u> silence.

Greg stood on the landing. He listened, and after a while there was another sound on the staircase.

"Mr. Brown?" he called.

"Yeah, it's me," came the answer. "I got their flashlight."

Greg <u>exhaled</u> in relief as Lemon Brown made his way slowly back up the stairs.

"You OK?"

"Few bumps and bruises," Lemon Brown said.

"I think I'd better be going," Greg said, his breath returning to normal. "You'd better leave, too, before they come back."

"They may hang around outside for a while," Lemon Brown said, "but they ain't getting their nerve up to come in here again. Not with crazy old rag men and howling spooks. Best you stay a while till the coast is clear. I'm heading out west tomorrow, out to East St. Louis."

"They were talking about treasures," Greg said. "You *really* have a treasure?"

"What I tell you? Didn't I tell you every man got a treasure?" Lemon Brown said. "You want to see mine?"

"If you want to show it to me," Greg shrugged.

"Let's look out the window first, see what them <u>scoundrels</u> be doing," Lemon Brown said.

© Pearson Education

## TAKE NOTES

### Short Story

The **climax** is the turning point of the story. Underline the turning point in the bracketed paragraph.

### Stop to Reflect

Lemon Brown gives Greg credit for helping scare off the bad men. Do you think Greg deserves credit? Explain.

_____

_____

_____

_____

### Short Story

A **motivation** is a reason for a character's actions. What is Lemon Brown's motivation for fighting the bad men?

_____

_____

_____

_____

_____

**Vocabulary Development**

**ominous** (AHM uh nuhs) *adj.* giving the feeling that something bad is about to happen

**exhaled** (eks HAYLD) *v.* breathed out

**scoundrels** (SKOWN druhlz) *n.* dishonest people, troublemakers

## Short Story

**Falling action** occurs in a story when the conflict lessens. Is there any conflict left in this story? Explain.

_____

_____

_____

_____

## Short Story

One **theme**, or message about life, in this story involves the meaning of a treasure. Why are the news clippings and harmonica a treasure to Lemon Brown?

_____

_____

_____

_____

## Stop to Reflect

How do the words in the bracketed passage relate to the conflict Greg had at the beginning of the story?

_____

_____

_____

_____

They followed the oval beam of the flashlight into one of the rooms and looked out the window. They saw the men who had tried to take the treasure sitting on the curb near the corner. One of them had his pants leg up, looking at his knee.

"You sure you're not hurt?" Greg asked Lemon Brown.

"Nothing that ain't been hurt before," Lemon Brown said. "When you get as old as me all you say when something hurts is, 'Howdy, Mr. Pain, sees you back again.' Then when Mr. Pain see he can't worry you none, he go on mess with somebody else."

Greg smiled.

"Here, you hold this." Lemon Brown gave Greg the flashlight.

He sat on the floor near Greg and carefully untied the strings that held the rags on his right leg. When he took the rags away, Greg saw a piece of plastic. The old man carefully took off the plastic and unfolded it. He revealed some yellowed newspaper clippings and a battered harmonica.

"There it be," he said, nodding his head. "There it be."

Greg looked at the old man, saw the distant look in his eye, then turned to the clippings. They told of Sweet Lemon Brown, a blues singer and harmonica player who was appearing at different theaters in the South. One of the clippings said he had been the hit of the show, although not the headliner. All of the clippings were reviews of shows Lemon Brown had been in more than 50 years ago. Greg looked at the harmonica. It was dented badly on one side, with the reed holes on one end nearly closed.

"I used to travel around and make money for to feed my wife and Jesse—that's my boy's name. Used to feed them good, too. Then his mama died, and he stayed with his mama's sister. He growed up to be a man, and when the war come he saw fit to go off and fight in it. I didn't have nothing to give him except these things that told him who I was, and what he come from. If you know your pappy did something, you know you can do something too.

"Anyway, he went off to war, and I went off still playing and singing. 'Course by then I wasn't as much as I used to be, not without somebody to make it worth the while. You know what I mean?"

"Yeah," Greg nodded, not quite really knowing.

"I traveled around, and one time I come home, and there was this letter saying Jesse got killed in the war. Broke my heart, it truly did.

"They sent back what he had with him over there, and what it was is this old mouth fiddle[7] and these clippings. Him carrying it around with him like that told me it meant something to him. That was my treasure, and when I give it to him he treated it just like that, a treasure. Ain't that something?"

"Yeah, I guess so," Greg said.

"You *guess* so?" Lemon Brown's voice rose an octave as he started to put his treasure back into the plastic. "Well, you got to guess 'cause you sure don't know nothing. Don't know enough to get home when it's raining."

"I guess . . . I mean, you're right."

"You OK for a youngster," the old man said as he tied the strings around his leg, "better than those scalawags[8] what come here looking for my treasure. That's for sure."

"You really think that treasure of yours was worth fighting for?" Greg asked. "Against a pipe?"

"What else a man got 'cepting what he can pass on to his son, or his daughter, if she be his oldest?" Lemon Brown said. "For a big-headed boy you sure do ask the foolishest questions."

Lemon Brown got up after patting his rags in place and looked out the window again.

"Looks like they're gone. You get on out of here and get yourself home. I'll be watching from the window so you'll be all right."

Lemon Brown went down the stairs behind Greg. When they reached the front door the old man looked out first, saw the street was clear and told Greg to scoot on home.

"You sure you'll be OK?" Greg asked.

"Now didn't I tell you I was going to East St. Louis in the morning?" Lemon Brown asked. "Don't that sound OK to you?"

"Sure it does," Greg said. "Sure it does. And you take care of that treasure of yours."

**Short Story**

Why are the news clippings and harmonica a treasure for Lemon Brown?

_____

_____

_____

_____

**Short Story**

How does the underlined sentence relate to a **theme** of the story?

_____

_____

_____

_____

_____

**Stop to Reflect**

Greg asks Lemon Brown whether he really thought his treasure was worth fighting for. Do you? Why or why not?

_____

_____

_____

_____

7. **mouth fiddle** slang term for a harmonica.

8. **scalawags** (SKAL uh wagz) *n.* people who cause trouble, scoundrels.

### Short Story

The **resolution** is the ending of the story and the conflict. What is the resolution of this story?

_____

_____

_____

_____

### Reading Check

The change in weather reflects a change in Greg's mood. Underline the sentence that tells the weather changed.

"That I'll do," Lemon said, the wrinkles about his eyes suggesting a smile. "That I'll do."

The night had warmed and the rain had stopped, leaving puddles at the curbs. Greg didn't even want to think how late it was. He thought ahead of what his father would say and wondered if he should tell him about Lemon Brown. He thought about it until he reached his stoop,[9] and decided against it. Lemon Brown would be OK, Greg thought, with his memories and his treasure.

Greg pushed the button over the bell marked Ridley, thought of the lecture he knew his father would give him, and smiled.

Reader's Response: Do you think a story like this one could really happen? Explain.

_____

_____

_____

_____

_____

_____

_____

_____

_____

_____

_____

9. **stoop** (stoop) *n.* porch or stairs in front of a house.

# Short Stories

1. **Respond:** Do you think Greg should tell his father about Lemon Brown? Explain your answer.

_____

_____

_____

_____

2. Complete the chart by telling what each treasure means to Brown and why the treasures are an important part of the story.

| Lemon Brown's Treasures | | |
| --- | --- | --- |
| What It Says | What It Means | Why It Is Important |
|  |  |  |

3. **Short Story:** What is the main **conflict** in this story?

_____

_____

4. **Short Story:** Which details of the **setting** of this story could be real?

_____

_____

## Create a Biographical Timeline

Follow these steps to create your **biographical timeline** of Walter Dean Myers's life.

- Go to the library. Use a computer to find a database for literature or biography. (If you need help, ask a librarian.) For example, you might find databases such as *Contemporary Authors, Contemporary Black Biography,* or *Major Authors and Illustrators for Children and Young Adults.* Find one or more entries for Walter Dean Myers in the databases. Record the information you find below.

**Date Born:** _____

**Book:** _____ **Date:** _____

**Book:** _____ **Date:** _____

**Book:** _____ **Date:** _____

**Award:** _____ **Date:** _____

**Award:** _____ **Date:** _____

- Use the Internet. Type in search terms such as *"Walter Dean Myers"* + *awards*. Screen your results, or "hits," for descriptions that match your research goal. Use reliable sites, such as those that end in .org (often libraries or nonprofit groups). Record the information you find below.

**Date Born:** _____

**Book:** _____ **Date:** _____

**Book:** _____ **Date:** _____

**Book:** _____ **Date:** _____

**Award:** _____ **Date:** _____

**Award:** _____ **Date:** _____

- Watch the video interview with Walter Dean Myers and review your source material. Use this information to record additional dates and facts for your timeline.

**Additional dates/facts:** _____

# The Bear Boy • Rikki-tikki-tavi

## Reading Skill

**Predicting** means making an intelligent guess about what will happen next in a story based on details in the text. You can also **use prior knowledge to make predictions.** For example, if a character in a story sees dark clouds, you can predict that there will be a storm because you know from prior knowledge that dark clouds often mean stormy weather.

## Literary Analysis

**Plot** is the related sequence of events in a short story and other works of fiction. A plot has the following elements:

- **Exposition:** introduction of the setting, the characters, and the basic situation
- **Rising Action:** events that introduce a **conflict**, or struggle, and increase the tension
- **Climax:** the story's high point, at which the eventual outcome becomes clear
- **Falling Action:** events that follow the climax
- **Resolution:** the final outcome and tying up of loose ends
  Fill in the lines of this chart to show the plot of the story.

Climax: _____

Event: _____    Event: _____

_____              _____

Event: _____    Event: _____

_____              _____

Event: _____

_____

Rising Action    Falling Action

Resolution

Exposition

# The Bear Boy
## Joseph Bruchac

**Summary** Kuo-Haya's father ignores him. Kuo-Haya becomes lost one day as he wanders outside his village. He finds a mother bear and her cubs. The bears teach Kuo-Haya things his father never showed him. Kuo-Haya's father tries to get back his son and learns how to be a good father.

### Writing About the Big Question

**Does every conflict have a winner?** In "The Bear Boy," a family of bears helps resolve a conflict by teaching a father how to care for his son. Complete this sentence:

When a person does not understand how to care for others, _____

_____ can be lost.

### Note-taking Guide

Use this chart to record how Kuo-Haya and his father changed during the story.

|  | How does he feel when the story starts? | What does he learn from the bears? | How does he feel when the story ends? |
|---|---|---|---|
| Kuo-Haya |  |  |  |
| Kuo-Haya's father |  |  |  |

# The Bear Boy

## Joseph Bruchac

Long ago, in a Pueblo village, a boy named Kuo-Haya lived with his father. But his father did not treat him well. In his heart he still <u>mourned</u> the death of his wife, Kuo-Haya's mother, and did not enjoy doing things with his son. He did not teach his boy how to run. He did not show him how to wrestle. He was always too busy.

As a result, Kuo-Haya was a <u>timid</u> boy and walked about stooped over all of the time. When the other boys raced or wrestled, Kuo-Haya slipped away. He spent much of his time alone.

Time passed, and the boy reached the age when his father should have been helping him get ready for his <u>initiation</u> into manhood. Still Kuo-Haya's father paid no attention at all to his son.

One day Kuo-Haya was out walking far from the village, toward the cliffs where the bears lived. Now the people of the village always knew they must stay away from these cliffs, for the bear was a very powerful animal. It was said that if someone saw a bear's tracks and followed them, he might never come back. But Kuo-Haya had never been told about this. When he came upon the tracks of a bear, Kuo-Haya followed them along an arroyo, a small canyon[1] cut by a winding stream, up into the mesas.[2] The tracks led into a little box canyon below some caves. There, he came upon some bear cubs.

When they saw Kuo-Haya, the little bears ran away. But Kuo-Haya sat down and called to them in a friendly voice.

### Vocabulary Development

**mourned** (mawrnd) *v.* was very sad about

**timid** (TIM id) *adj.* shy

**initiation** (i ni shee AY shun) *n.* process by which one becomes a member of a group

1. **canyon** (KAN yuhn) *n.* long narrow valley between high cliffs, often with a stream flowing through it.
2. **mesas** (MAY suhz) *n.* plateaus (or flat-topped hills) with steep sides.

---

## TAKE NOTES

**Activate Prior Knowledge**

How do you expect people and bears to interact?

_____

_____

_____

_____

**Literary Analysis**

The **plot** of a story is the series of events in the story. One element of a plot is the rising action that increases tension. Underline the sentences in the bracketed paragraph that build tension in the story.

**Stop to Reflect**

Kuo-Haya does not know that he should keep away from bear tracks. Who should have told him this?

_____

_____

**Reading Check**

Underline the sentence that tells why Kuo-Haya's father does not play with him.

## Reading Skill

**Predictions** are your thoughts about what will happen next in a story. Read the first bracketed paragraph. On the basis of your knowledge of bears, predict what might happen to Kuo-Haya.

_____

_____

_____

_____

## Literary Analysis 🔍

How does the second bracketed paragraph contribute to the **rising action** in the story?

_____

_____

_____

_____

_____

## Reading Check

How does Kuo-Haya come to live in the cave with the bears? Circle the sentence that gives the answer.

_____

"I will not hurt you," he said to the bear cubs. "Come and play with me." The bears walked back out of the bushes. Soon the boy and the bears were playing together. As they played, however, a shadow came over them. Kuo-Haya looked up and saw the mother bear standing above him.

"Where is Kuo-Haya?" the people asked his father.

"I do not know," the father said.

"Then you must find him!"

So the father and other people of the pueblo began to search for the missing boy. They went through the canyons calling his name. But they found no sign of the boy there. Finally, when they reached the cliffs, the best trackers found his footsteps and the path of the bears. They followed the tracks along the arroyo and up into the mesas to the box canyon. In front of a cave, they saw the boy playing with the bear cubs as the mother bear watched them <u>approvingly</u>, nudging Kuo-Haya now and then to encourage him.

The trackers crept close, hoping to grab the boy and run. But as soon as the mother bear caught their scent, she growled and pushed her cubs and the boy back into the cave.

"The boy is with the bears," the trackers said when they returned to the village.

"What shall we do?" the people asked.

"It is the <u>responsibility</u> of the boy's father," said the medicine man. Then he called Kuo-Haya's father to him.

"You have not done well," said the medicine man. "You are the one who must guide your boy to manhood, but you have <u>neglected</u> him. Now the mother bear is caring for your boy as you should have done all along. She is teaching him to be strong

### Vocabulary Development

**approvingly** (uh PROOV ing lee) *adv.* with support; thinking it is good

**responsibility** (ri spahn suh BIL uh tee) *n.* a duty or something that must be done

**neglected** (ni GLEKT id) *v.* failed to take care of

as a young man must be strong. If you love your son, only you can get him back."

Every one of the medicine man's words went into the father's heart like an arrow. He began to realize that he had been blind to his son's needs because of his own sorrow.

"You are right," he said. "I will go and bring back my son."

Kuo-Haya's father went along the arroyo and climbed the cliffs. When he came to the bears' cave, he found Kuo-Haya wrestling with the little bears. As the father watched, he saw that his son seemed more sure of himself than ever before.

"Kuo-Haya," he shouted. "Come to me."

The boy looked at him and then just walked into the cave. Although the father tried to follow, the big mother bear stood up on her hind legs and growled. She would not allow the father to come any closer.

So Kuo-Haya's father went back to his home. He was angry now. He began to gather together his weapons, and brought out his bow and his arrows and his lance.[3] But the medicine man came to his lodge and showed him the bear claw that he wore around his neck.

"Those bears are my relatives!" the medicine man said. "You must not harm them. They are teaching your boy how we should care for each other, so you must not be cruel to them. You must get your son back with love, not violence."

Kuo-Haya's father prayed for guidance. He went outside and sat on the ground. As he sat there, a bee flew up to him, right by his face. Then it flew away. The father stood up. Now he knew what to do!

"Thank you, Little Brother," he said. He began to make his preparations. The medicine man watched what he was doing and smiled.

**Reading Skill**

Read the first bracketed passage. Use your prior knowledge of weapons to **predict** what the father plans to do.

_____

_____

_____

_____

_____

**Literary Analysis**

Read the second bracketed passage. Circle the sentences that show the **climax** of the story.

How do you know that this is the climax?

_____

_____

_____

_____

_____

**Reading Skill**

Look at the second bracketed passage. Use what you know about how bears feel about honey to **predict** how Kuo-Haya's father's plans have changed.

_____

_____

_____

_____

**Vocabulary Development**

**violence** (VY uh luhns) _n._ actions meant to hurt someone

**guidance** (GYD uhns) _n._ help in finding a better way to do something

3. **lance** (LANS) _n._ long spear.

© Pearson Education

**Stop to Reflect**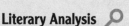

Read the underlined sentences in the first bracketed paragraph. What do you think is the lesson the father was beginning to learn?

_____

_____

_____

_____

_____

**Literary Analysis** 🔍

Read the second bracketed passage. Is this scene part of the **rising action**? Explain your answer.

_____

_____

_____

_____

_____

**Reading Check**

What have Kuo-Haya and his father learned from the bears? Underline the sentences that give the answer.

Kuo-Haya's father went to the place where the bees had their hives. He made a fire and put green branches on it so that it made smoke. Then he blew the smoke into the tree where the bees were. The bees soon went to sleep.

Carefully Kuo-Haya's father took out some honey from their hive. When he was done, he placed pollen and some small pieces of turquoise[4] at the foot of the tree to thank the bees for their gift. The medicine man, who was watching all this, smiled again. Truly the father was beginning to learn.

Kuo-Haya's father traveled again to the cliffs where the bears lived. He hid behind a tree and saw how the mother bear treated Kuo-Haya and the cubs with love. He saw that Kuo-Haya was able to hold his own as he wrestled with the bears.

He came out from his hiding place, put the honey on the ground, and stepped back. "My friends," he said, "I have brought you something sweet."

The mother bear and her cubs came over and began to eat the honey. While they ate, Kuo-Haya's father went to the boy. He saw that his little boy was now a young man.

"Kuo-Haya," he said, putting his hands on his son's shoulders, "I have come to take you home. The bears have taught me a lesson. I shall treat you as a father should treat his son."

"I will go with you, Father," said the boy. "But I, too, have learned things from the bears. They have shown me how we must care for one another. I will come with you only if you promise you will always be friends with the bears." The father promised, and that promise was kept. Not only was he friends with the bears, but he showed his boy the love a son deserves. And he taught him all the things a son should be taught.

**Vocabulary Development**

**pollen** (PAHL uhn) *n.* a powder made by flowers, which is carried by wind or insects to make other flowers produce seeds

4. **turquoise** (TER kwoyz) *n.* greenish-blue gemstone.

Everyone in the village soon saw that Kuo-Haya, the bear boy, was no longer the timid little boy he had been. Because of what the bears had taught him, he was the best wrestler among the boys. With his father's help, Kuo-Haya quickly became the greatest runner of all. To this day, his story is told to remind all parents that they must always show as much love for their children as there is in the heart of a bear.

Reader's Response: Is this story meant for children or for adults?

_____

Explain your answer.

_____

_____

_____

_____

**Literary Analysis**

Which details in this paragraph show how the story's conflict is resolved?

_____

_____

_____

_____

_____

_____

**Reading Check** ✐

What does Kuo-Haya's story remind parents to do? Circle the text that tells you.

# The Bear Boy

1. **Compare and Contrast:** How is Kuo-Haya's life with the bears different from his life in the village?

_____

_____

2. **Connect:** How does seeing a bee help the father decide how to get his son back?

_____

_____

3. **Reading Skill:** Write a **prediction** based on prior knowledge that you made as you read this story. Use this chart.

| Story Details | + | My Prior Knowledge | = | Prediction |
|---|---|---|---|---|
| | | | | |

4. **Literary Analysis:** Identify two events in the **plot** that increase the tension of the story.

_____

_____

_____

_____

_____

## Writing: Informative Article

Write an **informative article** about how a mother bear raises her cubs. Use details from the story to write your article. Focus on the answers to these questions to write your article.

- How did the mother bear treat her cubs?

  _____

  _____

- What did the mother bear teach Kuo-Haya?

  _____

  _____

## Listening and Speaking: Informal Debate

With your partner, hold an **informal debate** on the training of wild animals. In an informal debate, you and your partner exchange opinions on a topic. Choose whether you will argue for or against the training of wild animals. Write reasons why your partner should agree with your side of the argument. Use these notes during your debate.

- Write about times when animal training should be used.

  _____

  _____

- Write reasons that support your opinion.

  _____

  _____

- Write weaknesses in your position.

  _____

  _____

# Rikki-tikki-tavi
## Rudyard Kipling

**Summary** This story takes place in India. Teddy's family adopts a mongoose named Rikki-tikki-tavi. Two deadly cobras, Nag and Nagaina, plot to kill Teddy's family. They want to have the garden to themselves when their babies hatch. Rikki-tikki-tavi and his friends Darzee and Chuchundra protect the family from the cobras.

## Writing About the Big Question

**Does every conflict have a winner?** "Rikki-tikki-tavi" tells the story of a fierce battle between a mongoose and two cobras. Complete this sentence:

Sometimes in a conflict, innocent victims _____.

## Note-taking Guide

Use this chart to help you recall the events of the story.

| Clue | Event |
| --- | --- |
| Why does Rikki leave his home? | |
| Where does Rikki go to live? | |
| What creatures does Rikki meet in his new home? | |
| How does Rikki protect his adopted family? | |

# Rikki-tikki-tavi

1. **Compare:** How are Rikki and the cobras alike? How are they different?

_____

_____

_____

2. **Evaluate:** Many people have read this short story. It has been popular for a long time. Do you think it deserves to be a popular story? Explain.

_____

_____

_____

3. **Reading Skill:** Use this chart to write a **prediction** based on what you know as you read this story.

| Story Details | + | My Prior Knowledge | = | Prediction |
|---|---|---|---|---|
| | | | | |

4. **Literary Analysis:** Name two events in the **plot** that increase tension between Rikki and Nag. Reread the story before you answer the question.

_____

_____

## Writing: Informative Article

Write a short **informative article** about mongooses. Write for an audience of third graders.

- What do you think third graders would like to know about mongooses?

_____

_____

_____

- Write three facts from the story that you think would interest third graders.

_____

_____

_____

Use your notes to write an informative article for third graders.

## Listening and Speaking: Informal Debate

Engage in a **debate** about whether the cobra or the mongoose is a more interesting animal. Use the following T-chart to record reasons and facts to support your opinion.

My Viewpoint:

| Reasons | Facts |
| --- | --- |
| | |

**Summary:**

_____

_____

_____

# Letters from Rifka • Two Kinds

## Reading Skill

A **prediction** is an informed guess about what will happen. Use details in the text to make predictions as you read. Then, **read ahead to verify predictions**—to check whether your predictions are correct.

- As you read, ask yourself whether new details support your predictions. If they do not, revise your predictions according to the new information.
- If the predictions you make turn out to be wrong, **reread to look for details** that you might have missed.

Use this graphic organizer to record and verify predictions as you read the story.

| Prediction | Details |
| --- | --- |
| Revised or Confirmed Prediction | New Details |
| Actual Outcome | Details From Rereading (if necessary) |

## Literary Analysis

A **character** is a person or an animal that takes part in the action of a literary work.

- A **character's motives** are the emotions or goals that drive him or her to act one way or another.
- **Character traits** are the individual qualities that make each character unique.

Characters' motives and traits influence what characters do and how they interact with others. As you read, think about what the characters are like and why they do what they do.

# Letters from Rifka
## Karen Hesse

**Summary** Rifka is a young girl who lives in Russia. Her family is leaving their home suddenly. Her father does not want her brothers to fight in the Russian Civil War. Her letters to her cousin tell of Rifka's bravery and loyalty to her family.

### ? Writing About the Big Question

**Does every conflict have a winner?** In *Letters from Rifka*, a family must escape from their country after a war. Complete this sentence:

The struggles of war sometimes cause people to _____.

### Note-taking Guide

Use this chart to record the events that lead up to Rifka's being on the train.

Beginning

_____

_____

_____

_____

_____

on the train

# Letters from Rifka
## Karen Hesse

September 2, 1919
Russia

My Dear Cousin Tovah,

We made it! If it had not been for your father, though, I think my family would all be dead now: Mama, Papa, Nathan, Saul, and me. At the very best we would be in that <u>filthy</u> prison in Berdichev,[1] not rolling west through Ukraine on a freight train bound for Poland.

I am sure you and Cousin Hannah were glad to see Uncle Avrum come home today. How worried his daughters must have been after the locked doors and whisperings of last night.

Soon Bubbe Ruth, my dear little grandmother, will hear of our escape. I hope she gives a big pot of Frusileh's cream to Uncle Avrum. How better could she thank him?

When the sun rose above the trees at the train station in Berdichev this morning, I stood alone outside a boxcar, my heart knocking against my ribs.

I stood there, trying to look older than my twelve years. Wrapped in the new shawl Cousin Hannah gave to me, still I trembled.

"Wear this in health," Hannah had whispered in my ear as she draped the shawl over my shoulders early this morning, before we slipped from your house into the dark.

"Come," Papa said, leading us through the woods to the train station.

I looked back to the <u>flickering</u> lights of your house, Tovah.

"Quickly, Rifka," Papa whispered. "The boys, and Mama, and I must hide before light."

## Vocabulary Development

**filthy** (FIL thee) *adj.* very dirty
**flickering** (FLIK er ing) *v.* unsteady; going on and off

1. **Berdichev:** a city in Russia, now Ukraine.

## TAKE NOTES

### Activate Prior Knowledge

Why do people write letters to relatives and friends?

_____

_____

_____

_____

_____

### Literary Analysis

A **character** is a person or an animal who takes part in the action of a story. **Character traits** are qualities that a character has. You can identify character traits by noticing what a character says and does. Read the bracketed paragraph. What can you tell about Rifka's character from what she writes about her grandmother and Uncle Avrum?

_____

_____

_____

_____

### Reading Check

To whom is Rifka writing her letter? Circle the answer.

### Stop to Reflect 📖

Read the first bracketed paragraph. How does the author show that the family is afraid?

_____

_____

_____

_____

### Literary Analysis 🔍

A **character's motives** are the emotions or goals that drive him or her to act a certain way. Read the second bracketed paragraph. Why might Rifka choose to hold the book in her hands?

_____

_____

_____

### Reading Skill 📖

Read the third bracketed paragraph. **Predict** why the soldiers are looking for Nathan.

_____

_____

_____

_____

_____

"You can distract the guards, can't you, little sister?" Nathan said, putting an arm around me. In the darkness, I could not see his eyes, but I felt them studying me.

"Yes," I answered, not wanting to disappoint him.

At the train station, Papa and Mama hid behind bales of hay in boxcars to my right. My two giant brothers, Nathan and Saul, crouched in separate cars to my left. Papa said that we should hide in different cars. If the guards discovered only one of us, perhaps the others might still escape.

Behind me, in the dusty corner of a boxcar, sat my own rucksack. It waited for me, holding what little I own in this world. I had packed Mama's candlesticks, wrapped in my two heavy dresses, at the bottom of the sack.

Your gift to me, the book of Pushkin, I did not pack. I kept it out, holding it in my hands.

I would have liked to fly away, to race back up the road, stopping at every door to say good-bye, to say that we were going to America.

But I could not. Papa said we must tell no one we were leaving, not even Bubbe Ruth. Only you and Hannah and Uncle Avrum knew. I'm so glad at least you knew, Tovah.

As Papa expected, not long after he and Mama and the boys had hidden themselves, two guards emerged from a wooden shelter. They thundered down the platform in their heavy boots climbing in and out of the cars, making their search.

They did not notice me at first. Saul says I am too little for anyone to notice, but you know Saul. He never has a nice word to say to me. And I am small for a girl of twelve. Still, my size did not keep the guards from noticing me. I think the guards missed seeing me at first because they were so busy in their search of the train. They were searching for Nathan.

### Vocabulary Development

**distract** (di STRAKT) *v.* draw attention in another direction
**emerged** (i MERJD) *v.* came into view; became visible

You know as well as I, Tovah, that when a Jewish boy deserts the Russian Army, the army tries hard to find him. They bring him back and kill him in front of his regiment[2] as a warning to the others. Those who have helped him, they also die.

Late last night, when Nathan slipped away from his regiment and appeared at our door, joy filled my heart at seeing my favorite brother again. Yet a troubled look worried Nathan's face. He hugged me only for a moment. His dimpled smile vanished as quickly as it came.

"I've come," he said, "to warn Saul. The soldiers will soon follow. They will take him into the army."

I am ashamed, Tovah, to admit that at first hearing Nathan's news made me glad. I wanted Saul gone. He drives me crazy. From his big ears to his big feet, I cannot stand the sight of him. Good riddance, I thought.

How foolish I was not to understand what Nathan's news really meant to our family.

"You should not have come," Mama said to Nathan. "They will shoot you when you return."

Papa said, "Nathan isn't going to return. Hurry! We must pack!"

We all stared at him.

"Quickly," Papa said, clapping his hands. "Rifka, run and fill your rucksack[3] with all of your belongings." I do not know what Papa thought I owned.

Mama said, "Rifka, do you have room in your bag for my candlesticks?"

"The candlesticks, Mama?" I asked.

"We either take them, Rifka, or leave them to the greedy peasants. Soon enough they will swoop down like vultures to pick our house bare," Mama said.

© Pearson Education

## Vocabulary Development

**deserts** (di ZERTS) *v.* leaves without permission

**dimpled** (DIM puhld) *adj.* with little pockets in the chin or cheeks, often from smiling

2. **regiment** (REJ uh muhnt) *n.* large group of soldiers.

3. **rucksack** (RUK sak) *n.* backpack.

---

## TAKE NOTES

### Literary Analysis

What do Nathan's actions in the bracketed paragraphs tell you about his **character traits**?

_____

_____

_____

_____

_____

### Reading Skill

**Predict** what Nathan's news might mean for the family.

_____

_____

_____

_____

### Reading Check

What does Rifka think about her brother Saul? Circle the sentences that give the answer. How do you think she really feels? Explain.

_____

_____

_____

## Stop to Reflect 📖

Read the first bracketed passage. What does Rifka's father mean when he says, "There is no time for papers"?

_____

_____

_____

_____

_____

## Reading Skill 📖

**Predict** how the soldier's remarks in the second bracketed paragraph will make Rifka feel.

_____

_____

_____

_____

_____

## Literary Analysis 🔍

What **motive** for future action does Rifka feel in response to the soldiers' talk about Nathan? Circle the answer.

Papa said, "Your brothers in America have sent for us, Rifka. It is time to leave Russia and we are not coming back. Ever."

"Don't we need papers?" I asked.

Papa looked from Nathan to Saul. "There is no time for papers," he said.

Then I began to understand.

We <u>huddled</u> in your cellar through the black night, planning our escape. Uncle Avrum only shut you out to protect you, Tovah.

Hearing the guards speak this morning, I understand his <u>precaution</u>. It was dangerous enough for you to know we were leaving. We could not risk telling you the details of our escape in case the soldiers came to question you.

The guards were talking about Nathan. They were saying what they would do to him once they found him, and what they would do to anyone who had helped him.

Nathan hid under a stack of <u>burlap</u> bags, one boxcar away from me. I knew, no matter how frightened I was, I must not let them find Nathan.

**Reader's Response:** Why might the author have chosen to write this book as a series of letters?

_____

_____

_____

_____

### Vocabulary Development

**huddled** (HUD ld) *v.* crowded or nestled close together

**precaution** (pri KAW shun) *n.* an action taken to keep something bad from happening

**burlap** (BUHR lap) *n.* a rough, thick cloth

# Letters from Rifka

1. **Speculate:** How do you think Nathan felt as he appeared at his family's door? Explain.

   _____

   _____

2. **Analyze:** How do you think Rifka's age affects the way she feels about the story's events?

   _____

   _____

3. **Reading Skill:** At what point in the story were you able to **predict** the family's reason for leaving Russia?

   _____

   _____

4. **Literary Analysis:** Record Rifka's **character traits** in this diagram. Support your answers with details from the story.

   _____

   _____

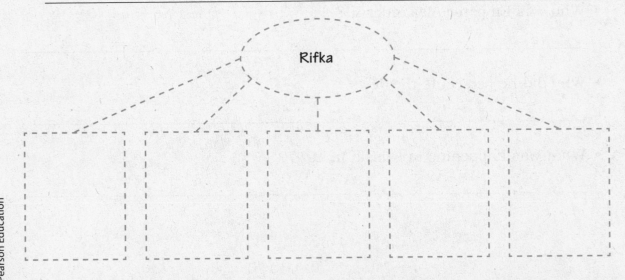

## Writing: Journal Entry

- Write a **journal entry** as if you were one of Rifka's famly members—Nathan, Saul, Mama, or Papa.

- Fill out this chart to organize the order of events for your journal entry.

- Add details about the events.

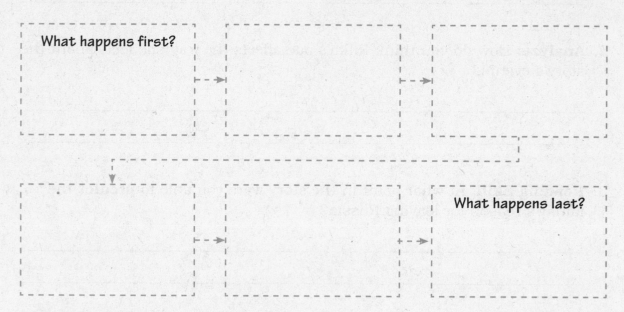

## Research and Technology: Outline

Make an **outline** of the persecution of Jews in Russia in the early twentieth century. Use library or Internet resources to find the answers to these questions:

- Who was Emperor Alexander III?

_____

- Why did he persecute the Jews?

_____

- What was happening in Russia in 1917?

_____

# Two Kinds
### Amy Tan

**Summary** This story is about a conflict between a Chinese woman and her American-born daughter, Jing-mei. The mother wants Jing-mei to be famous. Jing-mei refuses to do what her mother wants. This leads to an argument. Jing-mei realizes that she wants to follow her own path.

 **Writing About the Big Question**
**Does every conflict have a winner?**
In "Two Kinds," the narrator's mother has dreams of greatness for her daughter. Complete this sentence:

   Parents and children have disagreements about _____.

## Note-taking Guide
Use this chart to record the characters' actions in the story.

| Mother's Plans | Daughter's Response |
| --- | --- |
| She wants her daughter to be a Chinese Shirley Temple. | |
| | |
| | |

# Two Kinds

1. **Draw Conclusions:** How does the difference in the attitudes of the mother and daughter create problems?

_____

_____

_____

2. **Make a Judgment:** Should the narrator's mother have pushed Jing-mei as she did? Explain.

_____

_____

3. **Literary Analysis:** Using this diagram, identify Jing-mei's **character traits.** Support your answers with story details.

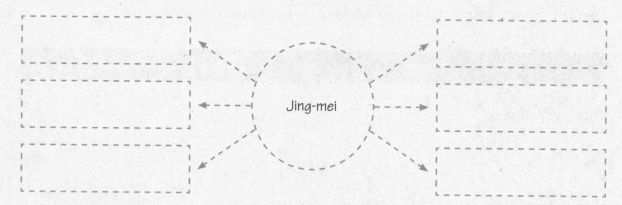

4. **Reading Skill:** What **prediction** did you make about how the narrator would perform at the piano recital? Explain why it was accurate or not.

_____

_____

_____

### Writing: Journal Entry

- Write a **journal entry** that the narrator might have made on the night after the piano recital. Fill in this chart to organize the order of events for your journal entry.

- Add details about the events. Also describe who was there and what each person said.

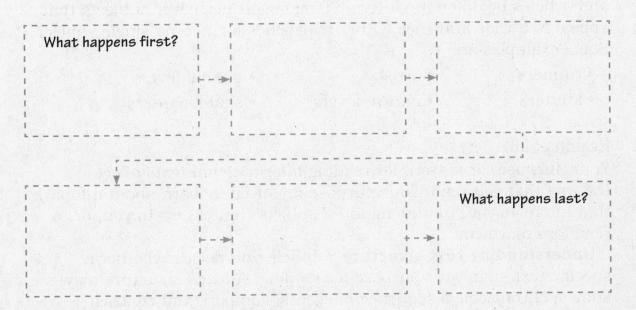

What happens first?

What happens last?

### Research and Technology: Outline

Use the following chart to record information for your **outline.** List information about traditional Chinese beliefs about the roles of parents and children.

| Father's Role | Mother's Role | Daughter's Role | Son's Role |
|---|---|---|---|
| | | | |

# Magazine Articles

## About Magazine Articles

A **magazine** is a form of print media published on a regular schedule. Magazines can be published weekly, monthly, or even quarterly (four times a year). They usually contain photographs, advertisements, and articles by different writers. Some magazines cover subjects that appeal to a wide audience. Other magazines focus on a single subject. Some examples are

- runners
- knitters
- artists
- nature lovers
- animal lovers
- skateboarders

## Reading Skill

Your **purpose,** or reason, for reading informational texts affects the way that you read. Your purpose might be to learn about a topic that interests you, to understand a subject that is new to you, or to read for enjoyment.

**Understanding text structure** will help you decide whether a specific text suits your purpose for reading. A text's structure may show a chronological sequence of events, compare and contrast information, or show causes and effects. **Text features** organize and highlight important information. Before reading, look through the text for the features shown in the chart.

| Text Features | Description |
|---|---|
| Title | The name of the article, which often gives clues about the topic |
| Subtitles | Titles of sections that identify the main idea of each section |
| Photographs, illustrations, captions | Images and their labels that give additional information |
| Charts, graphs, diagrams | Information that is presented visually |
| Maps, legends | Images that show information about places |

# Mongoose on the Loose

### Larry Luxner

In 1872 a Jamaican sugar planter imported nine furry little mongooses from India to eat the rats which were devouring his crops. They did such a good job, the planter started breeding his exotic animals and selling them to eager farmers on neighboring islands.

## Population Explodes

With no natural predators—like wolves, coyotes, or poisonous snakes—the mongoose population exploded, and within a few years, they were killing not just rats but pigs, lambs, chickens, puppies, and kittens. Dr. G. Roy Horst, a U.S. expert on mongooses, says that today mongooses live on seventeen Caribbean islands as well as Hawaii and Fiji, where they have attacked small animals, threatened endangered species, and have even spread minor rabies epidemics.

In Puerto Rico there are from 800,000 to one million of them. That is about one mongoose for every four humans. In St. Croix, there are 100,000 mongooses, about twice as many as the human population. "It's impossible to eliminate the mongoose population, short of nuclear war," says Horst. "You can't poison them, because cats, dogs, and chickens get poisoned, too. I'm not a prophet crying in the wilderness, but the potential for real trouble is there," says Horst.

According to Horst, great efforts have been made to rid the islands of mongooses, which have killed off a number of species including the Amevia lizard on St. Croix, presumed extinct for several decades.

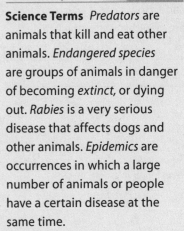

© Pearson Education

**Text Structure**

Special features in magazine articles guide the reader. The title and photo help you know what the article is about. Subtitles break the article into smaller parts so that it is easier to read. What can you tell about this article from the title and subtitle?

_____

_____

_____

_____

_____

**Fluency Builder**

Quotations, or words spoken by a person interviewed for the article, appear between quotation marks (" "). Underline the quotations in the bracketed paragraph. With a partner, take turns reading aloud the quotations, with expression.

**Vocabulary Builder**

**Science Terms** *Predators* are animals that kill and eat other animals. *Endangered species* are groups of animals in danger of becoming *extinct,* or dying out. *Rabies* is a very serious disease that affects dogs and other animals. *Epidemics* are occurrences in which a large number of animals or people have a certain disease at the same time.

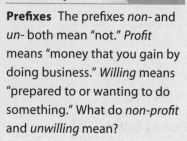

On Hawaii, the combination of mongooses and sports hunting has reduced the Hawaiian goose, or nene, to less than two dozen individuals.

### Scientist Studies Problem

The fifty-nine-year-old biology professor, who teaches at Potsdam College in upstate New York, recently finished his third season at the 500-acre Cabo Rojo National Wildlife Refuge in southwestern Puerto Rico, using microchips to study the life cycle and reproductive habits of the Caribbean mongoose. (He is also doing similar work at the Sandy Point Fish and Wildlife Refuge on St. Croix in the U.S. Virgin Islands.) "I want to know what happens when you take a small animal and put him in an area with no competition. This is a model that doesn't exist anywhere else in the world."

Horst's five-year, $60,000 study is being sponsored by Earthwatch Incorporated, a non-profit group that has funded some 1,300 research projects in eighty-seven countries. Volunteers pay $1,500 each (not including airfare) to come to Puerto Rico for ten days and help Horst set out mongoose traps, study the animals, and keep records. Often he and his volunteers spend a sweaty day walking about ten miles while setting out mongoose traps in the wilderness. Later, they perform surgery on their unwilling subjects to implant the electronic devices that will allow them to track the animal's habits.

> " . . . This is a model that doesn't exist anywhere else in the world."

Horst has tagged more than 400 mongooses with PITs (permanently implanted transponders),

**A mongoose is tagged.**

a new microchip **technology,** which he says has changed his work dramatically. "You couldn't do this with ear tags. It was very hard to permanently mark these animals until this technology came along," he said.

Horst has caught thousands of mongooses and has reached some interesting **conclusions.** Among them: mongooses have a life expectancy of six to ten years, much longer than the previously accepted figure of three years. Horst says his research will provide local and federal health officials[1] with extremely valuable information if they ever decide to launch a **campaign** against rabies in Puerto Rico or the U.S. Virgin Islands.

---

**Everyday Words**

**technology** (tek NAHL uh jee) *n.* new machines, equipment, and ways of doing things that are based on modern knowledge about science and computers

**conclusions** (kuhn KLOO shuhnz) *n.* things that you decide after considering all the information that you have

**campaign** (kam PAYN) *n.* a series of actions intended to achieve a particular result

---

1. **local and federal health officials** officials who work for local and national government

---

## TAKE NOTES

**Text Structure**

Pictures and captions help you know more about the content of an article. Underline the text that tells you what the scientist is doing in the photo.

**Vocabulary Builder**

**Suffixes** The suffixes *-ally* and *-ly* both mean "in a particular way." *Dramatic* means "great and sudden." *Permanent* means "continuing to exist for a long time or for all time in the future." *Previous* means "having happened before the event or time that you are talking about." What do the underlined phrases mean?

_____

_____

_____

_____

**Comprehension Builder**

Draw a box around the sentence that tells you one thing Horst learned by studying mongooses.

# Thinking About the Magazine Article

1. Explain your purpose for reading the magazine article.

_____

_____

_____

2. Explain how the background information in the first paragraph helps you understand "Mongoose on the Loose."

_____

_____

_____

### (TALK ABOUT IT) Reading Skill

3. What does the subhead "Scientist Studies Problem" tell about the article?

_____

_____

_____

### WRITE ABOUT IT  Timed Writing: Description (15 minutes)

Write a description of a mongoose. Make a list of specific details from the article about the mongoose's appearance and behavior. Use vivid words and phrases to create strong pictures for readers. What are some examples of vivid words or phrases? List at least five.

_____

_____

# The Third Wish • Amigo Brothers

## Reading Skill

Short story writers do not directly tell you everything there is to know about the characters, setting, and events. Instead, they leave it to you to **make inferences**, or logical guesses, about unstated information.

- To form inferences, you must **recognize details** in the story and consider their importance.
- As you read, use this chart to record details that can help you make inferences.

| Details |
| --- |
|  |
|  |

↓

| Inference |
| --- |
|  |

## Literary Analysis

Most fictional stories center on a **conflict**—a struggle between opposing forces. There are two kinds of conflict:

- When there is an **external conflict**, a character struggles with an outside force such as another character or nature.
- When there is an **internal conflict**, a character struggles with himself or herself to overcome opposing feelings, beliefs, needs, or desires. The **resolution**, or outcome of the conflict, often comes toward the end of the story, when the problem is settled in some way.

A story can have smaller conflicts that build the main conflict.

# The Third Wish

## Joan Aiken

**Summary** Mr. Peters rescues the King of the Forest. The King gives three leaves to Mr. Peters that he can use to make three wishes. The King warns that wishes often cause problems. Mr. Peters tries to be careful when using his wishes. He learns that making wishes can have unexpected results.

 ## Writing About the Big Question

**Does every conflict have a winner?** In "The Third Wish," wishes granted do not necessarily bring happiness to everyone involved. Complete this sentence:

When we desire something for another's happiness we should consider

_____.

## Note-taking Guide

Use this chart to help you record the effects of the three wishes.

| Wish | Result |
| --- | --- |
| 1. | |
| 2. | |
| 3. | |

# The Third Wish

## Joan Aiken

Once there was a man who was driving in his car at dusk on a spring evening through part of the forest of Savernake. His name was Mr. Peters. The primroses were just beginning but the trees were still bare, and it was cold; the birds had stopped singing an hour ago.

As Mr. Peters entered a straight, empty stretch of road he seemed to hear a faint crying, and a struggling and thrashing, as if somebody was in trouble far away in the trees. He left his car and climbed the mossy bank beside the road. Beyond the bank was an open slope of beech trees leading down to thorn bushes through which he saw the gleam of water. He stood a moment waiting to try and discover where the noise was coming from, and presently heard a rustling and some strange cries in a voice which was almost human—and yet there was something too hoarse about it at one time and too clear and sweet at another. Mr. Peters ran down the hill and as he neared the bushes he saw something white among them which was trying to extricate[1] itself; coming closer he found that it was a swan that had become <u>entangled</u> in the thorns growing on the bank of the canal.

The bird struggled all the more frantically as he approached, looking at him with hate in its yellow eyes, and when he took hold of it to free it, it hissed at him, pecked him, and thrashed dangerously with its wings which were powerful enough to break his arm. Nevertheless he managed to release it from the thorns, and carrying it tightly with one arm, holding the snaky head well away with the other hand (for he did not wish his eyes pecked out), he took it to the <u>verge</u> of the canal and dropped it in.

---

**Vocabulary Development**

**entangled** (in TANG guhld) *v.* wrapped up or caught in something and not able to get out

**verge** (verj) *n.* the edge

---

1. **extricate** (EKS truh kayt) *v.* set free.

**Activate Prior Knowledge**

Imagine that you are granted three wishes. What would one of your wishes be?

_____

_____

_____

_____

**Reading Skill**

When you **make an inference**, you make a guess by using information in the story. What can you infer about Mr. Peters's character?

_____

_____

_____

_____

**Reading Check**

Circle the text that tells what happens after Mr. Peters frees the swan.

## Stop to Reflect

Would you have stopped to talk to the little man in green? Explain why or why not.

_____

_____

_____

_____

## Literary Analysis

A **conflict** is a struggle between opposing forces. What is the **conflict** in the bracketed passage?

_____

_____

_____

_____

_____

## Reading Check

What does the King of the Forest throw into the air? Circle the answer in the story.

The swan instantly assumed great dignity and sailed out to the middle of the water, where it put itself to rights with much <u>dabbling</u> and <u>preening</u>, smoothing its feathers with little showers of drops. Mr. Peters waited, to make sure that it was all right and had suffered no damage in its struggles. Presently the swan, when it was satisfied with its appearance, floated in to the bank once more, and in a moment, instead of the great white bird, there was a little man all in green with a golden crown and long beard, standing by the water. He had fierce glittering eyes and looked by no means friendly.

"Well, Sir," he said threateningly, "I see you are <u>presumptuous</u> enough to know some of the laws of magic. You think that because you have rescued—by pure good fortune—the King of the Forest from a difficulty, you should have some fabulous reward."

"I expect three wishes, no more and no less," answered Mr. Peters, looking at him steadily and with composure.[2]

"Three wishes, he wants, the clever man! Well, I have yet to hear of the human being who made any good use of his three wishes—they mostly end up worse off than they started. Take your three wishes then"—he flung three dead leaves in the air—"don't blame me if you spend the last wish in undoing the work of the other two."

Mr. Peters caught the leaves and put two of them carefully in his briefcase. When he looked up, the swan was sailing about in the middle of the water again, flicking the drops angrily down its long neck.

Mr. Peters stood for some minutes reflecting on how he should use his reward. He knew very well that the gift of three magic wishes was one which brought

### Vocabulary Development

**dabbling** (DAB uhl ing) *v.* playing around with something without being serious about it

**preening** (PREEN ing) *v.* when a bird cleans and smoothes its feathers

**presumptuous** (pri ZUMP choo uhs) *adj.* overconfident; arrogant

2. **composure** (kuhm POH zher) *n.* calmness of mind.

trouble more often than not, and he had no <u>intention</u> of being like the forester who first wished by <u>mistake</u> for a sausage, and then in a rage wished it on the end of his wife's nose, and then had to use his last wish in getting it off again. Mr. Peters had most of the things which he wanted and was very content with his life. The only thing that troubled him was that he was a little lonely, and had no companion for his old age. He decided to use his first wish and to keep the other two in case of an emergency. Taking a thorn he pricked his tongue with it, to remind himself not to utter <u>rash</u> wishes aloud. Then holding the third leaf and gazing round him at the dusky undergrowth, the primroses, great beeches and the blue-green water of the canal, he said:

"I wish I had a wife as beautiful as the forest."

A tremendous quacking and splashing broke out on the surface of the water. He thought that it was the swan laughing at him. Taking no notice he made his way through the darkening woods to his car, wrapped himself up in the rug and went to sleep.

When he awoke it was morning and the birds were beginning to call. Coming along the track towards him was the most beautiful creature he had ever seen, with eyes as blue-green as the canal, hair as dusky as the bushes, and skin as white as the feathers of swans.

"Are you the wife that I wished for?" asked Mr. Peters.

"Yes, I am," she replied. "My name is Leita."

She stepped into the car beside him and they drove off to the church on the <u>outskirts</u> of the forest, where they were married. Then he took her to his house in a remote and lovely valley and showed her all his treasures—the bees in their white hives, the Jersey cows, the hyacinths, the silver candlesticks, the blue cups and the luster bowl for putting primroses in. She admired everything, but what pleased her most was the river which ran by the foot of his garden.

## Vocabulary Development

**intention** (in TEN shuhn) *n.* something a person means to do or plans on doing

**rash** (rash) *adj.* thoughtless, reckless

**outskirts** (OWT skerts) *n.* edge

---

## TAKE NOTES

### Literary Analysis

An **internal conflict** occurs inside a character. What **internal conflict** will be resolved if Mr. Peters has a wife?

_____

_____

_____

_____

_____

### Stop to Reflect

Did Mr. Peters make a wise choice with his first wish? Explain.

_____

_____

_____

_____

_____

### Reading Check

What does Mr. Peters do to remind himself not to make rash wishes? Underline the answer.

**Stop to Reflect**

How can you tell when someone is unhappy?

**Literary Analysis**

Sometimes the **conflict**, or struggle, in a story is within a character. Explain what Leita's conflict is.

_____

_____

_____

_____

**Reading Skill**

"When a human being marries a bird it always leads to sorrow." What can you **infer** about the ending of the story from that sentence?

_____

_____

_____

_____

**Reading Check**

What does Mr. Peters find out about Leita? Put an arrow next to the sentence in the text.

"Do swans come up there?" she asked.

"Yes, I have often seen swans there on the river," he told her, and she smiled.

Leita made him a good wife. But as time went by Mr. Peters began to feel that she was not happy. She seemed <u>restless</u>, wandered much in the garden, and sometimes when he came back from the fields he would find the house empty and she would return after half an hour or so with no explanation of where she had been. On these occasions she was always especially tender and would put out his slippers to warm and cook his favorite dish—Welsh rarebit[3] with wild strawberries—for supper.

One evening he was returning home along the river path when he saw Leita in front of him, down by the water. A swan had sailed up to the verge and she had her arms round its neck and the swan's head rested against her cheek. She was weeping, and as he came nearer he saw that tears were rolling, too, from the swan's eyes.

"Leita, what is it?" he asked, very troubled.

"This is my sister," she answered. "I can't bear being separated from her."

Now he understood that Leita was really a swan from the forest, and this made him very sad because when a human being marries a bird it always leads to sorrow.

"I could use my second wish to give your sister human shape, so that she could be a companion to you," he suggested.

"No, no," she cried, "I couldn't ask that of her."

"Is it so very hard to be a human being?" asked Mr. Peters sadly.

"Very, very hard," she answered.

"Don't you love me at all, Leita?"

"Yes, I do, I do love you," she said, and there were tears in her eyes again. "But I missed the old life in the forest, the cool grass and the mist rising off the

© Pearson Education

**Vocabulary Development**

**restless** (REST lis) *adj.* wanting to be in motion, unable to stay still

3. **Welsh rarebit:** a dish of melted cheese served on crackers or toast.

river at sunrise and the feel of the water sliding over my feathers as my sister and I drifted along the stream."

"Then shall I use my second wish to turn you back into a swan again?" he asked, and his tongue pricked to remind him of the old King's words, and his heart swelled with <u>grief</u> inside him.

"Who will take care of you?"

"I'd do it myself as I did before I married you," he said, trying to sound cheerful.

She shook her head. "No, I could not be as unkind to you as that. I am partly a swan, but I am also partly a human being now. I will stay with you."

Poor Mr. Peters was very distressed on his wife's account and did his best to make her life happier, taking her for drives in the car, finding beautiful music for her to listen to on the radio, buying clothes for her and even suggesting a trip round the world. But she said no to that; she would prefer to stay in their own house near the river.

He noticed that she spent more and more time baking wonderful cakes—jam puffs, petits fours, eclairs and meringues. One day he saw her take a basketful down to the river and he guessed that she was giving them to her sister.

He built a seat for her by the river, and the two sisters spent hours together there, <u>communicating</u> in some wordless manner. For a time he thought that all would be well, but then he saw how thin and pale she was growing.

One night when he had been late doing the account he came up to bed and found her weeping in her sleep and calling:

"Rhea! Rhea! I can't understand what you say! Oh, wait for me, take me with you!"

Then he knew that it was hopeless and she would never be happy as a human. He stooped down and kissed her goodbye, then took another leaf from his notecase, blew it out of the window, and used up his second wish.

© Pearson Education

**Vocabulary Development**

**grief** (greef) *n.* sadness
**communicating** (kuh MYOO ni kayt ing) *v.* talking or sharing ideas and feelings

---

## TAKE NOTES

**Literary Analysis**

Read the bracketed passage. Underline the two emotions described in the passage. What is Mr. Peters's internal **conflict** here?

_____

_____

_____

**Stop to Reflect**

Think about the characters in the story. How do you feel about them?

_____

_____

_____

**Reading Skill**

Make an **inference** about why Leita prefers to stay in her own house.

_____

_____

_____

**Reading Check**

Mr. Peters tries to do four things to make Leita happy. Number these items in the text.

© Pearson Education

## Literary Analysis 🔍

How does Mr. Peters resolve his **conflict**?

_____

_____

_____

## Reading Skill 📖

Make an **inference** about why the birds carried off the thieves from Mr. Peters's house.

_____

_____

_____

_____

## Stop to Reflect 📖

Why do you think people were a little afraid of Mr. Peters?

_____

_____

_____

_____

## Reading Check ✏️

How does Leita thank Mr. Peters for turning her back into a swan? Circle the answer in the story.

Next moment instead of Leita there was a sleeping swan lying across the bed with its head under its wing. He carried it out of the house and down to the <u>brink</u> of the river, and then he said, "Leita! Leita!" to waken her, and gently put her into the water. She gazed round her in astonishment for a moment, and then came up to him and rested her head lightly against his hand; next instant she was flying away over the trees towards the heart of the forest.

He heard a <u>harsh</u> laugh behind him, and turning round saw the old King looking at him with a <u>malicious</u> expression.

"Well, my friend! You don't seem to have managed so wonderfully with your first two wishes, do you? What will you do with the last? Turn yourself into a swan? Or turn Leita back into a girl?"

"I shall do neither," said Mr. Peters calmly. "Human beings and swans are better in their own shapes."

But for all that he looked sadly over towards the forest where Leita had flown, and walked slowly back to his house.

Next day he saw two swans swimming at the bottom of the garden, and one of them wore the gold chain he had given Leita after their marriage; she came up and rubbed her head against his hand.

Mr. Peters and his two swans came to be well known in that part of the country; people used to say that he talked to swans and they understood him as well as his neighbors. Many people were a little frightened of him. There was a story that once when thieves tried to break into his house they were set upon by two huge white birds which carried them off bodily and dropped them into the river.

As Mr. Peters grew old everyone wondered at his contentment. Even when he was bent with rheumatism[4] he would not think of moving to a drier spot, but went slowly about his work, with the two swans always somewhere close at hand.

### Vocabulary Development

**brink** (bringk) *n.* the edge

**harsh** (hahrsh) *adj.* rough, unkind

**malicious** (muh LI shuhs) *adj.* spiteful; hateful

4. **rheumatism** (ROO muh tizm) *n.* pain and stiffness of the joints and muscles.

Sometimes people who knew his story would say to him:

"Mr. Peters, why don't you wish for another wife?"

"Not likely," he would answer serenely. "Two wishes were enough for me, I reckon[5]. I've learned that even if your wishes are granted they don't always better you. I'll stay faithful to Leita."

One autumn night, passers-by along the road heard the mournful sound of two swans singing. All night the song went on, sweet and harsh, sharp and clear. In the morning Mr. Peters was found peacefully dead in his bed with a smile of great happiness on his face. In his hands, which lay clasped on his breast, were a withered leaf and a white feather.

Reader's Response: Would you have made the same wishes as Mr. Peters? Explain.

_____

_____

_____

_____

_____

_____

© Pearson Education

**Vocabulary Development**
**serenely** (suh REEN lee) *adv.* quietly, calmly, peacefully
**mournful** (MAWRN fuhl) *adj.* full of sadness
**clasped** (klaspd) *v.* held tightly

5. **I reckon** I figure, I think.

## TAKE NOTES

**Literary Analysis** 🔍

Recall Mr. Peters's **internal conflict** at the beginning of the story. How is his situation the same at the end of the story?

_____

_____

_____

_____

How does Mr. Peters resolve his conflict?

_____

_____

_____

_____

**Reading Skill**

Mr. Peters dies with a leaf and a white feather in his hand. What can you **infer** about the white feather?

_____

_____

_____

_____

The Third Wish  **131**

# The Third Wish

1. **Speculate:** Why do you think Mr. Peters does not wish for money?

   _____

   _____

2. **Reading Skill:** List two details in the story that support the **inference** that Mr. Peters loves Leita more than he loves himself.

   _____

   _____

3. **Reading Skill:** List two details in the story that support the **inference** that Leita still loves Mr. Peters even after changing back into a swan.

   _____

   _____

4. **Literary Analysis:** In this chart, identify two smaller **conflicts** that build toward Mr. Peters's main conflict, and tell how each is resolved.

| Smaller Conflict | Resolution |
|---|---|
|  |  |
|  |  |

Main Conflict

## Writing: Anecdote

- Write an **anecdote**, or brief story, using the three-wishes pattern. Brainstorm for ideas about what you would wish for.

_____

_____

- Think about what problems might happen if you made three wishes. Would people follow you around if you were famous? How would it make you feel to never be alone with your family and friends?

_____

_____

- How would you solve the problem?

_____

_____

- The characters in an anecdote usually learn something from the problem and solution. Write what you might learn from your wish.

_____

_____

## Listening and Speaking: News Story

Write a **news story** that announces the death of Mr. Peters and hails him as a local hero. Use details from "The Third Wish" to give details about Mr. Peters.

- **Whom** was the story about? _____

- **What** was the story about? _____

- **When** did the story take place? _____

- **Where** did the story take place? _____

- **Why** was the story covered? _____

# Amigo Brothers
## Piri Thomas

**Summary** This story is about two friends who must box each other. Felix and Antonio grew up together. For years they have trained together. Now, they must fight each other in the finals. They do what they can to make sure that their friendship will last no matter who wins.

 **Writing About the Big Question**

**Does every conflict have a winner?** In "Amigo Brothers," two good friends compete against each other in a boxing match. Complete this sentence:

When close friends compete _____

_____.

## Note-taking Guide

Felix and Antonio are very much alike. Use this chart to show how they are different from each other.

|  | Felix | Antonio |
|---|---|---|
| Physical Traits |  |  |
| Fighting Style |  |  |
| Fighting Gear (Clothes) |  |  |

# Amigo Brothers

1. **Draw Conclusions:** The boys plan to stay apart for a while before the fight. What are the advantages and disadvantages of this plan?

   _____

   _____

2. **Speculate:** Do you think the boys' solution was a good one? Why or why not?

   _____

   _____

3. **Literary Analysis:** What **conflicts** do the boys have? They have a main conflict and some smaller conflicts. Use this chart to show two smaller conflicts that lead to the main conflict.

   | Smaller Conflict | Resolution |
   |---|---|
   |  |  |
   |  |  |

   | Main Conflict |
   |---|
   |  |

4. **Reading Skill:** You can **infer**, or guess, from the story that Felix and Antonio care for each other. List two details that show that the boys care for each other.

   _____

   _____

## Writing: Anecdote

Write an **anecdote**, or brief story, that tells what might have happened if Antonio or Felix had been knocked out.

- Create a small outline that details how many scenes the anecdote will have.

_____

_____

- A good anecdote has a good ending. You must decide which boy gets knocked out and what lesson is learned. Fill in the chart below.

| Antonio Gets Knocked Out | Felix Gets Knocked Out |
|---|---|
| Lesson learned | Lesson learned |
|  |  |

## Listening and Speaking: News Story

Present a **news story** about the fight between Antonio and Felix.

- **News stories** answer who, what, why, where, and when. Use this chart to fill in the details.

| What is the event? | Who was fighting? | Why were they fighting? | Where was the fight? | When was the fight? |
|---|---|---|---|---|
|  |  |  |  |  |

# Zoo • Ribbons

## Reading Skill

An **inference** is your best guess, based on what the text tells you, about things not stated directly in the text. For example, suppose a story opens with a man running down a dark alley while looking over his shoulder. You can infer from these details that the man is trying to get away from someone or something.

- One way to make inferences is to **read between the lines by asking questions** such as "Why does the writer include these details?" and "Why does the writer leave out certain information?"

- As you read, jot down questions and answers in this chart.

| Why Does the Writer . . . | Answer (inference) |
|---|---|
|  |  |
|  |  |
|  |  |

## Literary Analysis

A story's **theme** is its central idea, message, or insight into life. Occasionally, the author states the theme directly. More often, however, the theme is implied.

As you read, look at what the characters say and do, where the story takes place, and objects that seem important to help you determine the theme—what the author wants to teach you about life.

# Zoo
### Edward D. Hoch

**Summary** Every year Professor Hugo's Interplanetary Zoo comes to Earth. People pay to see creatures from other planets. Afterwards, the spaceship returns the creatures to their homes. The creatures remark how much they enjoyed the Earth zoo. Both Earth people and space creatures enjoy the zoo.

## Writing About the Big Question

**Does every conflict have a winner?** In "Zoo," human and alien cultures have conflicting ideas about each other. Complete this sentence:

When two groups that are very different come together, misunderstandings

can result because _____.

## Note-taking Guide

Fill in this Venn diagram. Tell how the horse-spider people and the Earth people are the same and different.

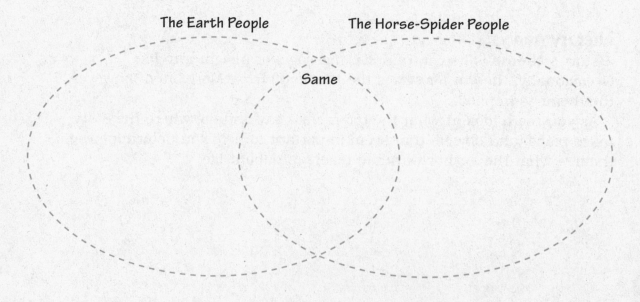

The Earth People          The Horse-Spider People

Same

# Zoo
## Edward D. Hoch

The children were always good during the month of August, especially when it began to get near the twenty-third. It was on this day that the great silver spaceship carrying Professor Hugo's Interplanetary Zoo settled down for its annual six-hour visit to the Chicago area.

Before daybreak the crowds would form, long lines of children and adults both, each one clutching his or her dollar and waiting with wonderment[1] to see what race of strange creatures the Professor had brought this year.

In the past they had sometimes been treated to three-legged creatures from Venus, or tall, thin men from Mars, or even snakelike horrors from somewhere more distant. This year, as the great round ship settled slowly to earth in the huge tri-city parking area just outside of Chicago, they watched with awe as the sides slowly slid up to reveal the familiar barred cages. In them were some wild breed of nightmare—small, horse-like animals that moved with quick, jerking motions and constantly chattered in a high-pitched tongue[2]. The citizens of Earth clustered around as Professor Hugo's crew quickly collected the waiting dollars, and soon the good Professor himself made an appearance, wearing his many-colored rainbow cape and top hat. "Peoples of Earth," he called into his microphone. The crowd's noise died down and he continued. "Peoples of Earth, this year you see a real treat for your single dollar— the little-known horse-spider people of Kaan— brought to you across a million miles of space at great expense. Gather around, see them, study them,

© Pearson Education

**Vocabulary Development**

**interplanetary** (in ter PLAN uh ter ee) *adj.* between planets

**awe** (aw) *n.* fear and wonder

**expense** (ik SPENS) *n.* cost

1. **wonderment** (WUN der ment) *n.* astonishment
2. **tongue** (tung) *n.* language

**Activate Prior Knowledge**

What do you know about zoos?

_____

_____

_____

_____

_____

**Reading Skill**

An **inference** is an intelligent guess. You base an inference on clues that you find in a story. Make an inference about why the children are being good.

_____

_____

_____

_____

**Reading Check**

Underline the text that describes the horse-spider people.

## Reading Skill

Read the bracketed paragraph. Based on the details, what **inference** can you make about Professor Hugo's life?

_____

_____

## Reading Check

Underline the words that show how the humans react to the creatures from Kaan.

## Reading Skill

What can you **infer** about the people of Kaan and why they are a part of the zoo?

_____

_____

_____

_____

listen to them, tell your friends about them. But hurry! My ship can remain here only six hours!"

And the crowds slowly filed by, at once horrified and <u>fascinated</u> by these strange creatures that looked like horses but ran up the walls of their cages like spiders. "This is certainly worth a dollar," one man remarked, hurrying away. "I'm going home to get the wife."

All day long it went like that, until ten thousand people had filed by the barred cages set into the side of the spaceship. Then, as the six-hour limit ran out, Professor Hugo once more took the microphone in hand. "We must go now, but we will return next year on this date. And if you enjoyed our zoo this year, telephone your friends in other cities about it. We will land in New York tomorrow, and next week on to London, Paris, Rome, Hong Kong, and Tokyo. Then on to other worlds!"

He waved farewell to them, and as the ship rose from the ground, the Earth peoples agreed that this had been the very best Zoo yet. . . .

Some two months and three planets later, the silver ship of Professor Hugo settled at last onto the familiar jagged rocks of Kaan, and the odd horse-spider creatures filed quickly out of their cages. Professor Hugo was there to say a few parting words, and then they scurried away in a hundred different directions, seeking their homes among the rocks.

In one house, the she-creature was happy to see the return of her mate and offspring. She <u>babbled</u> a greeting in the strange tongue and hurried to <u>embrace</u> them. "It was a long time you were gone. Was it good?"

And the he-creature nodded. "The little one enjoyed it especially. We visited eight worlds and saw many things."

---

**Vocabulary Development**

**fascinated** (FAS suh nayt id) *adj.* very interested

**babbled** (BAB buhld) *v.* talked in a way that could not be understood

**embrace** (im BRAYS) *v.* to put arms around, as in a hug

The little one ran up the wall of the cave. "On the place called Earth it was the best. The creatures there wear garments over their skins, and they walk on two legs."

"But isn't it dangerous?" asked the she-creature.

"No," her mate answered. "There are bars to protect us from them. We remain right in the ship. Next time you must come with us. It is well worth the nineteen commocs it costs."

And the little one nodded. "It was the very best Zoo ever. . . ."

Reader's Response: Would you choose to visit Hugo's Interplanetary Zoo? Why or why not?

_____

_____

_____

_____

_____

_____

_____

_____

_____

_____

Reading Skill

What can you **infer** about why the people of Kaan are a part of the zoo?

_____

_____

_____

_____

Literary Analysis

Underline the text on this page that is similar to text that appeared in an earlier part of the story.

How do these sentences tie in with the story's **theme**?

_____

_____

_____

Stop to Reflect

Do you think that the ending of the story is successful? Explain your answer.

_____

_____

_____

_____

_____

# Zoo

1. **Interpret:** Why does the crowd view the creatures as "some wild breed of nightmare"?

   _____

   _____

2. **Draw Conclusions:** What does the label "some wild breed of nightmare" say about how humans view things that look different from them?

   _____

   _____

3. **Reading Skill:** What **inference** can you make from the first two sentences of the story?

   _____

   _____

4. **Literary Analysis:** What **theme** does the story convey about people and their differences? Using this graphic organizer, give details about the setting and characters that support the theme.

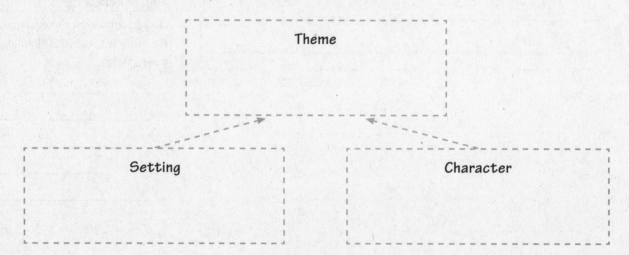

## Writing: Letter to the Editor

A letter to the editor expresses an opinion. The editor of a publication may publish the letter. Write a **letter to the editor** about whether zoo animals should live in natural habitats or in cages.

- Research two zoos that use cages and two zoos that use natural habitats.
  - What is one benefit that cages have over natural habitats?

    _____

    _____

  - What is one benefit that natural habitats have over cages?

    _____

    _____

Use these answers to support your position in your letter.

## Research and Technology: Poster

Answer the following questions to help you gather information for your zoo **poster.**

- Where is the zoo located?

  _____

- When is the zoo open?

  _____

- How much does it cost to see the zoo?

  _____

- What animals will people see?

  _____

- Which special exhibits will you feature?

  _____

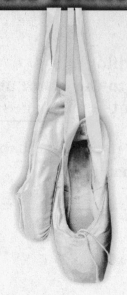

# Ribbons
## Laurence Yep

**Summary** This story is about a misunderstanding that Stacy and her grandmother have. Stacy's grandmother comes from Hong Kong to live with the family. It is difficult for Grandmother to adjust. She gets upset about Stacy's ribboned ballet shoes. Stacy learns why Grandmother is upset. She helps Grandmother understand ballet.

 **Writing About the Big Question**

**Does every conflict have a winner?** In "Ribbons," a granddaughter and a grandmother struggle to overcome their differences. Complete this sentence:

Family members from different generations often struggle to _____

_____.

## Note-taking Guide

Use this chart to help you recall Grandmother's actions in the story. Give two answers to each question.

| What does Grandmother do to show her feelings for Ian? | What does Grandmother do to show her feelings for Stacy? |
|---|---|
| | |
| | |

# Ribbons

1. **Evaluate:** Things in the house change when Grandmother arrives. What are the most difficult changes for Stacy to accept?

_____

_____

2. **Deduce:** How do Stacy and her grandmother come to understand one another?

_____

_____

3. **Reading Skill:** Grandmother carried her daughter on her back to Hong Kong to escape her enemy. What questions might you ask to help you make an **inference** about Grandmother's life?

_____

_____

4. **Literary Analysis:** How does the character of the daughter show the **theme** of this story? Use this chart to list her traits and motives. Then show how they relate to the theme of the story.

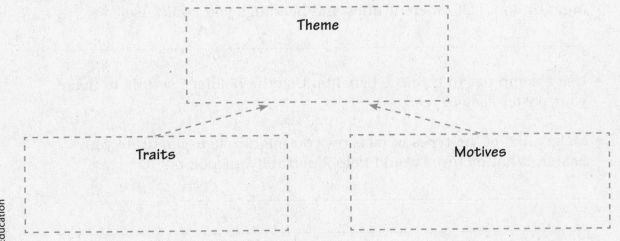

## Writing: Letter to the Editor

Use these guidelines to help you draft your **letter to the editor.**

- State your position in the first paragraph. For example, "I think that students my age should. . . ." Write a sentence stating your position.

_____

_____

- List your most important reason first. An example is "Sports are good exercise. They help us stay strong."

_____

_____

- List two or three reasons to support your position. Tell why the other activity is not a good choice.

_____

- Brainstorm three words you could use to persuade the editor of the newspaper. Use a dictionary and a thesaurus to help you.

_____

## Research and Technology: Poster

Use these suggestions to help make your **poster** on ballet.

- Use a title and headings on your poster to draw attention and create organization. List different titles and headings you could use.

_____

- Use a computer to type the benefits. Use the boldface setting to make your poster easy to read.

- Make a list of the types of pictures you might use to illustrate your poster. What pictures would help illustrate your points?

_____

# Government Publications

## About Government Publications

The United States government prepares many publications on many topics. These **government publications** might be articles, booklets, or books.

Examples of government publications include:

- Explanations of new and proposed laws
- Details of how money will be spent
- Notes from a city council meeting
- Tips on testing drinking water

The President's Council on Physical Fitness and Sports published this government publication about walking.

## Reading Skill

Writers do not often tell you everything about a subject. Instead, they leave it to you to fill in the missing information. You make an **inference** when you guess based on information that the writer gives you and on your own knowledge.

When you apply an inference in a general way, you make a **generalization.** A generalization is a broad statement that applies to many examples.

Let's say that you read a story about friendly dogs. Your pet dog is very friendly. Your neighbor's pet dog is friendly. You could make a generalization that *most dogs are friendly.*

The words *always, all, none, never,* and *most* signal a generalization. Use this chart to make a generalization about information in the government publication. Record the facts that support your generalization.

| Evidence | + | Evidence | + | Evidence | = | Generalization |
|----------|---|----------|---|----------|---|----------------|
|          |   |          |   |          |   |                |

## Text Structure

The name of a government office appears on most government publications. Circle the government office responsible for this publication.

## Fluency Builder

Words in parentheses are often read aloud in a different tone of voice. Put an asterisk next to a group of words in parentheses on this page. Practice reading aloud the sentence.

## Vocabulary Builder

**Word Families** Words that share a common base word make up a word family. *Popular* and *popularity* are in the same word family. *Popular* means "liked by many people." What does *popularity* mean?

_____

_____

# Walking for Exercise and Pleasure

## The President's Council on Physical Fitness and Sports

### Walking: An Exercise for All Ages

Walking is easily the most popular form of exercise. Other activities generate more conversation and media coverage, but none of them approaches walking in number of participants.[1] Approximately half of the 165 million American adults (18 years of age and older) claim they exercise regularly, and the number who walk for exercise is increasing every year.

Walking is the only exercise in which the rate of participation does not decline in the middle and later years. In a national survey, the highest percentage of regular walkers (39.4%) for any group was found among men 65 years of age and older.

Unlike tennis, running, skiing, and other activities that have gained great popularity fairly recently, walking has been widely practiced as a recreational and fitness activity throughout recorded history. Classical and early English literature seems to have been written largely by men who were prodigious walkers,[2] and Emerson

1. **participants** (pahr TIS uh puhnts) *n.* people who take part in an activity or event
2. **prodigious** (pruh DI juhs) **walkers** *n.* people who are very good at walking and better than most people

and Thoreau helped carry on the tradition in America. Among American presidents, the most famous walkers included Jefferson, Lincoln, and Truman.

## Walking: The Slower, Surer Way to Fitness

People walk for many reasons: for pleasure . . . to rid themselves of tensions[3] . . . to find solitude[4] . . . or to get from one place to another. Nearly everyone who walks regularly does so at least in part because of a conviction[5] that it is good exercise.

Often dismissed in the past as being "too easy" to be taken seriously, walking recently has gained new respect as a means of improving physical fitness. Studies show that, when done briskly on a regular schedule, it can improve the body's ability to consume oxygen during exertion,[6] lower the resting heart rate, reduce blood pressure, and increase the efficiency of the heart and lungs. It also helps burn excess calories.

Walking burns approximately the same amount of calories per mile as does running, a fact particularly appealing to those who find it difficult to sustain the jarring effects of long distance jogging. Briskly walking one mile in 15 minutes burns just about the same number of calories as jogging an equal distance in 8 1/2 minutes. In weightbearing activities like walking, heavier individuals will burn more calories than lighter persons. For example, studies show that a 110-pound person burns about half as many calories as a 216-pound person walking at the same pace for the same distance.

In addition to the qualities it has in common with other activities, walking has several unique advantages. Some of these are:

*Almost everyone can do it.* You don't have to take lessons to learn how to walk.

3. **tensions** (TEN shunz) *n.* feelings of nervousness or tightness in the muscles
4. **solitude** (SAH luh tood) *n.* a place where a person is alone and enjoys it
5. **conviction** (kuhn VIK shuhn) *n.* a very strong belief or opinion
6. **exertion** (ig ZER shuhn) *n.* a great deal of physical or mental effort

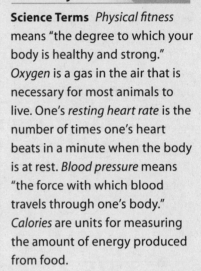

### TAKE NOTES

**Vocabulary Builder**

**Science Terms** *Physical fitness* means "the degree to which your body is healthy and strong." *Oxygen* is a gas in the air that is necessary for most animals to live. One's *resting heart rate* is the number of times one's heart beats in a minute when the body is at rest. *Blood pressure* means "the force with which blood travels through one's body." *Calories* are units for measuring the amount of energy produced from food.

**Comprehension Builder**

Underline four reasons that people walk.

**Vocabulary Builder**

**Compound Adjectives** In the bracketed paragraph, *110-pound* and *216-pound* are compound adjectives. A hyphen (-) connects two words that together describe the noun *person*. The hyphens make clear that the words go together as an adjective. A *110-pound person* means "a person who weighs 110 pounds." What does a *216-pound person* mean?

_____

_____

### Text Structure

Beginning on the previous page, the author calls out important information—four advantages of walking—by indenting four paragraphs differently from the rest of the text. The author also makes the first line of each of those paragraphs *italic*. What are the four advantages of walking that the author wants to emphasize?

_____

_____

_____

_____

### Vocabulary Builder

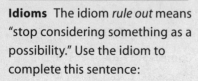

**Idioms** The idiom *rule out* means "stop considering something as a possibility." Use the idiom to complete this sentence:

Extreme weather can_____

_____ some activities.

### Text Structure

What does the subheading *Listen to Your Body* tell you about the information in the paragraph?

_____

_____

_____

Probably all you need to do to become a serious walker is step up your pace and distance and walk more often.

*You can do it almost anywhere.* All you have to do to find a place to walk is step outside your door. Almost any sidewalk, street, road, trail, park, field, or shopping mall will do. The variety of settings available is one of the things that makes walking such a **practical** and pleasurable activity.

*You can do it almost anytime.* You don't have to find a partner or get a team together to walk, so you can set your own schedule. Weather doesn't pose the same problems and uncertainties that it does in many sports. Walking is not a seasonal activity, and you can do it in extreme temperatures that would rule out other activities.

*It doesn't cost anything.* You don't have to pay fees or join a private club to become a walker. The only equipment required is a **sturdy,** comfortable pair of shoes.

### Listen to Your Body

Listen to your body when you walk. If you develop dizziness, pain, nausea, or any other unusual **symptom,** slow down or stop. If the problem persists, see your physician before walking again. The most important thing is simply to set aside part of each day and walk. No matter what your age or condition, it's a practice that can make you healthier and happier.

**Everyday Words**

**practical** (PRAK ti kuhl) *adj.* likely to be effective in a situation

**sturdy** (STER dee) *adj.* strong, well-made, and not easily broken

**symptom** (SIMP tuhm) *n.* something wrong with your body or mind that shows that you have a certain illness

# Thinking About the Government Publication

1. Name one way that walking is good for your health.

_____

2. When should you slow down or stop when you walk? Explain how your body tells you to slow down.

_____

_____

_____

### Reading Skill

3. What **generalization** can you make about why so many people walk for exercise?

_____

4. What fact from this article supports the **generalization** that you should "listen to your body"?

_____

_____

**WRITE ABOUT IT** **Timed Writing: Persuasion (10 minutes)**

Write an open letter to your neighbors about starting a walking group in your neighborhood. Use persuasive language to convince them how important your goal is. Include facts and details that support your arguments. What facts or details do you think would be persuasive to your neighbors?

_____

_____

_____

_____

# What Makes a Rembrandt a Rembrandt?

Nonfiction writing is about real people, places, ideas, and events. Nonfiction writing takes these forms:

**Letters** and **journals** contain personal thoughts and feelings.

**Biographies** and **autobiographies** are life stories.

- A **biography** is the story of someone else's life.

- An **autobiography** is the story of the author's own life.

**Media accounts** are nonfiction stories for magazines, newspapers, television, or radio.

**Essays** and **articles** are short, nonfiction works on one subject. They may include these kinds of writing:

- **Expository writing** explains facts, ideas, or a process.

- **Persuasive writing** convinces the reader that he or she should take an action or accept a point of view.

- **Reflective writing** tells a writer's insights about events or experiences.

- **Humorous writing** makes people laugh. Sometimes, it also makes a serious point.

- **Narrative writing** retells real-life experiences.

- **Descriptive writing** helps a reader experience something through the five senses.

- **Analytical writing** breaks an important idea into parts in order to explain it.

## Elements of Nonfiction

There are several ways to organize nonfiction writing.

| Organization | Definition | Example |
| --- | --- | --- |
| Chronological | presents events and details in time order | a vacation journal |
| Comparison-and-contrast | shows ways that the subjects are alike and different | an essay about two planets, two animals, or three branches of government |
| Cause-and-effect | shows how one or more things cause something to happen or how one or more things result from a cause | an article about what led up to the Civil War and what happened as a result of the war |
| Problem-and-solution | identifies a problem and presents one or more solutions | a magazine story that discusses how a city faces a major problem and plans to solve it |

The **author's purpose** is the author's reason for writing. In nonfiction, writers present information to explain, entertain, inform, or persuade.

# What Makes a Rembrandt a Rembrandt?
### Richard Mühlberger

**Summary** The Dutch artist Rembrandt changed painting. His most famous painting shows Captain Frans Banning Cocq's militia company. Rembrandt adds excitement by showing extra people and even a dog. He shows activity by using contrasts of light and shadow and bright and dark colors.

## Note-taking Guide
Use this chart to record details from the article.

Rembrandt's techniques as shown in *The Night Watch*

contrasts light and dark

# What Makes a Rembrandt a Rembrandt?

### Richard Mühlberger

## Citizen Soldiers

A Dutch poet of Rembrandt's day wrote, "When the country is in danger, every citizen is a soldier." That was the idea behind the militia, or civic guard companies, which trained citizens how to fight and shoot in case their city was attacked. Each company drilled in archery, the crossbow, or the musket. By Rembrandt's time, militia companies were as much social clubs as military organizations.

Captain Frans Banning Cocq, out to impress everyone, chose Rembrandt to paint his militia company, with members of the company paying the artist to have their portraits included in the painting. The huge canvas was to be hung in the new hall of the militia headquarters, where it would be seen at receptions and celebrations along with other militia paintings.

By the mid-seventeenth century, there were more than one hundred big militia paintings hanging in public halls in the important cities of the Netherlands. In all of these group portraits, the men were evenly lined up so that each face got equal attention, just as they had been in traditional anatomy lesson paintings. Rembrandt did not like this way of presenting the scene. He had seen militia companies in action, and there were always people milling[1] about who were not militiamen but who took part in their exercises and parades. To add realism to the piece, he decided to include some of these people, as well as a dog. There was room on the wall for a canvas about sixteen feet wide, large enough for

---

## Vocabulary Development

**receptions** (ri SEP shuhnz) *n.* formal parties

**portraits** (PAWR trits) *n.* pictures of people

---

1. **milling** (MIL ing) *v.* moving around without a clear purpose.

**Activate Prior Knowledge**

Think of people lined up for a family portrait. If you were painting the scene, how would you make it interesting?

_____

_____

_____

_____

_____

**Nonfiction**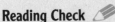

What **problem** did Rembrandt see with the usual way of doing group portraits? Underline the sentence that tells the problem. Then tell Rembrandt's **solution**.

_____

_____

_____

_____

**Reading Check** 

What did Frans Banning Cocq hire Rembrandt to paint? Underline the answer.

Rembrandt to do what no other painter had ever done before. His idea was to show the exciting <u>commotion</u> before a parade began.

**Two Handsome Officers**

Everywhere in the painting, Rembrandt used sharp <u>contrasts</u> of dark and light. Everything that honors the citizen soldiers and their work is <u>illuminated</u>; everything else is in shadow. Captain Frans Banning Cocq is the man dressed in black with a red sash under his arm, striding forward in the center. Standing next to him is the most brightly lighted man in the painting, Lieutenant Willem van Ruytenburgh, attired in a glorious gold and yellow uniform, silk sash, soft leather cavalry boots, and a high hat with white ostrich plumes. His lancelike weapon, called a partisan, and the steel gorget[2] around his neck—a leftover from the days when soldiers wore full suits of armor—are the only hints that he is a military man. Rembrandt links him to Banning Cocq by contrasting the colors of their clothing and by painting the shadow of Banning Cocq's hand on the front of van Ruytenburgh's coat. The captain is giving orders to his lieutenant for the militia company to march off.

Banning Cocq is dressed in a black suit against a dark background, yet he does not disappear. Rembrandt made him the most important person in the composition. Van Ruytenburgh turns to listen to him, which shows his respect for his commander. Banning Cocq's face stands out above his bright red sash and white collar. How well Rembrandt knew that darkness makes faces shine! The captain's self-assured pace, the movement of the tassels at his knees, and the angle of his walking staff are proof of the energy and dignity of his stride.

### Nonfiction

Nonfiction often presents **comparisons and contrasts**, or similarities and differences, between two or more subjects. How do the "two handsome officers" contrast with everything else in the painting?

_____

_____

_____

How are the two handsome officers linked, or shown to be alike? Underline the sentence that gives the answer.

### Nonfiction

**Causes** are reasons that explain why something happens. The results are **effects**. Circle the sentences in the bracketed passage that tell the effect. What effect does Van Ruytenburgh's position have?

### Reading Check

What makes Banning Cocq's face stand out or shine? Underline the reason.

---

**Vocabulary Development**

**commotion** (kuh MOH shuhn) *n.* loud noise and much activity
**contrasts** (KAHN trasts) *n.* differences
**illuminated** (i LOOM uh nayt id) *v.* lit up

2. **gorget** (GAWR jit) *n.* a piece of armor for the throat.

## Muskets and Mascots

On either side of these two handsome officers, broad paths lead back into the painting.

Rembrandt knew that when the huge group scene was placed above eye level on the wall of the militia headquarters, these empty areas would be the first to be seen. He wanted them to lead the eyes of viewers to figures in the painting who did not have the advantage of being placed in the foreground.[3] In the middle of one of these paths is a man in red pouring gunpowder into the barrel of his musket.[4] Behind the captain, only partially seen, another man shoots his gun into the air, and a third militiaman, to the right of van Ruytenburgh, blows on his weapon to clean it. Loading, shooting, and cleaning were part of the standard drill for musketeers, and so they were included in the painting to demonstrate the men's mastery of their weapons.

Walking in a stream of bright light down the path on the left is a blond girl dressed in yellow with a dead chicken tied to her waist. She has a friend in blue behind her. In their public shows, the militia would choose two young girls to carry the emblems[5] of their company, here the claws of a bird. The yellow and blue of the girls' costumes are the militia's colors. In the parade that is being organized, these mascots will take a prominent place, the fair-haired girl holding aloft the chicken's claws.

Many of the background figures stand on stairs so that their faces can be seen. The man above the girl in yellow is Jan Corneliszoon Visscher, after Banning Cocq and van Ruytenburgh the highest-ranking person in the militia company. He waves a flag that combines the colors of the militia company with the three black crosses of Amsterdam. While Rembrandt did not pose him in bright light, he made him important by placing him high up on the stairs, by showing the sheen in his costume, and by giving him the large flag to unfurl.

### Vocabulary Development

**sheen** (sheen) *n.* smooth and shiny look
**unfurl** (un FERL) *v.* unroll or open a flag

---

3. **foreground** (FAWR grownd) *n.* the part of a picture that seems closest to you.
4. **musket** (MUS kit) *n.* a type of gun used in earlier times.
5. **emblems** (EM bluhmz) *n.* pictures or objects that represent a country, a group, or an idea.

**Stop to Reflect**

The author thinks of Rembrandt as a great painter. How does the first bracketed passage help show Rembrandt's greatness?

_____

_____

_____

**Nonfiction**

**Descriptive writing** helps a reader experience something through the five senses. Read the second bracketed passage. List three details about the girls that you can see.

_____

_____

_____

**Reading Check**

How did Rembrandt show the importance of Jan Corneliszoon Visscher, the third most important person in the militia company? Underline the sentence that tells what Rembrandt did.

## Nonfiction

The bracketed paragraph is an **expository** paragraph, a paragraph that presents and explains facts. What are these facts about?

_____

_____

One sentence in the bracketed paragraph is **reflective**: it includes the writer's insights. Underline the sentence.

## Stop to Reflect

How are the costumes or uniforms of these soldiers similar to those worn today? How are they different?

_____

_____

_____

_____

_____

_____

## Reading Check

Why is *Night Watch* the wrong name for the painting of the militia company? Underline one reason in the text.

---

### A Red Ribbon and Fine Old Clothes

In spite of his partial appearance, the drummer on the right seems ready to come forward to lead a march with his staccato[6] beat. The sound seems to bother the dusty dog below. Behind the drummer, two men appear to be figuring out their places in the formation. The one in the white collar and black hat outranks many of the others in the scene. His prestige is signaled in an unusual way: A red ribbon dangles over his head, tied to the lance of the man in armor behind van Ruytenburgh. Additional lances can be counted in the darkness, some leaning against the wall, others carried by militiamen. Their crisscross patterns add to the feeling of commotion that Rembrandt has captured everywhere on the huge canvas.

The costumes worn in this group portrait are much more ornate and colorful than what Dutchmen ordinarily wore every day. Some, like the breeches and helmet of the man shooting his musket behind Banning Cocq, go back a hundred years to the beginnings of the militia company. In the eyes of many Dutchmen, clothing associated with a glorious past brought special dignity to the company. What an opportunity for Rembrandt, perhaps the greatest lover of old clothes in Amsterdam!

### Not a Night Watch

*Night Watch* is a mistaken title that was given to the painting over a hundred years after Rembrandt died, but it has stuck, and is what the painting is almost universally called. Although the exaggerated chiaroscuro[7] does give an impression of night time, there is daylight in the scene. It comes from the left, as the shadows under Banning Cocq's feet prove.

---

**Vocabulary Development**

**prestige** (pres TEEZH) *n.* honor; respect from others

**ornate** (or NAYT) *adj.* very decorative

**universally** (yoo nuh VER suh lee) *adj.* in all of the world; in all of a certain group

---

6. **staccato** (stuh KAHT oh) *adj.* short, brief.

7. **chiaroscuro** (kee ahr uh SKOOR oh) *n.* a dramatic style of light and shade in a painting or drawing.

And it is clear that no one in the painting is on watch, alert to the approach of an enemy. The official title of the painting is *Officers and Men of the Company of Captain Frans Banning Cocq and Lieutenant Willem van Ruytenburgh.*

Rembrandt completed the painting in 1642, when he was thirty-six years old. He probably had no idea that it would be the most famous Dutch painting of all time. In 1678, one of his former students wrote that it would "outlive all its <u>rivals</u>," and within another century the painting was considered one of the wonders of the world.

**Stop to Reflect**

What painting or photograph do you think is great? Explain your answer.

_____

_____

_____

_____

_____

_____

**Stop to Reflect**

How old was Rembrandt when he painted *The Night Watch*? Circle the answer.

**Reader's Response:** If you could see a Rembrandt painting in a museum, what whould you look for in it?

_____

_____

_____

_____

_____

**Vocabulary Development**

**rivals** (RY vuhlz) *n.* people or things that compete with one another

# What Makes a Rembrandt a Rembrandt?

1. **Respond:** Now that you have read the essay, what new title would you give to *The Night Watch*? Explain.

_____

_____

_____

2. **Generalize:** How did Rembrandt change the way military group portraits were painted?

_____

_____

_____

3. **Interpret:** How did Rembrandt use light and shadow to indicate rank?

_____

_____

4. Use this chart to list examples of the types of writing Mühlberger uses in this essay.

| Examples of Description | Examples of Exposition |
|---|---|
|  |  |
|  |  |
|  |  |

### Plan a Panel Discussion

Follow these steps to gather information for your panel discussion.

- Go to the library. Use a computer and the online catalog. Select an author search, and type *Mühlberger, Richard* into the search box. Press enter. A list of Mühlberger's books will come up. Record some of them below.

**Book:** _____

**Book:** _____

**Book:** _____

**Book:** _____

**Book:** _____

- Use the Internet. Type in search terms such as "*Richard Mühlberger*" + *career*, "*Richard Mühlberger*" + *background*, or "*Richard Mühlberger*" + *education*. Screen your results, or "hits," for descriptions that match your research goal. Use reliable sites, such as those that end in *.edu*, *.gov*, or *.org*. Record your findings below.

**What I learned:** _____

_____

_____

_____

_____

_____

- Watch the video interview with Richard Mühlberger, and review your source material. Use this information to record additional information for your panel discussion.

**Additional information:** _____

_____

_____

_____

_____

# Life Without Gravity • Conversational Ballgames

## Reading Skill

The **main idea** is the central point of a passage or text. The main idea of a paragraph is usually stated in a **topic sentence** that identifies the key point. **Supporting details** give examples, explanations, or reasons.

When reading nonfiction, **adjust your reading rate to recognize main ideas and key points**.

- **Skim**, or look over the text quickly, to get a sense of the main idea before you begin reading.
- **Read closely** to learn what the main ideas are.
- **Scan**, or run your eyes over the text, to find answers to questions, to clarify, or to find supporting details.

Fill in this chart as you look for main ideas.

| Reading Rate | What to Look for | Example From Text |
|---|---|---|
| Skimming before reading | organization, topic sentences, repeated words | |
| Close reading | key points, supporting details | |
| Scanning | particular word or idea | |

## Literary Analysis

An **expository essay** is a short piece of nonfiction that explains, defines, or interprets ideas, events, or processes. The organization and presentation of information depends on the specific topic of the essay.

# Life Without Gravity
## Robert Zimmerman

**Summary** How does weightlessness affect the body? The author explains the challenges that living without gravity brings to astronauts. Weightlessness is uncomfortable at first for astronauts. It poses special problems for muscles, bones, blood, and even for eating food. Astronauts get used to living without gravity over time.

 ## Writing About the Big Question

**What should we learn?** In "Life Without Gravity," the author describes the ways that astronauts adjust to being weightless in space. Complete this sentence:

Reading about other people's experiences can help us explore our ideas

about _____.

## Note-taking Guide

Use this cluster diagram to list the effects of weightlessness on the body.

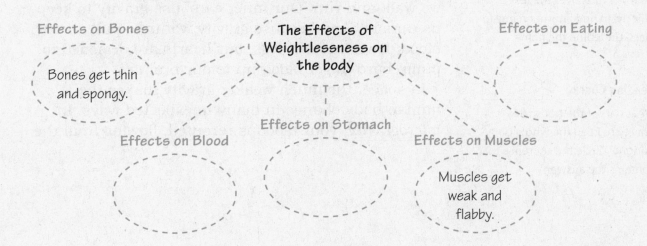

Effects on Bones

Bones get thin and spongy.

The Effects of Weightlessness on the body

Effects on Eating

Effects on Blood

Effects on Stomach

Effects on Muscles

Muscles get weak and flabby.

## Activate Prior Knowledge

Would you like to be an astronaut? Explain your choice.

_____

_____

_____

_____

## Literary Analysis

An **expository essay** is a short piece of nonfiction. It explains or defines ideas, events, or processes. What is the topic of this expository essay?

_____

_____

_____

_____

## Reading Skill

**Skim,** or look over the text quickly, to find another name for Mars. Underline the name.

## Reading Check

What part of the body uses gravity to keep the whole body upright? Circle the sentence that contains the answer.

# Life Without Gravity
## Robert Zimmerman

Being weightless in space seems so exciting. Astronauts bounce about from wall to wall, flying! They float, they weave, they do somersaults and acrobatics without effort. Heavy objects can be lifted like feathers, and no one ever gets tired because nothing weighs anything. In fact, everything is fun, nothing is hard.

NOT! Since the first manned space missions in the 1960s, scientists have discovered that being weightless in space isn't just flying around like Superman. Zero gravity is alien stuff. As space tourist Dennis Tito said when he visited the international space station, "Living in space is like having a different life, living in a different world."

Worse, weightlessness can sometimes be downright unpleasant. Your body gets upset and confused. Your face puffs up, your nose gets stuffy, your back hurts, your stomach gets upset, and you throw up. If astronauts are to survive a one-year journey to Mars—the shortest possible trip to the Red Planet— they will have to learn how to deal with this weird environment.

Our bodies are adapted to Earth's gravity. Our muscles are strong in order to overcome gravity as we walk and run. Our inner ears[1] use gravity to keep us upright. And because gravity wants to pull all our blood down into our legs, our hearts are designed to pump hard to get blood up to our brains.

In space, the much weaker gravity makes the human body change in many unexpected ways. In microgravity, your blood is rerouted, flowing from the

### Vocabulary Development
**survive** (ser VYV) *v.* live through
**microgravity** (my kroh GRAV i tee) *n.* the near-weightlessness that astronauts experience as their spacecraft orbits Earth

1. **inner ears** internal parts of the ears that give people a sense of balance.

legs, which become thin and sticklike, to the head, which swells up. The extra liquid in your head also makes you feel like you're hanging upside down or have a stuffed-up nose.

The lack of gravity causes astronauts to routinely "grow" between one and three inches taller. Their spines[2] straighten out. The bones in the spine and the disks between them spread apart and relax.

But their bones also get thin and spongy. The body decides that if the muscles aren't going to push and pull on the bones, it doesn't need to lay down as much bone as it normally does. Astronauts who have been in space for several months can lose 10 percent or more of their bone tissue.[3] If their bones got much weaker, they would snap once the astronauts returned to Earth.

And their muscles get weak and flabby. Floating about in space is too easy. If astronauts don't force themselves to exercise, their muscles become so feeble that when they return to Earth they can't even walk.

Worst of all is how their stomachs feel. During the first few days in space, the inner ear—which gives people their sense of balance—gets confused. Many astronauts become nauseous. They lose their appetites. Many throw up. Many throw up a lot!

Weightlessness isn't all bad, however. After about a week people usually get used to it. Their stomachs settle down. Appetites return (though astronauts always say that food tastes blander in space). The heart and spine adjust.

Then, flying around like a bird becomes fun! Rooms suddenly seem much bigger. Look around you: The space above your head is pretty useless on

**Stop to Reflect**

In what sort of physical shape should a person be in to become an astronaut? Support your answer with details from the text.

_____

_____

_____

_____

**Reading Skill**

The **main idea** is the central point of a text, passage, or paragraph. A **topic sentence** usually identifies the main idea of a paragraph. Underline the topic sentence in the bracketed paragraph.

**Literary Analysis**

Which of the following does this **expository essay** explain? Circle your answer.

**idea    event    process**

Explain your choice.

_____

_____

_____

**Vocabulary Development**

**routinely** (roo TEEN lee) _adv._ regularly, usually

**feeble** (FEE buhl) _adj._ weak

**blander** (BLAND er) _adj._ having less taste

2. **spines** (spynz) _n._ backbones.

3. **tissue** (TI shoo) _n._ the material that makes up plant and animal cells.

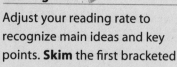

## Reading Skill

Adjust your reading rate to recognize main ideas and key points. **Skim** the first bracketed passage to get a sense of its main idea. Then, read the passage closely. Write a sentence that tells its main idea.

_____

_____

_____

_____

_____

## Literary Analysis 🔍

What process does the second bracketed paragraph explain?

_____

_____

_____

_____

## Reading Check

What happens if you do not tie something down in space? Circle the answer.

Earth. You can't get up there to work, and anything you attach to the ceiling is simply something you'll bump your head on.

In space, however, that area is useful. In fact, equipment can be <u>installed</u> on every inch of every wall. In weightlessness you choose to move up or down and left or right simply by pointing your head. If you turn yourself upside down, the ceiling becomes the floor.

And you can't drop anything! As you work you can let your tools float around you. But you'd better be organized and neat. If you don't put things back where they belong when you are finished, tying them down securely, they will float away. Air currents will then blow them into nooks and crannies, and it might take you days to find them again.

In microgravity, you have to learn new ways to eat. Don't try pouring a bowl of cornflakes. Not only will the flakes float all over the place, the milk won't pour. Instead, big balls of milk will form. You can drink these by taking big bites out of them, but you'd better finish them before they slam into a wall, splattering apart and covering everything with little tiny milk globules.[4]

Some meals on the space station are eaten with forks and knives, but scooping food with a spoon doesn't work. If the food isn't gooey enough to stick to the spoon, it will float away.

Everyone in space drinks through a straw, since liquid simply refuses to stay in a glass. The straw has to have a clamp at one end, or else when you stop drinking, the liquid will continue to flow out, spilling everywhere.

To prevent their muscles and bones from becoming too weak for life on Earth, astronauts have to follow a boring two-hour exercise routine

**Vocabulary Development**

**installed** (in STAWLD) *v.* put a piece of equipment in place

4. **globules** (GLAHB yoolz) *n.* small drops.

every single day. Imagine having to run on a treadmill for one hour in the morning and then ride an exercise bicycle another hour before dinner. As Russian astronaut Valeri Ryumin once said, "Yeech!"

Even after all this exercise, astronauts who spend more than two months in space are usually weak and uncomfortable when they get back to Earth. Jerry Linenger, who spent more than four months on the Russian space station, Mir, struggled to walk after he returned. "My body felt like a 500 pound barbell," he said. He even had trouble lifting and holding his fifteen-month-old son, John.

When Linenger went to bed that first night, his body felt like it was being smashed into the mattress. He was constantly afraid that if he moved too much, he would float away and out of control.

And yet, Linenger <u>recovered</u> quickly. In fact, almost two dozen astronauts have lived in space for more than six months, and four have stayed in orbit for more than a year. These men and women faced the <u>discomforts</u> of weightlessness and overcame them. And they all readapted to Earth gravity without problems, proving that voyages to Mars are possible . . . Even if it feels like you are hanging upside down the whole time!

## Literature in Context

### Weighted Down

Your weight in pounds is actually the measure of the downward force of gravity on you. How much force gravity puts on you depends on the size and mass of the planet on which you are standing.

Imagine that on Earth you weigh 100 pounds. Because the surface gravity of Jupiter is 2.64 times that of Earth, you would weigh 264 pounds on

© Pearson Education

### Vocabulary Development
**recovered** (ri KUV erd) *v.* got better; healed
**discomforts** (dis KUM ferts) *n.* slight pains; uncomfortable things

**Literary Analysis**

The end of this **expository essay** explains an idea. What is the idea?

_____
_____
_____
_____
_____

**Reading Skill**

**Scan,** or run your eyes over the bracketed paragraph. Look for details that support the main idea. Underline and number two **supporting details**.

**Stop to Reflect**

What would you miss if you spent several months in space?

_____
_____
_____

**Reading Check**

What determines the force of gravity on you? Circle the answer.

_____

Jupiter without eating a forkful more. On the other hand, surface gravity on the moon is one-sixth of Earth's gravity. That means your moon weight would be just under 17 pounds, though you would look just the same.

Of course, when you are not on a planet or moon, you are out of gravity's pull, so you weigh nothing at all.

### Stop to Reflect

Where would you rather live—on Earth, on Jupiter, or on the moon? Explain your choice.

_____

_____

_____

_____

_____

_____

### Reading Check

How is the moon's gravity different from that on Earth? Circle the answer in the text.

**Reader's Response:** Think of your answer to the first question for this selection. Has this essay changed your thought or feelings about wanting to be an astronaut? Explain your decision.

_____

_____

_____

_____

_____

_____

# Life Without Gravity

1. **Cause and Effect:** Describe the causes of bone loss, upset stomach, and flabby muscles that occur during weightlessness.

   _____

   _____

   _____

2. **Connect:** What new choices does living in a weightless environment give an astronaut?

   _____

   _____

3. **Reading Skill:** What is the **main idea** of the article?

   _____

   _____

4. **Literary Analysis:** Fill out this chart to organize the information in this **expository essay**.

| What is Weightlessness? | What are Its Advantages? | What Are Its Disadvantages? | Author's Conclusions |
|---|---|---|---|
| zero gravity | | | |

## Writing: Problem-and-Solution Essay

Write a brief **problem-and-solution essay** about the difficulties of being an astronaut in space. Use this chart to list problems and solutions.

| Astronauts | Problems Faced | Solutions |
|---|---|---|
| While in space | | |
| After returning from space | | |

## Listening and Speaking: Oral Summary

Prepare and deliver an **oral summary** of Zimmerman's expository essay.

- To what type of audience will you give your oral summary? Consider presenting to younger students, classmates, older students, or adults.

  _____

- What are the needs of your audience? Do they need visual aids to help them understand the concepts? What terms will you have to define?

  _____

  _____

# Conversational Ballgames

## Nancy Masterson Sakamoto

**Summary** The author has trouble holding a conversation in Japanese until she learns the rules. She compares the rules in the United States and Japan to the rules of different ballgames. To win, you must know when it is your turn to keep the conversational ball "rolling."

 **Writing About the Big Question**

**What should we learn?** In "Converational Ballgames," the author explains the difference between western and Japanese styles of conversation. Complete this sentence:

Understanding conversational "rules" can be helpful because _____

_____.

## Note-taking Guide

List ways in which the author compares western-style conversation and volleyball. List ways in which the author compares Japanese-style conversation and bowling. Use this chart.

| Western-style conversation | Volleyball | Japanese-style conversation | Bowling |
|---|---|---|---|
| conversation topic | volleyball | conversation topic | |
| People expect that others will comment on their opinions. | Teams hit the ball back and forth over the net. | People expect that no one will comment on their opinions. | |
| People speak whenever they wish. | | | Players wait their turn to bowl. |

# Conversational Ballgames

1. **Draw Conclusions:** What misunderstandings took place when the author first tried to join a conversation in Japan?

   _____

   _____

2. **Evaluate:** Suppose that two people from different cultures hold a conversation. Explain which person has the greater responsibility for playing by the culture's "conversational rules": the newcomer or the person already living there.

   _____

   _____

   _____

3. **Reading Skill:** What is the **main idea** of the article?

   _____

   _____

4. **Literary Analysis:** Fill out this chart to organize information about conversations at dinner.

| Describe Polite Conversation in the United States | Describe Polite Conversation in Japan | Author's Conclusion |
|---|---|---|
|  |  |  |

## Writing: Problem-and-Solution Essay

Write a brief **problem-and-solution essay** about the difficulties that Japanese and Westerners have when speaking with one another. Use this chart to list problems and solutions.

|  | Problems Faced | Solutions |
|---|---|---|
| Japanese speaking to Westerners |  |  |
| Westerners speaking to Japanese |  |  |

## Listening and Speaking: Presentation

You will give a **presentation** in which you provide an oral summary of "Conversational Ballgames." Use the following chart to record important ideas and details. Complete your chart on another sheet of paper.

| Main Idea: | |
|---|---|
| Supporting Details: | Visual Aids |
|  |  |

# I Am a Native of North America • Volar: To Fly

## Reading Skill

The **main idea** is the most important idea in a work. Authors often state the main idea directly. They provide key points that support the main idea. Details, such as examples and descriptions, support these points. The main idea may be unstated. The author gives you only the key points or supporting details.

**Make connections between key points and supporting details.** Notice how the writer groups details. Look for sentences that pull details together. Use this chart to help show the connections.

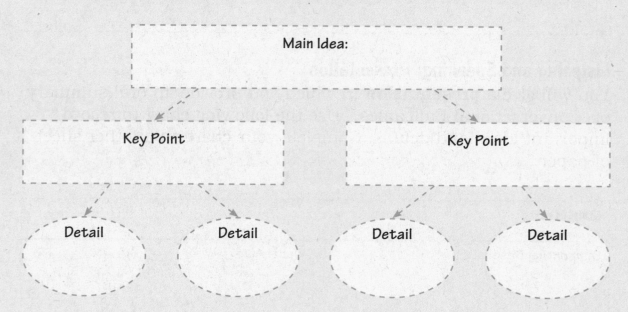

## Literary Analysis

A **reflective essay** is a short work.

- It shows a writer's feelings and thoughts or reflections about an experience or an idea.
- Writers want readers to respond with thoughts and feelings of their own.

# I Am a Native of North America

## Chief Dan George

**Summary** The author reflects on the lessons he learned from his Native American culture. He wonders whether people from white culture know how to love. He asks people from both cultures to love and forgive one another.

 **Writing About the Big Question**

**What should we learn?** In "I Am a Native of North America," Chief Dan George recalls the traditions and beliefs that his culture values above all. Complete this sentence:

It is important to discover the traditions and beliefs of people from a

different culture because _____.

## Note-taking Guide

Chief Dan George compares his Native American culture and white American culture. See the example given in the Venn diagram. Use the extra space to list more differences that he names between the two cultures.

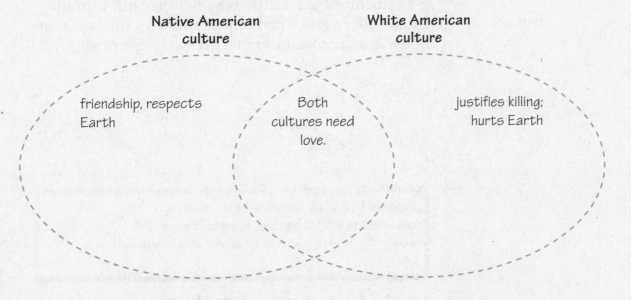

Native American culture

White American culture

friendship, respects Earth

Both cultures need love.

justifies killing; hurts Earth

# I Am a Native of North America

## Chief Dan George

**Activate Prior Knowledge**

What important goal should the United States accomplish in the future? Write your answer below.

_____

_____

_____

**Reading Skill**

The **main idea** is the most important thought or concept in a passage of text. Read the underlined sentence. It tells that people learned how to treat one another well by living together in close quarters. Circle three details in the same paragraph that tell about Chief George's grandfather's house.

**Reading Check**

How large was Chief George's grandfather's house? Draw a box around the answer.

In the course of my lifetime I have lived in two distinct cultures.[1] I was born into a culture that lived in communal houses. My grandfather's house was eighty feet long. It was called a smoke house, and it stood down by the beach along the inlet.[2] All my grandfather's sons and their families lived in this large dwelling. Their sleeping apartments were separated by blankets made of bull rush reeds, but one open fire in the middle served the cooking needs of all. In houses like these, throughout the tribe, people learned to live with one another; learned to serve one another; learned to respect the rights of one another. And children shared the thoughts of the adult world and found themselves surrounded by aunts and uncles and cousins who loved them and did not threaten them. My father was born in such a house and learned from infancy how to love people and be at home with them.

And beyond this acceptance of one another there was a deep respect for everything in nature that surrounded them. My father loved the earth and all its creatures. The earth was his second mother. The earth and everything it contained was a gift from See-see-am[3] . . . and the way to thank this great spirit was to use his gifts with respect.

I remember, as a little boy, fishing with him up Indian River and I can still see him as the sun rose above the mountain top in the early morning . . .

**Vocabulary Development**

**distinct** (di STINGKT) *adj.* clearly different or separate
**communal** (kuh MYOO nl) *adj.* shared by a group of people
**infancy** (IN fuhn see) *n.* the time in a child's life before he or she can walk or talk

1. **cultures** (KUL cherz) *n.* the art, beliefs, behavior, and ideas of a certain group of people.
2. **inlet** (IN let) *n.* narrow strip of water extending into a piece of land from a river, a lake, or an ocean.
3. **See-see-am** the name of the Great Spirit, or "The Chief Above," in the Salishan language of Chief George's people.

I can see him standing by the water's edge with his arms raised above his head while he softly moaned . . . "Thank you, thank you." It left a deep impression on my young mind.

And I shall never forget his disappointment when once he caught me gaffing for fish[4] "just for the fun of it." "My Son," he said, "the Great Spirit gave you those fish to be your brothers, to feed you when you are hungry. You must respect them. You must not kill them just for the fun of it."

This then was the culture I was born into and for some years the only one I really knew or tasted. This is why I find it hard to accept many of the things I see around me.

I see people living in smoke houses hundreds of times bigger than the one I knew. But the people in one apartment do not even know the people in the next and care less about them.

It is also difficult for me to understand the deep hate that exists among people. It is hard to understand a culture that justifies the killing of millions in past wars, and is at this very moment preparing bombs to kill even greater numbers. It is hard for me to understand a culture that spends more on wars and weapons to kill, than it does on education and welfare to help and develop.

It is hard for me to understand a culture that not only hates and fights its brothers but even attacks nature and abuses her. I see my white brother going about blotting out nature from his cities. I see him strip the hills bare, leaving ugly wounds on the face of mountains. I see him tearing things from the

**Literary Analysis**

In this **reflective essay**, the writer reflects on an experience he had with his father. What lesson from his culture does the writer learn?

_____

_____

**Stop to Reflect**

What can you and your family do to get to know people who live near you?

_____

_____

_____

_____

_____

**Reading Skill**

Remember to **make connections between key points and supporting details.** Circle the key point in the bracketed paragraph.

Underline the supporting details.

---

**Vocabulary Development**

**impression** (im PRESH uhn) *n.* opinion or feeling you have about something from the way it seems

**exists** (ig ZISTS) *v.* happens or is present in certain situations or places

**justifies** (JUS tuh fyz) *v.* excuses; explains

4. **gaffing for fish** using a barbed spear to catch river fish.

© Pearson Education

**Reading Skill**

What key word is repeated on this page? Circle this word. How does the key word help you determine the essay's **main idea**?

_____

_____

_____

**Literary Analysis**

Chief Dan George has experienced two cultures. List some of his thoughts in this **reflective essay** about what these cultures are like.

_____

_____

_____

_____

**Reading Check**

What will happen to people if they do not love fully? Underline the answer.

bosom of mother earth as though she were a monster, who refused to share her treasures with him. I see him throw poison in the waters, indifferent to the life he kills there; and he chokes the air with deadly fumes.

My white brother does many things well for he is more clever than my people but I wonder if he knows how to love well. I wonder if he has ever really learned to love at all. Perhaps he only loves the things that are his own but never learned to love the things that are outside and beyond him. And this is, of course, not love at all, for man must love all creation or he will love none of it. Man must love fully or he will become the lowest of the animals. It is the power to love that makes him the greatest of them all . . . for he alone of all animals is capable of love.

Love is something you and I must have. We must have it because our spirit feeds upon it. We must have it because without it we become weak and faint. Without love our <u>self-esteem</u> weakens. Without it our courage fails. Without love we can no longer look out confidently at the world. Instead we turn inwardly and begin to feed upon our own <u>personalities</u> and little by little we destroy ourselves.

You and I need the strength and joy that comes from knowing that we are loved. With it we are creative. With it we march tirelessly. With it, and with it alone, we are able to <u>sacrifice</u> for others.

There have been times when we all wanted so desperately to feel a reassuring hand upon us . . . there have been lonely times when we so wanted a strong arm around us . . . I cannot tell you how

**Vocabulary Development**

**self-esteem** (self i STEEM) *n.* being satisfied with your abilities; feeling that you should be liked and respected

**personalities** (per suh NAL uh teez) *n.* characters, how people behave toward other people

**sacrifice** (SAK ruh fys) *v.* willingly give something up for something that is more important

deeply I miss my wife's presence when I return from a trip. Her love was my greatest joy, my strength, my greatest blessing.

I am afraid my culture has little to offer yours. But my culture did prize friendship and companionship. It did not look on privacy as a thing to be clung to, for privacy builds up walls and walls promote distrust. My culture lived in big family communities, and from infancy people learned to live with others.

My culture did not prize the <u>hoarding</u> of private possessions; in fact, to hoard was a shameful thing to do among my people. The Indian looked on all things in nature as belonging to him and he expected to share them with others and to take only what he needed.

Everyone likes to give as well as receive. No one wishes only to receive all the time. We have taken much from your culture . . . I wish you had taken something from our culture . . . for there were some beautiful and good things in it.

Soon it will be too late to know my culture, for integration[5] is upon us and soon we will have no values but yours. Already many of our young people have forgotten the old ways. And many have been <u>shamed</u> of their Indian ways by <u>scorn</u> and ridicule. My culture is like a wounded deer that has crawled away into the forest to bleed and die alone.

**Reading Skill**

An author should back up his statements with **support**. What information does the author provide to support his claim that his culture prized friendship and companionship?

_____

_____

_____

_____

_____

**Stop to Reflect**

Suppose that you were to move to a culture different from yours. Could you maintain your cultural identity while living there? Explain.

_____

_____

_____

_____

**Reading Check** ✐

Underline the sentence that tells what Chief Dan George's culture prized.

**Vocabulary Development**

**hoarding** (HAWRD ing) *v.* collecting a large amount of something and keeping it in a secret place

**shamed** (shaymd) *v.* embarrassed or made to feel bad

**scorn** (skawrn) *n.* words or looks indicating that something is foolish or not as good as something else

5. **integration** (in tuh GRAY shuhn) *n.* process of combining or placing individual parts into one entire piece.

© Pearson Education

**I Am a Native of North America   179**

## Literary Analysis

Authors show their feelings and thoughts in a **reflective essay**. Briefly summarize Chief Dan George's thoughts about the cultures he has experienced.

_____

_____

_____

_____

_____

_____

_____

## Reading Check

Underline the author's description of *brotherhood*.

The only thing that can truly help us is <u>genuine</u> love. You must truly love us, be patient with us and share with us. And we must love you—with a genuine love that forgives and forgets . . . a love that forgives the terrible sufferings your culture brought ours when it swept over us like a wave crashing along a beach . . . with a love that forgets and lifts up its head and sees in your eyes an answering love of trust and acceptance.

This is brotherhood . . . anything less is not worthy of the name.

I have spoken.

**Reader's Response:** Do you agree that "the power to love" is the most important human quality? Explain.

_____

_____

_____

_____

_____

_____

**Vocabulary Development**

**genuine** (JEN yoo in) *adj.* real or true

# I Am a Native of North America

1. **Analyze:** What is the "brotherhood" that Chief Dan George talks about at the end of the essay?

   _____

   _____

2. **Interpret:** When Chief Dan George says "My white brother . . . is more clever than my people," what does he mean by *clever*?

   _____

   _____

3. **Reading Skill:** What is the **main idea** of the essay?

   _____

   _____

4. **Literary Analysis:** In the left column of the chart below, write Chief George's reflections on two points. Use the reflection provided, and add one more. In the middle column, write your response to each reflection. Then, reread the paragraph that includes each reflection. Identify any feelings that Chief George expresses in the reflection. In the third column, explain whether your responses changed on the basis of your rereading.

| Chief George's Reflections | My responses | After Rereading |
|---|---|---|
| Father gives thanks on fishing trip. | | |
| | | |

### Writing: Outline

Write an **outline** of "I Am a Native of North America."

- Skim the passage. Identify the most important thought in the passage. This is the main idea. You may need to write it in your own words.

_____

- Look at each paragraph. Pay attention only to ideas that support the main idea. Write three key points here.

_____

_____

The key points will follow Roman numerals in your outline.

### Listening and Speaking: Response

Present a **response** to the essay. State whether you agree or disagree with the author's message.

- Sometimes reasons may not be clear to an audience. Details are often necessary. Develop details into a response to "I Am a Native of North America." Fill in the chart below. Think about *why* you use a certain reason to support your response. Doing so will help you identify important details.

My Response:

Reason 1:

Reason 2:

# Volar: To Fly

## Judith Ortiz Cofer

**Summary** In "Volar: To Fly," a girl and her mother both want to fly but for different reasons. The girl dreams that she is a superhero who can fly high above her neighborhood. Her mother wishes to return to Puerto Rico to visit her family and friends.

## Writing About the Big Question

**What should we learn?** In "Volar: To Fly," a mother and a daughter dream of flying—for very different reasons. Complete this sentence:

Our hopes and dreams help us to examine what is important in our lives

because they show us _____.

## Note-taking Guide

Use this chart to describe what happens to the author in her dream.

| In what way *does the author's appearance change?* | What powers does the author have? |
| --- | --- |
|  |  |

# Volar: To Fly

1. **Analyze:** What is the significance of the words "To Fly" in the title of this essay?

_____

_____

2. **Respond:** Do you think the author enjoyed her dreams? Explain.

_____

_____

3. **Reading Skill:** The **main idea** is the most important concept in a work. What is the main idea of this essay?

_____

_____

4. **Literary Analysis:** A **reflective essay** tells how a writer thinks or feels about a topic. Analyze the reflective essay. Use this chart. In the first column, write Cofer's reflections on two points. Write your responses in the middle column. Then, reread the paragraphs that include Cofer's reflections. Think about any feelings that she expresses in these reflections. Now, describe your responses after you have reread.

| Cofer's Reflections | My Responses | After Rereading |
| --- | --- | --- |
| She could control her Supergirl dreams. | | |

## Writing: Outline

Write an **outline** for "Volar: To Fly."

- Skim the selection. Identify the main idea. Write it in your own words.

  _____

  _____

- Read each paragraph. Look for key points that support the main idea. Write these key points here.

  _____

  _____

  _____

- Look at the paragraphs in which you found key points. List any details that support each key point. Write these supporting details here.

  _____

  _____

  Use these notes to write an outline.

## Listening and Speaking: Response

Present a **response** to the essay. State whether you agree or disagree with the message.

Develop details into a response to "Volar: To Fly." Fill in the following chart.

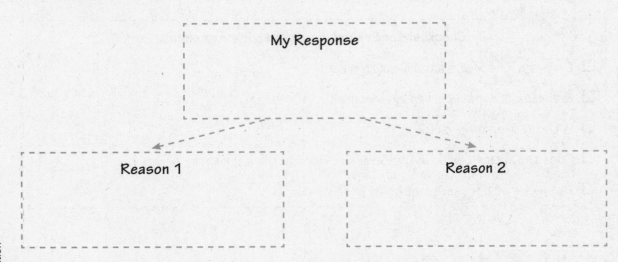

# Problem-and-Solution Essays

## About Problem-and-Solution Essays

A **problem-and-solution essay** identifies and explains a problem and then presents one or more possible solutions to it.

Look for the following in a problem-and-solution essay:

- a clearly stated problem and an explanation of the situation
- step-by-step solutions
- evidence that supports each suggested solution
- a consistent, logical organization

## Reading Skill

First, **identify the problem** that the author presents. The title or the introduction usually names the problem. Next, **find the possible solutions** that the author describes. Look for the details and evidence that the author provides to support or oppose each solution. Use these questions as you analyze the author's argument.

- What problem is the author trying to solve?
- What solutions does the author present?
- What evidence does the author provide to support or oppose each solution?
- Is the author's argument well organized and convincing?

---

### Checklist for Evaluating an Author's Argument

❑ Does the author present a clear argument?

❑ Is the argument supported by evidence?

❑ Is the evidence believable?

❑ Does the author use sound reasoning to develop the argument?

❑ Do I agree with the message? Why or why not?

---

# Keeping It Quiet

A construction worker uses a jackhammer; a woman waits in a noisy airport; a spectator watches a car race. All three experience noise pollution. In the United States alone, 40 million people face danger to their health from noise pollution.

People start to feel pain at about 120 decibels.[1] But noise that "doesn't hurt" can still damage your hearing. Exposure to 85 decibels (a kitchen blender) can slowly damage the hair cells in your cochlea. As many as 9 million Americans have hearing loss caused by noise. What can be done about noise pollution?

## The Issues

### What Can Individuals Do?

Some work conditions are noisier than others. Construction workers, airport employees, and truck drivers are all at risk. Workers in noisy environments can help themselves by using ear protectors, which can reduce noise levels by 35 decibels.

Many leisure activities also pose a risk. A listener at a rock concert or someone riding a motorbike can prevent damage by using ear protectors. People can also reduce noise at the source. They can buy quieter machines and avoid using lawn mowers or power tools at quiet times of the day. Simply turning down the volume on head phones for radios and CD players can help prevent hearing loss in young people.

1. **decibels** (DES uh buhlz) *n.* units for measuring the loudness of sound

**TAKE NOTES**

**Comprehension Builder**

What is the problem discussed in this essay? Underline it.

**Text Structure**

What does the subheading tell you about the information in the bracketed passage? What will the reader learn?

_____

_____

_____

**Vocabulary Builder**

**Compound Words** *Jackhammer* and *head phones* are compound words. A compound word is formed by joining two words. Sometimes a blank space or a hyphen separates the two words. Circle three more compound words found on this page.

## TAKE NOTES

### Fluency Builder

A writer may use dashes (—) to set off extra information, such as an explanation or a list, in a sentence. The information adds to your understanding, but it does not change the meaning of the sentence. When reading, you should pause after each dash. With a partner, take turns reading aloud the first paragraph. Pause briefly after each dash as well as after other punctuation marks.

### Comprehension Builder

Underline the main idea in the bracketed passage.

### Vocabulary Builder

**Compound Words** *Federal* means "national" or "central." What does the compound word *federal government* mean?

## What Can Communities Do?

Transportation—planes, trains, trucks, and cars—is the largest source of noise pollution. About 15 million Americans live near airports or under airplane flight paths. Careful planning to locate airports away from dense populations can reduce noise. Cities can also prohibit late-night flights.

Many communities have laws against noise that exceeds a certain decibel level, but these laws are hard to enforce. In some cities, "noise police" can give fines to people who use noisy equipment.

## What Can the Government Do?

A National Office of Noise Abatement and Control was set up in the 1970s. It required labels on power tools to tell how much noise they made. But in 1982, this office lost its funding. In 1997, lawmakers proposed The Quiet Communities Act to bring the office back and set limits to many types of noise. But critics say that national laws have little effect. They want the federal government to encourage—and pay for—research into making quieter vehicles and machines.

© Pearson Education

# Thinking About the Problem-and-Solution Essay

1. What is the largest source of noise pollution? Support your answer with details from the essay.

   _____

   _____

2. Explain why pain is not necessarily a sign of hearing damage.

   _____

   _____

## TALK ABOUT IT  Reading Skill

3. What solution does the author propose for individuals?

   _____

   _____

4. How does the author organize the essay to make his or her augument?

   _____

   _____

## WRITE ABOUT IT  Timed Writing: Summary (10 minutes)

Write a brief summary of "Keeping It Quiet."

- First, write a sentence that states the problem.
- Next, list the author's solutions to the problem.
- Then, explain the evidence that shows that there is a problem and the evidence that supports the suggested solutions.
- Finally, finish your summary with a sentence that states your conclusion about the problem and the author's solutions.

# All Together Now • The Eternal Frontier

## Reading Skill

When you read nonfiction, you must be able to distinguish between fact and opinion.

- A **fact** is something that can be proved.
- An **opinion** is a person's judgment or belief. It may be supported by factual evidence, but it cannot be proved.

As you read, **recognize clues that indicate an opinion**, such as *I believe* or *in my opinion*. Words such as *always*, *never*, *must*, and *all* may signal a personal judgment. Emotional statements are often clues to opinion.

## Literary Analysis

A **persuasive essay** is a piece of nonfiction that presents a series of arguments to convince readers that they should believe or act in a certain way. In the chart below, give an example from the story for each technique. Some rows may not have an answer.

| Persuasive Techniques | | Appeals to Reason |
|---|---|---|
| **Appeals to Authority** | | uses logical arguments backed by facts |
| uses opinions of experts and well-known people | | |
| **Appeals to Emotion** | | |
| uses words that appeal to strong feelings | | |

# All Together Now
## Barbara Jordan

**Summary** Barbara Jordan challenges Americans to understand other groups of people. She encourages readers to make friends with people of different backgrounds. She asks parents to teach tolerance to their children. She believes that people can work together. They can make the world a more loving and peaceful place.

## Writing About the Big Question

**What should we learn?** In *All Together Now*, Barbara Jordan discusses how people can make a difference in improving race relations. Complete this sentence:

When we examine the ways that all people are similar, we discover that

accepting others is _____.

## Note-taking Guide

Use this chart to help you define tolerance.

| Tolerance | | |
|---|---|---|
| **What is it?** | **How can we achieve it?** | **Why is it important?** |
| harmony in society | | |

# All Together Now

1. **Interpret:** What does Jordan mean when she says "I have yet to find a racist baby"?

   _____

2. **Evaluate:** Do you think that Jordan's ideas could work to promote tolerance? Explain.

   _____

   _____

3. **Reading Skill:** The chart below shows two **opinions** that Jordan expresses in her essay. List another opinion and the clues that help identify each opinion.

| Opinion | Clues |
|---|---|
| "I don't believe that the task of bringing us all together can be accomplished by government." | "I don't believe" |
| "The best way to get this country faithful to the American dream of tolerance and equality is to start small." | |
| | |

4. **Literary Analysis:** Identify one appeal to authority, one appeal to emotion, and one appeal to reason that Jordan uses in this **persuasive essay**.

   _____

   _____

## Writing: Persuasive Letter

Write a **persuasive letter** to a community leader, advising him or her on ways that people in the community can promote tolerance. Use business letter format.

- Clearly identify several steps that people can take at home.

  _____

  _____

- Explain several challenges that people might face in trying to achieve their goal of a tolerant society.

  _____

  _____

Use these notes to write a persuasive letter.

## Listening and Speaking: Public Service Announcement

A **public service announcement** is similar to an editorial. The point of your PSA is to persuade people to support and agree with your message. Use the following prompts to write ideas for your message and ways in which you will appeal to readers.

Message:

Appeals

1. To authority:

2. To emotion:

3. To reason:

# The Eternal Frontier
## Louis L'Amour

**Summary** Louis L'Amour answers this question: Where is the frontier now? He argues that the next frontier is outer space. He writes that many products and technologies that people use are linked to space research. He believes that people are ready to take the next step into the future—outer space.

 **Writing About the Big Question**

**What should we learn?** In "The Eternal Frontier," the author discusses new discoveries that came about because of people's desire to explore space. Complete this sentence:

Space exploration (is/is not) important because _____

_____.

## Note-taking Guide
Use this chart to list the author's reasons for supporting space exploration.

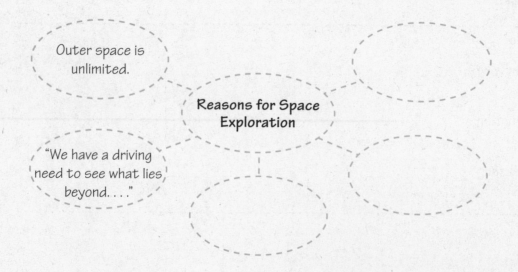

Outer space is unlimited.

Reasons for Space Exploration

"We have a driving need to see what lies beyond. . . ."

# The Eternal Frontier
## Louis L'Amour

The question I am most often asked is, "Where is the frontier now?"

The answer should be obvious. Our frontier lies in outer space. The moon, the asteroids, the planets, these are mere stepping stones, where we will test ourselves, learn needful lessons, and grow in knowledge before we attempt those frontiers beyond our solar system. Outer space is a frontier without end, the eternal frontier, an everlasting challenge to explorers not [only] of other planets and other solar systems but also of the mind of man.

All that has gone before was preliminary. We have been preparing ourselves mentally for what lies ahead. Many problems remain, but if we can avoid a devastating war we shall move with a rapidity[1] scarcely to be believed. In the past seventy years we have developed the automobile, radio, television, transcontinental and transoceanic flight, and the electrification of the country, among a multitude of other such developments. In 1900 there were 144 miles of surfaced road in the United States. Now there are over 3,000,000.

Paved roads and the development of the automobile have gone hand in hand, the automobile being civilized man's antidote to overpopulation.

What is needed now is leaders with perspective; we need leadership on a thousand fronts, but they must be men and women who can take the long view and

## TAKE NOTES

### Activate Prior Knowledge

Tell how you think ways of life in the future will be different from the way people live today.

_____

_____

_____

_____

### Reading Skill

A **fact** is something that can be proved. An **opinion** is a person's judgment or belief. Circle two opinions in the bracketed paragraph. Underline four facts.

### Reading Check

Where does the author believe the frontier now lies? Circle the answer.

## Vocabulary Development

**frontier** (fruhn TEER) *n.* area beyond what people know well

**preliminary** (pri LIM uh ner ee) *adj.* coming before or leading up to the main action

**devastating** (DEV uh stayt ing) *adj.* causing heavy damage or harm

1. **rapidity** (ruh PID uh tee) *n.* speed.

The Eternal Frontier 195

## Literary Analysis

A **persuasive essay** presents arguments to convince readers that they should think or act in a certain way. Writers use various ways to get readers to accept their ideas. These ways include appeals to authority, emotion, and reason. Which of these ways does the author use in the underlined sentence?

_____

_____

## Stop to Reflect

What does the author mean when he says that "we are a people born to the frontier"?

_____

_____

## Reading Check

Where would we be now if we had limited ourselves to the known world? Circle the answer.

help to shape the outlines of our future. <u>There will always be the nay-sayers, those who cling to our lovely green planet as a baby clings to its mother, but there will be others like those who have taken us this far along the path to a limitless future.</u>

We are a people born to the frontier. It has been a part of our thinking, waking, and sleeping since men first landed on this continent. The frontier is the line that separates the known from the unknown wherever it may be, and we have a driving need to see what lies beyond . . . .

A few years ago we moved into outer space. We landed men on the moon; we sent a vehicle beyond the limits of the solar system, a vehicle still moving farther and farther into that limitless distance. If our world were to die tomorrow, that tiny vehicle would go on and on forever, carrying its mighty message to the stars. Out there, someone, sometime, would know that once we existed, that we had the vision and we made the effort. Mankind is not bound by its atmospheric envelope or by its gravitational field, nor is the mind of man bound by any limits at all.

One might ask—why outer space, when so much remains to be done here? If that had been the spirit of man we would still be hunters and food gatherers, growling over the bones of <u>carrion</u> in a cave somewhere. It is our destiny to move out, to accept the challenge, to dare the unknown. It is our destiny to achieve.

Yet we must not forget that along the way to outer space whole <u>industries</u> are springing into being that did not exist before. The computer age has <u>arisen</u> in part from the space effort, which gave

### Vocabulary Development

**carrion** (KAR ee uhn) *n.* dead or decaying meat
**industries** (IN duh streez) *n.* businesses or companies that make a product
**arisen** (uh RIZ uhn) *v.* appeared, developed

great <u>impetus</u> to the development of computing devices. Transistors, chips, integrated circuits, Teflon, new medicines, new ways of treating diseases, new ways of performing operations, all these and a multitude of other developments that enable man to live and to live better are linked to the space effort. Most of these developments have been so <u>incorporated</u> into our day-to-day life that they are taken for granted, their origin not considered.

If we are content to live in the past, we have no future. And today is the past.

---

*Reader's Response:* Has this essay changed the way you thik or will act? Explain your response.

_____

_____

_____

_____

_____

_____

© Pearson Education

**Vocabulary Development**

**impetus** (IM puh tus) *n.* driving force

**incorporated** (in KAWR puh rayt id) *adv.* made part of something

---

**Literary Analysis**

This **persuasive essay** uses an appeal to reason in the bracketed paragraph. Number three facts that the author uses to back his argument.

**Reading Skill**

Words such as *always, never, must, cannot, best, worst,* and *all* are **clues that indicate an opinion**. What two clues that indicate an opinion do you recognize in the bracketed paragraph?

_____

_____

List two **facts** that the author uses to support his opinion.

_____

_____

_____

# The Eternal Frontier

1. **Infer:** In what ways would leaders who have "perspective" support space travel?

   _____

   _____

2. **Draw Conclusions:** What message about space travel does the essay convey? Explain.

   _____

   _____

3. **Reading Skill:** The chart below shows three **opinions** that L'Amour expresses in his essay. List the clue words that help identify each opinion.

| Opinion | Clue Words |
|---|---|
| "All that has gone before was preliminary." | |
| "There will always be the nay-sayers." | |
| "They must be men and women who can take the long view . . . It is our destiny to achieve." | |

4. **Literary Analysis:** Identify one appeal to emotion and one appeal to reason that L'Amour uses in this **persuasive essay**.

   _____

   _____

   _____

## Writing: Persuasive Letter

Write a **persuasive letter** that advises the government about space travel.

- Decide whether you are for or against space travel. List your reasons.

  _____

  _____

- Brainstorm for a list of goals that you want to achieve with your letter.

  _____

  _____

- Offer reasons to support each goal.

  _____

  _____

## Listening and Speaking: Public Service Announcement

Plan a **public service announcement** that encourages space travel.
- Include interesting facts that highlight the importance of space travel.
- Select the persuasive technique that will best express each point.
- Use this chart to organize your information.

| Importance of Space Travel | Facts About Space Travel | Persuasive Technique |
|---|---|---|
| | | |
| | | |
| | | |
| | | |

Use these notes from the chart to write a public service announcement.

# The Real Story of a Cowboy's Life
## • Rattlesnake Hunt

## Reading Skill

A **fact** is information that you can prove. An **opinion** is a judgment.

- **Fact:** The room is 10 feet by 12 feet.
- **Opinion:** Green is the best color for the room.

Some writers state opinions as facts. To get to the truth, **use resources to check facts**.

The resources listed in this chart can help you decide whether a statement is true. As you read, identify statements that give information. Then, write the statement next to the resource that you could use to check the facts. Some boxes may not have answers.

| Resources | Statement in Text |
|---|---|
| almanac | |
| atlas or map | |
| biographical dictionary | "Teddy Blue was born Edward C. Abbott in England." |
| dictionary | |
| encyclopedia | |
| reliable Web site | |

## Literary Analysis

The words a writer uses—the **word choice**—can make writing seem difficult or easy, formal or informal. **Diction** includes the writer's word choice as well as the way that he or she puts the words together. The answers to these questions shape a writer's diction:

- *What does the audience already know about the topic?* The writer may have to define terms or use simpler language.

- *What feeling will this work express to the reader?* Word choice can make a work serious or funny, formal or personal. The length and style of the sentences can make a work seem simple or difficult.

Notice how word choice or diction affects your response to this text.

# The Real Story of a Cowboy's Life
### Geoffrey C. Ward

**Summary** The true life of a cowboy on the trails was very challenging. He faced cattle stampedes and angry settlers with guns. Few trail bosses allowed drinking or gambling. There was little recreation except singing with trail mates. To be a cowboy required courage, strength, and love for life on the trail.

## Writing About the Big Question

**What should we learn?** "The Real Story of a Cowboy's Life" describes the duties and dangers that cowboys experienced in the 1800s. Complete this sentence:

The facts that we can learn from historical accounts are important

because _____.

## Note-taking Guide
Use this cluster diagram to understand what a cowboy's life was really like.

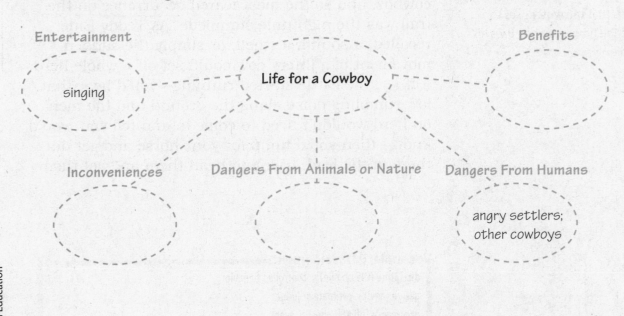

Entertainment

singing

Life for a Cowboy

Benefits

Inconveniences

Dangers From Animals or Nature

Dangers From Humans

angry settlers; other cowboys

# The Real Story of a Cowboy's Life
## Geoffrey C. Ward

**Activate Prior Knowledge**

What images come to mind when you hear the word *cowboy*? List your ideas.

_____

_____

_____

**Stop to Reflect**

Why do you think cowboys had to work as a team?

_____

_____

**Literary Analysis**

**Diction** includes both the writer's word choice and the way that he or she puts the words into sentences. **Word choice** is the specific vocabulary a writer uses. Read the bracketed paragraph. Underline three words that the writer uses to describe how a cowboy uses his saddle.

A drive's success depended on <u>discipline</u> and planning. According to Teddy Blue,[1] most Texas herds numbered about 2,000 head with a trail boss and about a dozen men in charge—though herds as large as 15,000 were also driven north with far larger escorts. The most experienced men rode "point" and "swing," at the head and sides of the long herd; the least experienced brought up the rear, riding "drag" and eating dust. At the end of the day, Teddy Blue remembered, they "would go to the water barrel . . . and rinse their mouths and cough and spit up . . . black stuff. But you couldn't get it up out of your lungs."

They had to learn to work as a team, keeping the herd moving during the day, resting peacefully at night. Twelve to fifteen miles a day was a good pace. But such steady progress could be interrupted at any time. A cowboy had to know how to <u>gauge</u> the temperament of his cattle, how to chase down a stray without alarming the rest of the herd, how to lasso a steer using the horn of his saddle as a tying post. His saddle was his most prized possession; it served as his chair, his workbench, his pillow at night. Being dragged to death was the most common death for a cowboy, and so the most feared <u>occurrence</u> on the trail was the nighttime stampede. As Teddy Blue recalled, a sound, a smell, or simply the sudden movement of a jittery cow could set off a whole herd.

If . . . the cattle started running—you'd hear that low rumbling noise along the ground and the men on herd wouldn't need to come in and tell you, you'd know—then you'd jump for your horse and get out there in the lead, trying to head them and get them

**Vocabulary Development**

**discipline** (DIS uh plin) *n.* controlled behavior
**gauge** (gayj) *v.* estimate or judge
**occurrence** (uh KER uhns) *n.* event

1. **Teddy Blue** Edward C. Abbot; a cowboy who rode in a successful trail drive in the 1880s.

into a mill[2] before they scattered. It was riding at a dead run in the dark, with cut banks and prairie dog holes all around you, not knowing if the next jump would land you in a shallow grave.

Most cowboys had guns, but rarely used them on the trail. Some outfits made them keep their weapons in the chuck wagon[3] to eliminate any chance of gunplay. Charles Goodnight[4] was still more emphatic: "Before starting on a trail drive, I made it a rule to draw up an article of agreement, setting forth what each man was to do. The main clause stipulated[5] that if one shot another he was to be tried by the outfit and hanged on the spot, if found guilty. I never had a man shot on the trail."

Regardless of its <u>ultimate</u> destination, every herd had to <u>ford</u> a series of rivers—the Nueces, the Guadalupe, the Brazos, the Wichita, the Red.

A big herd of longhorns swimming across a river, Goodnight remembered, <u>"looked like a million floating rocking chairs,"</u> and <u>crossing those rivers one after another, a cowboy recalled, was like climbing the rungs of a long ladder reaching north.</u>

"After you crossed the Red River and got out on the open plains," Teddy Blue remembered, "it was sure a pretty sight to see them strung out for almost a mile, the sun shining on their horns." Initially, the land immediately north of the Red River was Indian territory, and some tribes charged tolls for herds crossing their land—payable in money or beef. But Teddy Blue remembered that the homesteaders, now pouring onto the Plains by railroad, were far more nettlesome:

<u>There was no love lost between settlers and cowboys on the trail.</u> Those jay-hawkers would take up a claim right where the herds watered and charge us for water. They would plant a crop alongside the

## Vocabulary Development
**ultimate** (UL tuh mit) *adj.* final
**ford** (fawrd) *v.* cross a river at a shallow point

2. **mill** slow movement in a circle.

3. **chuck wagon** (CHUK WAG uhn) *n.* wagon that carried food and supplies.

4. **Charles Goodnight** cowboy who rode successful trail drives beginning in the 1860s.

5. **stipulated** (STIP yuh layt id) *v.* stated as a rule.

---

### Reading Skill

A **fact** is information you can prove. An **opinion** is a judgment. Read the first group of underlined sentence parts. Decide whether each underlined part is a **fact** or an **opinion**. Mark each part with F for Fact or O for Opinion.

### Literary Analysis 🔍

Read the second underlined sentence. Using different **word choice**, write a new sentence that has the same meaning as the underlined sentence.

_____

_____

_____

_____

_____

### Reading Check

Cowboys were never shot on Charles Goodnight's trail drives. Why not? Circle the answer.

### Reading Skill

You can use **resources to check facts**. This can help you decide whether a statement is a fact or an opinion. Read the bracketed paragraph. Circle the resource or resources in which you might check facts about quarantine lines.

atlas   dictionary   encyclopedia

Read the first underlined sentence. Could you use the same resources to find out about Canyon City?

_____

If not, what other resources would you use for Canyon City?

_____

### Literary Analysis 🔍

Read the second underlined sentence. Does the speaker use formal or informal **word choice**?

_____

Circle the words that support your answer.

### Reading Check ✏️

Circle the diversions that cowboys were not allowed to have on the trail.

trail and plow a furrow around it for a fence, and then when the cattle got into their wheat or their garden patch, they would come cussing and waving a shotgun and yelling for damages. And the cattle had been coming through there when they were still raising punkins in Illinois.

The settlers' hostility was entirely understandable. The big herds ruined their crops, and they carried with them a disease, spread by ticks and called "Texas fever," that devastated domestic livestock. Kansas and other territories along the route soon established quarantine lines, called "deadlines," at the western fringe of settlement, and insisted that trail drives not cross them. Each year, as settlers continued to move in, those deadlines moved farther west.

Sometimes, farmers tried to enforce their own, as John Rumans, one of Charles Goodnight's hands, recalled:

Some men met us at the trail near Canyon City, and said we couldn't come in. There were fifteen or twenty of them, and they were not going to let us cross the Arkansas River. We didn't even stop. . . . Old man [Goodnight] had a shotgun loaded with buckshot and led the way, saying: "John, get over on that point with your Winchester and point these cattle in behind me." He slid his shotgun across the saddle in front of him and we did the same with our Winchesters. He rode right across, and as he rode up to them, he said: "I've monkeyed as long as I want to with you," and they fell back to the sides, and went home after we had passed.

There were few diversions on the trail. Most trail bosses banned liquor. Goodnight prohibited gambling, too. Even the songs for which cowboys became famous grew directly out of doing a job, remembered Teddy Blue:

The singing was supposed to soothe [the cattle] and it did; I don't know why, unless it was that a sound

**Vocabulary Development**

**hostility** (hah STIL uh tee) *n.* unfriendly or angry behavior
**quarantine** (KWAWR uhn teen) *n.* lines or boundaries created to prevent the spread of disease
**diversions** (duh VER zhunz) *n.* amusements, fun things

they was used to would keep them from spooking at other noises. I know that if you wasn't singing, any little sound in the night—it might be just a horse shaking himself—could make them leave the country; but if you were singing, they wouldn't notice it.

The two men on guard would circle around with their horses on a walk, if it was a clear night and the cattle was bedded down and quiet, and one man would sing a verse of song, and his partner on the other side of the herd would sing another verse; and you'd go through a whole song that way. . . . "Bury Me Not on the Lone Prairie" was a great song for awhile, but . . . they sung it to death. It was a saying on the range that even the horses nickered it and the coyotes howled it; it got so they'd throw you in the creek if you sang it.

The number of cattle on the move was sometimes staggering: once, Teddy Blue rode to the top of a rise from which he could see seven herds strung out behind him; eight more up ahead; and the dust from an additional thirteen moving parallel to his. "All the cattle in the world," he remembered, "seemed to be coming up from Texas."

At last, the herds neared their destinations. After months in the saddle—often wearing the same clothes every day, eating nothing but biscuits and beef stew at the chuck wagon, drinking only water and coffee, his sole companions his fellow cowboys, his herd, and his horse—the cowboy was about to be paid for his work, and turned loose in town.

> Reader's Response: Describe something new you have learned about a cowboy's life.
>
> _____
>
> _____
>
> _____
>
> _____
>
> _____
>
> _____

## Literary Analysis

**Diction** and, especially, **word choice** give writing a certain feeling. Circle each word that describes the feeling of the first bracketed paragraph.

serious          funny

formal           personal

academic         informal

_____

Underline words in the paragraph that give the writing this feeling.

## Reading Skill

Write one **fact** and one **opinion** from the second bracketed paragraph.

_____

_____

_____

_____

## Reading Check

Over time, what would happen to cowboys who sang "Bury Me Not on the Lone Prairie"? Circle the answer.

# The Real Story of a Cowboy's Life

1. **Evaluate:** What qualifies Teddy Blue as a reliable source of information about cattle drives?

2. **Interpret:** According to the information from the story, what are three characteristics of a successful cowboy?

_____

_____

_____

3. **Reading Skill:** How do **facts** and **opinions** help the writer paint a full picture of his subject?

_____

_____

_____

4. **Literary Analysis:** Review the author's **word choice** and **diction** by completing this chart.

| Technical Vocabulary | Formal Language | Informal Language |
|---|---|---|
| "point"; "swing" | "A drive's success depended on discipline and planning." | |

## Writing: Adaptation
Write an **adaptation** of one of the incidents narrated in the essay.

- What resource will give you definitions for words? What resource will help you find words that are similar to or different from one another?

  _____

  _____

- Pictures may help support your adaptation. What library books or Internet sites provide information on and pictures of the real lives of cowboys?

  _____

  _____

## Research and Technology: Help-Wanted Ad
Write a **help-wanted ad** for a modern job involving cattle or horses.

- Where will you go to research your sources?

  _____

  _____

- What books or articles tell about the modern cattle or horse industry?

  _____

  _____

  _____

- What technology is used in the modern cattle or horse industry?

  _____

  _____

  _____

- What Web sites provide profiles of people who work with cattle or horses, such as cowboys, farmers, or racehorse trainers?

  _____

  _____

  _____

# Rattlesnake Hunt
## Marjorie Kinnan Rawlings

**Summary** Marjorie Kinnan Rawlings agrees to go on a rattlesnake hunt with scientist Ross Allen. She is terrified of snakes at first. Allen shows Rawlings how to catch snakes safely. Finally, Rawlings catches her own snake.

### Writing About the Big Question

**What should we learn?** In "Rattlesnake Hunt," the author learns to manage her fear of rattlesnakes. Complete this sentence:

When we evaluate how we feel after trying something that scares us, we

sometimes find that our feelings have changed because _____

_____.

### Note-taking Guide

Use this chart to list the events that help Rawlings lose her fear of snakes.

| Rawlings learns about snakes. | → | She holds a snake. | → | | → | |

# Rattlesnake Hunt

1. **Infer:** Why does the author say at the end of the hunt that she has won a victory?

   _____

   _____

   _____

2. **Analyze:** In what ways does the hunt change the way that Rawlings thinks about nature and herself?

   _____

   _____

3. **Reading Skill:** How do **facts** and **opinions** help the writer explain her experience with snakes?

   _____

   _____

4. **Literary Analysis:** Review the author's **word choice** and **diction** by completing this chart.

| Technical Vocabulary | Formal Language | Informal Language |
|---|---|---|
| herpetologist | "My courage was not adequate to inquire whether they were thrown in loose and might be expected to appear between our feet." | "It seemed to me that I should drop in my tracks." |
|  |  |  |

## Writing: Adaptation

For a new audience, write an **adaptation** of one of the incidents narrated in the essay. You retell a story when you write an adaptation. You use words that are easy for your audience to understand. Answer these questions before you write your adaptation.

- What resource will give you definitions for words? What resource will help you find words that are similar to or different from one another?

_____

- Pictures may help support your adaptation. What library books or Internet sites provide information on and pictures of rattlesnakes?

_____

_____

## Research and Technology: Help-Wanted Ad

Complete the following chart with information for your **help-wanted ad**.

| | |
|---|---|
| Job Responsibilities | |
| Education | |
| Experience | |
| Skills | |
| Personal Traits | |

# Manuals

## About Manuals

- A **manual** is a book of facts or instructions.
- Manuals tell you how to do something, such as write a term paper, use a camera, or fix a bicycle.
- Manuals often have diagrams, warnings, and step-by-step instructions.

This first-aid manual tells people in North America

- how to spot poisonous snakes
- how to treat snake bites

## Reading Skill

In order to understand information in a text, you need to **understand its structure and purpose.** A manual's title and table of contents will show its purpose. The structure of a text is the way it is organized. The structure of a manual often includes the following elements:

- Sections or chapters that have headings and subheadings
- Bulleted or numbered lists that highlight specific details or steps
- Visual aids such as photographs, diagrams, illustrations, and charts
- Text formatting such as **boldfaced,** *italicized,* or underlined words and phrases

| Purpose | Category | Structural Features |
|---------|----------|---------------------|
| to teach | instructional manual | • Bulleted lists that give essential information<br>• Numbered lists that show step-by-step instructions |

© Pearson Education

# How to Recognize Venomous Snakes in North America

## Vocabulary Builder

**Synonyms** *Venomous* and *poisonous* are synonyms. Synonyms are words that have the same meaning. Both *venomous* and *poisonous* mean "producing poison." Poison is a substance that can cause serious illness or death if it gets into your body.

## Text Structure

What do the labels on the illustrations of the snake identify?

_____

_____

_____

## Text Structure

What does each photograph on the page show?

_____

_____

_____

Most snakes in North America are not venomous. The two types of poisonous snakes you should be aware of, pit vipers and coral snakes, are described in this chart.

Rattlesnakes, copperheads, and cottonmouths are all *pit vipers.* You can recognize a pit viper by its triangular head, fangs, narrow, vertical pupils, and the pits between its nostrils and its eyes. The coral snake has round pupils and is not a pit viper; it does have fangs, but they may or may not be visible. Nonvenomous snakes have round pupils and no fangs, pits, or rattles.

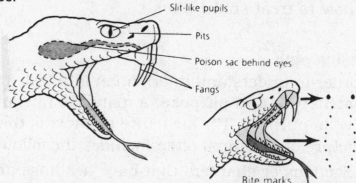

Slit-like pupils

Pits

Poison sac behind eyes

Fangs

Bite marks

Rattlers grow up to 8 feet long. There are about 30 species of rattlesnakes in the U.S., but any rattler can be recognized by the rattles at the end of its tail.

Copperheads grow up to 4 feet long and have diamond-shaped markings down their backs. They vibrate their tails when angry, but have no rattles.

The cottonmouth, also known as the water moccasin, grows up to 4 feet long. When alarmed, it opens its mouth, revealing the white lining for which it is named.

Coral snakes grow up to 3 feet long and have distinctive red, black, and yellow or white rings and a black nose. Other snakes have similar colors, but only the coral snake has red bands bordered by white or yellow.

© Brian Kenny

# First Aid for a Snake Bite

- Call EMS.
- Try to identify the type of snake. If it can be done quickly and without danger to you, kill the snake and have it identified. (Be aware that venomous snakes can bite reflexively even after they die.)
- Call ahead to the emergency department so that the correct antivenin can be prepared.

  **DO NOT** cut into a snake bite.

  **DO NOT** apply cold compresses to a snake bite.

  **DO NOT** apply a tourniquet.

  **DO NOT** raise the site of the bite above the level of the victim's heart.

  **DO NOT** give the victim aspirin, stimulants, or pain medication unless a physician says to.

  **DO NOT** allow the victim to exercise. If necessary, carry him or her to safety.

1. Check the victim's ABCs. Open the airway; check breathing and circulation. If necessary, begin rescue breathing, CPR, or bleeding control. (See the Emergency Action Guides on pages 199–210.)

2. If the victim is having breathing problems, keep his or her airway open. A conscious victim will naturally get into the position in which it is easiest to breathe.

3. Calm and reassure the victim. Anxiety aggravates all reactions.

4. Wash the bite with soap and water.

### Comprehension Builder

Writers often use parentheses to highlight extra information. This extra information may be very important. What warning does the author of this manual put in parentheses? Underline the answer. With a partner, discuss why this information is important.

### Fluency Builder

Remember that words formatted differently from the rest of the text may have special importance. What words are formatted differently in the bracketed passage?

_____

Read aloud the bracketed text, placing emphasis on the boldfaced words in all capital letters.

### Text Structure

The manual provides numbered instructions for caring for the victim of a snakebite. What is the first step in the numbered instructions?

_____

_____

**Comprehension Builder**

Why should you remove any rings or constricting items? Underline the answer.

**Vocabulary Builder**

**Multiple-Meaning Words**

*Shock* may mean "the feeling of surprise and disbelief that you have when something very unexpected happens." In this paragraph, *shock* means "a medical condition in which the victim is pale and his or her heart and lungs fail to work correctly, usually in response to a sudden, very unpleasant experience." Circle clues in the text that help you understand the meaning of *shock*.

**Text Structure**

What is the final step in the numbered instructions?

_____

_____

_____

5. Remove any rings or **constricting** items, since the bitten area may swell.

6. Take steps to slow the rate at which the venom spreads in the victim's body. Have the victim lie still. Place the injured site below the level of the victim's heart and **immobilize** it in a comfortable position.

7. Look for signs of shock, such as decreased alertness or increased paleness. If shock develops, lay the victim flat, raise his or her feet 8 to 12 inches, and cover the victim with a coat or blanket. Do not **elevate** the bitten area, and do not place the victim in this position if you suspect any head, neck, back, or leg injury or if the position makes the victim uncomfortable. (See **Shock** on page 172.)

8. Stay with the victim until you get medical help.

**Everyday Words**

**constricting** (kuhn STRIKT ing) *adj.* making something narrower or tighter
**immobilize** (ih MOH buh lyz) *v.* prevent someone or something from moving
**elevate** (EL uh vayt) *v.* lift someone or something to a higher position

# Thinking About the Manual

1. Why is it important to keep bite victims calm?

_____

_____

2. Compare and contrast the physical characteristics of venomous and nonvenomous snakes.

_____

_____

**TALK ABOUT IT Reading Skill**

3. Why does the author include photographs of snakes?

_____

_____

4. What information do the bulleted and numbered lists on pages 213 and 214 provide?

_____

_____

**WRITE ABOUT IT** ▷ **Timed Writing: Explanation (10 minutes)**

Explain what should be done if someone is bitten by a poisonous snake:

- Review the steps for first aid.
- Underline the most important steps.
- Draw a line through sentences that tell you what not to do.

Explain the important steps in complete sentences. Remember that you can have more than one step in the same sentence.

# Maestro • The Desert Is My Mother • Bailando

Poems are usually divided into lines. The lines often form groups called **stanzas**, or verses. Poems also use figurative language and sound devices.

| Figurative Language | Definition | Example |
| --- | --- | --- |
| Metaphor | describes one thing as if it were another | The house was a zoo! |
| Personification | gives human qualities to something that is not human | The wind whispered to us. |
| Simile | uses *like* or *as* to compare two unlike things | The stars were like a diamond necklace. |
| Symbol | uses one thing to stand for something else | A dove is a symbol of peace. |

Poems also use **sound devices**. Sound devices are qualities of language that you can hear.

| Sound Device | Definition | Example |
| --- | --- | --- |
| Alliteration | repetition of a consonant sound at the beginning of words | slippery slope |
| Repetition | repeated use of a sound, word, phrase, clause, or sentence | bells, bells, bells, bells |
| Assonance | repetition a vowel sound followed by different consonants in stressed syllables | close, home, alone, erode |
| Consonance | repetition of a consonant sound at the end of accented syllables | sand, wind, defend |
| Onomatopoeia | use of words that imitate sounds | crash, hiss |
| Rhyme | repetition of a sound at the end of words | near, year |
| Meter | the pattern of rhythm in the poem | Whose **woods** these **are I think I** know |

**Narrative poetry** tells a story. It has lines and stanzas. It also has characters and action.

**Haiku** are Japanese poems with three lines. The first and third lines each have five syllables. The second line has seven syllables.

**Free verse** is poetry that does not rhyme or have any set number of syllables per line. It has no pattern, such as four lines per stanza.

**Ballads** are poems that tell a story. They are like songs and may have a chorus. They often deal with adventure and romance.

**Concrete poems** are poems that create a picture on the page. The shape of the poem suggests the subject of the poem.

**Limericks** are humorous poems with five lines. They have a specific rhyme pattern.

**Rhyming couplets** are pairs of rhyming lines. The lines usually have the same number of syllables and the same rhythm.

# Maestro • The Desert Is My Mother • Bailando
## Pat Mora

**Summaries** In "Maestro," a violin player remembers playing music with his mother and father. The speaker in "The Desert Is My Mother" gives a series of commands to the desert. In "Bailando," the speaker remembers seeing her aunt dance at several different stages of her life.

## Note-taking Guide
Use this chart to record main ideas from the poems.

|  | Maestro | The Desert Is My Mother | Bailando |
|---|---|---|---|
| Speaker | A violinist |  |  |
| Memories or Commands | Remembers playing music years earlier with his father and mother |  |  |

# Maestro
## Pat Mora

He hears her
when he bows.
Rows of hands clap
again and again he bows
5   to stage lights and upturned faces
but he hears only his mother's voice

years ago in their small home
<u>singing Mexican songs</u>
one phrase at a time
10   while his father <u>strummed</u> the guitar
or picked the melody with quick fingertips.
Both cast their music in the air
for him to <u>snare</u> with his strings,
songs of lunas[1] and amor[2]
15   learned bit by bit.
<u>She'd nod, smile, as his bow slid</u>
note to note, then the trio
     voz,[3] guitarra,[4] violín[5]
would blend again and again
20   to the last pure note
sweet on the tongue.

### Vocabulary Development

**Maestro** (MY stroh) *n.* great musician

**strummed** (struhmd) *v.* played the strings of a musical instrument

**snare** (snayr) *v.* capture

1. **lunas** (loo nahs) *n.* Spanish for "moons."
2. **amor** (AH mohr) *n.* Spanish for "love."
3. **voz** (vohz) *n.* Spanish for "voice."
4. **guitarra** (GHE tawr uh) *n.* Spanish for "guitar."
5. **violín** (VEE ohl n) *n.* Spanish for "violin."

---

## TAKE NOTES

**Activate Prior Knowledge**

Think of something you learned from a parent or another adult. Tell what can bring back your memories of this learning process.

_____

_____

_____

**Poetry**

**Consonance** is the repetition of a consonant sound at the end of two or more words. List the words that create consonance in the first underlined text.

_____

**Poetry**

**Alliteration** is the repetition of consonant sounds at the beginning of words. Circle the words that create alliteration in the second underlined text.

**Reading Check** ✏️

When does the violinist hear his mother? Underline the answer.

## Poetry

**Personification** is the giving of human qualities to something that is not human. Write who "she" is in the poem.

_____

Underline three human things "she" does.

## Poetry

**Assonance** is the repetition of a vowel sound in the middle of words. List the words that create assonance in the underlined text.

_____

## Stop to Reflect

How does the speaker feel about the desert?

_____

_____

_____

# The Desert Is My Mother
## Pat Mora

I say feed me.
She serves red prickly pear[1] on a spiked cactus.

I say tease me.
She sprinkles raindrops in my face on a
    sunny day.

5   I say frighten me.
She shouts thunder, flashes lightning.

I say hold me. She whispers, "Lie in my arms."

I say heal me.
She gives me <u>chamomile</u>, oregano, peppermint.

10  I say caress me.
She strokes my skin with her warm breath.

I say make me beautiful.
She offers <u>turquoise</u> for my fingers,
a pink blossom for my hair.

15  I say sing to me.
She chants her windy songs.

I say teach me.
She blooms in the sun's glare,
<u>the snow's silence,</u>
20  <u>the driest sand.</u>

The desert is my mother.
_El desierto es mi madre._
The desert is my strong mother.

---

**Vocabulary Development**

**chamomile** (KAM uh myl) _n._ an herb often used to make tea
**turquoise** (TER kwoiz) _n._ a blue mineral often used to make jewelry such as rings

---

1. **prickly pear** _n._ a species of cactus with sharp spines and an edible fruit.

# El desierto es mi madre
## Pat Mora

Le digo, dame de comer.
Me sirve rojas tunas en nopal espinoso.

Le digo, juguetea conmigo.
Me salpica la cara con gotitas de lluvia en día
    asoleado.

5  Le digo, asústame.
Me grita con truenos y me tira relámpagos.

Le digo, abrázame.
Me susurra, "Acuéstate aquí."

Le digo, cúrame.
10  Me da manzanilla, orégano, yerbabuena.

Le digo, acaríciame.
Me roza la cara con su cálido aliento.

Le digo, hazme bella.
Me ofrece turquesa para mis dedos,
15    una flor rosada para mi cabello.

Le digo, cántame.
Me arrulla con sus canciones de viento.

Le digo, enséñame.
Y florece en el brillo del sol,
20  en el silencio de la nieve,
en las arenas más secas.

El desierto es mi madre.
El desierto es mi madre poderosa.

**Poetry**

**Repetition** is the repeated use of a sound, word, or phrase. Underline two words or phrases in the bracketed section that show repetition.

**Poetry**

**Sound devices** are qualities of language that you can hear. What sound devices do you notice in the poem? Explain?

_____

_____

_____

**Stop to Reflect**

What words do you associate with the desert?

_____

_____

_____

_____

# Bailando[1]
## Pat Mora

**Poetry**

**Free verse** is poetry without rhyme. Free verse also has stanzas with different numbers of lines or lines with different numbers of syllables. Tell why "Bailando" is free verse.

_____

_____

_____

_____

_____

_____

_____

**Poetry**

**Repetition** is the use of any sound, word, phrase, or sentence more than once. Circle the words that create repetition in the underlined text.

**Reading Check**

Whom does the speaker remember? Underline the answer.

I will remember you dancing,
spinning round and round
a young girl in Mexico,
your long, black hair free in the wind,
5  spinning round and round
a young woman at village dances
your long, blue dress swaying
to the beat of La Varsoviana,[2]
smiling into the eyes of your partners,
10  years later smiling into my eyes
when I'd reach up to dance with you,
my dear aunt. who years later
danced with my children,
you, white-haired but still young
15  waltzing on your ninetieth birthday,
more beautiful than the orchid
pinned on your shoulder,
tottering now when you walk
but saying to me, "Estoy[3] bailando,"
20  and laughing.

**Reader's Response:** Suppose you were to meet the woman who dances. What do you think she would be like?

_____

_____

**Vocabulary Development**

**tottering** (TAHT er ing) *adj.* moving as if about to fall over

1. **Bailando** (by LAHN doh) *v.* Spanish for "dancing."

2. **La Varsoviana** (lah vahr soh vee AH nah) *n.* a lively folk dance.

3. **Estoy** (es TOY) Spanish for "I am."

# Poetry

1. **Interpret:** The musician remembers his childhood during his performance. What causes that to happen?

_____

_____

2. **Analyze:** The poem "Bailando" is about dancing. What else is it about?

_____

3. **Poetry:** Find one example of **repetition** in each poem.

_____

_____

_____

4. **Poetry:** Find examples of **personification** in "The Desert Is My Mother." Use this chart to compare and contrast the language used to describe the desert.

Words that show the desert is . . .

. . . a woman          both          . . . a hot and dry region

## Author Booklet

Follow these steps to gather information for an **author booklet** on Pat Mora.

- Go to the library. Use a computer to find a database for literature or biography. (If you need help, ask a librarian.) For example, you might find databases such as *Contemporary Authors, Dictionary of Hispanic Biography,* or *Major Authors and Illustrators for Children and Young Adults*. Find one or more entries for Pat Mora in the databases. Use the lines below to record the information that you find.

**Details About Her Life:** _____

_____

**Awards:** _____

- Go to the library. Find a computer and the online catalog. Select an author search, and type *Mora, Pat* into the search box. Press the enter key. A list of Mora's books will come up. Use the call numbers to find one or more of the books on the shelf. Select one or two poems. Write their titles here, and copy the poems in a notebook.

**Poem:** _____

**Poem:** _____

- Use the Internet. Type in search terms such as *"Pat Mora" + biography* or *"Pat Mora" + awards*. Screen your results, or "hits," for descriptions that match your research goal. Use reliable sites, such as those that end in *.edu, .gov,* or *.org*. Use the lines below to record the information that you find.

**What I learned:** _____

_____

- Watch the video interview with Pat Mora, and review your source material. Use this information to record additional information for your author booklet.

**Additional information:** _____

_____

# Poetry Collection 1 • Poetry Collection 2

## Reading Skill

**Drawing conclusions** means arriving at an overall judgment or idea by pulling together several details. By drawing conclusions, you recognize meanings that are not directly stated. **Asking questions** such as the following can help you identify details and draw conclusions.

- What details does the writer include and emphasize?
- How are the details related?
- What do the details mean all together?

Use this chart to draw conclusions from details in the poems.

| Detail | Detail | Detail |
|---|---|---|

**How are the details related?**

**CONCLUSION**

## Literary Analysis

There are many different **forms of poetry**.

- A **lyric poem** expresses the poet's thoughts and feelings about a single image or idea in vivid, musical language.
- The poet arranges the words in a **concrete poem** to create a visual image that suggests the poem's subject.
- **Haiku** is a traditional form of Japanese poetry that is often about nature. The first and third lines each have five syllables. The second line has seven syllables.

# Poetry Collection 1

**Summaries** The speaker in "The Rider" is a bicycle rider. He wonders whether he can escape loneliness by riding fast. The poet of "Seal" uses the concrete form of a seal-like curve to create an image of a seal. He describes the seal as quick, playful, and clever. The speaker in "Haiku" talks about nature. The haiku describe a warning to ducklings, a still forest, and shadows in a forest.

## Writing About the Big Question

**What is the best way to communicate?** In "Poetry Collection 1," three poets use different forms to share their thoughts or observations. Complete these sentences:

Through poetry, writers can express _____

_____

_____.

## Note-taking Guide

Use this chart to list the topics and actions in the poems.

| | | |
|---|---|---|
| The Rider | | |
| Seal | | |
| Haiku | | |

# The Rider

## Naomi Shihab Nye

A boy told me
if he rollerskated fast enough
his loneliness couldn't catch up to him,

the best reason I ever heard
5  for trying to be a champion.

What I wonder tonight
pedaling hard down King William Street
is if it translates to bicycles.

A victory! To leave your loneliness
10  panting behind you on some street corner
while you float free into a cloud of sudden
    azaleas,
luminous pink petals that have
    never felt loneliness,
no matter how slowly they fell.

© Pearson Education

**Vocabulary Development**

**luminous** (LOO muh nuhs) *adj.* giving off light

---

## TAKE NOTES

### Activate Prior Knowledge

These poems all have strong images. What kinds of images inspire you? Describe something you've seen that might be a good subject for a poem.

_____

_____

_____

_____

### Reading Skill

**Asking questions** can help you find the most important details in a poem. Ask yourself this question: What makes the speaker feel less lonely? Underline the details that answer this question.

### Literary Analysis

There are many different **forms of poetry.** "The Rider" is a **lyric poem.** It expresses the feelings inspired by one image or idea. What image or idea inspires this poem?

_____

_____

_____

## Seal
### William Jay Smith

See how he dives
  From the rocks with a zoom!
 See how he darts
  Through his watery room
5  Past crabs and eels
   And green seaweed,
   Past fluffs of sandy
   Minnow feed![1]
  See how he swims
10  With a <u>swerve</u> and a twist,
   A flip of the flipper,
   A flick of the wrist!
  Quicksilver-quick,
  Softer than spray,
15  Down he plunges
  And sweeps away;
 Before you can think,
 Before you can <u>utter</u>
Words like "Dill pickle"
20  Or "Apple butter,"
 Back up he swims
  Past Sting Ray and Shark,
  Out with a zoom,
  A whoop, a bark;
25  Before you can say
   Whatever you wish,
   He plops at your side
    With a mouthful of fish!

**Literary Analysis**

"Seal" is a **concrete poem**. What does this mean?

_____

_____

_____

Why do you think the poet arranged the lines of the poem this way?

_____

_____

_____

**Reading Skill**

**Drawing conclusions** means arriving at an overall judgment. You can use details to draw conclusions about a poem. What conclusion can you draw from the details in the underlined text?

_____

_____

_____

**Reading Check** ✐

The seal in this poem zooms, plunges, and plops. Circle the line in which the seal makes a sound all its own.

**Vocabulary Development**

**swerve** (swerv) *n.* curving motion
**utter** (ut ter) *v.* speak

1. **feed** (feed) *n.* tiny particles that minnows feed on.

# Haiku
## Buson

O foolish ducklings,
you know my old green pond is
watched by a weasel!

Deep in a windless
wood, not one leaf dares to move. . . .
Something is afraid.

After the moon sets,
slow through the forest, shadows
drift and disappear.

Reader's Response: This collection includes a lyric poem, a concrete poem, and three haiku. Which of the poems do you like best? What do you like about it?

_____

_____

_____

_____

© Pearson Education

**Vocabulary Development**

**weasel** (WEE zuhl) *n.* a small mammal that eats rats, mice, birds, and eggs

**Reading Skill**

Poems do not always state their meaning directly. To find the meaning, you may have to **draw a conclusion**. What is the speaker of the bracketed haiku worried about?

_____

_____

_____

Conclusions are based on the poem's details. Underline the details that told you what the speaker was worried about.

**Stop to Reflect**

The speaker of the second haiku says, "Something is afraid." What do you think is afraid? Why would it be afraid?

_____

_____

_____

**Literary Analysis**

**Haiku** is one **form of poetry.** Haiku always have three lines. The first line has five syllables, the second line has seven syllables, and the third line has five syllables. Count and circle the syllables in the third haiku.

# Poetry Collection 1

1. **Compare:** What do the two sports discussed in "The Rider" have in common?

   _____

2. **Infer:** How would you describe the mood or feeling that the words "darts," "zoom," "flip," "flick," and "plops" create in "Seal"?

   _____

3. **Reading Skill:** A **conclusion** about "The Rider" is "The speaker in 'The Rider' values speed." Identify a question that helps you draw the conclusion given.

   _____

   _____

4. **Literary Analysis:** Place a checkmark on the chart below each characteristic of the **poetic form** that classifies each poem.

| Poem | Characteristics of Poem | | | | |
|---|---|---|---|---|---|
| | Musical language | Single image or idea | Thoughts of one speaker | Lines shaped like subject | Three lines; 17 syllables |
| The Rider (lyric) | | | | | |
| Seal (concrete) | | | | | |
| Haiku (haiku) | | | | | |

## Writing: Lyric Poem, Concrete Poem, or Haiku

Write a **lyric poem**, **concrete poem**, or **haiku** to share your thoughts in new, creative ways.

- List five subjects that interest you. Write a sentence next to each subject. The sentence should explain why the subject interests you.

_____

_____

_____

_____

- Review the three forms of poetry. Ask yourself which poetic form will best express your subject.

- Write the subject and poetic form that you have chosen.

_____

Use your notes to draft your poem in the form you have chosen.

## Listening and Speaking: Presentation

Listen to a recording of a poet reading one of his or her lyric poems. Then, prepare a **presentation** about what you liked from the poet's reading. Give reasons for your opinions. Answer the following questions.

- What emotion does the poet's voice express?

_____

- What words did the poet emphasize?

_____

Use your answers when preparing your presentation.

_____

# Poetry Collection 2

**Summaries** "Winter" tells how both animals and humans get ready for winter. "Forsythia" uses the letters of the word *forsythia* to create an image of the flowering plant. The three poems in "Haiku" celebrate spring. They describe a sunrise, misty mountains, and a lovely spring evening.

## Writing About the Big Question

**What is the best way to communicate?** In "Poetry Collection 2," each poem describes an aspect of nature. Complete this sentence:

Descriptive language can **contribute** to _____

_____.

## Note-taking Guide

Use this diagram to record the main idea of each poem and two details that support it.

| | Main Idea | Supporting Details |
|---|---|---|
| Winter | Both animals and humans prepare for winter | |
| Forsythia | | |
| Haiku | | |

# Poetry Collection 2

1. **Interpret:** Tell the meaning of the lines that grow out of the bottom line of "Forsythia."

   _____

   _____

2. **Analyze:** How would you describe Bashō's attitude toward nature in the three haiku?

   _____

   _____

3. **Reading Skill:** Identify a question that helps you **draw the conclusion** that forsythia grows in a tangled, wild way.

   _____

4. **Literary Analysis:** Place a checkmark on this chart under each characteristic of the **poetic form** that classifies each poem.

| Poem | Characteristics of Poem | | | | |
|---|---|---|---|---|---|
| | Musical language | Single image or idea | Thoughts of one speaker | Lines shaped like subject | Three lines; 17 syllables |
| Winter | | | | | |
| Forsythia | | | | | |
| Haiku | | | | | |

### Writing: Lyric Poem, Concrete Poem, or Haiku

Write a **lyric poem**, **concrete poem**, or **haiku** to share your thoughts in new, creative ways.

- List five subjects that interest you. Write a sentence next to each subject. The sentence should explain why the subject interests you.

_____

_____

_____

_____

_____

- Review the three forms of poetry. Ask yourself which poetic form will best express your subject.

- Write the subject and poetic form that you have chosen.

_____

Use your notes to draft your poem in the form that you have chosen.

### Listening and Speaking: Presentation

Use the following chart to record what you like about the poem that you will listen to. Then, use your notes to contribute to the **presentation**.

| |
| --- |
| Poem: |
| Why I Like the poem: |
| Examples of . . . <br>     interesting words: <br><br>     sounds or rhymes: <br><br>     memorable images: |

# Poetry Collection 3 • Poetry Collection 4

## Reading Skill

A **conclusion** is a decision or an opinion that you reach after considering details in a literary work. **Connecting the details** can help you draw conclusions as you read. For example, if the speaker in a poem describes beautiful flowers, bright sunshine, and happy children playing, you might conclude that he or she has a positive outlook. As you read, identify important details. Then, look at the details together and draw a conclusion about the poem or the speaker.

## Literary Analysis

**Figurative language** is language that is not meant to be taken literally. Writers use figures of speech to express ideas in vivid and imaginative ways. Common figures of speech include the following:

- A **simile** compares two unlike things using *like* or *as*.
- A **metaphor** compares two unlike things by stating that one thing is another.
- **Personification** gives human characteristics to a nonhuman subject.
- A **symbol** is an object, a person, an animal, a place, or an image that represents something other than itself.

As you read the poems, write an example of each figure of speech. Use this chart.

| Simile | Personification |
|---|---|
| | |
| **Metaphor** | **Symbol** |
| | |

# Poetry Collection 3

**Summaries** "Life" compares life to a watch. "The Courage That My Mother Had" compares the bravery of the poet's mother to the granite hills of New England. "Loo-Wit" compares an old woman to an erupting volcano.

## Writing About the Big Question

**What is the best way to communicate?** In "Poetry Collection 3," each poem includes one or more comparisons between objects or ideas. Complete this sentence:

Sometimes, a comparison between seemingly unrelated things can

express the idea that _____

_____.

## Note-taking Guide

Use this chart to record details about the poems. First describe the topic of each poem. Then, list descriptive words about the topic.

| Title of Poem | Topic of Poem | Words Used to Describe Topic |
|---|---|---|
| Life | | |
| The Courage That My Mother Had | | |
| Loo-Wit | A volcano. | |

# Life
### Naomi Long Madgett

Life is but a toy that swings on a bright gold
   chain
Ticking for a little while
To amuse a <u>fascinated</u> infant,
Until the keeper, a very old man,
5  Becomes tired of the game
And lets the watch run down.

# The Courage That My Mother Had
### Edna St. Vincent Millay

The courage that my mother had
Went with her, and is with her still:
Rock from New England quarried;[1]
Now granite in a granite hill.

5  The golden brooch[2] my mother wore
She left behind for me to wear;
I have no thing I treasure more:
Yet, it is something I could spare.

Oh, if instead she'd left to me
10  The thing she took into the grave!—
That courage like a rock, which she
Has no more need of, and I have.

© Pearson Education

## Vocabulary Development
**fascinated** (FA suh nayt id) *adj.* very interested

1. **quarried** (KWAWR eed) *adj.* carved out of the ground.
2. **brooch** (brohch) *n.* large ornamental pin.

**Activate Prior Knowledge**

These poems are about mysterious, powerful forces. Describe life, courage, or a volcano in your own words.

_____

_____

**Reading Skill**

A **conclusion** is an opinion that you reach after considering details. Details in a poem can help you draw conclusions. How does the speaker feel about life?

_____

_____

**Literary Analysis** 🔍

Language that is not meant to be taken literally is called **figurative language**. One kind of figurative language is a **simile**. A simile compares two things using the words *like* or *as*. Underline the simile in the bracketed stanza.

**Stop to Reflect**

What do you think happens when the keeper lets the watch run down?

_____

_____

# Loo-Wit[1]
## Wendy Rose

The way they do
this old woman
no longer cares
what others think
5  but spits her black tobacco
any which way
stretching full length
from her bumpy bed.
Finally up
10  she sprinkles ashes
on the snow,
cold buttes[2]
promise nothing
but the walk
15  of winter.
Centuries of cedar
have bound her
to earth,
huckleberry ropes
20  lay prickly
on her neck.
<u>Around her
machinery growls,
snarls and plows
25  great patches
of her skin.</u>
She crouches
in the north,
her trembling
30  the source
of dawn.
Light appears
with the shudder
of her slopes,

## Reading Skill

**Connecting details** means seeing how details fit together. Doing this can help you figure out a poem's meaning. Read lines 1–21. What details about the old woman seem to be most important?

_____

_____

_____

What **conclusion** can you draw about the old woman, based on the details in the underlined text?

_____

_____

_____

## Literary Analysis 🔍

**Symbols** are one kind of **figurative language**. A symbol is a person, place, or thing that stands for something more than itself. What might the machinery stand for?

_____

_____

## Reading Check

What does the old woman do that shows she does not care what others think? Circle the answer.

---

**Vocabulary Development**

**crouches** (KROW chez) *v.* stoops or bends low

---

1. **Loo-Wit** name given by the Cowlitz people to Mount St. Helens, an active volcano in Washington State. It means "lady of fire."

2. **buttes** (byoots) *n.* steep hills standing alone in flat land.

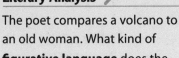

35  the movement
of her arm.
Blackberries <u>unravel</u>,
stones <u>dislodge</u>;
it's not as if
40  they weren't warned.
She was sleeping
but she heard the boot scrape,
the creaking floor,
felt the pull of the blanket
45  from her thin
shoulder.
With one free hand
she finds her weapons
and raises them high;
clearing the twigs from her
throat
50  she sings, she
sings,
shaking the sky
like a blanket about her
Loo-wit sings and sings and
sings!

**Literary Analysis**

The poet compares a volcano to an old woman. What kind of **figurative language** does the poet use?

_____

_____

Underline two details that compare a volcano to an old woman.

**Reading Skill**

This poem ends with Loo-wit singing. What **conclusion** can you draw about Loo-wit's singing?

_____

_____

_____

**Reading Check** ✏

The old woman, Loo-wit, "was sleeping." Circle the lines that say what wakes her up.

**Reader's Response:** The poems in this collection have vivid images. What image did you find most striking? Explain why this image was so powerful.

_____

_____

_____

**Vocabulary Development**

**unravel** (un RAV uhl) *v.* become untangled or separated

**dislodge** (dis LAHDJ) *v.* force from a position or place

# Poetry Collection 3

1. **Interpret:** In the poem "Life," what does the image of a watch suggest about life?

_____

_____

2. **Analyze Causes and Effects:** According to the poem "Loo-Wit," what causes the volcano's eruption?

_____

_____

_____

3. **Reading Skill:** Use this graphic organizer to **connect details** from the poem "Life" to reach the conclusion that is given.

| Detail | Detail | Detail |
|--------|--------|--------|
|        |        |        |

**Conclusion:** The speaker believes that people lose interest in life as they grow older.

4. **Literary Analysis:** What is a **symbol** for strength in "The Courage That My Mother Had"?

_____

_____

### Writing: Metaphor

Write a **metaphor** about life. Decide what you want to say about life. A metaphor compares two things that are not alike by saying that one thing is another thing.

- List three things that you like about life.

_____

_____

_____

- List three challenges that life brings.

_____

_____

_____

- Look at your lists. Decide on something that you can compare to your ideas about life.

_____

### Research and Technology: Scientific Explanation

Prepare a **scientific explanation** about volcanic eruptions. List three questions that you need to answer for your topic. Then, list the answers to the questions. For example, if your topic is famous eruptions, one question may be "When did a famous eruption happen?" Use this chart to help you organize the research.

| | Answers |
|---|---|
| Question 1: | |
| Question 2: | |
| Question 3: | |

# Poetry Collection 4

**Summaries** The speaker in "Mother to Son" shares her experience of a hard life with her son. "The Village Blacksmith" describes the working life of a village blacksmith. "Fog" describes fog as a cat in a city landscape.

## ? Writing About the Big Question

**What is the best way to communicate?**
In "Poetry Collection 4," the poets use evocative language that makes their poems memorable. Complete this sentence:

Sometimes writers choose to write poems about people who enrich

their lives because _____.

## Note-taking Guide

Use this chart to record details about the poems. Describe the topic of each poem. Then, list descriptive words about each topic.

|  | Topic of Poem | Words Used to Describe Topic |
|---|---|---|
| Mother to Son | a mother's encouragement to her son | "don't you set down on the steps" |
| The Village Blacksmith |  |  |
| Fog |  |  |

# Poetry Collection 4

1. **Connect:** What qualities of fog make it a good subject for a poem?

_____

_____

2. **Analyze:** What qualities does the mother in "Mother to Son" demonstrate through her words and actions?

_____

_____

3. **Reading Skill:** Use this graphic organizer to connect details from "Mother to Son" to reach the **conclusion** that is given.

| Detail | Detail | Detail |
|--------|--------|--------|
|        |        |        |

**Conclusion:** Life has not been easy for the speaker.

4. **Literary Analysis:** Which type of **figurative language** is included in the following lines from "The Village Blacksmith"?

> You can hear him swing his heavy sledge,
> With measured beat and slow,
> Like a sexton ringing the village bell,
> When the evening sun is low.

_____

_____

## Writing: Metaphor

A **metaphor** compares two things that are not alike by saying that one thing *is* another thing. Write a metaphor about a quality or an idea, such as love, kindness, or fear.

- Think of a subject.

_____

- Write a sentence that compares your subject to something else. It might be an object, an idea, or an animal.

_____

_____

- Extend the metaphor by making one or two connected comparisons.

_____

_____

_____

Use your notes to write your metaphor.

## Research and Technology: Scientific Explanation

Your scientific explanation should include facts that explain what fog and smog are. Use the following chart to record information as you research.

| Fog | Smog |
| --- | --- |
| Types: | Types: |
| Characteristics: | Characteristics: |

# Technical Directions

## About Technical Directions

**Technical directions** tell you how to put something together, how to fix something, or how to perform another specific task. The directions describe the steps to complete the task in the order that you need to do them. Technical directions also list necessary tools or materials.

Technical directions often include:

- illustrations
- diagrams
- warnings

## Reading Skill

Read all of the directions carefully before you try to perform a task. **Follow the instructions** in the order in which they are listed. Check off each step as you complete it before moving on to the next step. Technical directions may provide instructions for more than one task. Subheadings identify each task. **Skim,** or quickly read through, the subheadings to find the instructions that you need.

---

### Checklist for Following Technical Directions

❑ Read all the directions completely before starting to follow them.

❑ Look for clues such as bold type or capital letters that point out specific sections or important information.

❑ Use diagrams to locate and name the parts of the product.

❑ Follow each step in the exact order given.

❑ Do not skip any steps.

---

# How to Download Ringtones for a Cell Phone

Technical Directions

**Features:**

- step-by-step instructions for the use of a mechanical device
- tips or warnings
- some technical language
- text written for a general or a specific audience

## The Built-in Method

**Instructions**

- **STEP 1:** Determine if your wireless carrier provides you with a built-in method for downloading ringtones right from your phone. This is usually the most expensive method, but quite simple.
- **STEP 2:** Press the "Web" or "Internet" button on your phone. Once it loads, go to the "Downloads" section. From there, there should be a section for ringtones.
- **STEP 3:** Preview and download new tones for your phone from the ringtones section.

> Directions are provided in sequential order.

## Free Ringtones

> Subheads identify different methods of downloading ringtones.

**Instructions**

- **STEP 1:** Access a computer with Internet.
- **STEP 2:** Go to your favorite search engine and search for "free ringtones." You will get lots of results.
- **STEP 3:** Choose a site that does not require registration. If you do have to register, make sure that any boxes that would sign you up for emails or additional services are NOT checked.
- **STEP 4:** Find ringtones you like and have them sent to your phone. This will require entering your carrier and phone number if you haven't already. The new ringtones will be sent to your phone.

**Tips & Warnings**

- You may need to be in your home service area to receive these tones.

# Setting Your New Ringtones

## Instructions

Bold type and capital letters help to call out the steps of the process.

- **STEP 1:** Decide if you want to set one ringtone as a universal ring, which will play every time you receive a call, or whether you want to set specific ringtones to correspond to specific entries in your phonebook. That way different ringtones will play when different people call you.

- **STEP 2:** Set a universal ringtone in the settings section of your phone. If you cannot find how to do this, consult the manual for your phone. If you do not have the manual, you can probably find it online at either the manufacturer's site or your carrier's site.

- **STEP 3:** Set a ring that is specific to a caller by first finding that person in your phonebook. Select the person for which you want the special ring. Select "Edit." Scroll down in the phonebook entry and select "Ring." Choose the ringtone you want to play when that person calls.

## Overall Tips & Warnings

- If at any point you are having trouble, consult the documentation that came with your phone.

### What is the best way to communicate?

**(a)** According to the technical directions, what two methods can you use to download ringtones?
**(b)** How do the directions make this information clear?

# Thinking About Technical Directions

1. Why might someone want to set different ringtones instead of a universal ringtone?

_____

_____

2. What tips and warnings do the technical directions provide?

_____

_____

**TALK ABOUT IT** **Reading Skill**

3. What is the first step that you need to complete in order to use the built-in method for downloading ringtones?

_____

4. How many steps do you need to complete to set a new ringtone?

_____

**WRITE ABOUT IT** **Timed Writing: Explanation (15 minutes)**

Think of something that you like to make. Write instructions for completing that process. You might explain how to cook or prepare a food, how to do an art project, or how to build something.

• Identify the tools and materials that you need:

_____

• Make sure that your instructions follow a logical order.
• Number the steps:

   1. _____

   2. _____

   3. _____

# Poetry Collection 5 • Poetry Collection 6

## Reading Skill

When you **paraphrase,** you restate something in your own words. To paraphrase a poem, you must first understand it. **Reading aloud according to punctuation** can help you identify complete thoughts in a poem. Observe the following rules when you read poetry:

- Keep reading when a line has no end punctuation.
- Pause at commas, dashes, and semicolons.
- Stop at periods, question marks, or exclamation points.

As you read, note the punctuation to help you paraphrase.

## Literary Analysis

**Sound devices** create musical effects that appeal to the ear. Here are some common sound devices used in poetry:

- **Onomatopoeia** is the use of words whose sounds suggest their meanings.
- **Alliteration** is the repetition of sounds at the beginning of words.
- **Repetition** is the repeated use of words, phrases, or rhythms.

The chart gives examples of each type of sound device. As you read each poem, add a second example of each sound device.

| Sound Devices | | |
|---|---|---|
| Onomatopoeia | Alliteration | Repetition |
| The *shooshing of skis in the fresh snow* | *maggie and millie and molly and may* Went down to the beach *(to play one day)* | To the swinging and the ringing *Of the bells, bells, bells, Of the bells, bells, bells* |
|  |  |  |

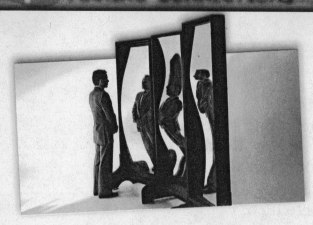

# Poetry Collection 5

**Summaries** "Sarah Cynthia Sylvia Stout" is about a girl who absolutely refuses to take out the garbage. "Weather" is about a rainstorm that starts out drop by drop. The poet describes his individuality in "One."

## Writing About the Big Question

**What is the best way to communicate?** In "Poetry Collection 5," the poems have a pleasing musical quality. Complete this sentence:

Poets and song writers might use musical language in their work because

it can produce _____

_____ for readers.

## Note-taking Guide

Use this chart to record details about the poems. Explain what each poem is about in the second column. Then, list descriptive words about the topic in the third column.

| Title of Poem | Topic of Poem | Words Used to Describe Topic |
|---|---|---|
| Sarah Cynthia Sylvia Stout . . . | | |
| Weather | the sound of raindrops | dot, spack, splatter |
| One | | |

# Sarah Cynthia Sylvia Stout Would Not Take the Garbage Out

### Shel Silverstein

Sarah Cynthia Sylvia Stout
Would not take the garbage out!
She'd scour[1] the pots and scrape the pans,
Candy[2] the yams and spice the hams,
5   And though her daddy would scream and shout,
She simply would not take the garbage out.
And so it piled up to the ceilings:
Coffee grounds, potato peelings,
Brown bananas, rotten peas,
10   Chunks of sour cottage cheese.
It filled the can, it covered the floor,
It cracked the window and blocked the door
With bacon rinds[3] and chicken bones,
Drippy ends of ice cream cones,
15   Prune pits, peach pits, orange peel,
Gloppy glumps of cold oatmeal,
Pizza crusts and withered greens,
Soggy beans and tangerines,
Crusts of black burned buttered toast,
20   Gristly bits of beefy roasts . . .
The garbage rolled on down the hall,
It raised the roof, it broke the wall . . .
Greasy napkins, cookie crumbs,
Globs of gooey bubblegum,
25   Cellophane from green baloney,
Rubbery blubbery macaroni,
Peanut butter, caked and dry,
Curdled milk and crusts of pie,
Moldy melons, dried up mustard,
30   Eggshells mixed with lemon custard,
Cold french fries and rancid meat,
Yellow lumps of Cream of Wheat.

## TAKE NOTES

### Activate Prior Knowledge

These poems use word sounds to make readers laugh. Think of some of the silliest words you know. Write a sentence using as many funny-sounding words as you can.

_____

_____

_____

### Literary Analysis

**Sound devices** make musical effects with words. What sound device is used in the title of this poem?

_____

Explain how this device is present in the title.

_____

_____

### Reading Skill

**Reading according to punctuation** can help you make sense of a poem. The underlined text make two sentences. Circle the beginning and end of each sentence. Also circle the punctuation in the two sentences.

© Pearson Education

---

**Vocabulary Development**

**withered** (WITH erd) _adj._ dried up

**rancid** (RAN sid) _adj._ spoiled and bad-smelling

---

1. **scour** (SKOW er) _v._ clean by rubbing vigorously.

2. **candy** (KAN dee) _v._ coat with sugar.

3. **rinds** (rynds) _n._ tough outer layers or skins.

At last the garbage reached so high
That finally it touched the sky.
35 And all the neighbors moved away,
And none of her friends would come to play.
And finally Sarah Cynthia Stout said,
"OK, I'll take the garbage out!"
But then, of course, it was too late
40 The garbage reached across the state,
From New York to the Golden Gate
And there, in the garbage she did hate
Poor Sarah met an awful fate,
That I cannot right now relate[4]
45 Because the hour is much too late.
But children, remember Sarah Stout
And always take the garbage out!

### Literary Analysis

**Alliteration** is the use of the same sound to begin several words. Circle the repeated sounds in the underlined words.

### Reading Skill

Restating something in your own words is called **paraphrasing**. Paraphrase the first bracketed stanza.

_____

_____

_____

### Literary Analysis

The second bracketed stanza is very musical. What **sound devices** does the poet use?

_____

_____

### Reading Check

What is the rain hitting? Circle the answer in the first stanza.

# Weather
## Eve Merriam

Dot a dot dot    dot a dot dot
Spotting the windowpane.
Spack a spack speck    flick a flack fleck
Freckling the windowpane.

5 A spatter a scatter    a wet cat a clatter
A splatter a rumble outside.
Umbrella umbrella umbrella umbrella
Bumbershoot barrel of rain.

Slosh a galosh    slosh a galosh
10 Slither and slather and glide
A puddle a jump a puddle a jump
A puddle a jump puddle splosh
A juddle a pump a luddle a dump a
Puddmuddle jump in and slide!

4. **relate** (ree LAYT) v. tell.

# One

## James Berry

Only one of me
and nobody can get a second one
from a photocopy machine.

Nobody has the fingerprints I have.
5  Nobody can cry my tears, or laugh my laugh
or have my expectancy when I wait.

But anybody can mimic my dance with my dog.
Anybody can howl how I sing out of tune.
And mirrors can show me multiplied
10  many times, say, dressed up in red
or dressed up in grey.

Nobody can get into my clothes for me
or feel my fall for me, or do my running.
Nobody hears my music for me, either.

15  I am just this one.
Nobody else makes the words
I shape with sound, when I talk.

But anybody can act how I stutter in a rage.
Anybody can copy echoes I make.
20  And mirrors can show me multiplied
many times, say, dressed up in green
or dressed up in blue.

**Reader's Response:** All of the poems in this collection have musical qualities. Which poem's sounds do you like best? Explain why you like the way this poem sounds.

_____

_____

_____

© Pearson Education

**Vocabulary Development**

**stutter** (STUT er) *v.* speak in a hesitant or faltering way

## TAKE NOTES

**Literary Analysis**

One way poets create rhythms is to repeat key words or phrases. This **sound device** is called **repetition**. Circle the words the poet repeats in the first bracketed stanza.

**Reading Skill**

Read the second bracketed stanza. Stop reading at the end of each line. You will not understand what the speaker "shapes" when he talks. Now, practice **reading aloud according to punctuation**. Write what the speaker shapes when he talks.

_____

**Paraphrase** the second bracketed stanza.

_____

_____

_____

**Reading Check**

What is there only one of? Underline the answer.

# Poetry Collection 5

1. **Analyze:** Do you think Silverstein intended to teach a lesson with "Sarah Cynthia . . ."? Why or why not?

_____

_____

2. **Interpret:** How do you think the poet of "One" feels about the words *mimic* (line 7), *act* (line 18), and *copy* (line 19)? Are these good or bad actions?

_____

_____

3. **Reading Skill:** Write an example from each poem in which you **read according to punctuation** rather than stopping at the end of a line. Then, **paraphrase** each example. Use this chart.

| Poem | Example from Poem | Paraphrase |
|---|---|---|
| Sarah Cynthia Sylvia Stout . . . | | |
| Weather | | |
| One | "Dot a dot dot    dot a dot dot Spotting the windowpane." | Drops of rain are hitting the window. |

4. **Literary Analysis:** List two examples of the **sound device onomatopoeia** in "Weather" that imitate the sound of water.

_____

_____

## Writing: Poem

Write a **poem** called "Alliteration" that defines the term and gives examples of this sound device. Alliteration is the repetition of beginning consonant sounds. Sometimes the use of certain sounds creates silly, scary, or even sad feelings. The line, "suffer a sea change/Into something rich and strange" repeats the *s* sound. The feeling is mysterious.

Use this chart to help you brainstorm examples of alliteration for your poem.

| Examples of funny or silly alliteration | Examples of sad alliteration | Examples of exciting alliteration | Examples of scary alliteration | Other examples you can think of |
|---|---|---|---|---|
| | | | | |

## Listening and Speaking: Poetry Reading

First, review the poems in this collection, and choose one that you really like. Then use the following guidelines to help you with your **poetry reading**.

- Read the poem aloud. Pause at commas, dashes, and semicolons, and stop at periods.

- Vary your reading rate depending on structure.

- Notice the rhythm of the poem. Follow this rhythm as you read.

- Practice reading loudly and clearly. Be sure to make eye contact with your audience.

# Poetry Collection 6

**Summaries** "Full Fathom Five," a song from Shakespeare's play *The Tempest*, explains that a young prince's father has drowned. "Onomatopoeia" describes the sounds and look of water dripping from a faucet. "Train Tune" tracks the movement of a train through time and place.

 **Writing About the Big Question**

**What is the best way to communicate?** In "Poetry Collection 6," each poem uses sound to create an image or to bring about a certain mood. Complete this sentence:

Sound can entertain us, but it can also express _____

_____.

## Note-taking Guide

Use this chart to record visual and sound details in the three poems.

| Poem | Visual Details | Aural (sound) Descriptions |
|------|----------------|----------------------------|
| Full Fathom Five | "bones are coral made" | Ding-dong |
| Onomatopoeia | | |
| Train Tune | | |

# Poetry Collection 6

1. **Interpret:** Why does the poet call the changes that happened to the father in "Full Fathom Five" "rich and strange"?

_____

_____

2. **Speculate:** Why do you think the poet includes the detail about love in "Train Tune"?

_____

_____

3. **Reading Skill:** In this chart, write an example from each poem in which you **read according to punctuation** rather than stopping at the end of a line. Then, **paraphrase** each example.

| Poem | Example from Poem | Paraphrase |
|------|-------------------|------------|
| Full Fathom Five | | |
| Onomatopoeia | | |
| Train Tune | | |

4. **Literary Analysis:** List three words not used in "Onomatopoeia" that use **onomatopoeia** to imitate the sound of water.

_____

_____

## Writing: Poem

Write a **poem** called "Alliteration" that defines the term and gives examples of this sound device. Alliteration is the repetition of beginning consonant sounds. Sometimes the use of certain sounds creates silly, scary, or even sad feelings. The line, "suffer a sea change/Into something rich and strange" repeats the s sounds. The feeling is mysterious.

Use this chart to help you brainstorm examples of alliteration.

| Examples of funny or silly alliteration | Examples of sad alliteration | Examples of exciting alliteration | Examples of scary alliteration | Other examples you can think of |
|---|---|---|---|---|
| | | | | |

Share your finished poem with a partner.

## Listening and Speaking: Poetry Reading

Present a poem from *Poetry Collection 2* in a **poetry reading**. Fill in this chart to help you decide how to read this poem.

| Poem's title | What emotions or feelings can I express in the poem? | What visual details can I act out? | How does the poem sound if I read it quickly? | How does it sound if I read it slowly? |
|---|---|---|---|---|
| | | | | |

Use your notes in the chart to help you improve your reading of the poem. Then, practice the **poetry reading** in front of a mirror.

# Poetry Collection 7 • Poetry Collection 8

## Reading Skill

To **paraphrase** means to restate something in your own words to make the meaning clear to yourself. If you are unsure of a poem's meaning, **reread** the parts that are difficult.

- Look up unfamiliar words and replace them with words you know.
- Restate the line or passage using your own, everyday words.
- Reread the passage to make sure that your version makes sense.

As you read, use this chart to help you paraphrase.

| Original | Unfamiliar Words | Dictionary Definitions of Unfamiliar Words | Paraphrase |
|---|---|---|---|
| | | | |
| | | | |
| | | | |

## Literary Analysis

Rhythm and rhyme make poetry musical. **Rhythm** is a poem's pattern of stressed ( ´ ) and unstressed ( ˘ ) syllables.

**Meter** is a poem's rhythmical pattern. It is measured in *feet*, or single units of stressed and unstressed syllables.

**Rhyme** is the repetition of sounds at the ends of words. In the example, the words *sire* and *fire* create a rhyme.

Hálf / ĭn dreáms / hĕ sáw / hĭs síre /

Wíth / hĭs gréat / hănds fúll / ŏf fĭre.

# Poetry Collection 7

**Summaries** The speaker in "Annabel Lee" mourns for the woman he loves who has died. "Martin Luther King" is about civil rights leader Dr. Martin Luther King, Jr. The speaker in "I'm Nobody" scorns being a somebody, or a celebrity.

## Writing About the Big Question

**What is the best way to communicate?**
In "Poetry Collection 7," the poets present people and ideas about which they feel passionate. Complete these sentences:

Using words to express our feelings about others can help us reveal

_____.

## Note-taking Guide

Use this chart to record details about the poems. Describe the topic of the poem in the second column. Then, list words to describe how the speaker in the poem feels about that topic.

| Title of Poem | Topic of Poem | Feelings the Speaker Has for the Topic |
|---|---|---|
| Annabel Lee | mourning the death of Annabel Lee | sadness; longing |
| Martin Luther King | | |
| I'm Nobody | | |

# Annabel Lee
## Edgar Allan Poe

*Poe's biographer, Kenneth Silverman, believes that the woman in this poem "represents all of the women he loved and lost." Poe finished the poem about a year after his wife's death and published it in a New York newspaper.*

It was many and many a year ago,
    In a kingdom by the sea.
That a maiden there lived whom you may know
    By the name of Annabel Lee;—
And this maiden she lived with no other thought
    Than to love and be loved by me.

*She* was a child and *I* was a child,
    In this kingdom by the sea.
5 But we loved with a love that was more than love—
    I and my Annabel Lee—
With a love that the winged seraphs[1] of Heaven
    Coveted her and me.

And this was the reason that, long ago,
    In this kingdom by the sea,
A wind blew out of a cloud by night
    Chilling my Annabel Lee;
So that her highborn kinsmen[2] came
    And bore her away from me,
10 To shut her up in a sepulcher[3]
    In this kingdom by the sea.

### Activate Prior Knowledge

Poems often have strong rhythms that make musical sounds from the words. Songs also have strong rhythms. Write two or three lines from your favorite song.

_____

_____

_____

### Literary Analysis

When you read a poem aloud, the syllables you say with more force are stressed syllables. The ones you say more softly are unstressed syllables. The poem's **rhythm** is the pattern of stressed and unstressed syllables. Read the underlined text. Circle each stressed syllable.

### Reading Skill

**Rereading** parts of poems that are difficult can help you paraphrase. Reread the group of bracketed lines. Use the words in the vocabulary box and the footnotes to help you understand the lines.

_____

_____

## Vocabulary Development

**maiden** (maydn) *n.* a young woman who is not married

**coveted** (KUV it tid) *v.* wanted greatly

**bore** (bawr) *v.* carried

1. **seraphs** (SER uhfs) *n.* angels.
2. **highborn kinsmen** relatives of noble birth.
3. **sepulcher** (SEP uhl ker) *n.* vault for burial; grave; tomb.

**Reading Skill**

**Reread** the underlined text. What words or phrases are confusing?

_____

_____

To **paraphrase** means to put writing into your own words to make the meaning clearer. Paraphrase the bracketed lines. Replace unfamiliar words with easier ones.

_____

_____

_____

**Literary Analysis**

Words **rhyme** if they end with the same sound. Circle the rhyming words in the bracketed stanza. Draw lines to connect words that rhyme.

**Reading Check**

What does the speaker see when he sees the stars? Underline the answer.

The angels, not half so happy in Heaven,
    Went envying her and me:—
Yes! that was the reason (as all men know,
    In this kingdom by the sea)
That the wind came out of a cloud, chilling
    And killing my Annabel Lee.

But our love it was stronger by far than the love
    Of those who were older than we—
    Of many far wiser than we—
15 And neither the angels in Heaven above
    Nor the demons down under the sea,
Can ever dissever[4] my soul from the soul
    Of the beautiful Annabel Lee:—

For the moon never beams without bringing
    me dreams
Of the beautiful Annabel Lee;
And the stars never rise but I see the bright eyes
    Of the beautiful Annabel Lee;
20 And so, all the nighttide,[5] I lie down by the side
Of my darling, my darling, my life and my bride,
    In her sepulcher there by the sea—
    In her tomb by the side of the sea.

---

**4. dissever** (dis SE ver) *v.* separate.

**5. nighttide** (NYT tyd) *n.* an old-fashioned way of saying nighttime.

© Pearson Education

# Martin Luther King

### Raymond Richard Patterson

He came upon an age
Beset by grief, by rage—

His love so deep, so wide,
He could not turn aside.

5   His passion, so profound.
He would not turn around.

He taught a suffering earth
The measure of man's worth.

For this he was slain.
10  But he will come again.

# I'm Nobody

### Emily Dickinson

I'm Nobody! Who are you?
Are you—Nobody—too?
Then there's a pair of us!
Don't tell! they'd banish us—you know!

5   How dreary—to be—Somebody!
How public—like a Frog—
To tell your name—the livelong June—
To an admiring Bog!

**Literary Analysis**

The **rhythm** in this poem is very regular. Circle the stressed syllables in the first bracketed stanza.

**Reading Skill**

Read the second bracketed stanza. Then, **reread** them. Write words or phrases that are unfamiliar or confusing.

_____

_____

**Paraphrase** the second bracketed stanza. Replace unfamiliar words with words you know.

_____

_____

**Reading Check**

What would happen if people knew about the pair of nobodies? Underline the answer.

Reader's Response: These poems all have strong, musical rhythms. Which of these poems would make the best song? Explain.

_____

_____

_____

# Poetry Collection 7

1. **Interpret:** In "Martin Luther King," what does the poet mean by King's "passion, so profound"?

_____

_____

2. **Apply:** In what way does "I'm Nobody" suggest some of the difficulties celebrities face?

_____

_____

3. **Reading Skill:** Reread lines 9–10 in "Annabel Lee." Then, **paraphrase** them.

_____

_____

4. **Literary Analysis:** Use this chart to analyze the **rhyme** in each poem.

| Poem | Rhyming Words |
|------|---------------|
| Annabel Lee | |
| Martin Luther King | |
| I'm Nobody | you, too; Frog, bog |

### Writing: Paraphrase

Write a **paraphrase** of one of the poems in this collection. To *paraphrase* means to retell in your own words.

- Reread the poems. Paraphrase the main idea of each poem.

  _____

  _____

  _____

- Choose the poem that you understand best. Then, answer the following questions:

  - Who is the speaker of the poem?

    _____

  - What is the topic of the poem?

    _____

  - What action happens in the poem?

    _____

    _____

### Research and Technology: Conduct a Survey

Use the following chart to tally the results for your survey.

| Category | "Annabel Lee" | "Martin Luther King" | "I'm Nobody" |
|---|---|---|---|
| Best character description | | | |
| Best use of language | | | |
| Best rhythm | | | |
| Best rhyme | | | |
| Best meter | | | |

# Poetry Collection 8

**Summaries** "Jim" recalls a son's care and love for his mother. "Father William" is a silly look at how young people think that older people should act. "Stopping by Woods on a Snowy Evening" tells of a traveler's thoughts on stopping in the woods.

## Writing About the Big Question

**What is the best way to communicate?**
In "Poetry Collection 8," each poem uses rhythm and rhyme to create a musical quality. Complete this sentence:

Messages that **entertain** as well as **inform** _____

_____.

## Note-taking Guide

Use this chart to record important details about the characters and actions in each poem.

| | Characters in poem | Actions in poem |
|---|---|---|
| Jim | Mrs. Jackson's Jim Mother-dear | |
| Father William | | |
| Stopping by Woods . . . | | |

# Poetry Collection 8

1. **Infer:** What detail tells you that Jim is not selfish?

_____

_____

2. **Analyze:** How does Father William's appearance make his actions seem especially surprising?

_____

_____

3. **Reading Skill: Reread** lines 11–12 of "Stopping by Woods on a Snowy Evening." Then, **paraphrase** them.

_____

_____

_____

_____

4. **Literary Analysis:** Use this chart to analyze the **rhyme** in each poem.

| Poem | Rhyming Words |
|------|---------------|
| Jim | |
| Father William | |
| Stopping by Woods . . . | |

## Writing: Paraphrase a Poem

Write a **paraphrase** of one of the poems in this collection. To *paraphrase* means to retell in your own words.

- Reread the poems. Paraphrase the main idea of each poem.

  _____

  _____

  _____

- Choose the poem that you understand best. Then, answer the following questions:

  - Who is the speaker of the poem?

    _____

  - What is the topic of the poem?

    _____

  - What action happens in the poem?

    _____

    _____

## Research and Technology: Conduct a Survey

Plan a survey. A *survey* is a set of questions that you ask to find out what people think about a certain topic. For example, which poem had the best character description? Which poem was the most musical?

- Complete a list of questions for your survey. Include several questions.

- Be sure to ask those who complete the survey to explain their choices.

- If possible, have classmates complete the survey.

# Magazine Articles

## About Magazine Articles

A **magazine article**

- gives information and analysis about a topic.
- is printed in a magazine. The magazine may be published weekly, monthly, or even quarterly (four times a year).
- may be about current issues and events.
- may appeal to a general audience.
- may be a good source of information for research.

## Reading Skill

The main idea is the most important idea in the text. To **determine the main idea** in a magazine article, follow these steps:

1. Read the article.

2. Note important facts, details, and opinions as you read.

3. Look for a statement of the main idea in the introduction or conclusion.

4. Ask: Do the facts, details, and opinions support this main idea?

5. Write the main idea in your own words.

| Sentence or Passage | Replacement Words | Paraphrase |
|---|---|---|
| Rap is about words, but rhythm makes them more powerful. | rhythm = beat<br><br>more powerful = stronger<br><br>but = although | Although words are the point of rap, its beat makes it stronger. |

# The Rhythms of Rap
### Kathiann M. Kowalski

### Text Structure

Photographs add interest to the page. They help the ideas in the article come to life. Look at the photograph. What looks interesting?

_____

_____

### Fluency Builder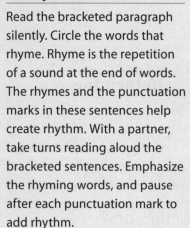

Read the bracketed paragraph silently. Circle the words that rhyme. Rhyme is the repetition of a sound at the end of words. The rhymes and the punctuation marks in these sentences help create rhythm. With a partner, take turns reading aloud the bracketed sentences. Emphasize the rhyming words, and pause after each punctuation mark to add rhythm.

### Comprehension Builder

You should know when an article was published. This will tell you how up-to-date the information is. What is the name of this magazine? What is the issue date of this article? Underline the information.

Rap is about society; some songs get notoriety. But do your feet tap, when you hear rap?

Lots of rap tracks make you move along with them. Rap is about words, but rhythm makes them more powerful.

"Rhythm is the feeling of movement in time," explains Miami University (OH) music professor Chris Tanner. "Rhythm is the term we use in music for dividing time. Music can't exist without rhythm." In other words, one sound with no break is just noise. Play a sequence of notes for a certain time each, and you get music.

As music moves forward in time, your brain notes the duration of individual sounds and groups them together into bunches that let you perceive rhythm in the music. It could be the hammering lyrics of a rap artist. Or, it could be the beginning of Beethoven's *Fifth Symphony:* "Bum, bum, bum, bummm. Bum, bum, bum, bummm."

## Saying Their Songs

Rap as a popular music style started in the late 1970s. But, notes music professor Adam Krims at the University of Alberta, "In some form or another, this kind of music has been around for about 250 years. It continues very old practices of rhyming and rhythm among African Americans."

*Odyssey Magazine* March 2002

Rap's style of rhythmic delivery sets it apart from talking or other styles of *declamatory* (words recited with music) delivery. "In rap, you're not just talking," notes Krims, "You're really fore-grounding [bringing up front] the rhythmic aspects of what you're doing."

It's somewhat like the difference between reading a textbook and reading Dr. Seuss's *Green Eggs and Ham* aloud. However, stresses Krims, "Rap actually takes a lot of practice to do even slightly well." Effective rhythmic phrasing really draws listeners into the lyrics of an MC ("MC" is the same as "emcee" and stands for "master of ceremonies"—a name rap artists commonly use).

Often an MC works with words' natural emphasis. Other times, the artist may deform words. "You purposely deliver them in a way that's a little perverse," explains Krims. So instead of "California," an MC might say "Californ-eye-ay."

## In the Background

Sampling serves up yet more rhythms in rap. "Sampling is taking a little bit of music from another source," says Krims. Sampling may be the artist's own composition. It may be a segment from another popular song or even a classical piece.

The musician then makes a "loop" of the segment, which means that it's played over and over. Sampling adds background melody and harmony. Each bit of sampling also adds its own rhythms to a rap song.

## The Beat Goes On

Underlying rap and almost all music is its pulse, or beat. "There are all kinds of rhythms going on in a *Sousa* march, but what do people march to?" says Tanner. It's not the rhythmic phrasing of the melody. Instead, he says, "They move their feet to the underlying pulse of the music."

Rap and other popular music forms often spell out the beat explicitly with drums. "Any popular

### Vocabulary Builder

**Multiple-Meaning Words**
The noun *delivery* may mean "the act of taking something to someone's house or workplace." It may also mean "the way in which someone speaks or performs in public." Which meaning does *delivery* have in the bracketed paragraph?

_____

_____

### Text Structure

Magazine articles are usually divided by headings. The headings are of a different size or color. Headings give a hint about the main idea of what follows. What is the main idea of the text under the heading **In the Background?**

_____

_____

### Vocabulary Builder

**Musical Terms** A *melody* is a song or a tune. *Harmony* is combinations of musical notes that sound good together.

music that we're used to usually has that characteristic," notes Tanner. "That's why it's fun to dance to. In fact, popular music is often designed for movement."

"Meter is simply organizing pulses into a regular cyclical pattern," adds Tanner. Instead of an endless series of beats, the musician may play cycles of "ONE, two, Three, four." This meter, known as "common time," stresses the first beat most. The third beat gets slight emphasis, too. Meter sets up a hierarchy, which the listener's brain can then remember and anticipate. That makes it possible for you to tap your foot or clap in time with the music.

*Tempo* is how fast a piece of music delivers its meter. Too slow, and a rap song sounds like a *dirge*, or funeral song. Too fast, and the brain can't perceive individual sounds. The music becomes one big blur. Choose a tempo that's just quick enough, and listeners want to move with the music. Speed it up slightly or slow it down in places, and listeners respond to the music's different moods.

## What Makes It Cool?

Hearing rhythm patterns in a song, listeners form expectations of what comes next. If music doesn't give enough for listeners to form those expectations, it sounds chaotic and grating. If music gets too predictable, however, it becomes boring.

Sophisticated rap music provides an innovative mix that satisfies and sometimes surprises listeners' expectations. With lyrics, an MC might stop in the middle of a line or give some offbeat accents. Sampling or the drum track may stress different notes than those that would usually be emphasized in the meter—a technique called *syncopation*.

Revel in the rhythms of your favorite music. Innovative rhythms not only move music forward in time, but they also make rap—and many other types of music—cool.

# Thinking About the Magazine Article

1. Remember that tempo is how fast a piece of music delivers its meter. Why is the tempo important to a rap song?

_____

_____

2. How does the brain help people understand rap music?

_____

_____

## TALK ABOUT IT Reading Skill

3. What is one important idea in the text under the heading **The Beat Goes On?**

_____

_____

4. What is the main idea of the article? Write your answer in one sentence.

_____

_____

## WRITE ABOUT IT  Timed Writing: Persuasion (15 minutes)

Think about this question: Is rap music simple or complicated? Then, write an answer that tells your opinion of rap music.

- Begin your writing by clearly stating your opinion in a complete sentence.
- Find three details or reasons in the article that support your opinion.
- Paraphrase information in this article to explain each of your reasons.
- Write a conclusion that summarizes your writing and brings it to a close.

# from Dragonwings

Drama is a story told in dialogue by performers in front of an audience. The following elements make drama come to life.

| Element | Definition | Example |
|---|---|---|
| Playwright | the author of a play | William Shakespeare |
| Actors | people who perform the drama | Brad Pitt, Halle Berry |
| Acts | units of action | Act I |
| Scenes | Acts are divided into these parts. | Act I, scene ii |
| Characterization | playwright's method for creating believable characters | A character speaks loudly and walks with her head up to show that she is confident and in control. |
| Dramatic speech | **dialogue:** a conversation between or among characters<br>**monologue:** a long speech by a single character that reveals his or her thoughts and feelings | **dialogue:**<br>BIFF: Let's go to sleep.<br>HAPPY: I guess we didn't settle anything, did we?<br>BIFF: We can figure it out tomorrow. Let's rest now. |
| Stage directions | information about where the action takes place or how it is done | U (upstage or rear of stage)<br>C (center stage) |
| Theater | place where plays are performed | Wilbur Theater |
| Set | everything on stage that suggests the time and place | a cozy living room with furniture from the 1940s |
| Props | small items that the actors use or carry to make their actions seem real | a doctor's bag |

There are three main types of drama.

- A **comedy** is a drama with a happy ending. Comedies are written to entertain and make people laugh. Comedies often point out faults in people or society.

- A **tragedy** is an unhappy drama that ends with the downfall of the main character. The main character can be an average person or a person of great importance. Often, the main character is a heroic figure.

- A **drama** is written about serious subjects such as events that happen in everyday life. Dramas may not have a comedic or a tragic tone.

Drama often takes place on a stage in a theater. Stage plays require actors, costumes, lights, and sets. Other types of drama are not performed on stage.

- **Screenplays** are scripts for films. Screenplays include directions not only for actors but also for camera operators. They usually have more scene changes than a stage play.

- **Teleplays** are scripts for television. They also include directions for camera operators and have more scene changes than a stage play.

- **Radio plays** are scripts for radio broadcasts. They include sound effects. Radio plays do not require sets, costumes, or directions for actors or camera operators about movement.

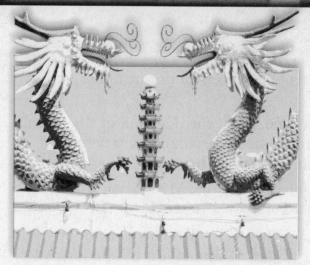

# from Dragonwings
## Laurence Yep

**Summaries** In the novel, the narrator awakes to a knock on his door. Outside, in the cold fog, his uncle and friends bring ropes, food, and an empty wagon up the hill. They have come to help the narrator and his father move their flying machine. In the play, Moon Shadow and his father are about to lose their home and their flying machine, Dragonwings. Yep adapts the story of his novel. He uses dialogue to show how Moon Shadow's family and friends come together to launch the flying machine.

## Note-taking Guide

Use this chart to compare and contrast the novel and the dramatic versions of Yep's *Dragonwings*.

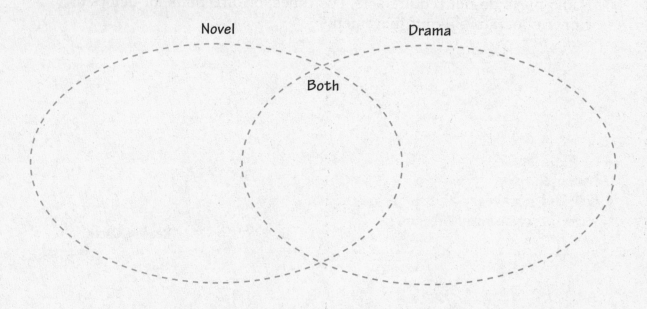

Novel          Drama

Both

# from the novel
# Dragonwings
## Laurence Yep

I do not know when I fell asleep, but it was already way past sunrise when I woke up. The light crept through the cracks in the walls and under the shutters and seemed to delight especially in dancing on my eyes. Father lay huddled, rolled up in his blanket. He did not move when the knock came at our door. I was still in my clothes because it was cold. I crawled out of the blankets and opened the side door.

The fog lay low on the hill. Tendrils drifted in through the open doorway. At first I could not see anything but shadows, and then a sudden breeze whipped the fog away from the front of our barn. Hand Clap stood there as if he had appeared by magic. He bowed.

"There you are." He turned and called over his shoulder. "Hey, everybody, they're here."

I heard the clink of harness and the rattle of an old wagon trying to follow the ruts in the road. Toiling up the hill out of the fog was Red Rabbit, and behind him I saw Uncle on the wagon seat. The rest of the wagon was empty—I suppose to give Red Rabbit less of a load to pull. Behind the wagon came the Company, with coils of ropes over their shoulders and baskets of food. I ran down the hill, my feet pounding against the hard, damp earth. I got up on the seat and almost bowled Uncle over. For once Uncle did not worry about his dignity but caught me up and returned my hug.

"Ouch," he said, and pushed me away. He patted himself lightly on his chest. "I'm not as young as I used to be."

Then Hand Clap, Lefty, and White Deer crowded around.

"Am I ever glad you're here," I said. "Poor Father—"

Uncle held up his hands. "We know. That's why we came."

"But how? Why?" I was bursting with a dozen questions all at once.

"Why, to help you get that thing up to the top of the hill," Uncle said. "Why else would we close up

---

**Activate Prior Knowledge**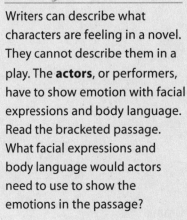

If you built a flying machine, where would you try to fly it?

_____

_____

_____

_____

_____

**Fiction**

Writers can describe what characters are feeling in a novel. They cannot describe them in a play. The **actors**, or performers, have to show emotion with facial expressions and body language. Read the bracketed passage. What facial expressions and body language would actors need to use to show the emotions in the passage?

_____

_____

_____

**Reading Check**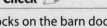

Who knocks on the barn door? Circle the text that tells you.

## Stop to Reflect

Uncle comes even though he does not believe in flying machines. What does that show about him?

_____

_____

_____

_____

_____

## Drama

A **scene** is a unit of action in a drama. Where is this scene set? Underline the time. Circle the place.

## Reading Check ✎

Why are Moon Shadow and his father about to lose Dragonwings? Underline the reasons.

---

our shop and take a boat and climb this abominable hill, all on the coldest, wettest day ever known since creation?"

"But you don't believe in flying machines."

"I still don't," Uncle said sternly. "But I still feel as if I owe you something for what was done to you by that man who once was my son.[1] I'll be there to haul your machine up the hill, and I'll be there to haul it back down when it doesn't fly."

"We were all getting fat anyway," White Deer said, "especially Uncle."

# from the dramatization of
# Dragonwings
## Laurence Yep

### Cast of Characters

**RED RABBIT**   a horse that pulls the company's laundry wagon

**UNCLE BRIGHT STAR**   another laundry owner

**WHITE DEER**   the third laundry owner

**MOON SHADOW**   the narrator of the story

**MISS WHITLAW**   owner of a stable in San Francisco where the narrator and his father live

**WINDRIDER**   Moon Shadow's father

### Scene 9

*Piedmont, later that day outside the stable.*

**MOON SHADOW.** September twenty-second, Nineteen-ought-nine. Dear Mother. I have bad news. We are going to lose Dragonwings before father can fly it. Black Dog stole all we have, and the landlord will not give us an extension on our rent. So we'll have to move and leave Dragonwings behind. We have asked Miss Whitlaw for help, but her new house has taken up all of her money. And even if Uncle would speak to us, he has probably spent all he has on rebuilding his laundry.

(UNCLE BRIGHT STAR *and* MISS WHITLAW *enter from L.*)

---

1. **man who was my son** Black Dog, who robbed the narrator and his father.

**MISS WHITLAW.** I could have gotten down from the wagon by myself.

**UNCLE BRIGHT STAR.** Watch gopher hole.

**MISS WHITLAW.** I'm younger than you.

**MOON SHADOW.** Uncle, Miss Whitlaw!

**MISS WHITLAW.** How are you?

*(Shaking MOON SHADOW's hand. WINDRIDER enters from U. He now wears a cap.)*

**WINDRIDER.** Come to laugh, Uncle?

**UNCLE BRIGHT STAR.** I came to help you fly your contraption.

**MOON SHADOW.** But you don't believe in flying machines.

**UNCLE BRIGHT STAR.** And I'll haul that thing back down when it doesn't fly. Red Rabbit and me were getting fat anyway. But look at how tall you've grown. And how thin. And ragged. *(Pause.)* But you haven't broken your neck which was more than I ever expected.

**MISS WHITLAW.** As soon as I told your uncle, we hatched the plot together. You ought to get a chance to fly your aeroplane.

**UNCLE BRIGHT STAR.** Flat purse, strong backs.

**WINDRIDER.** We need to pull Dragonwings to the very top.

**UNCLE BRIGHT STAR.** That hill is a very steep hill.

**WINDRIDER.** It has to be that one. The winds are right.

**UNCLE BRIGHT STAR.** Ah, well, it's the winds.

**WINDRIDER.** Take the ropes. *(Pantomimes taking a rope over his shoulder as he faces the audience.)* Got a good grip?

**OTHERS.** *(Pantomiming taking the ropes.)* Yes, right, etc.

**WINDRIDER.** Then pull.

*(They strain. MOON SHADOW stumbles but gets right up. Stamping his feet to get better footing, he keeps tugging.)*

**MOON SHADOW.** *(Giving up.)* It's no good.

**UNCLE BRIGHT STAR.** Pull in rhythm. As we did on the railroad.[1] *(In demonstration, UNCLE BRIGHT STAR*

---

1. **railroad** Uncle Bright Star had helped dig tunnels through the mountains for the railroad.

**Drama**

**Stage directions** give information about where the action takes place or how it is done. What do the underlined stage directions tell about Windrider?

_____

_____

_____

**Drama**

**Dialogue** is conversation between characters. What does the dialogue tell about Uncle Bright Star?

_____

_____

_____

_____

_____

_____

**Stop to Reflect**

How hard or easy is it to move the flying machine? Explain your answer.

_____

_____

_____

_____

_____

## Drama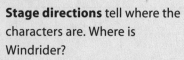

**Characterization** helps make characters believable. What is believable about the characters?

_____

_____

_____

_____

_____

## Drama

**Stage directions** tell where the characters are. Where is Windrider?

_____

_____

## Reading Check

Does the flying machine reach the top of the hill? Underline dialogue that tells you.

stamps his feet in a slow rhythm to set the beat and the others repeat. The rhythm picks up as they move.)
Ngúng, ngúng.
Dew gùng.

**OTHERS.** Ngúng, ngúng.
Dew gùng.

**UNCLE BRIGHT STAR.** *(Imitating the intonation of the Cantonese.)* Púsh, púsh.
Wòrk, wòrk.

**OTHERS.** Púsh, púsh.
Wòrk, wòrk.

**UNCLE BRIGHT STAR.** Seen gà,
Gee gà.

*(High rising tone on the last syllable.)*

**OTHERS.** Seen gà,
Gee gà.

*(High rising tone on the last syllable.)*

**UNCLE BRIGHT STAR.** Get rìch,
Go hóme.

**OTHERS.** Get rìch,
Go hóme.

*(MOON SHADOW, WINDRIDER, UNCLE BRIGHT STAR and MISS WHITLAW arrive D.)*

**MOON SHADOW.** *(Panting.)* We made it. Tramp the grass down in front.

*(WINDRIDER stands C as the others stamp the grass. They can't help smiling and laughing a little.)*

**WINDRIDER.** That's enough.

**MOON SHADOW.** *(To MISS WHITLAW.)* Take that propeller.

*(MISS WHITLAW takes her place before the right propeller with her hands resting on the blade. MOON SHADOW takes his place beside the left propeller. WINDRIDER faces U., his back to the audience.)*

**MISS WHITLAW.** Listen to the wind on the wings.

**UNCLE BRIGHT STAR.** It's alive.

**WINDRIDER.** All right.

*(MOON SHADOW and MISS WHITLAW pull down at the propellers and back away quickly. We hear a motor cough into life. Propellers begin to turn with a roar.)*

UNCLE BRIGHT STAR. *(Slowly turning.)* What's wrong? Is it just going to roll down the hill?

*(MISS WHITLAW crosses her fingers as they all turn to watch the aeroplane.)*

MISS WHITLAW. He's up!

*(WINDRIDER starts to do his flight ballet.)*

MOON SHADOW. *(Pointing.)* He's turning.

UNCLE BRIGHT STAR. He's really flying.

MISS WHITLAW. I never thought I'd see the day. A human up in the sky. Off the ground.

*(They turn and tilt their heads back.)*

MISS WHITLAW. *(Cont'd.)* Free as an eagle.

UNCLE BRIGHT STAR. *(Correcting her.)* Like dragon.

MOON SHADOW. Father, you did it. *(Wonderingly.)* You did it.

*(The aeroplane roars loudly overhead. MOON SHADOW as adult steps forward and addresses the audience.)*

MOON SHADOW. I thought he'd fly forever and ever. Up, up to heaven and never come down. But then some of the guy wires[2] broke, and the right wings separated. Dragonwings came crashing to earth. Father had a few broken bones, but it was nothing serious. Only the aeroplane was wrecked. Uncle took him back to the laundry to recover. Father didn't say much, just thought a lot—I figured he was busy designing the next aeroplane. But when Father was nearly well, he made me sit down next to him.

WINDRIDER. Uncle says he'll make me a partner if I stay. So the western officials would have to change my immigration class. I'd be a merchant, and merchants can bring their wives here. Would you like to send for Mother?

MOON SHADOW. *(Going to WINDRIDER.)* But Dragonwings?

WINDRIDER. When I was up in the air, I tried to find you. You were so small. And getting smaller. Just disappearing from sight. *(Handing his cap to MOON*

---

2. **guy wires** wires that help steady the plane's two sets of wings.

**Drama**

**Stage directions** often tell the actors what to do. Read the bracketed passage. What stage directions are given to the **actors**?

_____

_____

_____

_____

**Drama**

A **monologue** is a long speech by only one character. How do you know that the second bracketed passage is a monologue? Underline the stage directions that tell whom Moon Shadow addresses.

**Reading Check**

Does the flying machine actually fly? Underline the text that tells you.

*SHADOW.)* Like you were disappearing from my life. *(He begins his ballet again.)* I knew it wasn't the time. The Dragon King[3] said there would be all sorts of lessons.

*(MOON SHADOW turns to audience as an adult.)*

**MOON SHADOW.** We always talked about flying again. Only we never did. *(Putting on cap.)* But dreams stay with you, and we never forgot.

*(WINDRIDER takes his final pose. A gong sounds.)*

## Stop to Reflect

What does Windrider realize about flying?

_____

_____

_____

_____

Reader's Response: Do you think this is a good ending for the story? Explain.

_____

_____

_____

_____

_____

_____

3. **Dragon King** In Chinese legends, most dragons are not evil creatures. Earlier in the story, Windrider relates a dream sequence in which he was given his name by the Dragon King and learned he had once been a flying dragon.

# Drama

1. **Compare:** In the scene from the novel, Uncle and the others use a horse and rope to move the flying machine up the hill. In the scene from the play, what helps the audience understand how Dragonwings will be moved to the top of the hill?

_____

_____

2. **Interpret:** In the play, Moon Shadow says to the audience, "Dreams stay with you, and we never forget." What do you think he means?

_____

_____

3. **Drama:** Explain the ways in which the **drama** enhances the emotion of the situation.

_____

_____

4. **Drama:** Use this chart to list examples of **dialogue** and its uses. In the first column, list two examples that show action. In the second column, list two examples that reveal a character's thoughts or feelings. In the third column, list two examples that describe the setting.

| To Show Action | To Reveal Thoughts and Feelings | To Describe Setting |
|---|---|---|
| | | |
| | | |

## Plan an Exhibit

Plan an **exhibit** of books, audiocassettes, and CDs of at least five examples of Laurence Yep works. Follow these steps to gather information for your **exhibit**.

- Go to the library. Use a computer and select the online catalog. Select an author search. Type *Yep, Laurence* into the search box. Hit the enter key. A list of his works will come up. Click on the title of each work that interests you. Read a short description of it. List titles and descriptions that interest you below.

  **Title:** _____ **Description:** _____

  _____

  **Title:** _____ **Description:** _____

  _____

  **Title:** _____ **Description:** _____

  _____

  **Title:** _____ **Description:** _____

  _____

  **Title:** _____ **Description:** _____

  _____

- Check out the titles that interest you. Include at least one book on audiocassette and one book on CD. Name the book on audiocassette and the book on CD below.

  **Book on audiocassette:** _____

  **Book on CD:** _____

- Watch the video interview with Laurence Yep. Review your source material. Use this information to record additional information for your exhibit.

  **Additional information:** _____

  _____

  _____

  _____

# A Christmas Carol: Scrooge and Marley, Act I

## Reading Skill

**Setting a purpose** gives you a focus as you read. You may set one or more of the purposes shown.

- to learn about a subject
- to be entertained
- to gain understanding
- to make a decision
- to be inspired
- to complete a task

   **Preview a text** before reading. Look at the title, the pictures, the captions, the organization, and the beginnings of passages. Previewing can help you decide whether the text will fit your purpose. Previewing can also help you determine a reason for reading a text. Use this chart to jot down notes on details you notice as you preview. Then, use your notes to set one or more purposes.

| Elements in Work | What Is Suggested About the Work? |
|---|---|
| Title | This play will be about the holidays. |
| Picture | |
| Organization, Structure, Literary Form | |
| Beginnings of Passages | |

## Literary Analysis

**Dialogue** is a conversation between characters. In a play, the characters are developed entirely through dialogue. Dialogue also advances the action of the plot and develops the conflict.

   In the script of a dramatic work, you can tell which character is speaking by the name that appears before the character's lines. Look at this example:

   **Mrs. Perez.** Come on, kids! We're leaving.

   **Jen.** Wait for me!

# A Christmas Carol: Scrooge and Marley, Act I

## Israel Horovitz

### from A Christmas Carol by Charles Dickens

**Summary** It is Christmas Eve. Ebenezer Scrooge is a greedy old man who refuses to celebrate Christmas. The ghost of Jacob Marley, Scrooge's former business partner, appears. Marley warns that Scrooge will also become a miserable ghost unless he changes his ways. Marley tells Scrooge that three spirits will visit him that night. Act I reveals what happens when the Ghost of Christmas Past calls on Scrooge.

 **Writing About the Big Question**

**Do others see us more clearly than we see ourselves?** In Act 1 of *A Christmas Carol,* Scrooge is visited by a ghost who warns him to change his ways. Complete this sentence:

When we reflect on our actions towards others, we can learn _____

_____.

## Note-taking Guide

Use this chart to list details that describe Scrooge and how he changes.

| Scrooge's Character | Evidence |
|---|---|
| Scrooge is a stingy, greedy, and cold-hearted man. | |
| Scrooge was not always so stingy and grumpy. | |
| Scrooge begins to regret the choices he has made. | |

# A Christmas Carol: Scrooge and Marley, Act I

## Israel Horovitz

### adapted from A Christmas Carol
### by Charles Dickens

**JACOB MARLEY,** a specter

**EBENEZER SCROOGE,** not yet dead, which is to say still alive

**BOB CRATCHIT,** Scrooge's clerk

**FRED,** Scrooge's nephew

**THIN DO-GOODER**

**PORTLY DO-GOODER**

**SPECTERS (VARIOUS),** carrying money-boxes

**THE GHOST OF CHRISTMAS PAST**

**FOUR JOCUND TRAVELERS**

**A BAND OF SINGERS**

**A BAND OF DANCERS**

**LITTLE BOY SCROOGE**

**YOUNG MAN SCROOGE**

**FAN,** Scrooge's little sister

**THE SCHOOLMASTER**

**SCHOOLMATES**

**FEZZIWIG,** a fine and fair employer

**DICK,** young Scrooge's co-worker

**YOUNG SCROOGE**

**A FIDDLER**

**MORE DANCERS**

**SCROOGE'S LOST LOVE**

**SCROOGE'S LOST LOVE'S DAUGHTER**

**SCROOGE'S LOST LOVE'S HUSBAND**

**THE GHOST OF CHRISTMAS PRESENT**

**SOME BAKERS**

**MRS. CRATCHIT,** Bob Cratchit's wife

**BELINDA CRATCHIT,** a daughter

**MARTHA CRATCHIT,** another daughter

**PETER CRATCHIT,** a son

**TINY TIM CRATCHIT,** another son

**SCROOGE'S NIECE,** Fred's wife

**THE GHOST OF CHRISTMAS FUTURE,** a mute Phantom

**THREE MEN OF BUSINESS**

**DRUNKS, SCOUNDRELS, WOMEN OF THE STREETS**

**A CHARWOMAN**

**MRS. DILBER**

**JOE,** an old second-hand goods dealer

**A CORPSE,** very like Scrooge

**AN INDEBTED FAMILY**

**ADAM,** a young boy

**A POULTERER**

**A GENTLEMAN**

**SOME MORE MEN OF BUSINESS**

*THE PLACE OF THE PLAY* Various locations in and around the City of London, including Scrooge's Chambers and Offices; the Cratchit Home; Fred's Home; Scrooge's School; Fezziwig's Offices; Old Joe's Hide-a-Way.

### Activate Prior Knowledge

*A Christmas Carol* begins with the ghost of Jacob Marley. Think of other fictional ghosts you know from movies, plays, or stories. What role do ghosts usually play in stories? Which ghost do you remember best?

_____

_____

_____

_____

### Stop to Reflect

A list of characters always comes at the beginning of a play. Why might a list of characters be helpful to the reader?

_____

_____

_____

### Reading Skill

**Preview a text** before reading. By looking over key elements, you can get a sense of what to expect in a text. Circle the names of the characters that tell you most about what the play will be like.

## Reading Skill

**Setting a purpose** for reading means figuring out what you expect from a text before you read it. What is your purpose for reading this play?

_____

_____

_____

## Literary Analysis

The words characters say are called **dialogue**. Dialogue in a play is written for actors to say for an audience. A play does not include "he said" or "she said" to tell readers who is speaking. Who says the first words in this play? Circle the text that tells whom is speaking.

## Reading Check

Underline the passages that describe when this play takes place.

THE TIME OF THE PLAY *The entire action of the play takes place on Christmas Eve, Christmas Day, and the morning after Christmas, 1843.*

### Scene 1

*(Ghostly music in auditorium. A single spotlight on* JACOB MARLEY, D.C. *He is ancient; awful, dead-eyed. He speaks straight out to auditorium.)*

**MARLEY.** *(Cackle-voiced)* My name is Jacob Marley and I am dead. *(He laughs.)* Oh, no, there's no doubt that I am dead. The register of my burial was signed by the clergyman, the clerk, the undertaker . . . and by my chief mourner . . . Ebenezer Scrooge . . . *(Pause; remembers)* I am dead as a doornail.

*(A spotlight fades up, Stage Right, on* SCROOGE, *in his countinghouse,[1] counting. Lettering on the window behind* SCROOGE *reads:* "SCROOGE AND MARLEY, LTD." *The spotlight is tight on* SCROOGE's *head and shoulders. We shall not yet see into the offices and setting. Ghostly music continues, under.* MARLEY *looks across at* SCROOGE; *pitifully. After a moment's pause)*

I present him to you: Ebenezer Scrooge . . . England's most tightfisted hand at the grindstone, Scrooge! a squeezing, wrenching, grasping, scraping, clutching, covetous, old sinner! secret, and self-contained, and solitary as an oyster. The cold within him freezes his old features, nips his pointed nose, shrivels his cheek, stiffens his gait; makes his eyes red, his thin lips blue; and speaks out shrewdly in his grating voice. Look at him. Look at him . . .

*(SCROOGE counts and mumbles.)*

**SCROOGE.** They owe me money and I will collect. I will have them jailed, if I have to. They owe me money and I will collect what is due me.

*(MARLEY moves towards SCROOGE; two steps. The spotlight stays with him.)*

**MARLEY.** *(Disgusted)* He and I were partners for I don't know how many years. Scrooge was my sole executor, my sole administrator, my sole

---

1. **countinghouse** office for keeping financial records and writing business letters.

assign, my sole residuary legatee,[2] my sole friend
and my sole mourner. But Scrooge was not so
cut up by the sad event of my death, but that
he was an excellent man of business on the very
day of my funeral, and solemnized[3] it with an
undoubted bargain. *(Pauses again in disgust)* He
never painted out my name from the window.
There it stands, on the window and above the
warehouse door: Scrooge and Marley. Sometimes
people new to our business call him Scrooge and
sometimes they call him Marley. He answers to
both names. It's all the same to him. And it's
cheaper than painting in a new sign, isn't it?
*(Pauses; moves closer to SCROOGE)* Nobody has ever
stopped him in the street to say, with gladsome
looks, "My dear Scrooge, how are you? When will
you come to see me?" No beggars <u>implored</u> him
to bestow a trifle, no children ever ask him what
it is o'clock, no man or woman now, or ever in
his life, not once, inquire the way to such and
such a place. *(MARLEY stands next to SCROOGE now.
They share, so it seems, a spotlight.)* But what
does Scrooge care of any of this? It is the very
thing he likes! To edge his way along the crowded
paths of life, warning all human sympathy to
keep its distance.

*(A ghostly bell rings in the distance. MARLEY moves
away from SCROOGE, now, heading d. again. As he
does, he "takes" the light: SCROOGE has disappeared
into the black void beyond. MARLEY walks d.c., talking
directly to the audience. Pauses)*

The bell tolls and I must take my leave. You must
stay a while with Scrooge and watch him play
out his scroogey life. It is now the story: the once-
upon-a-time. Scrooge is busy in his counting
house. Where else? Christmas eve and Scrooge is

**Vocabulary Development**

**implored** (im PLAWRD) *v.* begged

2. **my sole executor** (ig ZEK yuht er) **my sole administrator, my sole assign** (uh SYN), **my sole residuary legatee**
(ri ZID yoo er ee LEG uh tee) legal terms giving one person responsibility to carry out the wishes of another who
has died.

3. **solemnized** (SAHL uhm nyzd) *v.* honored or remembered. Marley is being sarcastic.

© Pearson Education

---

## TAKE NOTES

### Reading Skill

Your **purpose** for reading a text
is what you expect to get out of
it. For example, you might
expect to be entertained, or to
gain some kind of
understanding. Based on
Marley's speech to the audience,
what is your purpose for reading
the play that follows?

_____

_____

_____

### Stop to Reflect

The stage directions in this play
are printed in italics. They
describe the settings and the
characters' appearances and
actions. Why are the bracketed
stage directions important?

_____

_____

_____

### Reading Skill

Why is Marley's name still
painted on the window?
Underline the answer in the text.

**Stop to Reflect**

Read the underlined stage direction. Why do you think the author wants explosions when Marley comes and goes?

_____

_____

_____

**Literary Analysis**

What can you tell about Scrooge from his first words of **dialogue** in Scene 2?

_____

_____

_____

**Reading Check** ✎

Why is Bob Cratchit cold? Circle the answer in the text.

---

busy in his counting-house. It is cold, bleak, biting weather outside: foggy withal: and, if you listen closely, you can hear the people in the court go wheezing up and down, beating their hands upon their breasts, and stamping their feet upon the pavement stones to warm them . . .

*(The clocks outside strike three.)*

Only three! and quite dark outside already: it has not been light all day this day.

*(This ghostly bell rings in the distance again.* MARLEY *looks about him. Music in.* MARLEY *flies away.)*

### Scene 2

*(N.B.* MARLEY'S *comings and goings should, from time to time, induce the explosion of the odd flash-pot.* I.H.*)*

*(Christmas music in, sung by a live chorus, full. At conclusion of song, sound fades under and into the distance. Lights up in set: offices of Scrooge and Marley, Ltd.* SCROOGE *sits at his desk, at work. Near him is a tiny fire. His door is open and in his line of vision, we see* SCROOGE'S *clerk,* BOB CRATCHIT, *who sits in a dismal tank of a cubicle, copying letters. Near* CRATCHIT *is a fire so tiny as to barely cast a light: perhaps it is one pitifully glowing coal?* CRATCHIT *rubs his hands together, puts on a white comforter[4] and tries to heat his hands around his candle.* SCROOGE'S NEPHEW *enters, unseen.)*

SCROOGE. What are you doing, Cratchit? Acting cold, are you? Next, you'll be asking to replenish your coal from my coal-box, won't you? Well, save your breath, Cratchit! Unless you're prepared to find employ elsewhere!

NEPHEW. *(Cheerfully; surprising* SCROOGE*)* A merry Christmas to you, Uncle! God save you!

SCROOGE. Bah! Humbug![5]

NEPHEW. Christmas a "humbug," Uncle? I'm sure you don't mean that.

SCROOGE. I do! Merry Christmas? What right do you have to be merry? What reason have you to be merry? You're poor enough!

---

4. **comforter** (KUM fuhr tuhr) *n.* long, woolen scarf.

5. **Humbug** (HUM bug) *interj.* nonsense.

**NEPHEW.** Come, then. What right have you to be dismal? What reason have you to be <u>morose</u>? You're rich enough.

**SCROOGE.** Bah! Humbug!

**NEPHEW.** Don't be cross, Uncle.

**SCROOGE.** What else can I be? Eh? When I live in a world of fools such as this? Merry Christmas? What's Christmastime to you but a time of paying bills without any money; a time for finding yourself a year older, but not an hour richer. If I could work my will, every idiot who goes about with "Merry Christmas" on his lips, should be boiled with his own pudding, and buried with a stake of holly through his heart. He should!

**NEPHEW.** Uncle!

**SCROOGE.** Nephew! You keep Christmas in your own way and let me keep it in mine.

**NEPHEW.** Keep it! But you don't keep it, Uncle.

**SCROOGE.** Let me leave it alone, then. Much good it has ever done you!

**NEPHEW.** There are many things from which I have derived good, by which I have not profited, I daresay. Christmas among the rest. But I am sure that I always thought of Christmas time, when it has come round—as a good time: the only time I know of, when men and women seem to open their shut-up hearts freely, and to think of people below them as if they really were fellow passengers to the grave, and not another race of creatures bound on other journeys. And therefore, Uncle, though it has never put a scrap of gold or silver in my pocket, I believe that it has done me good, and that it will do me good; and I say, God bless it!

*(The clerk in the tank applauds, looks at the furious* SCROOGE *and pokes out his tiny fire, as if in exchange for the moment of impropriety.* SCROOGE *yells at him.)*

© Pearson Education

**Vocabulary Development**
**morose** (muh ROHS) *adj.* gloomy; ill-tempered

## TAKE NOTES

### Literary Analysis

What does the bracketed **dialogue** show readers about the nephew's attitude?

_____

_____

_____

What does the dialogue show readers about Scrooge's attitude?

_____

_____

_____

### Stop to Reflect

Scrooge and his nephew are from the same family. Why do you think they have such different personalities?

_____

_____

_____

### Reading Skill

One **purpose** you might have for reading this play is to learn a lesson about the meaning of Christmas. Underline a passage that would help meet this purpose.

## Literary Analysis

Read the bracketed **dialogue** between Scrooge and his nephew. What differences between them does it show?

_____

_____

_____

## Stop to Reflect

What is Scrooge's attitude toward love?

_____

_____

Why do you think he feels this way?

_____

_____

_____

## Reading Check

What does Scrooge say is more ridiculous than "Merry Christmas"? Circle the answer in the text.

---

**SCROOGE.** *(To the clerk)* Let me hear another sound from you and you'll keep your Christmas by losing your situation. *(To the nephew)* You're quite a powerful speaker, sir. I wonder you don't go into Parliament.[6]

**NEPHEW.** Don't be angry, Uncle. Come! Dine with us tomorrow.

**SCROOGE.** I'd rather see myself dead than see myself with your family!

**NEPHEW.** But, why? Why?

**SCROOGE.** Why did you get married?

**NEPHEW.** Because I fell in love.

**SCROOGE.** That, sir, is the only thing that you have said to me in your entire lifetime which is even more ridiculous than "Merry Christmas"! *(Turns from NEPHEW)* Good afternoon.

**NEPHEW.** Nay, Uncle, you never came to see me before I married either. Why give it as a reason for not coming now?

**SCROOGE.** Good afternoon, Nephew!

**NEPHEW.** I want nothing from you; I ask nothing of you; why cannot we be friends?

**SCROOGE.** Good afternoon!

**NEPHEW.** I am sorry with all my heart, to find you so resolute. But I have made the trial in homage to Christmas, and I'll keep my Christmas humor to the last. So A Merry Christmas, Uncle!

**SCROOGE.** Good afternoon!

**NEPHEW.** And A Happy New Year!

**SCROOGE.** Good afternoon!

**NEPHEW.** *(He stands facing SCROOGE.)* Uncle, you are the most . . . *(Pauses)* No, I shan't. My Christmas humor is intact . . . *(Pause)* God bless you, Uncle . . . *(NEPHEW turns and starts for the door; he stops at CRATCHIT's cage.)* Merry Christmas, Bob Cratchit . . .

**CRATCHIT.** Merry Christmas to you sir, and a very, very happy New Year . . .

---

6. **Parliament** (PAHR luh muhnt) national legislative body of Great Britain, in some ways like the United States Congress.

**SCROOGE.** *(Calling across to them)* Oh, fine, a perfection, just fine . . . to see the perfect pair of you: husbands, with wives and children to support . . . my clerk there earning fifteen shillings a week . . . and the perfect pair of you, talking about a Merry Christmas! *(Pauses)* I'll retire to Bedlam![7]

**NEPHEW.** *(To CRATCHIT)* He's impossible!

**CRATCHIT.** Oh, mind him not, sir. He's getting on in years, and he's alone. He's noticed your visit. I'll wager your visit has warmed him.

**NEPHEW.** Him? Uncle Ebenezer Scrooge? Warmed? You are a better Christian than I am, sir.

**CRATCHIT.** *(Opening the door for NEPHEW; two DO-GOODERS will enter, as NEPHEW exits)* Good day to you, sir, and God bless.

**NEPHEW.** God bless . . . *(One man who enters is portly, the other is thin. Both are pleasant.)*

**CRATCHIT.** Can I help you, gentlemen?

**THIN MAN.** *(Carrying papers and books; looks around CRATCHIT to SCROOGE)* Scrooge and Marley's, I believe. Have I the pleasure of addressing Mr. Scrooge, or Mr. Marley?

**SCROOGE.** Mr. Marley has been dead these seven years. He died seven years ago this very night.

**PORTLY MAN.** We have no doubt his liberality[8] is well represented by his surviving partner . . . *(Offers his calling card)*

**SCROOGE.** *(Handing back the card; unlooked at)* . . . Good afternoon.

**THIN MAN.** This will take but a moment, sir . . .

**PORTLY MAN.** At this festive season of the year, Mr. Scrooge, it is more than usually desirable that we should make some slight provision for the poor and <u>destitute</u>, who suffer greatly at

© Pearson Education

---

**Vocabulary Development**

**destitute** (DES tuh toot) *adj.* used as n. people living in complete poverty

---

7. **Bedlam** (BED luhm) hospital in London for the mentally ill.

8. **liberality** (lib uhr AL i tee) generosity.

---

**Reading Skill**

You are beginning to get an idea of what kind of person Scrooge is from his relationship with Cratchit and his nephew. What **purpose** for reading do you have at this point in the play?

_____

_____

What questions do you want answered?

_____

_____

_____

**Literary Analysis** 🔍

Sometimes even short pieces of **dialogue** can tell you something about a character. Read the bracketed passage. What do Cratchit's words to the nephew tell you about Cratchit?

_____

_____

_____

**Reading Check**

How long ago did Marley die? Circle the answer in the text.

## Literary Analysis

What a character says tells you about his or her beliefs and feelings. What does the bracketed **dialogue** tell you about Scrooge's attitude toward the poor?

_____

_____

## Stop to Reflect

What do you think life was like for poor people in the time and place this play takes place?

_____

_____

_____

## Reading Skill

One **purpose** you might have for reading this play is to find out what will happen to Scrooge. What lesson do you think Scrooge will learn as the play continues?

_____

_____

Underline any passages that make you expect Scrooge will learn a Christmas lesson.

the present time. Many thousands are in want of common necessities; hundreds of thousands are in want of common comforts, sir.

**SCROOGE.** Are there no prisons?

**PORTLY MAN.** Plenty of prisons.

**SCROOGE.** And aren't the Union workhouses still in operation?

**THIN MAN.** They are. Still. I wish that I could say that they are not.

**SCROOGE.** The Treadmill[9] and the Poor Law[10] are in full vigor, then?

**THIN MAN.** Both very busy, sir.

**SCROOGE.** Ohhh, I see. I was afraid, from what you said at first, that something had occurred to stop them from their useful course. *(Pauses)* I'm glad to hear it.

**PORTLY MAN.** Under the impression that they scarcely furnish Christian cheer of mind or body to the multitude, a few of us are endeavoring to raise a fund to buy the Poor some meat and drink, and means of warmth. We choose this time, because it is a time, of all others, when Want is keenly felt, and Abundance rejoices.
*(Pen in hand; as well as notepad)* What shall I put you down for, sir?

**SCROOGE.** Nothing!

**PORTLY MAN.** You wish to be left anonymous?

**SCROOGE.** I wish to be left alone! *(Pauses; turns away; turns back to them)* Since you ask me what I wish, gentlemen, that is my answer. I help to support the establishments that I have mentioned: they cost enough: and those who are badly off must go there.

**THIN MAN.** Many can't go there; and many would rather die.

---

9. **the Treadmill** (TRED mil) kind of mill wheel turned by the weight of people treading steps arranged around it; this device was used to punish prisoners.

10. **the Poor Law** the original 17th-century Poor Laws called for overseers of the poor in each neighborhood to provide relief for the needy. The New Poor Law of 1834 made the workhouses in which the poor sometimes lived and worked extremely hard and unattractive.

**SCROOGE.** If they would rather die, they had better do it, and decrease the surplus population. Besides—excuse me—I don't know that.

**THIN MAN.** But you might know it!

**SCROOGE.** It's not my business. It's enough for a man to understand his own business, and not to interfere with other people's. Mine occupies me constantly. Good afternoon, gentlemen! *(SCROOGE turns his back on the gentlemen and returns to his desk.)*

**PORTLY MAN.** But, sir, Mr. Scrooge . . . think of the poor.

**SCROOGE.** *(Turns suddenly to them. Pauses)* Take your leave of my offices, sirs, while I am still smiling.

*(The THIN MAN looks at the PORTLY MAN. They are undone. They shrug. They move to the door. CRATCHIT hops up to open it for them.)*

**THIN MAN.** Good day, sir . . . *(To CRATCHIT)* A merry Christmas to you, sir . . .

**CRATCHIT.** Yes. A Merry Christmas to both of you . . .

**PORTLY MAN.** Merry Christmas . . .

*(CRATCHIT silently squeezes something into the hand of the THIN MAN.)*

**THIN MAN.** What's this?

**CRATCHIT.** Shhhh . . .

*(CRATCHIT opens the door; wind and snow whistle into the room.)*

**THIN MAN.** Thank you, sir, thank you.

*(CRATCHIT closes the door and returns to his workplace. SCROOGE is at his own counting table. He talks to CRATCHIT without looking up.)*

**SCROOGE.** It's less of a time of year for being merry, and more a time of year for being loony . . . if you ask me.

**CRATCHIT.** Well, I don't know, sir . . . *(The clock's bell strikes six o'clock.)* Well, there it is, eh, six?

**SCROOGE.** Saved by six bells, are you?

**CRATCHIT.** I must be going home . . . *(He snuffs out his candle and puts on his hat.)* I hope you have a . . . very very lovely day tomorrow, sir . . .

**Stop to Reflect**

What do you think Cratchit squeezes into the thin man's hand?

_____

_____

What does this action tell you about Cratchit?

_____

_____

_____

**Literary Analysis** 🔍

Ellipses ( . . . ) are used on this page to show pauses in **dialogue**. Circle all of the ellipses on the page. Who does not pause in his speaking?

_____

Read the bracketed passage. What can you guess Cratchit wants to say to Scrooge in the places where he pauses?

_____

_____

**Reading Check**

Why doesn't Scrooge give the thin man money? Underline the answer.

## Literary Analysis

Read the bracketed **dialogue** between Scrooge and Cratchit. How does this dialogue help you learn about Scrooge's personality?

_____

_____

_____

## Stop to Reflect

Cratchit wishes Scrooge a merry Christmas, although Scrooge warns him not to. Underline the stage directions that show Cratchit is nervous about saying "Merry Christmas."

## Reading Check

Underline the sentence that tells what Cratchit agrees to.

**SCROOGE.** Hmmm. Oh, you'll be wanting the whole day tomorrow, I suppose?

**CRATCHIT.** If quite convenient, sir.

**SCROOGE.** It's not convenient, and it's not fair. If I was to stop half-a-crown for it, you'd think yourself ill-used, I'll be bound?

*(CRATCHIT smiles faintly.)*

**CRATCHIT.** I don't know, sir . . .

**SCROOGE.** And yet, you don't think me ill-used when I pay a day's wages for no work . . .

**CRATCHIT.** It's only but once a year . . .

**SCROOGE.** A poor excuse for picking a man's pocket every 25th of December! But I suppose you must have the whole day. Be here all the earlier the next morning!

**CRATCHIT.** Oh, I will, sir. I will. I promise you. And, sir . . .

**SCROOGE.** Don't say it, Cratchit.

**CRATCHIT.** But let me wish you a . . .

**SCROOGE.** Don't say it, Cratchit. I warn you . . .

**CRATCHIT.** Sir!

**SCROOGE.** Cratchit!

*(CRATCHIT opens the door.)*

**CRATCHIT.** All right, then, sir . . . well . . . *(Suddenly)* Merry Christmas, Mr. Scrooge!

*(And he runs out the door, shutting same behind him. SCROOGE moves to his desk; gathering his coat, hat, etc. A BOY appears at his window. . . .)*

**BOY.** *(Singing)* "Away in a manger . . ."

*(SCROOGE seizes his ruler and whacks at the image of the BOY outside. The BOY leaves.)*

**SCROOGE.** Bah! Humbug! Christmas! Bah! Humbug! (He shuts out the light.)

*A note on the crossover, following Scene 2:*

*(SCROOGE will walk alone to his rooms from his offices. As he makes a long slow cross of the stage, the scenery should change. Christmas music will be heard, various people will cross by SCROOGE, often smiling happily.*

There will be occasional pleasant greetings tossed at him.

SCROOGE, in contrast to all, will grump and mumble. He will snap at passing boys, as might a horrid old hound.

In short, SCROOGE's sounds and movements will define him in contrast from all other people who cross the stage: he is the misanthrope,[11] the malcontent, the miser. He is SCROOGE.

This statement of SCROOGE's character, by contrast to all other characters, should seem comical to the audience.

During SCROOGE's crossover to his rooms, snow should begin to fall. All passers-by will hold their faces to the sky, smiling, allowing snow to shower them lightly. SCROOGE, by contrast, will bat at the flakes with his walking-stick, as might an insomniac swat at a sleep-stopping, middle-of-the-night swarm of mosquitoes. He will comment on the blackness of the night, and, finally, reach his rooms and his encounter with the magical specter:[12] MARLEY, his eternal mate.)

## Scene 3

**SCROOGE.** No light at all . . . no moon . . . that is what is at the center of a Christmas Eve: dead black: void . . .

(SCROOGE puts his key in the door's keyhole. He has reached his rooms now. The door knocker changes and is now MARLEY's face. A musical sound; quickly: ghostly. MARLEY's image is not at all angry, but looks at SCROOGE as did the old MARLEY look at SCROOGE. The hair is curiously stirred; eyes wide open, dead: absent of focus. SCROOGE stares wordlessly here. The face, before his very eyes, does deliquesce.[13] It is a knocker again. SCROOGE opens the door and checks the back of same, probably for MARLEY's pigtail. Seeing nothing but screws and nuts, SCROOGE refuses the memory.)

Pooh, pooh!

(The sound of the door closing resounds throughout the house as thunder. Every room echoes the sound.

## Vocabulary Development
**void** (VOYD) n. emptiness

---

11. **misanthrope** (MIS uhn throhp) n. person who hates or distrusts everyone.

12. **specter** (SPEK tuhr) n. ghost.

13. **deliquesce** (del i KWES) v. melt away.

---

### TAKE NOTES

**Stop to Reflect**

The author says Scrooge is so different from other people he seems "comical." Do you find Scrooge funny? How would you describe him to a friend?

_____

_____

_____

**Reading Skill**

Based on the stage directions at the beginning of Scene 3, what is your **purpose** for reading?

_____

_____

_____

**Reading Check** ✏

A sound tells the audience that Marley's ghost has arrived in the house. Underline the stage direction that describes the sound.

Read the bracketed passage.
Based on Scrooge's dialogue,
what does he think of the sights
and sounds at the beginning of
this scene?

_____

_____

_____

Underline any details that
suggest Scrooge does not really
feel the way he says he feels.

**Stop to Reflect**

Why do you think Scrooge
refuses to believe that he is
hearing noises?

_____

_____

_____

**Reading Check**

Underline the sentence that
describes what Scrooge eats.

SCROOGE *fastens the door and walks across the hall
to the stairs, trimming his candle as he goes; and
then he goes slowly up the staircase. He checks
each room: sitting room, bedrooms, slumber room. He
looks under the sofa, under the table: nobody there.
He fixes his evening gruel on the hob,*[14] *changes his
jacket.* SCROOGE *sits near the tiny low-flamed fire,
sipping his gruel. There are various pictures on the
walls: all of them now show likenesses of* MARLEY.
SCROOGE *blinks his eyes.*)

Bah! Humbug!

(SCROOGE *walks in a circle about the room. The pictures
change back into their natural images. He sits down at
the table in front of the fire. A bell hangs overhead. It
begins to ring, of its own accord. Slowly, surely, begins
the ringing of every bell in the house. They continue
ringing for nearly half a minute.* SCROOGE *is stunned
by the phenomenon. The bells cease their ringing all
at once. Deep below* SCROOGE, *in the basement of
the house, there is the sound of clanking, of some
enormous chain being dragged across the floors;
and now up the stairs. We hear doors flying open.*)

Bah still! Humbug still! This is not happening! I
won't believe it!

(MARLEY'S GHOST *enters the room. He is horrible to
look at: pigtail, vest, suit as usual, but he drags an
enormous chain now, to which is fastened cash-boxes,
keys, padlocks, ledgers, deeds, and heavy purses
fashioned of steel. He is transparent.* MARLEY *stands
opposite the stricken* SCROOGE.)

How now! What do you want of me?

**MARLEY.** Much!

**SCROOGE.** Who are you?

**MARLEY.** Ask me who I was.

**SCROOGE.** Who were you then?

**MARLEY.** In life, I was your business partner: Jacob
    Marley.

**SCROOGE.** I see . . . can you sit down?

**MARLEY.** I can.

---

14. **gruel** (GROO uhl) **on the hob** (hahb) thin broth warming on a ledge at the back
    or side of the fireplace.

**SCROOGE.** *Do it then.*

**MARLEY.** I shall. *(MARLEY sits opposite SCROOGE, in the chair across the table, at the front of the fireplace.)* You don't believe in me.

**SCROOGE.** I don't.

**MARLEY.** Why do you doubt your senses?

**SCROOGE.** Because every little thing affects them. A slight disorder of the stomach makes them cheat. You may be an undigested bit of beef, a blot of mustard, a crumb of cheese, a fragment of an underdone potato. There's more of gravy than of grave about you, whatever you are!

*(There is a silence between them. SCROOGE is made nervous by it. He picks up a toothpick.)*

Humbug! I tell you: humbug!

*(MARLEY opens his mouth and screams a ghosty, fearful scream. The scream echoes about each room of the house. Bats fly, cats screech, lightning flashes. SCROOGE stands and walks backwards against the wall. MARLEY stands and screams again. This time, he takes his head and lifts it from his shoulders. His head continues to scream. MARLEY's face again appears on every picture in the room: all screaming. SCROOGE, on his knees before MARLEY.)*

Mercy! Dreadful apparition,[15] mercy! Why, O! why do you trouble me so?

**MARLEY.** Man of the worldly mind, do you believe in me, or not?

**SCROOGE.** I do. I must. But why do spirits such as you walk the earth? And why do they come to me?

**MARLEY.** It is required of every man that the spirit within him should walk abroad among his fellow-men, and travel far and wide; and if that spirit goes not forth in life, it is condemned to do so after death. *(MARLEY screams again; a tragic scream; from his ghosty bones.)* I wear the chain I forged in life. I made it link by link, and yard by yard. Is its pattern strange to you? Or would you know, you, Scrooge, the weight and length of the strong coil you bear yourself? It was full as heavy and long as this, seven Christmas Eves ago. You have labored on it, since. It is a ponderous chain.

15. **apparition** (ap uh RISH uhn) *n.* ghost.

## Literary Analysis

**Dialogue** shows audiences characters' attitudes. Read the first bracketed passage. How do you think Scrooge feels about ghosts?

_____

_____

_____

## Reading Skill

Read the second bracketed passage. What **purpose** for reading do you have after reading Scrooge's questions?

_____

_____

_____

## Reading Check

Scrooge says he does not believe in Marley. Underline the reasons that Scrooge gives for doubting what he sees.

## Literary Analysis 🔍

Read the first bracketed passage. What emotion does Marley show in his **dialogue**? Explain your answer.

_____

_____

_____

## Reading Skill 📖

Read the second bracketed passage. Summarize what Marley tells Scrooge in the underlined sentence.

_____

_____

_____

Based on this sentence, what **purpose** do you have for reading the rest of the play?

_____

_____

_____

_____

*(Terrified that a chain will appear about his body,* SCROOGE *spins and waves the unwanted chain away. None, of course, appears. Sees* MARLEY *watching him dance about the room.* MARLEY *watches* SCROOGE; *silently.)*

**SCROOGE.** Jacob. Old Jacob Marley, tell me more. Speak comfort to me, Jacob . . .

**MARLEY.** I have none to give. Comfort comes from other regions, Ebenezer Scrooge, and is <u>conveyed</u> by other ministers, to other kinds of men. A very little more, is all that is permitted to me. I cannot rest, I cannot stay, I cannot linger anywhere . . . *(He moans again.)* my spirit never walked beyond our countinghouse—mark me!—in life my spirit never roved beyond the narrow limits of our moneychanging hole; and weary journeys lie before me!

**SCROOGE.** But you were always a good man of business, Jacob.

**MARLEY.** *(Screams word "business"; a flash-pot explodes with him.)* BUSINESS!!! Mankind was my business. The common welfare was my business; charity, mercy, forbearance, <u>benevolence</u>, were, all, my business. *(*SCROOGE *is quaking.)* Hear me, Ebenezer Scrooge! My time is nearly gone.

**SCROOGE.** I will, but don't be hard upon me. And don't be flowery, Jacob! Pray!

**MARLEY.** How is it that I appear before you in a shape that you can see, I may not tell. I have sat invisible beside you many and many a day. That is no light part of my penance. <u>I am here tonight to warn you that you have yet a chance and hope of escaping my fate.</u> A chance and hope of my procuring, Ebenezer.

**SCROOGE.** You were always a good friend to me. Thank'ee!

**MARLEY.** You will be haunted by Three Spirits.

### Vocabulary Development

**conveyed** (kuhn VAYD) *v.* made known; expressed
**benevolence** (buh NEV uh luhns) *n.* kindliness

**SCROOGE.** Would that be the chance and hope you mentioned, Jacob?

**MARLEY.** It is.

**SCROOGE.** I think I'd rather not.

**MARLEY.** Without their visits, you cannot hope to shun the path I tread. Expect the first one tomorrow, when the bell tolls one.

**SCROOGE.** Couldn't I take 'em all at once, and get it over, Jacob?

**MARLEY.** Expect the second on the next night at the same hour. The third upon the next night when the last stroke of twelve has ceased to vibrate. Look to see me no more. Others may, but you may not. And look that, for your own sake, you remember what has passed between us!

*(MARLEY places his head back upon his shoulders. He approaches the window and beckons to SCROOGE to watch. Outside the window, specters fly by, carrying money-boxes and chains. They make a confused sound of lamentation. MARLEY, after listening a moment, joins into their mournful dirge. He leans to the window and floats out into the bleak, dark night. He is gone.)*

**SCROOGE.** *(Rushing to the window)* Jacob! No, Jacob! Don't leave me! I'm frightened!

*(He sees that MARLEY has gone. He looks outside. He pulls the shutter closed, so that the scene is blocked from his view. All sound stops. After a pause, he re-opens the shutter and all is quiet, as it should be on Christmas Eve. Carolers carol out of doors, in the distance. SCROOGE closes the shutter and walks down the stairs. He examines the door by which MARLEY first entered.)*

No one here at all! Did I imagine all that? Humbug! *(He looks about the room.)* I did imagine it. It only happened in my foulest dream-mind, didn't it? An undigested bit of . . .

*(Thunder and lightning in the room; suddenly)*

Sorry! Sorry!

*(There is silence again. The lights fade out.)*

*(Christmas music, choral, "Hark the Herald Angels Sing," sung by an onstage choir of children, spotlighted, d.c. Above, SCROOGE in his bed, dead to*

**Stop to Reflect**

Read the underlined stage directions. What conclusion can you draw from the many ghosts carrying money-boxes and chains?

_____

_____

_____

**Literary Analysis**

In a play, audiences can only learn about characters from their **dialogue**. What is the most revealing thing Scrooge says in this scene? Circle the line that shows you the most about Scrooge's character.

**Reading Skill**

Read the bracketed passage. Asking questions can help you set a **purpose**. What questions do you have about what will happen to Scrooge?

_____

_____

_____

## Literary Analysis

Sometimes, characters speak directly to the audience. This kind of **dialogue** is called an aside. What information does Marley give the audience in the bracketed lines?

_____

_____

_____

## Stop to Reflect

Underline the sentences that show whether or not Scrooge has changed after Marley's visit.

## Reading Check

Who can see Marley? Who cannot see him? Circle the answers in the text.

the world, asleep, in his darkened room. It should appear that the choir is singing somewhere outside of the house, of course, and a use of scrim[16] is thus suggested. When the singing is ended, the choir should fade out of view and MARLEY should fade into view, in their place.)

**MARLEY.** *(Directly to audience)* From this point forth . . . I shall be quite visible to you, but invisible to him. *(Smiles)* He will feel my presence, nevertheless, for, unless my senses fail me completely, we are—you and I—witness to the changing of a miser: that one, my partner in life, in business, and in eternity: that one: Scrooge. *(Moves to staircase, below SCROOGE)* See him now. He endeavors to pierce the darkness with his ferret eyes.[17] *(To audience)* See him, now. He listens for the hour.

*(The bells toll. SCROOGE is awakened and quakes as the hour approaches one o'clock, but the bells stop their sound at the hour of twelve.)*

**SCROOGE.** *(Astonished)* Midnight! Why this isn't possible. It was past two when I went to bed. An icicle must have gotten into the clock's works! I couldn't have slept through the whole day and far into another night. It isn't possible that anything has happened to the sun, and this is twelve at noon! *(He runs to window; unshutters same; it is night.)* Night, still. Quiet, normal for the season, cold. It is certainly not noon. I cannot in any way afford to lose my days. Securities come due, promissory notes,[18] interest on investments: these are things that happen in the daylight! *(He returns to his bed.)* Was this a dream?

*(MARLEY appears in his room. He speaks to the audience.)*

**MARLEY.** You see? He does not, with faith, believe in me fully, even still! Whatever will it take to turn the faith of a miser from money to men?

**SCROOGE.** Another quarter and it'll be one and Marley's ghosty friends will come. *(Pauses; listens)*

16. **scrim** (skrim) *n.* see-through fabric used to create special effects in the theater.

17. **ferret eyes** a ferret is a small, weasel-like animal used for hunting rabbits; this expression means to stare continously, the way a ferret hunts.

18. **promissory** (prahm i SAWR ee) **notes** written promises to pay someone a certain sum of money.

Where's the chime for one? *(Ding, dong)* A quarter past *(Repeats)* Half-past! *(Repeats)* A quarter to it! But where's the heavy bell of the hour one? This is a game in which I lose my senses! Perhaps, if I allowed myself another short doze . . .

**MARLEY.** . . . Doze, Ebenezer, doze.

*(A heavy bell thuds its one ring; dull and definitely one o'clock. There is a flash of light. SCROOGE sits up, in a sudden. A hand draws back the curtains by his bed. He sees it.)*

**SCROOGE.** A hand! Who owns it! Hello!

*(Ghosty music again, but of a new nature to the play. A strange figure stands before SCROOGE—like a child, yet at the same time like an old man: white hair, but unwrinkled skin, long, muscular arms, but delicate legs and feet. Wears white tunic; lustrous belt cinches waist. Branch of fresh green holly in its hand, but has its dress trimmed with fresh summer flowers. Clear jets of light spring from the crown of its head. Holds cap in hand. The Spirit is called PAST.)*

Are you the Spirit, sir, whose coming was foretold to me?

**PAST.** I am.

**MARLEY.** Does he take this to be a vision of his green grocer?

### Scene 4

**SCROOGE.** Who, and what are you?

**PAST.** I am the Ghost of Christmas Past.

**SCROOGE.** Long past?

**PAST.** Your past.

**SCROOGE.** May I ask, please, sir, what business you have here with me?

**PAST.** Your welfare.

**SCROOGE.** Not to sound ungrateful, sir, and really, please do understand that I am plenty obliged for your concern, but, really, kind spirit, it would have done all the better for my welfare to have been left alone altogether, to have slept peacefully through this night.

**PAST.** Your reclamation, then. Take heed!

**Reading Skill** 📖

Read the bracketed stage direction. What **purpose** would you set for reading this scene?

_____

_____

_____

**Literary Analysis** 🔍

How would you describe the **dialogue** between Scrooge and the Ghost of Christmas Past?

_____

_____

_____

What can you tell about how Scrooge has changed from the way he speaks to the ghost?

_____

_____

_____

_____

**SCROOGE.** My what?

**PAST.** *(Motioning to* SCROOGE *and taking his arm)* Rise! Fly with me! *(He leads* SCROOGE *to the window.)*

**SCROOGE.** *(Panicked)* Fly, but I am a mortal and cannot fly!

**PAST.** *(Pointing to his heart)* Bear but a touch of my hand here and you shall be upheld in more than this!

*(*SCROOGE *touches the spirit's heart and the lights dissolve into sparkly flickers. Lovely crystals of music are heard. The scene dissolves into another. Christmas music again)*

### Scene 5

*(*SCROOGE *and the* GHOST OF CHRISTMAS PAST *walk together across an open stage. In the background, we see a field that is open; covered by a soft, downy snow: a country road.)*

**SCROOGE.** Good Heaven! I was bred in this place. I was a boy here!

*(*SCROOGE *freezes, staring at the field beyond.* MARLEY'S *ghost appears beside him; takes* SCROOGE'S *face in his hands, and turns his face to the audience.)*

**MARLEY.** You see this Scrooge: stricken by feeling. Conscious of a thousand odors floating in the air, each one connected with a thousand thoughts, and hopes, and joys, and care long, long forgotten. *(Pause)* This one—this Scrooge—before your very eyes, returns to life, among the living. *(To audience, sternly)* You'd best pay your most careful attention. I would suggest rapt.[19]

*(There is a small flash and puff of smoke and* MARLEY *is gone again.)*

**PAST.** Your lip is trembling, Mr. Scrooge. And what is that upon your cheek?

**SCROOGE.** Upon my cheek? Nothing . . . a blemish on the skin from the eating of overmuch grease . . . nothing . . . *(Suddenly)* Kind Spirit of Christmas Past, lead me where you will, but quickly! To be stagnant in this place is, for me, unbearable!

---

**19. rapt**(RAPT) *adj.* giving complete attention; totally carried away by something.

## Reading Skill

Your **purpose** is what you expect to get from a text. Based on the first bracketed passage, what do you expect to happen in this scene?

_____

_____

## Literary Analysis

Circle the word Scrooge repeats in the second bracketed passage. Sometimes characters will repeat words that are important to them. How do Scrooge's words in this **dialogue** passage reveal feelings that he is trying to hide?

_____

_____

## Reading Check

Scene 5 begins in a new place. Underline the sentences that describe where Scrooge and the Ghost of Christmas Past are.

**PAST.** You recollect the way?

**SCROOGE.** Remember it! I would know it blindfolded!
My bridge, my church, my winding river! *(Staggers
about, trying to see it all at once. He weeps again.)*

**PAST.** These are but shadows of things that have
been. They have no consciousness of us.

*(Four jocund travelers enter, singing a Christmas song
in four-part harmony—"God Rest Ye Merry Gentlemen.")*

**SCROOGE.** Listen! I know these men! I know them! I
remember the beauty of their song!

**PAST.** But, why do you remember it so happily? It is
Merry Christmas that they say to one another!
What is Merry Christmas to you, Mr. Scrooge?
Out upon Merry Christmas, right? What good has
Merry Christmas ever done you, Mr. Scrooge? . . .

**SCROOGE.** *(After a long pause)* None. No good.
None . . . *(He bows his head.)*

**PAST.** Look, you, sir, a school ahead. The schoolroom
is not quite deserted. A solitary child, neglected
by his friends, is left there still.

*(SCROOGE falls to the ground; sobbing as he sees, and
we see, a small boy, the young SCROOGE, sitting and
weeping, bravely, alone at his desk: alone in a vast
space, a void.)*

**SCROOGE.** I cannot look on him!

**PAST.** You must, Mr. Scrooge, you must.

**SCROOGE.** It's me. *(Pauses; weeps)* Poor boy. He lived
inside his head . . . alone . . . *(Pauses; weeps)*
poor boy. *(Pauses; stops his weeping)* I wish . . .
*(Dries his eyes on his cuff)* ah! it's too late!

**PAST.** What is the matter?

**SCROOGE.** There was a boy singing a Christmas Carol
outside my door last night. I should like
to have given him something: that's all.

**PAST.** *(Smiles; waves his hand to SCROOGE)* Come.
Let us see another Christmas.

*(Lights out on little boy. A flash of light. A puff of
smoke. Lights up on older boy)*

**SCROOGE.** Look! Me, again! Older now! *(Realizes)* Oh,
yes . . . still alone.

**Stop to Reflect**

The Ghost of Christmas Past
brings Scrooge to visit his
childhood in this scene. How
would you feel visiting places
from your childhood?

_____

_____

_____

**Literary Analysis** 🔍

Read the bracketed passage.
Why do you think Scrooge
remembers the singing boy from
earlier in the play?

_____

_____

How does the bracketed
**dialogue** show changes in
Scrooge's attitude?

_____

_____

_____

**Reading Check**

Whom does Scrooge see that
makes him cry? Circle the stage
direction that describes who
he sees.

© Pearson Education

**Reading Skill**

Sometimes your **purpose** for reading is to find the answers to questions about a story. Read the first bracketed passage. Based on this passage, what questions do you have about Scrooge's family?

_____

_____

_____

**Stop to Reflect**

Underline the **dialogue** that shows Scrooge's feelings toward the Schoolmaster.

**Reading Check** ✐

How old is Fan in this Scene? Circle the answer in the text.

*(The boy—a slightly older SCROOGE—sits alone in a chair, reading. The door to the room opens and a young girl enters. She is much, much younger than this slightly older SCROOGE. She is, say, six, and he is, say, twelve. Elder SCROOGE and the GHOST OF CHRISTMAS PAST stand watching the scene, unseen.)*

**FAN.** Dear, dear brother, I have come to bring you home.

**BOY.** Home, little Fan?

**FAN.** Yes! Home, for good and all! Father is so much kinder than he ever used to be, and home's like heaven! He spoke so gently to me one dear night when I was going to bed that I was not afraid to ask him once more if you might come home; and he said "yes" . . . you should; and sent me in a coach to bring you. And you're to be a man and are never to come back here, but first, we're to be together all the Christmas long, and have the merriest time in the world.

**BOY.** You are quite a woman, little Fan!

*(Laughing; she drags at boy, causing him to stumble to the door with her. Suddenly we hear a mean and terrible voice in the hallway, Off. It is the SCHOOLMASTER.)*

**SCHOOLMASTER.** Bring down Master Scrooge's travel box at once! He is to travel!

**FAN.** Who is that, Ebenezer?

**BOY.** O! Quiet, Fan. It is the Schoolmaster, himself!

*(The door bursts open and into the room bursts with it the SCHOOLMASTER.)*

**SCHOOLMASTER.** Master Scrooge?

**BOY.** Oh, Schoolmaster. I'd like you to meet my little sister, Fan, sir . . .

*(Two boys struggle on with SCROOGE's trunk.)*

**FAN.** Pleased, sir . . . *(She curtsies.)*

**SCHOOLMASTER.** You are to travel, Master Scrooge.

**SCROOGE.** Yes, sir. I know sir . . .

*(All start to exit, but FAN grabs the coattail of the mean old SCHOOLMASTER.)*

**BOY.** Fan!

**SCHOOLMASTER.** What's this?

**FAN.** Pardon, sir, but I believe that you've forgotten to say your goodbye to my brother, Ebenezer, who stands still now awaiting it . . . *(She smiles, curtsies, lowers her eyes.)* pardon, sir.

**SCHOOLMASTER.** *(Amazed)* I . . . uh . . . harumph . . . uhh . . . well, then . . . *(Outstretches hand)* Goodbye, Scrooge.

**BOY.** Uh, well, goodbye, Schoolmaster . . .

*(Lights fade out on all but BOY looking at FAN; and SCROOGE and PAST looking at them.)*

**SCROOGE.** Oh, my dear, dear little sister, Fan . . . how I loved her.

**PAST.** Always a delicate creature, whom a breath might have withered, but she had a large heart . . .

**SCROOGE.** So she had.

**PAST.** She died a woman, and had, as I think, children.

**SCROOGE.** One child.

**PAST.** True. Your nephew.

**SCROOGE.** Yes.

**PAST.** Fine, then. We move on, Mr. Scrooge. That warehouse, there? Do you know it?

**SCROOGE.** Know it? Wasn't I apprenticed[20] there?

**PAST.** We'll have a look.

*(They enter the warehouse. The lights crossfade with them, coming up on an old man in Welsh wig: FEZZIWIG.)*

**SCROOGE.** Why, it's old Fezziwig! Bless his heart; it's Fezziwig, alive again!

*(FEZZIWIG sits behind a large, high desk, counting. He lays down his pen; looks at the clock: seven bells sound.)*

Quittin' time . . .

**FEZZIWIG.** Quittin' time . . . *(He takes off his waistcoat and laughs; calls off)* Yo ho, Ebenezer! Dick!

*(DICK WILKINS and EBENEZER SCROOGE—a young man version—enter the room. DICK and EBENEZER are FEZZIWIG's apprentices.)*

**SCROOGE.** Dick Wilkins, to be sure! My fellow- 'prentice! Bless my soul, yes. There he is. He was

© Pearson Education

20. **apprenticed** (uh PREN tist) *v.* received instruction in a trade as well as food and housing or wages in return for work.

---

## TAKE NOTES

### Literary Analysis

**Dialogue** can show audiences surprising things about a character. What surprising aspect of Scrooge's character does the bracketed dialogue show?

_____

_____

_____

### Stop to Reflect

Are you surprised to learn how much Scrooge loved Fan, his sister? Explain your answer.

_____

_____

_____

### Reading Check

What did Scrooge do at Fezziwig's? Circle the answer.

**Stop to Reflect**

Read the bracketed stage direction. Underline at least two details that help create the scene's mood.

**Literary Analysis** 🔍

Read the bracketed **dialogue**. What does it tell you about the young Scrooge's feelings for Fezziwig?

_____

_____

_____

_____

_____

_____

Do you find Scrooge's words surprising? Explain your answer.

_____

_____

_____

**Reading Check**

Seeing Fezziwig has an effect on Scrooge. Circle the word Scrooge says that shows his feelings are changing.

very much attached to me, was Dick. Poor Dick! Dear, dear!

**FEZZIWIG.** Yo ho, my boys. No more work tonight. Christmas Eve, Dick. Christmas, Ebenezer!

_(They stand at attention in front of_ FEZZIWIG; _laughing)_

Hilli-ho! Clear away, and let's have lots of room here! Hilli-ho, Dick! Chirrup, Ebenezer!

_(The young men clear the room, sweep the floor, straighten the pictures, trim the lamps, etc. The space is clear now. A fiddler enters, fiddling.)_

Hi-ho, Matthew! Fiddle away . . . where are my daughters?

_(The fiddler plays. Three young daughters of_ FEZZIWIG _enter followed by six young male suitors. They are dancing to the music. All employees come in: workers, clerks, housemaids, cousins, the baker, etc. All dance. Full number wanted here. Throughout the dance, food is brought into the feast. It is "eaten" in dance, by the dancers._ EBENEZER _dances with all three of the daughters, as does_ DICK. _They compete for the daughters, happily, in the dance._ FEZZIWIG _dances with his daughters._ FEZZIWIG _dances with_ DICK _and_ EBENEZER. _The music changes:_ MRS. FEZZIWIG _enters. She lovingly scolds her husband. They dance. She dances with_ EBENEZER, _lifting him and throwing him about. She is enormously fat. When the dance is ended, they all dance off, floating away, as does the music._ SCROOGE _and the_ GHOST OF CHRISTMAS PAST _stand alone now. The music is gone.)_

**PAST.** It was a small matter, that Fezziwig made those silly folks so full of gratitude.

**SCROOGE.** Small!

**PAST.** Shhh!

_(Lights up on_ DICK _and_ EBENEZER)

**DICK.** We are blessed, Ebenezer, truly, to have such a master as Mr. Fezziwig!

**YOUNG SCROOGE.** He is the best, best, the very and absolute best! If ever I own a firm of my own, I shall treat my apprentices with the same dignity and the same grace. We have learned a wonderful lesson from the master, Dick!

**DICK.** Ah, that's a fact, Ebenezer. That's a fact!

**PAST.** Was it not a small matter, really? He spent but a few pounds[21] of his mortal money on your small party. Three or four pounds, perhaps. Is that so much that he deserves such praise as you and Dick so lavish now?

**SCROOGE.** It isn't that! It isn't that, Spirit. Fezziwig had the power to make us happy or unhappy; to make our service light or burdensome; a pleasure or a toil. The happiness he gave is quite as great as if it cost him a fortune.

**PAST.** What is the matter?

**SCROOGE.** Nothing particular.

**PAST.** Something, I think.

**SCROOGE.** No, no. I should like to be able to say a word or two to my clerk just now! That's all!

*(EBENEZER enters the room and shuts down all the lamps. He stretches and yawns. The GHOST OF CHRISTMAS PAST turns to SCROOGE all of a sudden.)*

**PAST.** My time grows short! Quick!

*(In a flash of light, EBENEZER is gone, and in his place stands an OLDER SCROOGE, this one a man in the prime of his life. Beside him stands a young woman in a mourning dress. She is crying. She speaks to the man, with hostility.)*

**WOMAN.** It matters little . . . to you, very little. Another idol has displaced me.

**MAN.** What idol has displaced you?

**WOMAN.** A golden one.

**MAN.** This is an even-handed dealing of the world. There is nothing on which it is so hard as poverty; and there is nothing it professes to condemn with such severity as the pursuit of wealth!

**WOMAN.** You fear the world too much. Have I not seen your nobler aspirations fall off one by one, until the master-passion, Gain, engrosses you? Have I not?

**SCROOGE.** No!

**MAN.** What then? Even if I have grown so much wiser, what then? Have I changed towards you?

© Pearson Education

21. **pounds** (powndz) *n.* the money used in Great Britain at the time of the story.

---

**Literary Analysis**

Sometimes, audiences can learn about characters from what they try not to say. What can you learn about Scrooge's thoughts and feelings from the **dialogue** in the first bracketed passage?

_____

_____

_____

**Reading Skill** 📖

Read the second bracketed passage. Underline the details in this passage that let you know that the next memory will be sad. What is your **purpose** for reading past this point?

_____

_____

**Literary Analysis**

Read the third bracketed passage. What personal change in young Scrooge does this **dialogue** show?

_____

_____

_____

**Literary Analysis**

What do you learn about Scrooge's past from the **dialogue** in the bracketed passage?

_____

_____

_____

**Stop to Reflect**

Why do you think the younger Scrooge let the woman he loved go?

_____

_____

_____

**Reading Check** ✎

Does Scrooge wish the woman had let the younger Scrooge go? Underline the dialogue that shows how Scrooge feels about the woman.

**WOMAN.** No . . .

**MAN.** Am I?

**WOMAN.** Our contract is an old one. It was made when we were both poor and content to be so. You are changed. When it was made, you were another man.

**MAN.** I was not another man: I was a boy.

**WOMAN.** Your own feeling tells you that you were not what you are. I am. That which promised happiness when we were one in heart is fraught with misery now that we are two . . .

**SCROOGE.** No!

**WOMAN.** How often and how keenly I have thought of this, I will not say. It is enough that I have thought of it, and can release you . . .

**SCROOGE.** (*Quietly*) Don't release me, madame . . .

**MAN.** Have I ever sought release?

**WOMAN.** In words. No. Never.

**MAN.** In what then?

**WOMAN.** In a changed nature; in an altered spirit. In everything that made my love of any worth or value in your sight. If this has never been between us, tell me, would you seek me out and try to win me now? Ah, no!

**SCROOGE.** Ah, yes!

**MAN.** You think not?

**WOMAN.** I would gladly think otherwise if I could, heaven knows! But if you were free today, tomorrow, yesterday, can even I believe that you would choose a dowerless girl[22]—you who in your very confidence with her weigh everything by Gain; or, choosing her, do I not know that your repentance and regret would surely follow? I do; and I release you. With a full heart, for the love of him you once were.

**SCROOGE.** Please, I . . . I . . .

**MAN.** Please, I . . . I . . .

22. **a dowerless** (DOW uhr les) **girl** a girl without a dowry, the property or wealth a woman brought to her husband in marriage.

**WOMAN.** Please. You may—the memory of what is past half makes me hope you will—have pain in this. A very, very brief time, and you will dismiss the memory of it, as an unprofitable dream, from which it happened well that you awoke. May you be happy in the life that you have chosen for yourself . . .

**SCROOGE.** No!

**WOMAN.** Yourself . . . alone . . .

**SCROOGE.** No!

**WOMAN.** Goodbye, Ebenezer . . .

**SCROOGE.** Don't let her go!

**MAN.** Goodbye.

**SCROOGE.** No!

*(She exits.* SCROOGE *goes to younger man: himself.)*

You fool! Mindless loon! You fool!

**MAN.** *(To exited woman)* Fool. Mindless loon. Fool . . .

**SCROOGE.** Don't say that! Spirit, remove me from this place.

**PAST.** I have told you these were shadows of the things that have been. They are what they are. Do not blame me, Mr. Scrooge.

**SCROOGE.** Remove me! I cannot bear it!

*(The faces of all who appeared in this scene are now projected for a moment around the stage: enormous, flimsy, silent.)*

Leave me! Take me back! Haunt me no longer!

*(There is a sudden flash of light: a flare. The* GHOST OF CHRISTMAS PAST *is gone.* SCROOGE *is, for the moment, alone onstage. His bed is turned down, across the stage. A small candle burns now in* SCROOGE*'s hand. There is a child's cap in his other hand. He slowly crosses the stage to his bed, to sleep.* MARLEY *appears behind* SCROOGE, *who continues his long, elderly cross to bed.* MARLEY *speaks directly to the audience.)*

**MARLEY.** Scrooge must sleep now. He must surrender to the irresistible drowsiness caused by the recognition of what was. *(Pauses)* The cap he

## TAKE NOTES

### Literary Analysis

**Dialogue** shows how characters grow and change. What has changed in Scrooge in the years since the woman he loved left him?

_____

_____

How does the first bracketed passage show these changes?

_____

_____

_____

### Reading Skill

One **purpose** you may have for reading this scene is to be warned against making the mistakes Scrooge has made in his life. Underline the passage that you think meets this purpose.

What will be your **purpose** for reading Act II of this play?

_____

_____

_____

## Reading Check ✏️

Circle the details in Marley's speech that remind readers this is a play.

carries is from ten lives past: his boyhood cap . . . donned atop a hopeful hairy head . . . askew, perhaps, or at a rakish angle. Doffed now in honor of regret.[23] Perhaps even too heavy to carry in his present state of weak remorse . . .

*(SCROOGE drops the cap. He lies atop his bed. He sleeps. To audience)*

He sleeps. For him, there's even more trouble ahead. *(Smiles)* For you? The play house tells me there's hot cider, as should be your anticipation for the specter Christmas Present and Future, for I promise you both. *(Smiles again)* So, I pray you hurry back to your seats refreshed and ready for a miser—to turn his coat of gray into a blazen Christmas holly-red. *(A flash of lightning. A clap of thunder. Bats fly. Ghosty music. MARLEY is gone.)*

**Reader's Response:** How would you feel at this point in the play if you were Scrooge?

_____

_____

_____

_____

23. **donned . . . regret** To don and doff a hat means to put it on and take it off, *askew* means "crooked," and at a rakish angle means "having a dashing or jaunty look."

# A Christmas Carol: Scrooge and Marley, Act I

1. **Draw Conclusions:** Scrooge values money and nothing else at the beginning of the play. Do his values make Scrooge happy? Explain.

   _____

   _____

2. **Speculate:** How might Scrooge's future interactions with others differ from his interactions in the present?

   _____

   _____

3. **Reading Skill:** What is your **purpose for reading** this play?

   _____

   _____

4. **Literary Analysis: Dialogue** is what the characters in a play say. Use the chart below to explain an example of dialogue from the play. Write your example in the first column. Explain what the example means in the second column. Discuss why the example is important in the third column.

| What Does It Say? | What Does It Mean? | Why Is It Important? |
|---|---|---|
|  |  |  |
|  |  |  |

## Writing: Letter

Write a **letter** to Scrooge that tells him what he is missing by being cranky and mean to everybody around him.

- A good way to get Scrooge's attention is to tell him what he is missing in life. What do you think Scrooge is missing by being mean and selfish?

  _____

  _____

- You might want to tell Scrooge how much better his life could be if he changed his ways. What do you think Scrooge would gain by being kind to people?

  _____

  _____

  Use these notes to help you write your letter to Scrooge.

## Research and Technology: Costume Plans

When preparing your **costume plans**, you may want to consider these items.

| | | | |
|---|---|---|---|
| men's pants | men's vest | men's tie | women's dress |
| men's shirt | men's jacket | men's hat | women's hat |

Make sure that every group member has an article of clothing to research. Use the following chart to list details as you find information.

| Article of Clothing | Description |
|---|---|
| | |
| | |
| | |

# A Christmas Carol: Scrooge and Marley, Act II

## Reading Skill

**Setting a purpose** for reading is deciding before you read what you want to get out of a text. The purpose you set will affect the way you read. **Adjust your reading rate** to suit your purpose. For example, if you are reading directions to perform a task, you will read more slowly and carefully than if you are reading to be entertained.

- As you read drama, slow down to read stage directions carefully. They may reveal action that is not shown in the dialogue.

- Speed up to read short lines of dialogue quickly to create the feeling of conversation.

- Slow down to read longer speeches by a single character so that you can reflect on the character's words and look for clues to the message.

As you read, use this chart to help you decide what reading rate you should use.

| Types of Reading Material | + | Purpose for Reading | = | Reading Rate |
|---|---|---|---|---|
|  |  |  |  |  |

## Literary Skill

**Stage directions** are the words in a dramatic script that are not spoken by characters. When a play is performed, you can see the set, the characters, and the movements, and you can hear the sound effects. When you read a play, you get this information in the stage directions. Stage directions are usually written in italic type and set off by brackets or parentheses, as in this example.

*(Jen bursts through the door, stage left. There is a crack of thunder. Then the lights go dark.)*

# A Christmas Carol: Scrooge and Marley, Act II

## Israel Horovitz

from A Christmas Carol
by Charles Dickens

**Summary** It is Christmas Eve. Ebenezer Scrooge is a stingy businessman who despises Christmas. He has already been visited by the ghost of Jacob Marley and the Ghost of Christmas Past. Act II reveals what happens when the Ghosts of Christmas Present and Future show Scrooge the effects of his thoughtless ways.

 **Writing About the Big Question**

**Do others see us more clearly than we see ourselves?** In Act 2 of *A Christmas Carol*, Scrooge learns valuable lessons from his ghostly visitors. Complete this sentence:

In order to change, we must first **identify** how our behavior affects

_____ because _____.

## Note-taking Guide

Use this chart to write down details from the story that support statements about Scrooge.

| Statements About Scrooge | Details That Support These Statements |
| --- | --- |
| Scrooge is moved by what he sees at Bob Cratchit's house. | Scrooge says, "Spirit, tell me if Tiny Tim will live." |
| Scrooge fears what Future will show him. | |
| Scrooge is inspired to become a good man. | |

# A Christmas Carol: Scrooge and Marley, Act II

1. **Analyze:** Why does Scrooge care about the fate of Tiny Tim?

   _____

   _____

2. **Evaluate:** Scrooge promises at the end of the play to learn from his "lessons." How well does he live up to his promise?

   _____

   _____

3. **Reading Skill:** What happens to your **reading rate** when you read long speeches with difficult vocabulary? Explain.

   _____

   _____

4. **Literary Analysis:** Reread the **stage directions** at the beginning of Scene 1. Then, fill out this chart with information from the directions.

| Characters on Stage | Movement of Characters | Description of Lighting | Description of Sound | Other Special Effects |
|---------------------|------------------------|-------------------------|----------------------|-----------------------|
|                     |                        |                         |                      |                       |

## Writing: Tribute

Write a **tribute** to the changed Scrooge. Consider how Scrooge acts during each of the scenes in Act II as you prepare your tribute. Record his actions in this chart.

| Crachit's Home | Nephew's Home | Scoundrels Taking Possessions | The Tombstone |
|---|---|---|---|
|  |  |  |  |

## Listening and Speaking: Dramatic Monologue

Draft a **dramatic monologue** for Scrooge based on his experiences with one of the ghosts in Act II. Answer these questions after you select a scene.

- What do the stage directions tell you about the scene?

_____

_____

- How does the ghost challenge Scrooge in this scene?

_____

_____

_____

- What effect do you think the scene has had on Scrooge?

_____

_____

Review your notes as you prepare your monologue.

# Literary Criticism

## About Literary Criticism

**Literary criticism** is writing that examines literature. *Criticism* means making a judgment about the work. The judgment can be positive or negative. This type of writing is called a *review*. The writer is called a *critic*.

Most reviews contain these parts:

- a brief summary of the work
- a comparison or contrast to similar works
- a judgment about the work

## Reading Skill

An author's perspective is his or her attitude, or way of thinking, about something. An author's experiences may influence the way he or she thinks and writes about a topic. A writer who admires a well-known actor may write only good things about the actor. You need to **identify the author's perspective** so you can make judgments about a text.

Ask these questions to identify the author's perspective:

- Does the author have a negative or positive opinion about the subject?
- Does the author include opposing information or opinions?
- What experiences may have influenced what the author has written?

| Statement | Perspective |
|---|---|
| "A new take on an old classic always offers fresh insights." | The writer approaches classic story adaptations with a positive attitude. |
| "A retelling of a classic story can never live up to the original." | The writer approaches classic story adaptations with a negative attitude. |

## Text Structure

Quotations or excerpts from a text may be highlighted by placing them in the side margin or in a box. What does the text in the box tell you about the review?

_____

_____

## Vocabulary Builder

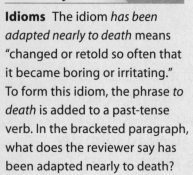

**Idioms** The idiom *has been adapted nearly to death* means "changed or retold so often that it became boring or irritating." To form this idiom, the phrase *to death* is added to a past-tense verb. In the bracketed paragraph, what does the reviewer say has been adapted nearly to death?

_____

_____

## Vocabulary Builder

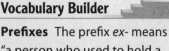

**Prefixes** The prefix *ex-* means "a person who used to hold a position." A *skipper* is the captain of an airplane, a ship, or in this case, a fictional spaceship. What does *ex-skipper* mean?

_____

_____

# A Christmas Carol
## TNT

**(Sun., Dec. 5, 8 p.m. ET)
Picks & Pans: Television**

Full text: COPYRIGHT
1999 Time, Inc.

> …this *Carol* feels more like Masterpiece Theatre than seasonal merchandise…

So you muttered "humbug" when you spied yet another version of *A Christmas Carol* on the TV schedule. Don't feel guilty. It doesn't take a spiritual descendant of Ebenezer Scrooge to notice that the Charles Dickens classic has been adapted nearly to death. (Two years ago, there was even a Ms. Scrooge.)

But TNT's *Carol* would be worth watching if only for the lead performance of Patrick Stewart. The ex-skipper of *Star Trek: The Next Generation* has been giving staged, one-man readings of *A Christmas Carol* for 10 years, and his approach to Scrooge is consistently interesting and intelligent. Early on, Stewart seems to be speaking on the misanthropic diatribes straight from Scrooge's flinty heart, rather than reciting thoroughly familiar quotations. And when Scrooge offers a boy a one-shilling tip, Stewart has the reformed miser feel a pang of the old parsimony. Filmed in England with a solid supporting cast (including Richard E. Grant as Bob Cratchit and Joel Grey as the Spirit of Christmas Past), this *Carol* feels more like Masterpiece Theatre than seasonal merchandise–except when the filmmakers embellish Scrooge's nocturnal visions with gratuitous special effects.

**Bottom line:** Old story well told.
–Terry Kelleher

*People Weekly*, Dec. 6, 1999

# Toned-down Christmas Carol has more spirit

## By John Sousanis
### Special to *The Oakland Press*

Director Debra Wicks has tinkered with Meadow Brook's recipe for *A Christmas Carol* just enough to make the old holiday fruitcake seem fresh. To be sure, Wicks's changes are subtle. Meadow Brook is still producing the Charles Nolte adaptation of Charles Dickens's Christmas classic that has been a mainstay of local theater for most of the last two decades.

The audience still is serenaded by a band of merry carolers in the lobby before the show. With its giant revolving set pieces and big bag of special effects, the production's script, set and costumes are unchanged from these many Christmases past.

But ironically, Wicks has infused the show with new energy by calming everything down a bit. In prior productions, the play's singing Londoners seemed positively hopped up on Christmas cheer to the point where one feared for the life of anyone not bubbling over with the spirit of the season.

Against this unebbing Yuletide, it was easy to forgive Scrooge of all his bah-hum-bugging. If only he had seen fit to give Tiny Tim a good spanking, we might all have enjoyed Christmas a little more. But Wicks has introduced a modicum of restraint into the Happy English populace, reducing the play's saccharine content considerably and making *A Christmas Carol* a more palatable holiday treat for adults and children.

Peter Hicks's set design for the show is, as always, enormous and gorgeous: Scrooge's storefront on a busy London street revolves to reveal the interior of the businessman's office and home, then opens on itself, providing the frame for scenes from Scrooge's boyhood, young adulthood and, of course, his potential end.

## Comprehension Builder

Read the first paragraph. Predict whether the critic will give a positive or negative review of the local production of *A Christmas Carol*. Underline text that helps you decide.

## Vocabulary Builder

**Drama Terms** An *audience* is a group of people who come to watch and listen to a performance. A *production* is a drama, or play, being performed. The *set* is the scenery, furniture, and other items used on the stage. The *script* is the written form of the play. *Costumes* are clothing and other items worn by actors in a play to make them look like something or someone.

## Fluency Builder

Words with many syllables can be difficult to read. Breaking words into syllables can make them easier to pronounce—for example, *un/ebb/ing, mod/i/cum, pop/u/lace*. Draw lines between the syllables in these words, and practice saying them aloud. With a partner, break *saccharine, considerably,* and *palatable* into syllables and mark them with lines.

_____

_____

_____

Now, take turns reading aloud the bracketed paragraph.

Meadow Brook's technical crew executes its stage magic without a hitch: Ghosts materialize and dematerialize in thick fogs and bolts of bright light, speaking to Scrooge in electronically altered voices and freezing the action onstage with a wave of their otherworldly hands.

The cast members take on multiple roles populating busy London in one scene, then visiting poor Scrooge in his dreams of Christmas Then, Now and Soon.

Standouts in the huge ensemble include John Biedenbach as Scrooge's put-upon assistant Bob Cratchit, Jodie Kuhn Ellison as Cratchit's fiercely loyal wife and Mark Rademacher, who pulls double duty as the Spirit of Christmas Present (the beefiest role in the play) and as a determined charity worker.

Scott Crownover, paying only passing attention to his English accent, takes an energetic turn as Scrooge's nephew, Fred, and Tom Mahard and Geoffrey Beauchamp have fun with a handful of roles they've been performing for years. Newcomer Sara Catheryn Wolf, fresh from three seasons at the Hilberry Theatre Company, provides an ethereal Spirit of Christmas Past.

The biggest change for longtime fans of the spectacle, however, is the replacement of Booth Coleman as Scrooge. Dennis Robertson's debut as the man in need of serious Christmas redemption is in perfect keeping with Wicks's toned-down production. If he's not quite as charismatic a miser as Coleman, Robertson is a much darker, even scarier Scrooge, which makes his ultimate transformation into an unabashed philanthropist that much more affecting.

All in all, *A Christmas Carol* is what it always has been: A well-produced, grand-scale event that is as much pageant as play. And like a beautifully wrapped gift under a well-decorated tree, it suits the season to a tee.

If you go, *A Christmas Carol* runs through December 24 at Meadow Brook Theatre, 127 Wilson Hall, Oakland University, Rochester Hills. Call 377-3300.

# Thinking About the Literary Criticism

1. Find one sentence in each review that supports this statement: Each critic thinks you already know the story of *A Christmas Carol*.

_____

_____

2. Terry Kelleher is the author of the first review. What is Kelleher's overall opinion of TNT's *A Christmas Carol*?

_____

_____

**TALK ABOUT IT** **Reading Skill**

3. Sousanis praises the Meadow Brook Theatre for "calming down" its production of *A Christmas Carol*. What does this tell you about Sousanis's personal preferences about plays?

_____

_____

4. If you learned that Kelleher admires Patrick Stewart's acting, how might that knowledge affect your reaction to his review?

_____

_____

**WRITE ABOUT IT** **Timed Writing: Summary (30 minutes)**

Write a summary of Kelleher's review of *A Christmas Carol*. Reread the review, and then answer these questions.

• What is Kelleher's opinion of the performance?

_____

• What parts of the performance did Kelleher like?

_____

• What parts of the performance did Kelleher dislike?

_____

# The Monsters Are Due on Maple Street

A **summary** is a brief statement that presents only the main ideas and the most important details. Summarizing helps you review and understand what you are reading.

First **distinguish between important and unimportant details**. Ask yourself questions.

- Is this detail necessary for my understanding of the work?
- Would the work hold together without this information?

Pause to think about and write down the key events and important details.

## Literary Analysis

A **character's motives** are the reasons for his or her actions. Motives are usually related to what a character wants, needs, or feels. The desire to win might motivate an athlete to practice daily for example. Powerful motives include love, anger, fear, greed, and jealousy.

Think about what motivates each of the characters. Use this diagram to explore each character's motives as you read.

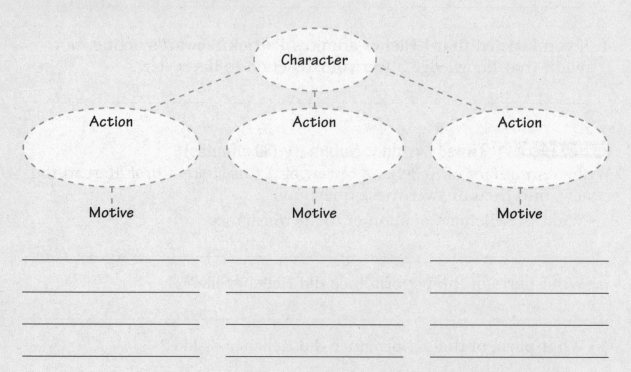

_____   _____   _____

_____   _____   _____

_____   _____   _____

_____   _____   _____

# The Monsters Are Due on Maple Street
## Rod Serling

**Summary** A strange object flashes across the sky over Maple Street. Then cars, telephones, and electricity fail to work. The neighbors gather. Pete Van Horn leaves to see whether other streets have lost power. One boy claims that monsters are coming from space and that one neighborhood family could be preparing the way for others. The neighbors become suspicious of one another. They actually do the work of the aliens.

 ## Writing About the Big Question

**Do others see us more clearly than we see ourselves?** In *The Monsters are Due on Maple Street*, mysterious events cause neighbors to become frightened and fearful. Complete this sentence:

Fear can influence our perception of others by _____

_____.

## Note-taking Guide
List the causes and effects of important events in Act 2.

| Cause | Effect/Cause | Effect/Cause | Effect/Cause |
|---|---|---|---|
| Something approaches, and so on. | Charlie shoots. | Everyone fights one another. | |

**Reading Check**

Underline the stage direction that describes how the homes are lit. Why are they lit this way?

_____

_____

# The Monsters Are Due on Maple Street

## Rod Serling

### Characters

NARRATOR
FIGURE ONE
FIGURE TWO

#### Residents of Maple Street

STEVE BRAND
CHARLIE'S WIFE
MRS. GOODMAN

MRS. BRAND
TOMMY
WOMAN
DON MARTIN
SALLY (TOMMY'S MOTHER)
MAN ONE
MAN TWO
PETE VAN HORN
CHARLIE
LES GOODMAN

### Act 2

(We see a medium shot of the GOODMAN entry hall at night. On the side table rests an unlit candle. MRS. GOODMAN walks into the scene, a glass of milk in hand. She sets the milk down on the table, lights the candle with a match from a box on the table, picks up the glass of milk, and starts out of scene.

MRS. GOODMAN comes through her porch door, glass of milk in hand. The entry hall, with table and lit candle, can be seen behind her.

Outside, the camera slowly pans down the sidewalk, taking in little knots of people who stand around talking in low voices. At the end of each conversation they look toward LES GOODMAN's house. From the various houses we can see candlelight but no electricity, and there's an all-pervading quiet that blankets the whole area, disturbed only by the almost whispered voices of the people as they stand around. The camera pans over to one group where CHARLIE stands. He stares across at GOODMAN's house.

We see a long shot of the house. Two men stand across the street in almost sentry-like poses. Then we see a medium shot of a group of people.)

SALLY. (A little timorously) It just doesn't seem right, though, keeping watch on them. Why . . . he was right when he said he was one of our neighbors. Why, I've known Ethel Goodman ever since they moved in. We've been good friends—

CHARLIE. That don't prove a thing. Any guy who'd spend his time lookin' up at the sky early in the morning—well, there's something wrong with that kind of person. There's something that ain't legitimate. Maybe under normal circumstances we could let it go by, but these aren't normal circumstances. Why, look at this street! Nothin' but candles. Why, it's like goin' back into the dark ages or somethin'!

*(STEVE walks down the steps of his porch, walks down the street over to LES GOODMAN's house, and then stops at the foot of the steps. GOODMAN stands there, his wife behind him, very frightened.)*

**GOODMAN.** Just stay right where you are, Steve. We don't want any trouble, but this time if anybody sets foot on my porch, that's what they're going to get—trouble!

**STEVE.** Look, Les—

**GOODMAN.** I've already explained to you people. I don't sleep very well at night sometimes. I get up and I take a walk and I look up at the sky. I look at the stars!

**MRS. GOODMAN.** That's exactly what he does. Why this whole thing, it's . . . it's some kind of madness or something.

**STEVE.** *(Nods grimly)* That's exactly what it is—some kind of madness.

**CHARLIE'S VOICE.** *(Shrill, from across the street)* You best watch who you're seen with, Steve! Until we get this all straightened out, you ain't exactly above suspicion yourself.

**STEVE.** *(Whirling around toward him)* Or you, Charlie. Or any of us, it seems. From age eight on up!

**WOMAN.** What I'd like to know is—what are we gonna do? Just stand around here all night?

**CHARLIE.** There's nothin' else we can do! *(He turns back looking toward STEVE and GOODMAN again.)* One of 'em'll tip their hand. They got to.

**STEVE.** *(Raising his voice)* There's something you can do, Charlie. You could go home and keep your mouth shut. You could quit strutting around like a self-appointed hanging judge and just climb into bed and forget it.

**Stop to Reflect**

Underline the stage directions describing Goodman and his wife. How do you think this fear would show in their actions?

_____

_____

_____

**Literary Analysis**

Read the second bracketed text. What does Charlie mean?

_____

_____

_____

**Reading Skill**

Why does Steve call Charlie a "hanging judge"?

_____

_____

_____

**Reading Skill** 📖

Read the bracketed text.
**Summarize** Steve's argument.

_____

_____

_____

**Reading Check** ✏️

What does Steve have in his basement? Underline the answer.

**Literary Analysis** 🔍

Underline Steve's answer to the question, "Who do I talk to?" Is his answer meant to be taken seriously?

_____

Explain.

_____

_____

_____

_____

**CHARLIE.** You sound real anxious to have that happen, Steve. I think we better keep our eye on you too!

**DON.** _(As if he were taking the bit in his teeth, takes a hesitant step to the front)_ I think everything might as well come out now. _(He turns toward_ STEVE.) Your wife's done plenty of talking, Steve, about how odd you are!

**CHARLIE.** _(Picking this up, his eyes widening)_ Go ahead, tell us what she's said.

_(We see a long shot of_ STEVE _as he walks toward them from across the street.)_

**STEVE.** Go ahead, what's my wife said? Let's get it all out. Let's pick out every idiosyncrasy of every single man, woman, and child on the street. And then we might as well set up some kind of kangaroo court.[1] How about a firing squad at dawn, Charlie, so we can get rid of all the suspects? Narrow them down. Make it easier for you.

**DON.** There's no need gettin' so upset, Steve. It's just that . . . well . . . Myra's talked about how there's been plenty of nights you spent hours down in your basement workin' on some kind of radio or something. Well, none of us have ever seen that radio—

_(By this time_ STEVE _has reached the group. He stands there defiantly close to them.)_

**CHARLIE.** Go ahead, Steve. What kind of "radio set" you workin' on? I never seen it. Neither has anyone else. Who you talk to on that radio set? And who talks to you?

**STEVE.** I'm surprised at you, Charlie. How come you're so dense all of a sudden? _(A pause)_ Who do I talk to? I talk to monsters from outer space. I talk to three-headed green men who fly over here in what look like meteors.

_(_STEVE_'s wife steps down from the porch, bites her lip, calls out.)_

---

1. **kangaroo court** unofficial court that does not follow normal rules.

**MRS. BRAND.** Steve! Steve, please. *(Then looking around, frightened, she walks toward the group.)* It's just a ham radio set, that's all. I bought him a book on it myself. It's just a ham radio set. A lot of people have them. I can show it to you. It's right down in the basement.

**STEVE.** *(Whirls around toward her)* Show them nothing! If they want to look inside our house— let them get a search warrant.

**CHARLIE.** Look, buddy, you can't afford to—

**STEVE.** *(Interrupting)* Charlie, don't tell me what I can afford! And stop telling me who's dangerous and who isn't and who's safe and who's a menace. *(He turns to the group and shouts.)* And you're with him, too—all of you! You're standing here all set to crucify—all set to find a scapegoat[2]—all desperate to point some kind of a finger at a neighbor! Well now look, friends, the only thing that's gonna happen is that we'll eat each other up alive—

*(He stops abruptly as* CHARLIE *suddenly grabs his arm.)*

**CHARLIE.** *(In a hushed voice)* That's not the only thing that can happen to us.

*(Cut to a long shot looking down the street. A figure has suddenly materialized in the gloom and in the silence we can hear the clickety-clack of slow, measured footsteps on concrete as the figure walks slowly toward them. One of the women lets out a stifled cry. The young mother grabs her boy as do a couple of others.)*

**TOMMY.** *(Shouting, frightened)* It's the monster! It's the monster!

*(Another woman lets out a wail and the people fall back in a group, staring toward the darkness and the approaching figure.*

*We see a medium group shot of the people as they stand in the shadows watching.* DON MARTIN *joins them, carrying a shotgun. He holds it up.)*

**DON.** We may need this.

**STEVE.** A shotgun? *(He pulls it out of* DON'*s hand.)* Good Lord—will anybody think a thought around

---

2. **scapegoat** person or group blamed for the mistakes or crimes of others.

**Literary Analysis**

Read the bracketed text. What do you think Steve is feeling at this point?

_____

_____

_____

**Reading Skill**

Circle what Don Martin brings to the group. Why is this information mentioned in the stage directions?

_____

_____

**Reading Check**

Does Steve think having a shotgun is a good idea? Underline the stage direction that gives you a clue to what he thinks.

© Pearson Education

**Reading Skill** 📖

What happens to Pete Van Horn?

_____

_____

_____


**Reading Check** ✏️

Underline what Charlie thought
Van Horn was.


**Literary Analysis** 🔍

What are Charlie's **motives**?

_____

_____

_____

_____

_____

here? Will you people wise up? What good would a shotgun do against—

(Now CHARLIE _pulls the gun from_ STEVE'_s hand._)

**CHARLIE.** No more talk, Steve. You're going to talk us into a grave! You'd let whatever's out there walk right over us, wouldn't yuh? Well, some of us won't!

(_He swings the gun around to point it toward the sidewalk. The dark figure continues to walk toward them._

_The group stands there, fearful, apprehensive, mothers clutching children, men standing in front of wives._ CHARLIE _slowly raises the gun. As the figure gets closer and closer he suddenly pulls the trigger. The sound of it explodes in the stillness. There is a long angle shot looking down at the figure, who suddenly lets out a small cry, stumbles forward onto his knees and then falls forward on his face._ DON, CHARLIE, _and_ STEVE _race forward over to him._ STEVE _is there first and turns the man over. Now the crowd gathers around them._)

**STEVE.** (_Slowly looks up_) It's Pete Van Horn.

**DON.** (_In a hushed voice_) Pete Van Horn! He was just gonna go over to the next block to see if the power was on—

**WOMAN.** You killed him, Charlie. You shot him dead!

**CHARLIE.** (_Looks around at the circle of faces, his eyes frightened, his face contorted_) But . . . but I didn't know who he was. I certainly didn't know who he was. He comes walkin' out of the darkness—how am I supposed to know who he was? (_He grabs_ STEVE.) Steve—you know why I shot! How was I supposed to know he wasn't a monster or something? (_He grabs_ DON _now._) We're all scared of the same thing. I was just tryin' to . . . tryin' to protect my home, that's all! Look, all of you, that's all I was tryin' to do. (_He looks down wildly at the body._) I didn't know it was somebody we knew! I didn't know—

(_There's a sudden hush and then an intake of breath. We see a medium shot of the living room window of_ CHARLIE'_s house. The window is not lit, but suddenly the house lights come on behind it._)

**WOMAN.** (*In a very hushed voice*) Charlie . . . Charlie . . . the lights just went on in your house. Why did the lights just go on?

**DON.** What about it, Charlie? How come you're the only one with lights now?

**GOODMAN.** That's what I'd like to know.

(*A pause as they all stare toward* CHARLIE.)

**GOODMAN.** You were so quick to kill, Charlie, and you were so quick to tell us who we had to be careful of. Well, maybe you had to kill. Maybe Peter there was trying to tell us something. Maybe he'd found out something and came back to tell us who there was amongst us we should watch out for—

(CHARLIE *backs away from the group, his eyes wide with fright.*)

**CHARLIE.** No . . . no . . . it's nothing of the sort! I don't know why the lights are on. I swear I don't. Somebody's pulling a gag or something.

(*He bumps against* STEVE, *who grabs him and whirls him around.*)

**STEVE.** A gag? A gag? Charlie, there's a dead man on the sidewalk and you killed him! Does this thing look like a gag to you?

(CHARLIE *breaks away and screams as he runs toward his house.*)

**CHARLIE.** No! No! Please!

(*A man breaks away from the crowd to chase* CHARLIE. *We see a long angle shot looking down as the man tackles* CHARLIE *and lands on top of him. The other people start to run toward them.* CHARLIE *is up on his feet, breaks away from the other man's grasp, lands a couple of desperate punches that push the man aside. Then he forces his way, fighting, through the crowd to once again break free, jumps up on his front porch. A rock thrown from the group smashes a window alongside of him, the broken glass flying past him. A couple of pieces cut him. He stands there perspiring, rumpled, blood running down from a cut on the cheek. His wife breaks away from the group to throw herself into his arms. He buries his face against her. We can see the crowd converging on the porch now.*)

**Stop to Reflect**

Read the underlined sentence. What do you think the people are thinking?

_____

_____

_____

**Reading Skill**

Why does Steve repeat himself? Why is this **detail** important?

_____

_____

**Literary Analysis**

Why do people think Charlie is the monster?

_____

_____

_____

**Reading Skill**

Read the bracketed stage direction. Summarize the action.

_____

_____

_____

_____

_____

**Literary Analysis** 🔍

Read the bracketed text. How do you know the people have become physically violent?

_____

_____

_____

_____

**Reading Check** ✏️

Who are the people who have been named as suspects? Underline the answers.

**VOICES.** It must have been him.
    He's the one.
    We got to get Charlie.

*(Another rock lands on the porch. Now* CHARLIE *pushes his wife behind him, facing the group.)*

**CHARLIE.** Look, look I swear to you . . . it isn't me . . . but I do know who it is . . . I swear to you, I do know who it is. I know who the monster is here. I know who it is that doesn't belong. I swear to you I know.

**GOODMAN.** *(Shouting)* What are you waiting for?

**WOMAN.** *(Shouting)* Come on, Charlie, come on.

**MAN ONE.** *(Shouting)* Who is it, Charlie, tell us!

**DON.** *(Pushing his way to the front of the crowd)* All right, Charlie, let's hear it!

*(*CHARLIE'S *eyes dart around wildly.)*

**CHARLIE.** It's . . . it's . . .

**MAN TWO.** *(Screaming)* Go ahead, Charlie, tell us.

**CHARLIE.** It's . . . it's the kid. It's Tommy. He's the one!

*(There's a gasp from the crowd as we cut to a shot of* SALLY *holding her son* TOMMY. *The boy at first doesn't understand and then, realizing the eyes are all on him, buries his face against his mother.)*

**SALLY.** *(Backs away)* That's crazy! That's crazy! He's a little boy.

**WOMAN.** But he knew! He was the only one who knew! He told us all about it. Well, how did he know? How could he have known?

*(The various people take this up and repeat the question aloud.)*

**VOICES.** How could he know?
    Who told him?
    Make the kid answer.

**DON.** It was Charlie who killed old man Van Horn.

**WOMAN.** But it was the kid here who knew what was going to happen all the time. He was the one who knew!

*(We see a close-up of* STEVE.*)*

**STEVE.** Are you all gone crazy? *(Pause as he looks about)* Stop.

© Pearson Education

*(A fist crashes at* STEVE's *face, staggering him back out of the frame of the picture.*

*There are several close camera shots suggesting the coming of violence. A hand fires a rifle. A fist clenches. A hand grabs the hammer from* VAN HORN's *body, etc. Meanwhile, we hear the following lines.)*

**DON.** Charlie has to be the one—Where's my rifle—

**WOMAN.** Les Goodman's the one. His car started! Let's wreck it.

**MRS. GOODMAN.** What about Steve's radio—He's the one that called them—

**MRS. GOODMAN.** Smash the radio. Get me a hammer. Get me something.

**STEVE.** Stop—Stop—

**CHARLIE.** Where's that kid—Let's get him.

**MAN ONE.** Get Steve—Get Charlie—They're working together.

*(The crowd starts to converge around the mother, who grabs the child and starts to run with him. The crowd starts to follow, at first walking fast, and then running after him.*

*We see a full shot of the street as suddenly* CHARLIE'S *lights go off and the lights in another house go on. They stay on for a moment, then from across the street other lights go on and then off again.)*

**MAN ONE.** *(Shouting)* It isn't the kid . . . it's Bob Weaver's house.

**WOMAN.** It isn't Bob Weaver's house. It's Don Martin's place.

**CHARLIE.** I tell you it's the kid.

**DON.** It's Charlie. He's the one.

*(We move into a series of close-ups of various people as they shout, accuse, scream, interspersing these shots with shots of houses as the lights go on and off, and then slowly in the middle of this nightmarish morass of sight and sound the camera starts to pull away, until once again we've reached the opening shot looking at the Maple Street sign from high above. The camera continues to move away until we dissolve to a shot looking toward the metal side of a space craft, which sits shrouded in darkness. An open door throws out a beam of light from the illuminated interior. Two figures silhouetted against the bright*

**Reading Skill**

Read the bracketed stage direction. Why do you think this **detail** is important?

_____

_____

_____

**Reading Check**

Who do Charlie and Don think is the alien? Circle the answer.

**Literary Analysis**

What **motivates** the people on this page?

_____

_____

_____

_____

_____

**Reading Skill** ✏️

Circle the weapons the Narrator mentions. Would you include them in a summary? Explain.

_____

_____

_____

_____

**Reading Check** ✏️

Underline the items that the Narrator mentions as "tools of conquest." Then circle the items that the Narrator says have fallout for children.

lights appear. We get only a vague feeling of form, but nothing more explicit than that.)

**FIGURE ONE.** Understand the procedure now? Just stop a few of their machines and radios and telephones and lawn mowers . . . throw them into darkness for a few hours, and then you just sit back and watch the pattern.

**FIGURE TWO.** And this pattern is always the same?

**FIGURE ONE.** With few variations. They pick the most dangerous enemy they can find . . . and it's themselves. And all we need do is sit back . . . and watch.

**FIGURE TWO.** Then I take it this place . . . this Maple Street . . . is not unique.

**FIGURE ONE.** *(Shaking his head)* By no means. Their world is full of Maple Streets. And we'll go from one to the other and let them destroy themselves. One to the other . . . one to the other . . . one to the other—

*(Now the camera pans up for a shot of the starry sky and over this we hear the NARRATOR'S VOICE.)*

**NARRATOR'S VOICE.** The tools of conquest do not necessarily come with bombs and explosions and fallout. There are weapons that are simply thoughts, attitudes, prejudices—to be found only in the minds of men. For the record, prejudices can kill and suspicion can destroy and a thoughtless frightened search for a scapegoat has a fallout all its own for the children . . . and the children yet unborn. *(A pause)* And the pity of it is . . . that these things cannot be confined to . . . The Twilight Zone!

---

**Reader's Response:** If you were a resident of Maple Street, how would you have responded to the strange events?

_____

_____

_____

# The Monsters Are Due on Maple Street

## Apply the Skills

1. **Infer:** How do the events of the play support this statement: "The tools of conquest do not necessarily come with bombs and explosions and fallout."

_____

_____

2. **Draw Conclusions:** Who are the monsters on Maple Street?

_____

_____

3. **Reading Skill:** Use this chart to create a **summary** of the play.

| Important Details from the Beginning | Important Details from the Middle | Important Details from the End |
|---|---|---|
| Summary: | | |

4. **Literary Analysis:** List two things that **motivate** the **characters** to finally turn on Tommy?

_____

_____

## Writing: Report

Write a report on the play.

Answer the following questions to help you organize information for your report.

- What happens on Maple Street? _____

_____

- When does the action take place? _____

- Where does the action take place? _____

- Why do the people act the way that they do? _____

_____

- How does the neighborhood change? _____

_____

Use these notes to help you complete the report.

## Research and Technology: Prepare for a Film Version

Prepare to film a scene from the play.

- List the events in the scene you choose.

- Decide on the best position for the camera.

- Describe special sound and lighting effects.

| Event in Play | Camera Position | Special Effects |
|---|---|---|
|  |  |  |
|  |  |  |
|  |  |  |
|  |  |  |

# Newspaper Articles

## ABOUT NEWSPAPER ARTICLES

**Newspapers** are printed publications that may also appear online. Most newspapers are published daily, but some may appear weekly. Newspapers offer different types of newspaper articles. **News articles** tell the facts about local and national events. **Feature articles** give facts and opinions about interesting people and places. **Editorials** give a writer's opinions about a topic. Editorial writers should support their opinions with facts, statistics, and examples.

## READING SKILL

When you read a newspaper article, analyze it carefully before you accept the information or the writer's opinion. I**dentify bias and stereotyping** that may be in the article. Bias is an opinion about whether something is good or bad that influences how you deal with it. A biased article may discuss only one **point of view.** It may present opinions without evidence. Stereotyping is making **generalizations,** or statements, about a group of people that are wrong or unfair.

To identify bias and stereotyping, look for

- articles with only one point of view presented.
- opinions without supporting evidence.
- generalizations about groups not based on facts.

|  | Example | How It Works |
|---|---|---|
| Bias | "He <u>won</u> the election with his plans on reform." <br><br>"He <u>stole</u> the election with a web of empty promises." | Two writers describe the same event differently, based on their personal feelings. |
| Stereotyping | "All teenagers are lazy." | The writer makes an unsupported claim about a group of people in order to sway readers' opinions. |

# Veteran Returns, Becomes Symbol

Editorial in the *Minneapolis Star and Tribune*, January 19, 1998

John Glenn went into orbit in 1962 and took America's hearts soaring with him. Who better to fire the nation's imagination again about the promise of space exploration?

NASA has done itself and its cause great good by announcing that Glenn, the astronaut-turned-U.S. senator, will fly into space once more. Though Glenn has represented Ohio in the Senate for five terms and run for president once, many Americans still consider his name synonymous with the nation's manned space program.

At a time when all astronauts were esteemed as America's best and brightest, Glenn stood out. Though not the first American in space, nor the one to seize the space-race prize—a moon landing—Glenn possessed an appeal that surpassed that of his peers.

Just as Glenn's orbital heroics inspired America when he was a young man, by joining the shuttle crew in October at age 77, he can inspire the nation again. He can reignite curiosity about the benefits and challenges for humankind that lie beyond Earth. He can let a watchful public share vicariously[1] his delight at leaving Earth's bounds once more.

And he can again be an exemplar for his generation—a generation already setting new standards for vigor and productivity past age 70. Glenn's flight should dramatically demonstrate that age is no limit to derring-do, nor to service to one's country.

Volunteering for a space ride isn't an option for most septuagenarians.[2] But many of Glenn's contemporaries are also volunteering, lending a hand to the young, old, sick and needy in their own communities. As American honors Glenn's past and future career in space, let the nation also take grateful note of the good works senior citizens are doing here on the ground.

---

1. **vicariously** (vī ker´ ē əs lē) *adv.* Indirectly; through the experience of another; by sympathy or imagination.
2. **septuagenarians** (sep´ toͦ ə jə ner´ ē ənz) *n.* Persons between the ages of 70 and 80.

---

**Do others see us more clearly than we see ourselves?**

**(a)** How does the author describe Glenn's planned space travel? **(b)** Does the author of the editorial have a favorable view of the proposed trip? **(c)** Do you agree with this assessment? **Explain.**

# Thinking About the Newspaper Article

1. Why does the writer say that John Glenn is a good choice to return to space?

_____

_____

2. Reread the title of the editorial. What might the writer say that Glenn symbolizes?

_____

_____

**TALK ABOUT IT** **Reading Skill**

3. What is the writer's bias? How do you know?

_____

_____

4. How does the writer stereotype astronauts? About what other group of people does the writer make generalizations?

_____

_____

**WRITE ABOUT IT** **Timed Writing: Editorial (20 minutes)**

Write an editorial on an issue about which you feel strongly.

• Choose an issue with more than one possible point of view.

• Choose one point of view, or side, and write a sentence stating your opinion.

_____

_____

• What facts, statistics, or examples support your opinion?

_____

_____

• Write a strong concluding sentence.

_____

_____

# Grasshopper Logic • The Other Frog Prince • duckbilled platypus vs. beefsnakstik®

The sharing of stories, cultures, and ideas by word of mouth is called the **oral tradition**. Stories in the oral tradition were created before the people who first told them knew how to write. People first told the stories to help explain their world. Stories also expressed their values. Then, these stories were passed along. Over time, these stories changed with many retellings.

The oral tradition includes stories about gods and goddesses, talking animals, great heroes, and amazing events. You will find these elements in stories that were once part of the oral tradition.

The **theme** is the message about life that is at the center of a story. Some themes are **universal themes**: They apply to every time and place. The themes are part of many different cultures.

A **moral** is a lesson about life taught in a story.

**Heroes and heroines** are men and women who do great and often seemingly impossible deeds.

**Storytelling** is an art. The storyteller has to hold the listeners' attention. Here are some ways that storytellers make stories more interesting and entertaining:

- **Hyperbole:** the use of exaggeration or overstatement. This device usually makes people laugh.
- **Personification:** the giving of human qualities to non-human objects
- **Allusion:** the mention of a well-known person, place, event, or work of art

| The Oral Tradition in Print | | |
|---|---|---|
| Type of Story | Definition | Example |
| Myths | • stories that explain the actions of gods, goddesses, and heroes <br> • can explain natural phenomena, such as earthquakes <br> • a culture's collection of myths is called a **mythology** | • the gods give King Midas the ability to turn all that he touches to gold <br> • how the Big Dipper was formed |
| Legends | • traditional stories about the past <br> • based on real-life events that have been twisted over time <br> • feature larger-than-life characters | Popo and Ixta |
| Folk tales | • stories about ordinary people <br> • reveal a culture's traditions and values <br> • often try to teach a lesson | The Force of Luck |
| Tall tales | • often focus on a hero who does impossible feats <br> • can contain **hyperbole**, or exaggeration, for comic effect | Paul Bunyan |
| Fables | • short stories that have speaking animals that act as people do <br> • often end with a moral or lesson | The Ant and the Grasshopper |
| Epics | • long poems about a larger-than-life hero who goes on a **quest**, or dangerous journey <br> • important to the history of a culture or nation | The Odyssey |

# Grasshopper Logic • The Other Frog Prince • duckbilled platypus vs. beefsnakstik®

## Jon Scieszka and Lane Smith

**Summaries** In "Grasshopper Logic," Grasshopper leaves a huge homework assignment until the night before it is due. Grasshopper Mom gets "hopping mad." A frog tells a princess that he is really a prince in "The Other Frog Prince." She kisses him and receives a surprise. A duckbilled platypus and a beefsnakstik® argue about who is better in "duckbilled platypus vs. beefsnakstik.®"

## Note-taking Guide
Use this chart to list main elements from each story.

|  | Grasshopper Logic | The Other Frog Prince | duckbilled platypus vs. beefsnakstik® |
|---|---|---|---|
| Characters | Grasshopper Mom Grasshopper |  |  |
| Problem |  | A frog says he is really a prince. |  |
| Moral |  |  | Just because you have a lot of stuff, do not think you are so special. |

# Grasshopper Logic
## from Squids Will Be Squids
### Jon Scieszka and Lane Smith

One bright and sunny day, Grasshopper came home from school, dropped his backpack, and was just about to run outside to meet his friends.

**"Where are you going?"** asked his mom.

"Out to meet some friends," said Grasshopper.

"Do you have any homework due tomorrow?" asked his mom.

"Just one small thing for History. I did the rest in class."

"Okay" said Mom Grasshopper. **"Be back at six for dinner."**

Grasshopper hung out with his friends, came home promptly at six, ate his dinner, then took out his History homework.

**His mom read the assignment and freaked out.**

"Rewrite twelve Greek myths as Broadway musicals. Write music for songs. Design and build all sets. Sew original costumes for each production."

**"How long have you known about this assignment?"** asked Mom Grasshopper, trying not to scream.

"I don't know," said Grasshopper.

© Pearson Education

**Activate Prior Knowledge**

List two or three things that can make a parent angry, or "hopping mad," at a child.

_____

_____

_____

**Oral Traditions**

**Personification** is giving human qualities to an animal or object. Underline the names of two talking animals in this story.

**Oral Traditions**

**Hyperbole** is exaggerating something to make it funny. Read the bracketed passage. Tell what is exaggerated.

_____

_____

**Reading Check**

For what class does Grasshopper say he has homework? Underline the answer.

### Oral Traditions

**Fables** are brief stories in which animals speak and act as humans do. Circle the type of animal that speaks as a human would.

### Oral Traditions

An **allusion** is a reference to something well-known. This story alludes to another story in which a princess kisses a frog. The frog then turns into a prince. What is funny about Jon Scieszka's allusion to this story?

_____

_____

_____

### Reading Check

Why does the princess kiss the frog? Underline the reason.

# The Other Frog Prince
# from The Stinky Cheese Man
# and Other Fairly Stupid Tales
## Jon Scieszka and Lane Smith

Once upon a time there was a frog.

One day when he was sitting on his lily pad, he saw a beautiful princess sitting by the pond. He hopped in the water, swam over to her, and poked his head out of the weeds.

"Pardon me, O beautiful princess," he said in his most sad and <u>pathetic</u> voice. "I wonder if you could help me."

The princess was about to jump up and run, but she felt sorry for the frog with the sad and pathetic voice.

So she asked, "What can I do to help you, little frog?"

"Well," said the frog. "I'm not really a frog, but a handsome prince who was turned into a frog by a wicked witch's spell. And the spell can only be broken by the kiss of a beautiful princess."

The princess thought about this for a second, then lifted the frog from the pond and kissed him.

"I was just kidding," said the frog. He jumped back into the pond and the princess wiped the frog <u>slime</u> off her lips.

**The End.**

**Vocabulary Development**

**pathetic** (puh THET ik) *adj.* sad enough to cause pity or tenderness
**slime** (slym) *n.* thick, sticky, slippery, and very unpleasant substance

# duckbilled platypus vs. beefsnakstik®
# from Squids Will Be Squids
## Jon Scieszka and Lane Smith

"I have a bill like a duck and a tail like a beaver," bragged Duckbilled Platypus.

"So what?" said BeefSnakStik®. "I have beef, soy protein concentrate[1], and dextrose[2]."

**"I also have webbed feet and fur,"** said Duckbilled Platypus.

**"Who cares?"** said BeefSnakStik®. **"I also have smoke flavoring, sodium erythorbate, and sodium nitrite.[3]**

**"I am one of only two mammals in the world that lay eggs,"** said Duckbilled Platypus.

**"Big deal,"** said BeefSnakStik®. **"I have beef lips."**

---

Reader's Response: Choose one of the characters from the fables. Write the character's name. Tell what you would like to say to the character if you ever met the character.

Character: _____

_____

_____

_____

_____

© Pearson Education

---

### Activate Prior Knowledge

**Personification** is giving human qualities to animals or objects. Circle the animal that has human qualities. Underline the thing that has human qualities.

### Stop to Reflect

Why are some lines printed **in bold type?**

_____

_____

_____

_____

_____

_____

### Reading Check

What is Duckbilled Platypus's tail like? Underline the text that tells you.

---

1. **soy protein concentrate** (SOY PROH teen KAHN suhn trayt) *n.* food ingredient for nutrition.

2. **dextrose** (DEKS trohs) *n.* type of sugar.

3. **smoke flavoring...nitrite** (NY tryt) *n.* other things added to food for flavor, color, or freshness.

# Themes in the Oral Tradition

1. **Respond:** Which tale is your favorite? Why?

   _____

   _____

2. **Infer:** Why does Grasshopper call his history assignment "small"?

   _____

   _____

3. **Oral Tradition:** What do you think is the **theme**, or message, of each fable? Explain.

   _____

   _____

   _____

4. **Oral Tradition:** Use this chart to list one example of **hyperbole** and **personification** used in each story.

| | Hyperbole | Personification |
|---|---|---|
| Grasshopper Logic | | |
| The Other Frog Prince | | |
| duckbilled platypus vs. beefsnakstik® | | |

## Bulletin Board Display

Follow these steps to gather information for a **bulletin board display** of Jon Scieszka's life and work.

- Select a search engine. Type *"Jon Scieszka" AND books AND family* in the search box. Carefully choose reliable sites when the results, or "hits," come up. These include sites that have information about the author and the sources used to make the site. Record information that you find.

**Scieszka's other books:** _____

_____

_____

**Scieszka's family:** _____

**Scieszka's education:** _____

- Go to the library. Find a computer and the online catalog. Select an author search. Type *Scieszka, Jon* in the search box. Press the enter key. A list of his books will come up. Click on highlighted titles to learn more about the books. Record on the lines below some of the information. Include the names of the books' illustrators. Then find the books on the shelf. Make copies of some of their illustrations.

**Book:** _____

_____

**Book:** _____

_____

**Book:** _____

_____

- Watch the video interview with Jon Scieszka. Review your source material. Use this information to record additional information for your bulletin board display.

**Additional information:** _____

_____

# Icarus and Daedalus • Demeter and Persephone

## Reading Skill

A **cause** is an event, an action, or a feeling that produces a result. That result is called an **effect**. Multiple causes can result in a single effect. Sometimes a single cause results in multiple effects. Effects can also become causes for events that follow. Causes and effects move the action forward.

**Ask questions to analyze cause-and-effect relationships**:

- What happened? Why?
- What will happen as a result of this?

Use this chart to record causes and effects as you read.

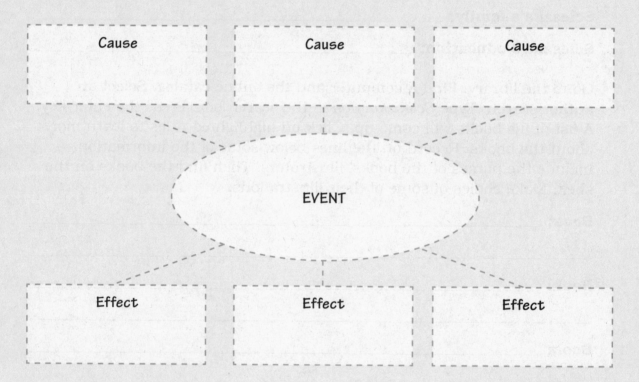

Cause   Cause   Cause

EVENT

Effect   Effect   Effect

## Literary Analysis

Since time began, people have tried to understand the world around them. Ancient people created **myths**. Myths are stories that explain natural occurrences. They also express beliefs about right and wrong.

Every culture has its own collection of myths, or *mythology*. Gods and goddesses have human traits in many of these myths. Human heroes may possess superhuman traits. Myths explore universal themes. They also explain the world in human terms.

# Icarus and Daedalus
## Josephine Preston Peabody

DEDALE PERD SON FILS ICARE.
Icare c'est en vain que ta foiblesse aspire,
Au Sacre cabinet des Merueilles des Dieux,
La seule foy te peut guinder iusques aux Cieux,
Autrement tu fondras ton aisleron de Cire.

**Summary** This story is a Greek myth. King Minos puts Daedalus and Daedalus' son Icarus in a prison on an island. Daedalus builds wings so that he and his son may escape. Icarus does not listen to his father's warning not to fly too close to the sun.

## Writing About the Big Question

**Community or individual: Which is more important?** In "Icarus and Daedalus," a boy ignores his father's advice. Complete this sentence:

When individuals become so focused on their own desires that they do

not listen to others _____.

## Note-taking Guide

Fill in this chart with details about the most important events in "Icarus and Daedalus."

**Beginning Event**

King Minos puts Daedalus and his son Icarus in prison on an island.

**Final Outcome**

# Icarus and Daedalus

## Josephine Preston Peabody

**Activate Prior Knowledge**

Describe a time when you tried to do something that was too hard for you.

_____

_____

_____

**Reading Skill**

Remember that a **cause** is an event, an action, or a feeling that produces a result. The result is the **effect**. What causes Daedalus to make wings to fly?

_____

_____

**Literary Analysis**

Human heroes can take on superhuman powers in **myths**. Read the bracketed paragraph. Underline the part that shows that Daedalus has superhuman power.

**Reading Check**

Circle the warning that Daedalus gives Icarus.

Among all those mortals who grew so wise that they learned the secrets of the gods, none was more cunning[1] than Daedalus.

He once built, for King Minos of Crete,[2] a wonderful Labyrinth[3] of winding ways so cunningly tangled up and twisted around that, once inside, you could never find your way out again without a magic clue. But the king's favor veered[4] with the wind, and one day he had his master architect imprisoned in a tower. Daedalus managed to escape from his cell; but it seemed impossible to leave the island, since every ship that came or went was well guarded by order of the king.

At length, watching the sea-gulls in the air—the only creatures that were sure of liberty—he thought of a plan for himself and his young son Icarus, who was captive with him.

Little by little, he gathered a store of feathers great and small. He fastened these together with thread, molded them in with wax, and so fashioned two great wings like those of a bird. When they were done, Daedalus fitted them to his own shoulders, and after one or two efforts, he found that by waving his arms he could winnow[5] the air and cleave it, as a swimmer does the sea. He held himself aloft, wavered this way and that with the wind, and at last, like a great fledgling,[6] he learned to fly.

Without delay, he fell to work on a pair of wings for the boy Icarus, and taught him carefully how to use them, bidding him beware of rash adventures among the stars. "Remember," said the father, "never to fly very low or very high, for the fogs about the earth would weigh you down, but the blaze of the sun will surely melt your feathers apart if you go too near."

1. **cunning** (KUN ing) *adj.* skillful; clever.
2. **King Minos** (KING MY nohs) **of Crete** King Minos was a son of the god Zeus. Crete is a Greek island in the eastern Mediterranean Sea, southeast of Greece.
3. **Labyrinth** (LAB uh RINTH) *n.* maze.
4. **veered** (veerd) *v.* changed directions.
5. **winnow** (WIN oh) *v.* beat, as with wings.
6. **fledgling** (FLEJ ling) *n.* young bird.

For Icarus, these cautions went in at one ear and out by the other. Who could remember to be careful when he was to fly for the first time? Are birds careful? Not they! And not an idea remained in the boy's head but the one joy of escape.

The day came, and the fair wind that was to set them free. The father bird put on his wings, and, while the light urged them to be gone, he waited to see that all was well with Icarus, for the two could not fly hand in hand. Up they rose, the boy after his father. The hateful ground of Crete sank beneath them; and the country folk, who caught a glimpse of them when they were high above the treetops, took it for a vision of the gods—Apollo,[7] perhaps, with Cupid[8] after him.

At first there was a terror in the joy. The wide <u>vacancy</u> of the air dazed them—a glance downward made their brains reel.

But when a great wind filled their wings, and Icarus felt himself <u>sustained</u>, like a halcyon bird[9] in the hollow of a wave, like a child uplifted by his mother, he forgot everything in the world but joy. He forgot Crete and the other islands that he had passed over: he saw but vaguely that winged thing in the distance before him that was his father Daedalus. He longed for one draft of flight to quench the thirst of his captivity: he stretched out his arms to the sky and made towards the highest heavens.

Alas for him! Warmer and warmer grew the air. Those arms, that had seemed to uphold him, relaxed. His wings wavered, drooped. He fluttered his young hands vainly—he was falling—and in that terror he remembered. The heat of the sun had melted the wax from his wings; the feathers were falling, one by one, like snowflakes; and there was none to help.

He fell like a leaf tossed down the wind, down, down, with one cry that overtook Daedalus far away.

## Vocabulary Development

**vacancy** (VAY kuhn see) *n.* emptiness

**sustained** (suh STAYND) *adj.* supported

---

7. **Apollo** (uh PAH loh) *n.* the Greek god of music, poetry, and medicine; identified with the sun.

8. **Cupid** (KYOO pid) *n.* in Roman mythology, the god of love, son of Venus.

9. **halcyon** (HAL see uhn) **bird** *n.* legendary sea bird, which the ancient Greeks believed could calm the sea by resting on it.

**Stop to Reflect**

Would Daedalus' plan have worked? Explain.

_____

_____

_____

**Reading Check**

What do the people of Crete think they see in the sky? Circle the answer in the text.

**Reading Skill**

What **effect** does the sun have in the myth?

_____

_____

© Pearson Education

**Reading Skill**

What **causes** Daedalus to know that his son has drowned?

_____

_____

**Reading Check** ✎

Why does Daedalus name an island Icaria? Underline the answer in the text.

When he returned, and sought high and low for his poor boy, he saw nothing but the birdlike feathers afloat on the water, and he knew that Icarus was drowned.

The nearest island he named Icaria, in memory of the child; but he, in heavy grief, went to the temple of Apollo in Sicily, and there hung up his wings as an offering. Never again did he attempt to fly.

> **Reader's Response:** How would you feel if you were Daedalus at the end of the story?
>
> _____
>
> _____
>
> _____

# Icarus and Daedalus

1. **Analyze:** How does Daedalus show how clever he is?

   _____

   _____

   _____

2. **Infer:** What do Icarus' actions reveal about his character?

   _____

   _____

   _____

3. **Reading Skill:** What is the **effect** of Icarus' crash on Daedalus?

   _____

   _____

   _____

4. **Literary Analysis:** Complete this chart to describe the lessons the characters learned in this **myth**.

| Character | Lesson | How Taught |
|-----------|--------|------------|
| Icarus | | |
| Daedalus | | |

## Writing: Myth

Write a short **myth** that explains something that happens in nature. Think of a natural phenomenon and a creative explanation for it. Respond to the following to help you write your myth.

- List three natural events.

  _____

- How does each event affect people or the natural world?

  _____

  _____

  _____

Then, decide how many characters your myth will have. Limit the number to keep the story simple. Describe your characters' appearance, actions, words, and the ways in which other characters relate to them. Plan the action of your story by identifying a problem and its solution.

## Listening and Speaking: Debate

Complete the following activity with your group to prepare for your **debate**.

- My group's argument: _____

- Support for argument: _____

  _____

  _____

- Possible opposing arguments: _____

  _____

  _____

- Response to opposing arguments: _____

  _____

  _____

# Demeter and Persephone
## Anne Terry White

**Summary** The myth "Demeter and Persephone" explains Earth's seasons. Pluto takes Demeter's daughter Persephone to his home in the underworld. Demeter is the goddess of the harvest. She becomes angry. Zeus asks Pluto to release Persephone as long as she has not eaten any food in the underworld. Persephone's mistake causes the change of seasons.

## Writing About the Big Question

**Community or individual: Which is more important?** In "Demeter and Persephone," Pluto's abduction of Persephone nearly caused the demise of humankind. Complete this sentence:

When making a decision that will affect the greater **community**, a person

is responsible for _____

_____ .

## Note-taking Guide
Use this chart to help you clarify the actions taken by the characters in the story.

| Character | Action |
|---|---|
| Eros | Causes Pluto to fall in love with Persephone |
| Pluto | |
| Demeter | |
| Persephone | |
| Zeus | |

# Demeter and Persephone

1. **Make a Judgment:** Demeter changes the earth so that plants are unable to grow. Do you think her actions were justifiable? Explain your answer.

_____

_____

2. **Synthesize:** How do the powerful emotions of the main characters account for the changing of the seasons?

_____

_____

3. **Reading Skill:** Persephone returns to Earth at the end of the myth. What is the **cause** of this event?

_____

_____

4. **Literary Analysis:** Use this chart to describe the lessons that the **myth** teaches through each character. Include the way that each lesson was taught.

| Character | Lesson | How Taught |
|-----------|--------|------------|
| Demeter | | |
| Persephone | | |
| Pluto | | |

## Writing: Myth

Write a short **myth** that explains something that happens in nature. Think of a natural phenomenon and a creative explanation for it. Respond to the following to help you write your myth.

- List three natural events.

_____

- How does each event affect people or the natural world?

_____

_____

   Then, decide on how many characters your myth will have. Limit the number to keep the story simple. Describe your characters' appearance, actions, words, and the ways other characters relate to them. Plan the action of your story by identifying a problem and its solution.

## Listening and Speaking: Debate

Plan a **debate** about whether or not Demeter was justified when she changed the weather on Earth. First, consider what the opposing arguments might be. Prepare to challenge these ideas. Record strengths and weaknesses of the arguments in this chart. Use the bottom box to develop an opening statement that summarizes your point.

| Strengths of Argument | Weaknesses of Argument |
|---|---|
| | |
| Opening Statement | |
| | |

# Tenochtitlan: Inside the Aztec Capital • Popocatepetl and Ixtlaccihuatl

## Reading Skill

A **cause** is an event or situation that produces a result. An **effect** is the result produced. In a story or an essay, each effect may eventually become a cause for the next event. This results in a cause-and-effect chain, which moves the action forward.

As you read, think about the causes and effects of events. If you do not clearly see the cause-and-effect relationships in a passage, **reread to look for connections** among the words and sentences. Some words that identify causes and effects are *because, due to, for this reason,* and *as a result.*

Notice the clue words in the cause-and-effect chain shown.

## Literary Analysis

A **legend** is a traditional story about the past. A **fact** can be proved to be true. Before legends were written down, they were passed on orally. Legends are based on facts that have grown into fiction in the many retellings over generations.

Every culture has developed its own legends to immortalize people who were famous. Most legends include the following elements:

- a human who seems larger than life
- fantastic elements
- roots or a basis in historical facts
- events that reflect the culture that created the story

---

**Cause/Effect**

*Because* the infant was crying, the mother woke up.

↓

**Effect/Cause**

She tripped in the dark and made a small groan.

↓

**Cause/Effect**

*As a result* of her groan, the father woke up.

---

# Tenochtitlan: Inside the Aztec Capital

### Jacqueline Dineen

**Summary** This nonfiction selection describes the Aztec city of Tenochtitlan. The Aztecs changed their surroundings so that they could live in the swampy land. At one time, 200,000 people lived in the capital. The people thrived by building floating gardens. They grew corn, tomatoes, beans, and prickly pear.

 ## Writing About the Big Question

**Community or individual: Which is more important?** "Tenochtitlan: Inside the Aztec Capital" describes how workers in Tenochtitlan built a ten-mile embankment to prevent crop damage and protect the city from flooding. Complete this sentence:

When people work together for a common cause, they can help not only

themselves but _____.

## Note-taking Guid

Use this chart to record details about the ancient city of Tenochtitlan.

| The Location | The Floating Gardens | The Homes | The Furniture and Decoration |
|---|---|---|---|
| an island in a swamp | | | |

## Tenochtitlan:[1] Inside the Aztec Capital

### Jacqueline Dineen

© Pearson Education

**Activate Prior Knowledge**

What do you know about how ancient people lived?

_____

_____

_____

**Reading Skill**

Remember that an **effect** is the result of a **cause**. What was the effect of the Aztec engineering skills on the Tenochtitlan area?

_____

_____

**Literary Analysis** 🔍

A **legend** is a traditional story about the past. Legends are usually based on **facts**. Facts are statements that can be proved. How might the Spaniards' reactions to their first sight of Tenochtitlan have sparked a legend?

_____

_____

_____

**Reading Check**

Who built the city of Tenochtitlan? Circle the text that tells you.

### The Lake City of Tenochtitlan

The city of Tenochtitlan began on an island in the middle of a swampy lake. There the Aztecs built their first temple to Huitzilopochtli.[2] The place was given the name Tenochtitlan, which means "The Place of the Fruit of the Prickly Pear Cactus." Later on the name was given to the city that grew up around the temple. The Aztecs rebuilt their temples on the same site every 52 years, so the first temple eventually became the great Temple Mayor[3] that stood at the center of the city.

The city started as a collection of huts. It began to grow after 1385, while Acamapichtli[4] was king. The Aztecs were excellent engineers. They built three causeways over the swamp to link the city with the mainland. These were raised roads made of stone supported on wooden pillars. Parts of the causeways were bridges. These bridges could be removed to leave gaps and this prevented enemies from getting to the city. Fresh water was brought from the mainland to the city along stone aqueducts.[5]

### Inside the City

The Spaniards' first view of Tenochtitlan was described by one of Cortés's[6] soldiers, Bernal Diaz: "And when we saw all those towns and level causeway leading into Mexico, we were astounded. These great towns and buildings rising from the water, all made of stone, seemed like an enchanted vision."

By that time Tenochtitlan was the largest city in Mexico. About 200,000 people lived there. The houses were one story high and had flat roofs. In the center of the city was a large square. The twin temple stood on one side, and the king's palace on another.

1. **Tenochtitlan** (te nohch tee TLAHN) *n.* ancient Aztec capital located in what is now Mexico City.
2. **Huitzilopochtli** (weet suh loh POHTCH tlee) *n.* Aztec sun and war god.
3. **Mayor** (may YOHR) *adj.* main.
4. **Acamapichtli** (uh kahm uh PEECH tlee)
5. **aqueducts** (AH kwuh dukts) *n.* large bridgelike structures made for bringing water from a distant source.
6. **Hernando Cortés** (huhr NAHN doh kohr TEZ) Spanish adventurer (1485–1547) who conquered what is now central and southern Mexico.

Officials' houses made of white stone also lined the square. There were few roads. People traveled in canoes along canals.

## Floating Gardens

Tenochtitlan was built in a huge valley, the Valley of Mexico, which was surrounded by mountains. Rivers flowed from the mountains into Lake Texcoco, where Tenochtitlan stood. The lake was linked to four other shallow, swampy lakes. The land around the lakes was dry because there was very little rain. The Aztecs dug ditches and piled up the earth to make islands in the shallow parts of the lake. These chinampas, or swamp gardens, could be farmed. The ditches carried water into larger canals that were used for irrigation[7] and as waterways to the city.

Texcoco and the lake to the south contained fresh water, but the northern lakes contained salt water, which was no good for irrigation. The Aztecs built an embankment[8] 10 miles long to keep out the salt water and also to protect the city from flooding.

## Feeding the People

Archaeologists think that when Tenochtitlan was at its greatest, about one million people lived in the Valley of Mexico. That included Tenochtitlan and the 50 or 60 city-states on the mainland surrounding the lakes. Food for all these people had to come from farming.

Historians are not sure how many people in Tenochtitlan were farmers, but they think it may have been between one third and one half of the population. The rest were the nobility, craftspeople, and others. Each chinampa was only big enough to grow food for one family. Most people in Tenochtitlan depended on food from outside the city.

As the city grew, more and more land was drained for farming and for building. Farmers had no tools except simple hoes and digging sticks, but the loose soil was fertile and easy to turn. The main crop was corn, but farmers also grew tomatoes, beans, chili peppers, and prickly pears. They grew maguey cactus

7. **irrigation** (ir uh GAY shuhn) *n.* supplying water with ditches, canals, or spinklers.

8. **embankment** (im BANGK muhnt) *n.* wall of earth built to keep water back.

**Stop to Reflect**

Why would the builders of Tenochtitlan have used waterways instead of streets for transportation?

_____

_____

_____

_____

**Literary Analysis**

What **fact** about the northern lakes made it necessary to build an embankment? Circle the text that tells the answer.

_____

_____

**Reading Skill**

Identify one **effect** of the city's growth.

_____

_____

_____

### Stop to Reflect

Why do you think that little information exists about Tenochtitlan's buildings?

_____

_____

_____

_____

### Literary Analysis

What sorts of records have provided the **facts** about the homes of the poor people of Tenochtitlan?

_____

_____

### Reading Check

What is adobe? Circle the sentence that tells the answer.

for its fibers and to make a drink called pulque. Cacao trees were grown in the hottest areas. The seeds were used for trading and to make a chocolate drink.

### Inside an Aztec Home

There were big differences between a rich Aztec home and a poor one. The nobles' houses were like palaces. They were one story high and built around a courtyard. Each of the four sides contained four or five large rooms. The courtyards were planted with flower and vegetable gardens. Some houses on the island in the center of the city were built of adobe— bricks made from mud and dried in the sun. Adobe is still used for building in Mexico today. These grand houses and palaces were whitewashed so that they shone in the sun. The Spanish soldier Bernal Diaz described buildings that looked like "gleaming white towers and castles: a marvelous sight."

There is very little evidence about the buildings in Tenochtitlan and hardly any about the poor people's houses. What we do know has been pieced together from scattered historical records such as documents that record the sale of building sites on the chinampa gardens. All of the poorer people's homes were built on the chinampas on the <u>outskirts</u> of the city. Because the chinampas would not take the weight of stone, houses had to be built of lighter materials such as wattle-and-daub. This was made by weaving <u>reeds</u> together and then plastering them with mud. We know that the outskirts of the city were divided into groups of houses inside walled areas, or compounds. A whole family lived in each compound. The family consisted of a couple, their married children, and their grandchildren. Every married couple in the family had a separate house of one or two rooms. All the houses opened onto an outdoor patio that belonged to the whole family.

Outside the house, the families often kept turkeys in pens. The turkeys provided eggs and meat. There

### Vocabulary Development

**outskirts** (OWT skerts) *n.* part of a district far from the center of a city

**reeds** (reedz) *n.* tall, slender grasses that grow in marshy land

was also a beehive for honey. Most families had a bathhouse in the garden.

## Furniture and Decoration

Aztec houses were very plain inside. Everyone slept on mats of reeds that were spread on the dirt floor at night. Families had cooking pots and utensils made of clay. There were <u>goblets</u> for pulque and other drinks, graters for grinding chilis, and storage pots of various designs. Reed baskets were also used for storage. Households had grinding stones for grinding corn into flour. There was also a household shrine with statues of the gods.

The houses had no windows or chimneys, so they must have been dark and smoky from the cooking fire. There were no doors, just an open doorway. Even the palaces had open doorways with cloths hanging over them.

Reader's Response: Which facts in this article might be used to create an interesting legend about Tenochtitlan? Explain your answer.

_____

_____

_____

_____

_____

TAKE NOTES

**Stop to Reflect**

Read the bracketed passage. Do you think it was difficult to live in an Aztec house? Why or why not?

_____

_____

_____

_____

**Reading Check**

What **caused** the Aztec homes to be dark and smoky? Circle the sentence that tells the answer.

**Vocabulary Development**

**goblets** (GAHB lits) *n.* bowl-shaped drinking containers without handles

# Tenochtitlan: Inside the Aztec Capital

1. **Respond:** You may still have questions about the article. Use the chart below to help answer them. Write your questions in the first column. Then, find details in the article that can help you answer each question. List these details in the second column. Finally, write your answers in the third column.

| Questions | Details | Understanding the Article |
|-----------|---------|---------------------------|
|           |         |                           |
|           |         |                           |
|           |         |                           |
|           |         |                           |

2. **Make a Judgment:** The Aztecs shaped their environment to suit their needs. How did this action improve their lives?

_____

_____

_____

3. **Reading Skill:** Reread the article. Find an **effect** for this cause: The city of Tenochtitlan was built on a lake.

_____

_____

4. **Literary Analysis:** Identify three **facts** from the article. Identify two predictions or assumptions made by archaeologists that are likely but cannot be proved to be true.

_____

_____

_____

## Writing: Description

Write a short **description** of the city of Tenochtitlan. Use the idea web to help you find ideas. Write your main idea in the center circle. Then, write details on the web's spokes.

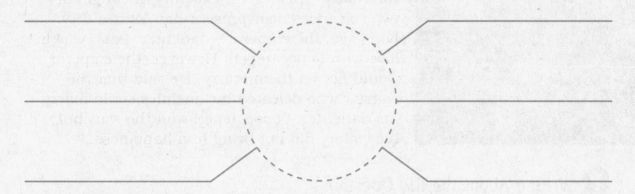

Use your notes to help write your description.

## Listening and Speaking: Persuasive Speech

You will give a **persuasive speech** in which you convince authorities that building a city on an island in the middle of a lake is a good idea. Use the following activity to prepare for your persuasive speech.

- Your position: _____

  _____

- Support for position: _____

  _____

  _____

  _____

- Words or phrases that will help me recall main points:

  _____

  _____

# Popocatepetl and Ixtlaccihuatl
## Juliet Piggott Wood

**Summary** This legend explains the origin of two volcanoes near present-day Mexico City. Long ago, the emperor's daughter, Ixtla, was in love with Popocatepetl. However, the emperor would not let them marry. He said that the warrior who defeated his enemies could marry his daughter. Popocatepetl won the war, but his victory did not bring him happiness.

 **Writing About the Big Question**

**Community or individual: Which is more important?** In "Popocatepetl and Ixtlaccihuatl," an Aztec emperor nearly brings his kingdom to ruin by stubbornly insisting that his daughter rule alone after his death. Complete this sentence:

**Tradition** and **duty** to one's **community** sometimes require a person to

_____.

## Note-taking Guide
Use this chart to record details about Popocatepetl.

| What Popo Says | What Popo Does | What Happens |
| --- | --- | --- |
|  |  |  |
|  |  |  |

# Popocatepetl and Ixtlaccihuatl

1. **Respond:** Use the chart below to gain a better understanding of "Popocatepetl and Ixtlaccihuatl." First, write your questions in the first column. Then, find details in the legend that can help answer each question. These details may be about the characters or their actions. List these details in the second column. Finally, use the details to help answer your questions. For each question, write the answer in the third column.

| Questions | Details | Understanding the Legend |
|---|---|---|
|  |  |  |

2. **Draw Conclusions:** Based on this legend, what traits do you think the Aztecs admired?

_____

_____

3. **Reading Skill:** What **causes** the smoke to rise from the volcano in this legend?

_____

_____

4. **Literary Analysis:** Identify two **facts** in this story. How do you know that they are facts?

_____

_____

## Writing: Description

Write a short **description** of the character of Ixtla. Use an idea web to record details. Write your main idea in the center circle. Then, write details about Ixtla on the web's spokes.

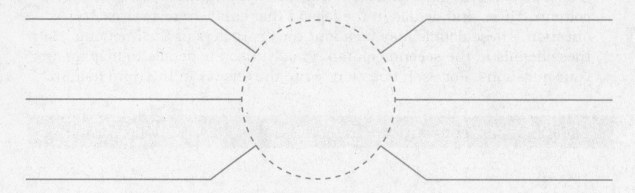

Use your notes to help write your description.

## Listening and Speaking: Persuasive Speech

Prepare a **persuasive speech** to convince the Emperor that Popo and Ixtla should be allowed to marry.

- Remember your audience when you prepare a persuasive speech. You must show respect when you talk to an emperor or other leader. Write three words or phrases that show respect.

_____

- People give persuasive speeches to persuade an audience to agree with them. What reason for the marriage will the emperor probably agree with? What reason will he probably not agree with?

_____

_____

- One way to persuade someone is to tell how other people feel. Do you suppose that the people of Tenochtitlan would like Ixtla and Popo to marry? Explain.

_____

# Textbooks

## About Textbooks

A **textbook** is nonfiction. It gives facts about a subject. Almost all textbooks have similar features.

- **Purpose:** A textbook provides information for students about a main topic or idea.
- **Structure:** Structure is the way that something is put together. Textbooks are put together in sections, such as chapters or units. A table of contents with the page numbers tells you where each section begins.
- **Format:** Format is the pattern for a book's pages. The format includes:

  - headings
  - highlighted terms
  - type size
  - diagrams and charts

## Reading Skill

Cause-and-effect organization is one way to organize information in a text. A **cause** is the reason for an action or event. An **effect** is what happens as a result of an action or event. To **analyze cause-and-effect organization,** look for words and phrases that are clues to causes and effects. These words include *because, as a result, led to, caused,* and *for this reason.* Also, look for connections between events, and ask yourself questions as you read. What happened before or after something else happened? What was the result of this action or event?

| Questions for Analyzing Cause-and-Effect Relationships ||
|---|---|
| What happened? | Winter |
| Why did this happen? (**cause**) | Earth's axis tilted away from the sun. |
| What has happened or will happen as a result? (**effect**) | Sunlight hit our hemisphere less directly; the days were colder. |

## Text Structure

Underline the main heading and the two subheadings on the page. What do they say you will learn from reading this page?

_____

_____

_____

## Vocabulary Builder

**Geography Terms** The *equator* is an imaginary line drawn around the middle of Earth. The equator is exactly the same distance from each of the *poles,* or the North Pole and the South Pole. The North Pole is the northernmost point on Earth. The South Pole is the southernmost point on Earth. Earth's *axis* is an imaginary line through the North and South Poles around which Earth turns.

## Text Structure

Illustrations show information in a way that is easy to understand. What information does Figure 1 show?

_____

_____

# The Seasons on Earth
## from *Prentice Hall Science Explorer*

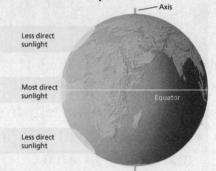

Axis

Less direct sunlight

Most direct sunlight

Equator

Less direct sunlight

**Figure 1 Sunlight Striking Earth's Surface** Near the equator, sunlight strikes Earth's surface more directly and is less spread out than near the poles.
**Relating Cause and Effect** Why is it usually colder near the poles than near the equator?

Most places outside the tropics and polar regions have four distinct seasons: winter, spring, summer, and autumn. But there are great differences in temperature from place to place. For instance, it is generally warmer near the equator than near the poles. Why is this so?

## How Sunlight Hits Earth

Figure 1 shows how sunlight strikes Earth's surface. Notice that sunlight hits Earth's surface most directly near the equator. Near the poles, sunlight arrives at a steep angle. As a result, it is spread out over a greater area. That is why it is warmer near the equator than near the poles.

## Earth's Tilted Axis

If Earth's axis were straight up and down relative to its orbit, temperatures would remain fairly constant year-round. There would be no seasons. Earth has seasons because its axis is tilted as it revolves around the sun.

Notice in Figure 2 that Earth's axis is always tilted at an angle of 23.5° from the vertical. As Earth revolves around the sun, the north end of its axis is tilted away from the sun for part of the year and toward the sun for part of the year.

Summer and winter are caused by Earth's tilt as it revolves around the sun. The change in seasons is not caused by changes in Earth's distance from the sun. In fact, Earth is farthest from the sun when it is summer in the Northern Hemisphere.

**Figure 2**

## The Seasons

The yearly cycle of the seasons is caused by the tilt of Earth's axis as it revolves around the sun.

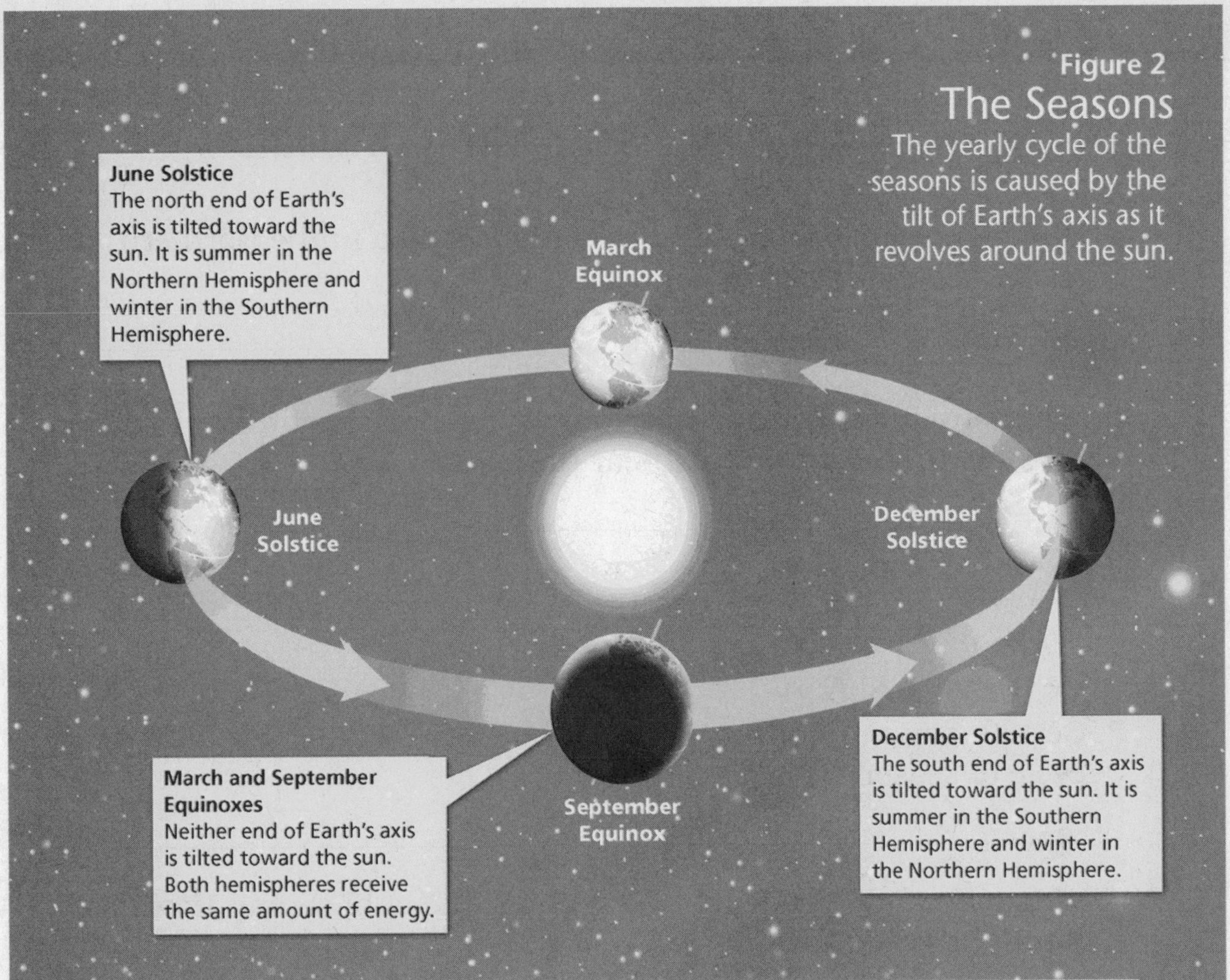
**June Solstice**
The north end of Earth's axis is tilted toward the sun. It is summer in the Northern Hemisphere and winter in the Southern Hemisphere.
March Equinox
June Solstice
December Solstice
September Equinox
**March and September Equinoxes**
Neither end of Earth's axis is tilted toward the sun. Both hemispheres receive the same amount of energy.
**December Solstice**
The south end of Earth's axis is tilted toward the sun. It is summer in the Southern Hemisphere and winter in the Northern Hemisphere.

The height of the sun above the horizon varies with the season. Interpreting Diagrams *When is the sun at its maximum height in the Northern Hemisphere?*

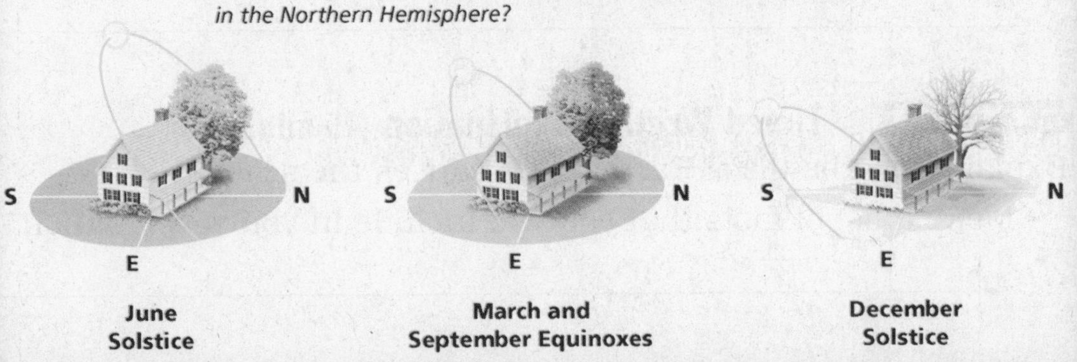
S
N
E
**June Solstice**
S
N
E
**March and September Equinoxes**
S
N
E
**December Solstice**

# Thinking About the Textbook

1. Study Figure 2. What will the weather be like in the Northern Hemisphere during the June solstice?

   _____

2. Why would people living near the equator wear lighter weight clothing than people living near the North Pole?

   _____

   _____

**TALK ABOUT IT** Reading Skill

3. Certain parts of Earth experience seasons. What causes the yearly cycle of seasons?

   _____

4. What effects do you learn about under the subheading **How Sunlight Hits Earth?**

   _____

   _____

**WRITE ABOUT IT** Timed Writing: Explanation **(15 minutes)**

Explain how the tilt of Earth's axis causes the seasons.

- Make a list of facts that you will include in your explanation.

   _____

   _____

- Write a first sentence that summarizes the cause of the seasons.

   _____

   _____

# Sun and Moon in a Box • How the Snake Got Poison

## Reading Skill

- A **comparison** tells how two or more things are alike.

- A **contrast** tells how two or more things are different.

By **using your prior knowledge to compare and contrast**, you can understand an unfamiliar concept. For example, you may understand an ancient culture better if you look for ways in which it is similar to and different from your own culture. You might also find similarities and differences between a story told long ago and one that is popular today. To help you compare and contrast stories, ask questions such as the following:

- What does this event bring to mind?

- Does this character make me think of someone I know or have read about?

## Literary Analysis

Stories such as fables, folk tales, and myths are influenced by the **cultural context**, or background, customs, and beliefs, of the people who originally told them. Recognizing the cultural context will help you understand and appreciate what you read. Use this chart to keep track of the cultural context of a literary work. You may not use every box for each work.

| Story Title: | |
|---|---|
| Time | Customs |
| Place | Beliefs |

# Sun and Moon in a Box
## Alfonso Ortiz and Richard Erdoes

**Summary** This Native American story tells how winter began. Coyote and Eagle took a box that contained the sun and the moon. Coyote tricked Eagle and opened the box. The sun and moon escaped and flew into the sky. Earth turned cold, snow fell, and winter settled in. Earth will now have summer and winter.

 **Writing About the Big Question**

**Community or individual: Which is more important?** In "Sun and Moon in a Box," Coyote betrays Eagle's trust. Complete this sentence:

When an individual puts his or her needs ahead of the community, the

results can be _____.

## Note-taking Guide

Use this chart to understand the causes and effects in the story.

| Cause | Effect/ Cause | Effect/ Cause | Effect/ Cause | Effect/ Cause | Effect |
|-------|------|------|------|------|--------|
| Eagle and Coyote see a box holding the sun and the moon. | | | | | Earth now has summer and winter. |

# Sun and Moon in a Box
## Zuni Folk Tale
### Alfonso Ortiz and Richard Erdoes

Coyote and Eagle were hunting. Eagle caught rabbits. Coyote caught nothing but grasshoppers. Coyote said: "Friend Eagle, my chief, we make a great hunting pair."

"Good, let us stay together," said Eagle.

They went toward the west. They came to a deep canyon. "Let us fly over it," said Eagle.

"My chief, I cannot fly," said Coyote. "You must carry me across."

"Yes, I see that I have to," said Eagle. He took Coyote on his back and flew across the canyon. They came to a river. "Well," said Eagle, "you cannot fly, but you certainly can swim. This time I do not have to carry you."

Eagle flew over the stream, and Coyote swam across. He was a bad swimmer. He almost drowned. He coughed up a lot of water. "My chief," he said, "when we come to another river, you must carry me." Eagle regretted to have Coyote for a companion.

They came to Kachina Pueblo.[1] The Kachinas were dancing. Now, at this time, the earth was still soft and new. There was as yet no sun and no moon. Eagle and Coyote sat down and watched the dance. They saw that the Kachinas had a square box. In it they kept the sun and the moon. Whenever they wanted light they opened the lid and let the sun peek out. Then it was day. When they wanted less light, they opened the box just a little for the moon to look out.

"This is something wonderful," Coyote whispered to Eagle.

"This must be the sun and the moon they are keeping in that box," said Eagle. "I have heard about these two wonderful beings."

"Let us steal the box," said Coyote.

"No, that would be wrong," said Eagle. "Let us just borrow it."

When the Kachinas were not looking, Eagle grabbed the box and flew off. Coyote ran after him on the

1. **Kachina Pueblo** (kuh CHEE nuh PWEB loh) Native American village.

---

## TAKE NOTES

### Activate Prior Knowledge

With what stories about the sun and moon are you familiar?

_____

_____

_____

### Literary Analysis 🔍

**Cultural context** is the background, customs, and beliefs of the people who originally told the story. Details within a story will help you understand the cultural context. What details show that this is a Native American story?

_____

_____

_____

### Reading Check

What do the Kachinas keep in the square box? Circle the sentence that tells the answer.

How does Coyote address Eagle in the bracketed paragraph? How is this a clue to the **cultural context** of this story?

_____

_____

_____

**Stop to Reflect**

How does Eagle feel about Coyote's request to carry the box?

_____

_____

_____

_____

**Reading Skill**

A **contrast** tells how things are different. Underline Eagle's and Coyote's comments about carrying the box. Contrast why each character wants to carry the box.

_____

_____

_____

_____

ground. After a while Coyote called Eagle: "My chief, let me have the box. I am ashamed to let you do all the carrying."

"No," said Eagle, "you are not <u>reliable</u>. You might be curious and open the box and then we could lose the wonderful things we borrowed."

For some time they went on as before—Eagle flying above with the box, Coyote running below, trying to keep up. Then once again Coyote called Eagle: "My chief, I am ashamed to let you carry the box. I should do this for you. People will talk badly about me, letting you carry this burden."

"No, I don't trust you," Eagle repeated. "You won't be able to refrain from opening the box. Curiosity will get the better of you."

"No," cried Coyote, "do not fear, my chief, I won't even think of opening the box." Still, Eagle would not give it to him, continuing to fly above, holding the box in his talons. But Coyote went on pestering Eagle: "My chief, I am really embarrassed. People will say: 'That lazy, disrespectful Coyote lets his chief do all the carrying.'"

"No, I won't give this box to you," Eagle objected. "It is too precious to entrust to somebody like you."

They continued as before, Eagle flying, Coyote running. Then Coyote begged for the fourth time: "My chief, let me carry the box for a while. My wife will scold me, and my children will no longer respect me, when they find out that I did not help you carry this load."

Then Eagle <u>relented</u>, saying: "Will you promise not to drop the box and under no circumstances to open it?"

"I promise, my chief, I promise," cried Coyote. "You can rely upon me. I shall not betray your trust."

Then Eagle allowed Coyote to carry the box. They went on as before, Eagle flying, Coyote running, carrying the box in his mouth. They came to a wooded area, full of trees and bushes. Coyote pretended to lag behind, hiding himself behind some bushes where

**Vocabulary Development**

**reliable** (ri LY uh buhl) *adj.* dependable
**relented** (ri LENT id) *v.* gave in

Eagle could not see him. He could not <u>curb</u> his curiosity. Quickly he sat down and opened the box. In a flash, Sun came out of the box and flew away, to the very edge of the sky, and at once the world grew cold, the leaves fell from the tree branches, the grass turned brown, and icy winds made all living things shiver.

Then, before Coyote could put the lid back on the box, Moon jumped out and flew away to the outer rim of the sky, and at once snow fell down from heaven and covered the plains and the mountains.

Eagle said: "I should have known better. I should not have let you persuade me. I knew what kind of low, cunning, stupid creature you are. I should have remembered that you never keep a promise. Now we have winter. If you had not opened the box, then we could have kept Sun and Moon always close to us. Then there would be no winter. Then we would have summer all the time."

---

**Reader's Response:** As you were reading the story, did you think that Eagle should give the box to Coyote? Why or why not?

_____

_____

_____

_____

_____

_____

_____

_____

_____

_____

**Vocabulary Development**
**curb** (kerb) *v.* check or control

**Reading Skill**

A **comparison** tells how two or more things are the same. Underline what Sun and Moon do after the box is opened. Write a comparison of the actions of Sun and Moon.

_____

_____

_____

**Literary Analysis**

The attitudes expressed in the story about summer and winter show **cultural context.** What attitudes does the story express about summer and winter?

_____

_____

Why do you think ancient people felt this way about these seasons?

_____

_____

**Reading Check**

Circle the sentence that tells why Coyote opened the box.

# Sun and Moon in a Box

1. **Infer:** Why do you think Eagle finally agrees to give the box to Coyote?

   _____

   _____

2. **Make a Judgment:** Explain whether Eagle shares any responsibility for the appearance of the first winter.

   _____

   _____

3. **Reading Skill: Compare** and **contrast** Eagle and Coyote. Think about how they look, what their abilities are, and how they react to responsibility. Use this Venn diagram.

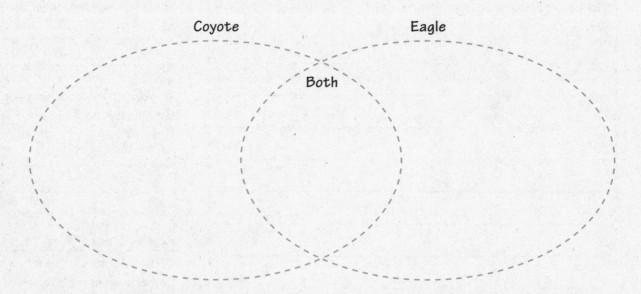

4. **Literary Analysis:** Eagle and Coyote spot the box at a Kachina Pueblo. How does this detail help you understand the **cultural context** of the story?

   _____

   _____

### Writing: Plot Summary

Write a **plot summary** for "Sun and Moon in a Box." Answer the following questions to help you complete the assignment.

- What is the conflict, or struggle, in the story?

  _____

  _____

  _____

- When is the critical moment in the story?

  _____

  _____

- Why is the box important to the story?

  _____

  _____

- How does this story explain the beginning of winter?

  _____

  _____

### Listening and Speaking: Story

Remember to include facts and characteristics of the animal without telling what the animal is. Use the following lines to write the facts and characteristics for your **story**.

**Fact/characteristic 1:** _____

**Fact/characteristic 2:** _____

**Fact/characteristic 3:** _____

**Fact/characteristic 4:** _____

**Fact/characteristic 5:** _____

**Ideas for dialogue:** _____

# How the Snake Got Poison
## Zora Neale Hurston

**Summary** This African American folk tale tells that God gave the snake poison to protect itself. The snake used the poison to kill small animals. The other animals complained to God. God resolved the matter by giving the snake a bell to tie to its tail. The bell alerted others that the snake was present.

### Writing About the Big Question

**Community or individual: Which is more important?** In "How the Snake Got Poison," God must mediate between the snake and the varmints. Complete these sentences:

When the needs of the **individual** and the needs of the larger **group** are

in conflict, it is helpful to _____

because _____.

### Note-taking Guide
Use this chart to write what the snake and varmints do in the story.

| Snake | Varmints |
|---|---|
| complains to God because he has no protection | |
| | |
| | |

# How the Snake Got Poison

1. **Analyze:** Explain why the varmints and the snake did not work out their problems together.

   _____

   _____

   _____

2. **Analyze:** Think about the answer to number one. What might this reveal about people and their ways of interacting?

   _____

   _____

3. **Reading Skill: Compare** and **contrast** the snake and the varmints at the beginning of the story. Use the diagram below.

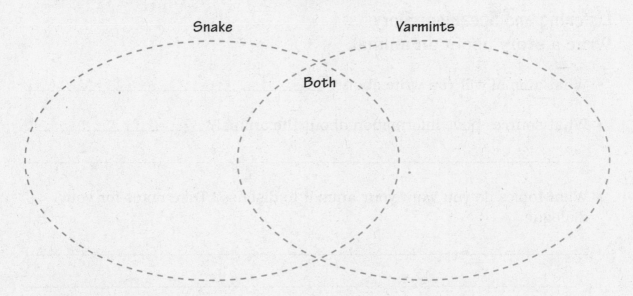

Snake          Varmints

Both

4. **Literary Analysis:** How does the the author's use of dialect help you understand the **cultural context** of the story?

   _____

   _____

## Writing: Plot Summary

Write a **plot summary** of "How the Snake Got Poison."

- Who are the characters involved in the story? _____

  _____

- What is the conflict, or struggle, in the story?

  _____

  _____

- Where does the story take place? _____

- How does this story explain how the snake got its poison and rattle?

  _____

  _____

  Use these notes to help you write a plot summary.

## Listening and Speaking: Story

Write a **story** about an animal.

- What animal will you write about? _____

- What sources have information about the animal? _____

  _____

- What topics do you want your animal to discuss? Take notes for your dialogue.

  _____

  _____

  Use these notes to help you write your story.

# The People Could Fly • All Stories Are Anansi's

## Reading Skill

When you **compare and contrast**, you recognize similarities and differences. You can compare and contrast elements in a literary work by **using a Venn diagram** to examine character traits, situations, and ideas.

- First, reread the text to locate the details you will compare.

- Then, write the details on the diagram below.

Recording these details will help you understand the similarities and differences in a literary work. You can also use a Venn diagram to compare and contrast elements of two different literary works.

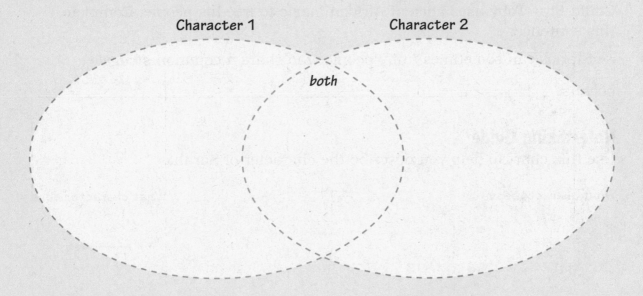

Character 1          Character 2

both

## Literary Analysis

A **folk tale** is a story that is composed orally and then passed from person to person by word of mouth. Although they originate in this **oral tradition**, most folk tales are eventually collected and written down. Similar folk tales are told by different cultures throughout the world, using common character types, plot elements, and themes. Folk tales often teach a lesson about life and present a clear separation between good and evil. Folk tales are part of the oral tradition that also includes fairy tales, legends, myths, fables, tall tales, and ghost stories.

HOEING

# The People Could Fly
## Virginia Hamilton

**Summary** The story tells that long ago in Africa people knew how to fly. Many came to America on slave ships. They lost their wings because the ships were too crowded. Enslaved African Americans worked hard in the fields in America. They were mistreated. Toby helps people remember how to fly. Those who cannot fly help tell the tale to others.

 **Writing About the Big Question**

**Community or individual: Which is more important?** In "The People Could Fly," Toby uses ancient African magic to free his people. Complete this sentence:

Stories can sometimes unify people who share a common struggle

because _____.

## Note-taking Guide
Use this chart to help you describe the character of Sarah.

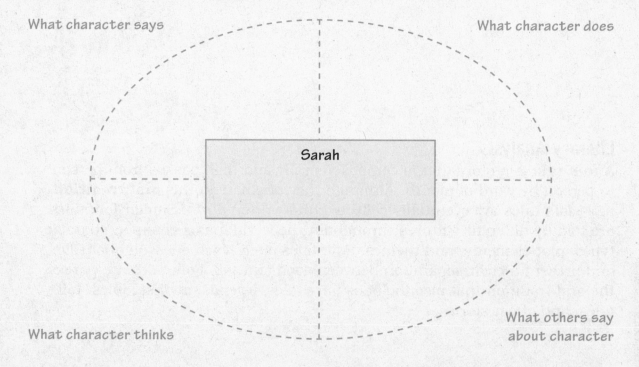

What character says

What character does

Sarah

What character thinks

What others say
about character

# The People Could Fly
## Virginia Hamilton

They say the people could fly. Say that long ago in Africa, some of the people knew magic. And they would walk up on the air like climbin up on a gate. And they flew like blackbirds over the fields. Black, shiny wings flappin against the blue up there.

Then, many of the people were captured for Slavery. The ones that could fly shed their wings. They couldn't take their wings across the water on the slave ships. Too crowded, don't you know.

The folks were full of misery, then. Got sick with the up and down of the sea. So they forgot about flyin when they could no longer breathe the sweet scent of Africa.

Say the people who could fly kept their power, although they shed their wings. They kept their secret magic in the land of slavery. They looked the same as the other people from Africa who had been coming over, who had dark skin. Say you couldn't tell anymore one who could fly from one who couldn't.

One such who could was an old man, call him Toby. And standin tall, yet afraid, was a young woman who once had wings. Call her Sarah. Now Sarah carried a babe tied to her back. She trembled to be so hard worked and scorned.

The slaves labored in the fields from sunup to sundown. The owner of the slaves callin himself their Master. Say he was a hard lump of clay. A hard, glinty[1] coal. A hard rock pile, wouldn't be moved. His Overseer[2] on horseback pointed out the slaves who were slowin down. So the one called Driver[3] cracked his whip over the slow ones to make them move faster. That whip was a slice-open cut of pain. So they did move faster. Had to.

---

## Vocabulary Development

**scorned** (skornd) *adj.* looked down upon

---

1. **glinty** (GLIN tee) *adj.* shiny; reflecting light.
2. **Overseer** (OH ver see er) *n.* someone who watches over and directs the work of others.
3. **Driver** (DRY ver) *n.* someone who forced (drove) the slaves to work harder.

 **TAKE NOTES**

### Activate Prior Knowledge

Think of a tale, story, or song about freedom. Retell it.

_____

_____

_____

### Literary Analysis

A **folk tale** is a story that was passed from person to person by word of mouth. The stories were eventually written. Some words were spelled in an unusual way to suggest how they would sound when spoken. Circle such a word in the first bracketed passage.

### Reading Skill

When you **compare and contrast**, you recognize similarities and differences. Read the second bracketed passage. Name a similarity or a difference between the Driver and the Overseer.

_____

_____

### Reading Check

The people from Africa could not fly any longer. Underline the sentence that tells why.

## Stop to Reflect

How would you feel if you were the woman or the baby described in the first bracketed passage? Why do you think the Driver is so cruel?

_____

_____

_____

_____

## Reading Check

What does Toby help Sarah to do? Underline the answer in the text.

## Literary Analysis

In the second bracketed passage, describe two examples of magic in this **folk tale**.

_____

_____

_____

_____

Sarah hoed and chopped the row as the babe on her back slept.

Say the child grew hungry. That babe started up bawling too loud. Sarah couldn't stop to feed it. Couldn't stop to soothe and quiet it down. She let it cry. She didn't want to. She had no heart to <u>croon</u> to it.

"Keep that thing quiet," called the Overseer. He pointed his finger at the babe. The woman scrunched low. The Driver cracked his whip across the babe anyhow. The babe hollered like any hurt child, and the woman fell to the earth.

The old man that was there, Toby, came and helped her to her feet.

"I must go soon," she told him.

"Soon," he said.

Sarah couldn't stand up straight any longer. She was too weak. The sun burned her face. The babe cried and cried, "Pity me, oh, pity me," say it sounded like. Sarah was so sad and starvin, she sat down in the row.

"Get up, you black cow," called the Overseer. He pointed his hand, and the Driver's whip snarled around Sarah's legs. Her sack dress tore into rags. Her legs bled onto the earth. She couldn't get up.

Toby was there where there was no one to help her and the babe.

"Now, before it's too late," panted Sarah. "Now, Father!"

"Yes, Daughter, the time is come," Toby answered. "Go, as you know how to go!"

He raised his arms, holding them out to her. "Kum . . . yali, kum buba tambe," and more magic words, said so quickly, they sounded like whispers and sighs.

The young woman lifted one foot on the air. Then the other. She flew clumsily at first, with the child now held tightly in her arms. Then she felt the magic, the African mystery. Say she rose just as free as a bird. As light as a feather.

The Overseer rode after her, hollerin. Sarah flew over the fences. She flew over the woods. Tall trees could not snag her. Nor could the Overseer. She flew

### Vocabulary Development

**croon** (kroon) v. sing or hum quietly and soothingly

like an eagle now, until she was gone from sight. No one dared speak about it. Couldn't believe it. But it was, because they that was there saw that it was.

Say the next day was dead hot in the fields. A young man slave fell from the heat. The Driver come and whipped him. Toby come over and spoke words to the fallen one. The words of ancient Africa once heard are never remembered completely. The young man forgot them as soon as he heard them. They went way inside him. He got up and rolled over on the air. He rode it awhile. And he flew away.

Another and another fell from the heat. Toby was there. He cried out to the fallen and reached his arms out to them. "Kum kunka yali, kum . . . tambe!" Whispers and sighs. And they too rose on the air. They rode the hot breezes. The ones flyin were black and shinin sticks, wheelin above the head of the Overseer. They crossed the rows, the fields, the fences, the streams, and were away.

"Seize the old man!" cried the Overseer. "I heard him say the magic words. Seize him!"

The one callin himself Master come runnin. The Driver got his whip ready to curl around old Toby and tie him up. The slaveowner took his hip gun from its place. He meant to kill old, black Toby.

But Toby just laughed. Say he threw back his head and said, "Hee, hee! Don't you know who I am? Don't you know some of us in this field?" He said it to their faces. "We are ones who fly!"

And he sighed the ancient words that were a dark promise. He said them all around to the others in the field under the whip,

". . . buba yali . . . buba tambe. . . ."

There was a great outcryin. The bent backs straightened up. Old and young who were called slaves and could fly joined hands. Say like they would ring-sing.[4] But they didn't <u>shuffle</u> in a circle. They didn't sing. They rose on the air. They flew in a flock that was black against the heavenly blue.

---

**Vocabulary Development**
**shuffle** (SHUF uhl) *v.* walk with dragging feet

---

4. **ring-sing** *v.* joining hands in a circle to sing and dance.

**Literary Analysis**

How do Toby's actions in the bracketed passage reveal the good and evil in this **folk tale**?

_____

_____

_____

_____

_____

**Reading Skill**

Read the second bracketed passage. **Contrast** how the Master acts and how Toby acts. Name one difference in the way they act.

_____

_____

_____

_____

**Reading Check**

Underline the sentence that tells why the Overseer called to have Toby seized.

### Reading Skill

Think about the **contrast** between the version of the story that the Overseer tells and the one that the Master tells. Why would the Master say "it was a lie"?

_____

_____

_____

_____

_____

### Literary Analysis

In the bracketed passage, underline the sentences that tell how this story was passed down in the **oral tradition**.

### Stop to Reflect

How did the ones who could not fly help future generations?

_____

_____

_____

_____

_____

Black crows or black shadows. It didn't matter, they went so high. Way above the plantation, way over the slavery land. Say they flew away to Free-dom.

And the old man, old Toby, flew behind them, takin care of them. He wasn't cryin. He wasn't laughin. He was the seer.[5] His gaze fell on the plantation where the slaves who could not fly waited.

"Take us with you!" Their looks spoke it but they were afraid to shout it. Toby couldn't take them with him. Hadn't the time to teach them to fly. They must wait for a chance to run.

"Goodie-bye!" The old man called Toby spoke to them, poor souls! And he was flyin gone.

So they say. The Overseer told it. The one called Master said it was a lie, a trick of the light. The Driver kept his mouth shut.

The slaves who could not fly told about the people who could fly to their children. When they were free. When they sat close before the fire in the free land, they told it. They did so love firelight and Free-dom, and tellin.

They say that the children of the ones who could not fly told their children. And now, me, I have told it to you.

**Reader's Response:** 1) How would you feel if you were one of the people who could fly? 2) How would you feel if you were one of the ones left behind?

_____

_____

_____

_____

_____

5. **seer** (SEE er) *n.* one who has supposed power to see the future; prophet.

# The People Could Fly

1. **Interpret:** Why do you think the author includes Toby's "magic words" in the story?

   _____

   _____

   _____

2. **Draw Conclusions:** What do you think "flying" refers to in the story?

   _____

   _____

   _____

3. **Reading Skill: Compare and contrast** the personalities of Toby and the Overseer. How are they similar? How are they different?

   _____

   _____

   _____

4. **Literary Analysis:** Use this chart to list elements of **folk tales** in this story.

| Elements: | Good | Evil | Lesson | Theme |
|-----------|------|------|--------|-------|
| Examples: | | | | |

## Writing: Review

- Some people will understand your review better if you can compare the story you are reviewing to another one that is similar. Use this chart to compare this story to another that is similar.

|  | This tale | A similar tale |
|---|---|---|
| Title |  |  |
| Plot |  |  |
| Characters |  |  |
| Other elements |  |  |

Use your notes to write your review of the folk tale.

## Listening and Speaking: Television News Report

First, watch a television news program. Answer the following questions about one news story:

- **Where** did the story take place? _____

- **When** did the story take place? _____

- **What** was the story about? _____

- **Whom** was the story about? _____

- **Who** saw the event happen? _____

_____

Then, answer the questions again using the events in "The People Could Fly." Use your answers to write your news report.

# All Stories Are Anansi's

## Harold Courlander

**Summary** This folk tale is about Anansi, a trickster spider who wants to own all of the stories. The Sky God, Nyame, currently owns the stories. He agrees to give the stories to Anansi for something in return. Anansi uses his tricky ways to win Nyame's challenge.

 **Writing About the Big Question**

**Community or individual: Which is more important?** In "All Stories Are Anansi's," Anansi uses trickery to capture the hornet, the python, and the leopard. Complete the sentence:

When an individual exploits others for personal gain, _____

_____.

## Note-taking Guide

Use this chart to help you record the ways in which Anansi plays a trickster.

| What does Anansi do to the hornets? | What does Anansi do to the python? | What does Anansi do to the leopard? |
|---|---|---|
| Anansi pours water on himself and the hornets' nest. | | |

# All Stories Are Anansi's

1. **Infer:** What can you infer about the hornets, the python, and the leopard from the fact that they listen to Anansi?

   _____

   _____

2. **Interpret:** How would you describe Anansi's personal code of behavior?

   _____

   _____

3. **Reading Skill: Compare and contrast** the hornets, the python, and the leopard. How are they similar? How are they different?

   _____

   _____

   _____

   _____

4. **Literary Analysis:** Use this chart to give examples of the elements of **folk tales** that you find in this story.

| Elements: | Good | Evil | Lesson | Theme |
|-----------|------|------|--------|-------|
| Examples: | | | | |

## Writing: Review

Write a review of "All Stories Are Anansi's" in which you tell other readers whether they will enjoy the folk tale. Fill in the blanks to help you determine your opinion.

- I like/do not like Anansi because _____ .

- I like/do not like the hornets/the pythons/the leopard because _____ .

- I think Nyame is _____ because _____ .

- I think the plot of the story is _____ .

- I like/do not like the way the writer _____ .

## Listening and Speaking: Television News Report

Prepare for your **television news report** by answering the following questions. Use this information to present the report.

- Where did the events take place? _____

- When did the events take place? _____

- What did Anansi want? _____

- What happened with the hornets? _____

- What happened with the python? _____

- What happened with the leopard? _____

- What happened at the end? _____

# Editorials

## About Editorials

**Editorials** are articles. They are about a topic that can prompt more than one possible point of view. Editorials tell the writers' opinions. Editorial writers support their opinions with

- facts
- statistics
- examples

Editorials try to persuade readers to agree with the writer's opinion. Newspapers and magazines may have editorials. Some editorials appear online.

## Reading Skill

An author's point of view is the way that he or she thinks about a subject. To **analyze point of view**, look for clues to the author's opinion. The author's point of view may affect the information in an editorial. Ask these questions:

- What is the author's opinion on the subject?
- What evidence does the author provide to support his or her opinion?
- Does the author include evidence that does not support his or her opinion?

| Techniques for Developing Point of View | Example |
|---|---|
| A clearly stated position | "School dress codes promote a sense of unity." |
| Supporting statistics, facts, and examples | "Students are more focused when distractions such as fashion choices are eliminated." |
| Persuasive techniques and language | "The self-confident manner of uniformed students makes a positive impression on visitors." |
| Arguments that address opposing views | "Some people believe that dress codes discourage individuality, yet, there are many other creative outlets." |
| A concluding statement that reinforces the author's point of view | "Schools with dress codes shift the focus from fashion to education, which is exactly where it should be." |

### Build Understanding

Knowing these words will help you read this editorial.

**captivity** (kap TIV i tee) *n.* the state of being a prisoner or being kept in a small place

**reverence** (REV ruhns) *n.* respect

# Zoos: Joys or Jails?
## Rachel F., San Diego, CA

Imagine your family lives in a luxurious mansion where all your needs are provided for. There are gardens and daily walks and all your favorite foods.

Suddenly, you're taken from your home and shipped to a place where people come from far and wide to ogle at you, thinking they are learning about your lifestyle. Sometimes, your captors force you to perform for thousands of people. Your life has changed drastically. Welcome to the zoo!

Although the circumstances and reasons for animals being in zoos vary, its concept has faults many don't notice during their visit with the animals. Animals in many zoos are kept in areas that are much smaller than their natural habitats.[1] As a result, animals behave differently than they would in their natural surroundings. Animals like big cats are accustomed to roaming territories of up to 10 square miles.

---

1. **natural habitats** (NA chuh ruhl HAB uh tats) places in which animals live in the wild

## Text Structure

Read the title of the editorial. Notice that the title has a question mark. In what way does the title suggest that the article will be an editorial?

_____

_____

_____

## Fluency Builder

Read the bracketed passage silently to yourself. As you read, think about what the writer is trying to express about the events. Then, read the passage aloud with expression.

## Vocabulary Builder

**Parts of Speech** *Faults* may be a noun meaning "flaws or problems that prevent something from working properly." *Faults* may also be a verb meaning "criticizes someone or something for a mistake." Which part of speech is *faults* in the underlined text?

_____

With a partner, discuss how you know the answer.

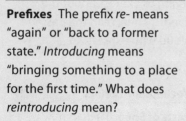
One of the best aspects of the zoo is its emphasis on education. Signs tell visitors about the animals and their behavior in the wild, but notice how the majority say the animals were born in the zoo. Unfortunately, the adaptive behavior[2] due to small cages gives visitors a skewed perception of how the animals actually behave in the wild. Although the idea of education to protect and preserve animals is excellent, is the zoo really setting a good example of treatment or representing the natural actions of these creatures?

Some advocates say that zoos protect and save endangered species. Despite today's advanced breeding techniques, animals raised in the zoo or other places of captivity are not learning the survival techniques they would in the wild. These animals would be very vulnerable if released and would encounter difficulties coping.[3] Would it not be more beneficial to raise them in their natural habitat?

In this way scientists wouldn't face as many risks in reintroducing captive animals raised into the wild.

Helping endangered species in the wild gives them a better chance for survival and reproduction. Scientists should only revert to the zoo if the necessary funding or habitat for breeding is not available.

Animals are not just brought to the zoo to protect their species, but also to provide entertainment. Many animals' lives will include performing for visitors. Four shows are performed every day at the San Diego Zoo. The zoo should be reserved for education and protecting endangered species, not an amusement park where animals are trained to perform.

2. **adaptive behavior** (uh DAHP tiv bee HAYV yer) the way in which people or animals change in order to make their lives easier in a new place

3. **very vulnerable . . . coping.** The animals would not know how to behave or keep themselves alive in the wild. This would put them in danger of being attacked by other animals and possibly dying.

Although the zoo is trying to be helpful in providing shows about the animals, it is harming those it intends to protect. The zoo has good intentions in its educational purposes, and in breeding endangered species, but animals shouldn't perform or be treated in a manner that could change their behaviors from how they act in the wild.

Though zoos are meant to be a joy to viewers and teach lessons about our earth, the zoo jails its inhabitants and passes on faulty knowledge.[4] The wild animals in our world are a wonder, and they must be preserved. At the zoo they are treated with care, but they should be treated with reverence.

Next time you visit a zoo, look at the enclosure of the tigers and watch the seals balance a ball on their noses, and then think about what you are really learning from your day at the zoo.

© Pearson Education

## TAKE NOTES

### Vocabulary Builder

**Verb Tenses** Read the underlined sentence. The verb *is trying* is in the present progressive tense, which describes an action that is happening now. The present progressive tense is formed by combining a helping verb such as *is* and a present participle such as *trying*. What other present-progressive-tense verb is in the same sentence?

_____

### Vocabulary Builder

**Parts of Speech** *Jails* may be a noun meaning "places where criminals are kept as part of their punishment." It may also be a verb meaning "puts someone in a jail" or "traps someone and prevents them from leaving, as if in a jail." Which part of speech is *jails* in the bracketed paragraph?

_____

### Text Structure

How does the photograph on this page relate to the text?

_____

_____

_____

# Thinking About the Editorial

1. What does the writer say are two mistakes that zoos make?

   _____

2. Think about the ways in which people can learn about animals. Why would this writer say that a movie about lions in the wild is more educational than seeing a lion in a zoo?

   _____

   _____

TALK ABOUT IT **Reading Skill**

3. What is the writer's opinion about zoos?

   _____

4. What evidence does the author provide to support her opinion?

   _____

   _____

WRITE ABOUT IT  **Timed Writing: Editorial (25 minutes)**

Write an editorial on an issue that you feel strongly about.

- Choose an issue with more than one "side."
- Choose one side and write a sentence stating your opinion.

   _____

- What facts, descriptions, or examples support your opinion?

   _____

   _____

- Write a strong concluding sentence.

   _____

   _____

The exercises and tools presented here are designed to help you increase your vocabulary. Review the instruction and complete the exercises to build your vocabulary knowledge. Throughout the year, you can apply these skills and strategies to improve your reading, writing, speaking, and listening vocabulary.

The following list contains common word roots with meanings and examples. On the blank lines, write other words you know that have the same roots. Write the meanings of the new words.

| Root | Meaning | Example and Meaning | Your Words | Meanings |
|------|---------|---------------------|------------|----------|
| -brev- | brief; short | *brevity:* the quality of lasting for a short time | | |
| -cede- | go | *recede:* move or go away or move or go back | | |
| -dict- | say or tell | *predict:* tell what might happen next | | |
| -fac- | make | *factory:* place where things are made | | |
| -fer- | bring; carry | *reference:* something you say or write that mentions another person or thing, something that brings or carries more information | | |
| -ject- | throw | *eject:* push or throw out with force | | |
| -manu- | hand | *manual:* operated or done by hand | | |

© Pearson Education

| Root | Meaning | Example and Meaning | Your Words | Meanings |
|------|---------|---------------------|------------|----------|
| -phon- | hearing; sound | *telephone:* a device that brings sound over long distances | | |
| -port- | carry | *support:* carry or hold something up | | |
| -scrib- | write | *scribble:* write something quickly in a messy way | | |
| -sequ- | follow | *consequence:* effect that follows a cause | | |
| -similis- | same | *similar:* alike in some way | | |
| -spec- | look; see | *inspect:* look carefully at something | | |
| -sum- | take; use | *assumption:* something that you think is true or take as true | | |
| -tele- | far; distant | *telescope:* instrument that makes distant objects look larger | | |
| -vali- | strong; worth | *valid:* true, based on strong reasons or facts | | |
| -ver- | truth | *verify:* make sure something is true | | |

The following list contains common prefixes with meanings and examples. On the blank lines, write other words you know that begin with the same prefixes. Write the meanings of the new words.

| Prefix | Meaning | Example and Meaning | Your Words | Meanings |
|--------|---------|---------------------|------------|----------|
| anti- | against | *antisocial*: not liking to meet and talk to people; against friendliness | | |
| aud- | hearing; sound | *auditorium*: a room for hearing concerts or speeches | | |
| con- | with; together | *concur*: agree with | | |
| de- | down; from | *decrease*: become less | | |
| dis- | not | *disorganized*: not organized | | |
| in- | without; not | *incapable*: not able | | |
| inter- | between | *intermission*: short period of time between the parts of a play or concert | | |
| ir- | without; not | *irregular*: not regular | | |

| Prefix | Meaning | Example and Meaning | Your Words | Meanings |
|---|---|---|---|---|
| mis- | wrong; bad | *misspell*: spell wrong; spell incorrectly | | |
| multi- | many | *multicolored*: having many colors | | |
| non- | without; not | *nonfat*: without fat | | |
| ob- | against | *obstacle*: something that works against another, something that makes it difficult for you to succeed | | |
| post- | after | *post-test*: a test given after instruction | | |
| pre- | before | *preview*: look before | | |
| re- | again | *remake*: make again | | |
| sub- | below, under | *submarine*: a ship that moves under the ocean | | |
| super- | above; over | *superior*: better than another | | |
| un-/an-/a- | not | *unbelievable*: not believable | | |

The following list contains common suffixes with meanings and examples. On the blank lines, write other words you know that have the same suffixes. Write the meanings of the new words.

| Suffix | Meaning | Example and Meaning | Your Words | Meanings |
| --- | --- | --- | --- | --- |
| -able/-ible | able to be | *movable*: able to be moved | | |
| -al | relating to | *financial*: relating to money | | |
| -ance/-ence | act of; state of; quality of | *assistance*: act of giving help | | |
| -ate | make | *motivate*: make someone feel eager to do something | | |
| -en | make | *weaken*: make something less strong | | |
| -er/-or | one who | *actor*: person who acts | | |
| -ful | filled with | *joyful*: filled with happiness | | |
| -hood | state or quality of | *manhood*: the state of being an adult male | | |

| Suffix | Meaning | Example and Meaning | Your Words | Meanings |
|--------|---------|---------------------|-----------|----------|
| -ic | like; pertaining to | *heroic:* like a hero; brave | | |
| -ish | resembling | *foolish:* not sensible | | |
| -ist | one who | *violinist:* person who plays the violin | | |
| -ize/-yze | make | *publicize:* make public; tell people about | | |
| -less | without | *powerless:* without power | | |
| -ly | in a way | *quickly:* done in a short amount of time | | |
| -ment | act or quality of | *excitement:* feeling of being excited | | |
| -ness | state or quality of | *kindness:* friendly and caring behavior | | |
| -ous | having; full of | *famous:* having fame; known and recognized by many people | | |
| -sion/-tion | act or process of | *persuasion:* act of convincing someone | | |

Use a **dictionary** to find the correct spelling, the meaning, the pronunciation, and the part of speech of a word. The dictionary will show you how the plural is formed if it is irregular. You can also find the word's history, or *etymology*, in a dictionary. Etymology explains how words change, how they are borrowed from other languages, and how new words are invented, or "coined."

Here is a sample entry from a dictionary. Notice what it tells about the word. Then, follow the instructions.

**lemon** (lem´ ən) **n.** [ME *lymon* < MFr *limon* < Ar *laimūn* < Pers *līmūn*] **1** a small, egg-shaped, edible citrus fruit with a yellow rind and a juicy, sour pulp, rich in ascorbic acid **2** the small, spiny, semitropical evergreen citrus tree (*Citrus limon*) bearing this fruit **3** pale yellow **4** [slang] something, esp. a manufactured article, that is defective or imperfect

1. Circle the *n.* in the dictionary entry. It stands for *noun.* Write what these other parts of speech abbreviations mean: *v.* _____, *adv.* _____, *adj.* _____, *prep.* _____.

2. Underline the origins of the word *lemon.* ME stands for Middle English, Ar stands for Arabic, and Pers. stands for Persian. What do you think MFr stands for? _____

3. Put a box around the pronunciation.

4. How many noun definitions does the entry have? _____

5. Which definition is slang? _____

6. Which definition of *lemon* is used in the following sentence? _____

   The car that my dad bought turned out to be a lemon.

**Activity:** Use a dictionary to learn about the origins of these words.

**Activity:** Use a dictionary to learn about the origins of these words.

**1. literature** _____ / _____ / _____
             pronunciation      main part of speech     original language(s)

_____ / _____
       1st meaning                      other meanings

_____

_____

_____

_____

**2. language** _____ / _____ / _____
             pronunciation      main part of speech     original language(s)

_____ / _____
       1st meaning                      other meanings

_____

_____

_____

**Activity:** Look up each of the following words in a dictionary. Then, write a definition of the word and a sentence using the word.

moment _____

_____

popular _____

_____

remedy _____

_____

blur _____

_____

lazy _____

_____

Use these word study cards to break big words into their parts. Write the word at the top of the card. Then, divide the word into its prefix, root, and suffix. Note that not all words have prefixes and suffixes. List the meaning of each part of the word. Next, find three words with the same root and write them on the card. Finally, write the word's part of speech and its definition. Use a dictionary to help you. One example has been done for you.

| Word: | invisible | |
|---|---|---|
| **Prefix** | **Root** | **Suffix** |
| **in**: not | **vis**: see | **ible**-able to be |

**Root-related Words**
1. vision
2. revise
3. visibility

**Definition:** invisible *adj.* not able to be seen

| Word: | | |
|---|---|---|
| **Prefix** | **Root** | **Suffix** |
| | | |

**Root-related Words**
1.
2.
3.

**Definition:**

**Word:**

| Prefix | Root | Suffix |
|---|---|---|

**Root-related Words**
1.
2.
3.

**Definition:**

**Word:**

| Prefix | Root | Suffix |
|---|---|---|

**Root-related Words**
1.
2.
3.

**Definition:**

**Word:**

| Prefix | Root | Suffix |
|---|---|---|

**Root-related Words**
1.
2.
3.

**Definition:**

**background** (BAK grownd) *n.* a person's experience or knowledge

**clarify** (KLAR uh fy) *v.* make clear

**context** (KAHN tekst) *n.* surrounding text or information

**establish** (uh STAB lish) *v.* determine; make sure of

**previous** (PREE vee uhs) *adj.* occurring before in time or order

**prior** (PRY uhr) *adj.* coming before in time; earlier

**recall** (ri KAWL) *v.* call back; remember

**reveal** (ri VEEL) *v.* make known

**significance** (sig NIF uh kuhns) *n.* meaning, importance

**verify** (VER uh fy) *v.* prove to be true

**A. True/False** For each of the following, mark T or F to indicate whether the italicized vocabulary word has been used correctly in the sentence. If you have marked F, correct the sentence by changing the words that make the statement wrong.

1. _____ You can use a dictionary to *clarify* the meaning of a word.

2. _____ If you had a *previous* experience playing on a team, you need to be introduced to the rules of the game.

3. _____ Photographs can help you *recall* who was at a party.

4. _____ Someone with a *background* in baking could explain how to make cookies.

5. _____ If you have an appointment *prior* to the first class in the morning, you can go after lunch.

6. _____ When learning new words as you read, pay no attention to the *context* of the paragraph.

7. _____ If you are giving a surprise party for a friend, it is best to *reveal* your plan to him.

8. _____ To *verify* the name of a book, look on the cover.

9. _____ If something has no *significance,* it is very important.

10. _____ Providing a list of teams  and the schedule of games helps to *establish* the league season.

**B. Completion** Complete each sentence that has been started for you. Your sentence completion should be logical and illustrate the meaning of the vocabulary word in italics.

1. It is important to know the *background* of an author to _____
   _____.

2. You can use an explanation to *clarify* _____
   _____.

3. The *context* of a word is _____
   _____.

4. If you want to *establish* a good reputation in school, you should _____
   _____.

5. Three of my *previous* teachers were _____
   _____.

6. One advantage of having *prior* knowledge of a story is _____
   _____.

7. I like to *recall* my favorite poem, which is _____
   _____.

8. If you *reveal* the secret location of the meeting, _____
   _____.

9. Please, explain the *significance* of _____
   _____.

10. To *verify* your identity, it is important to carry _____
    _____.

**anticipate** (an TIS uh payt) *v.* consider something before it happens

**conclude** (kuhn KLOOD) *v.* form an opinion or make a judgment based on

**evidence presented**

**credible** (KRED uh buhl) *adj.* easy to believe

**indicate** (IN di kayt) *v.* point something out or point to something

**object** (AHB jikt) *n.* a thing that can be seen or touched

**perspective** (puhr SPEK tiv) *n.* an assessment of a situation, especially from one person's point of view

**plot** (PLAHT) *n.* the sequence of events in a story

**predict** (pree DIKT) *v.* say what is going to happen in the future

**subject** (SUB jikt) *n.* the main idea or topic

**verify** (VER uh fy) *v.* check whether or not something is true

**A. True/False** For each of the following, mark T or F to indicate whether the italicized vocabulary word has been used correctly in the sentence. If you have marked F, correct the sentence by using the word properly.

1. _____ Matthew says that he is able to *anticipate* what happened yesterday.

2. _____ The *plot* of the story is confusing because events do not occur in time order.

3. _____ As the leaves changed colors, Sam began to *conclude* the first snowfall.

4. _____ The *subject* of a paragraph is often explained in the first sentence.

5. _____ I think that Molly told a *credible* story about the rollercoaster she rode.

6. _____ The story is told from the *perspective* of an old hunting dog.

7. _____ The *object* of all the attention was a tiny green worm.

8. _____ Please, *indicate* the dishes after you are through eating.

9. _____ Using DNA evidence, the scientist was able to *verify* the identity of the body.

10. _____ Use the left blinker to *predict* that you are going to turn left.

**B.** Use each academic vocabulary word in an original sentence that illustrates its meaning.

anticipate _____

_____

conclude _____

_____

credible _____

_____

indicate _____

_____

object _____

_____

perspective _____

_____

plot _____

_____

predict _____

_____

subject _____

_____

verify _____

_____

**almanac** (AWL muh nak) *n.* a yearly publication with details of events

**check** (CHEK) *v.* confirm that something is true or accurate

**evaluate** (ee VAL yoo ayt) *v.* examine something to make a judgment

**identify** (y DEN tuh fy) *v.* recognize something and be able to say what it is

**insignificant** (in sig NIF uh kuhnt) *adj.* having little or no meaning

**investigate** (in VES tuh gayt) *v.* examine in order to gain information

**irrelevant** (i REL uh vuhnt) *adj.* not having a connection with

**relevant** (REL uh vuhnt) *adj.* having a logical connection with

**significant** (sig NIF uh kuhnt) *adj.* having an important meaning

**valid** (VAL id) *adj.* justifiable, or logically correct

**A. Completion** Complete each sentence that has been started for you. Your sentence completion should be logical and illustrate the meaning of the vocabulary word in italics.

1. The *almanac* contained _____.

2. Go back to the house and *check* that _____.

3. The test is meant to *evaluate* _____.

4. Read the paragraph and i*dentify* _____.

5. The boy felt *insignificant* when _____.

6. The inspector will *investigate* the building to _____.

7. The most *irrelevant* information I have learned in school is _____
   _____.

8. The most *relevant* information I have learned in school is _____
   _____.

9. The most *significant* event of the day was _____.

10. A *valid* reason to go to school is _____.

**B.** Use each academic vocabulary word in an original sentence that illustrates its meaning.

almanac _____

_____

check _____

_____

evaluate _____

_____

identify _____

_____

insignificant _____

_____

investigate _____

_____

irrelevant _____

_____

relevant _____

_____

significant _____

_____

valid _____

_____

**conclude** (kuhn KLOOD) *v.* form an opinion based on evidence

**detect** (dee TEKT) *v.* notice or discover something

**emphasize** (EM fuh syz) *v.* stress the importance of something

**infer** (in FER) *v.* make a logical assumption based on evidence or reasoning

**highlight** (HY lyt) *v.* draw attention to something

**paraphrase** (PAR uh frayz) *v.* restate something in your own words

**passage** (PAS ij) *n.* a section of writing

**refer** (ri FER) *v.* 1. consult a source to find information; 2. mention a source of information

**restate** (ree STAYT) *v.* say something again; summarize

**transform** (trans FOHRM) *v.* change the shape or structure of

**A. True/False** For each of the following, mark T or F to indicate whether the italicized vocabulary word has been used correctly in the sentence. If you have marked F, correct the sentence by changing the words that make the statement wrong.

1. _____ If you *detect* an unusual smoky smell, you should report it.

2. _____ A list that *highlights* someone's strengths would indicate all the mistakes she has made.

3. _____ To *emphasize* your point, it is best to mumble.

4. _____ Before you *conclude* that the plan will work, you must review the ideas.

5. _____ To *paraphrase* the words of a song for an audience, read the lyrics out loud.

6. _____ Reading a *passage* of a story will take you longer than reading the whole story.

7. _____ If you want to learn more about a subject, you could *refer* to a textbook.

8. _____ If your friend came in to the classroom soaking wet, you might correctly *infer* there was a dust storm.

9. _____ Building an extra room onto a house would *transform* the way it looks.

10. _____ To prove you understand something, it is good to *restate* the main idea.

**B. Completion** Complete each sentence that has been started for you. Your sentence completion should be logical and illustrate the meaning of the vocabulary word in italics.

1. If you see that the door is open and the lights are on you can *conclude*

_____.

2. A bloodhound uses its nose to *detect* _____

_____.

3. When giving an oral report, it is important to *emphasize* _____

_____.

4. If you see dark clouds in the sky, you can *infer* _____

_____.

5. You would *highlight* sentences in a book that _____

_____.

6 When you *paraphrase* a poem, you _____

_____.

7. When I come across a long *passage* in a story, I _____

_____.

8. To find information on snakes, I would *refer* to _____

_____.

9. If you were to *restate* what you heard at a meeting, you would _____

_____.

10. A magician is able to *transform* _____

_____.

**assumption** (uh SUMP shuhn) *n.* the act of assuming or taking for granted

**characteristic** (kar uhk tuhr IS tik) *n.* a quality that makes something **recognizable**

**chronological** (krahn uh LAHJ i kuhl) *adj.* arranged in the order in which events occur

**conflict** (KAHN flikt) *n.* opposition between or among different forces, clash

**critique** (kri TEEK) *n.* an assessment, usually of a creative work

**focus** (FOH kuhs) *v.* look closely at

**involvement** (in VAHLV muhnt) *n.* participation

**reaction** (ree AK shuhn) *n.* an opposing action, a response

**sequence** (SEE kwuhns) *n.* one thing after another in logical or chronological order

**summarize** (SUM uh ryz) *v.* briefly state the most important events in a story

**A. True/False** For each of the following, mark T or F to indicate whether the italicized vocabulary word has been used correctly in the sentence. If you have marked F, correct the sentence by changing the words that make the sentence wrong.

1. _____ Most *assumptions* turn out to be accurate.

2. _____ One *characteristic* of winter in the Northeast is cold weather.

3. _____ *Chronological* order goes from most to least important.

4. _____ In many stories, there is a *conflict* between the characters and nature.

5. _____ When you write a *critique* of a poem, you only write facts.

6. _____ It is a good idea to watch television while you are studying to help you *focus*.

7. _____ Generally, *involvement* in a class is counted as part of your grade.

8. _____ An appropriate *reaction* to a scary movie is laughing.

9. _____ The numbers were in *sequence* from smallest to largest.

10. _____ When you *summarize* a story, you tell everything you can remember.

**B. Completion** Complete each sentence that has been started for you. Your sentence completion should be logical and illustrate the meaning of the vocabulary word in italics.

1. Student *involvement* in a classroom is good because _____.
   _____.

2. If you change the *sequence* of steps in a process, the end result might be
   _____.

3. We can't wait to see the movie again because our *reaction* the first time was
   _____.

4. After my friend *summarized* the story, I _____
   _____.

5. In a movie I liked, there was a *conflict* between _____
   _____.

6. An important *characteristic* of a rain storm is _____
   _____.

7. Writers can use *critiques* of their work to _____
   _____.

8. When you tell the *chronological* story of someone's life, the first event is
   _____.

9. One thing that can help you *focus* as you read is _____
   _____.

10. One *assumption* people often make about children is _____
    _____.

**affect** (uh FEKT) *v.* have an effect on someone or something

**alter** (AWL tuhr) *v.* adjust or make changes to

**analyze** (AN uh lyz) *v.* examine something in great detail

**aspect** (AS pekt) *n.* one feature or part of a whole

**characteristic** (kahr uhk tuhr IS tik) *n.* a quality that makes a person or thing recognizable

**consequence** (KAHN si kwens) *n.* something that follows as a result of something else

**detail** (DEE tayl) *n.* an individual part of something, such as one item of information in a story

**effect** (e FEKT) *n.* something that occurs as a direct result of an action

**occur** (uh KER) *v.* happen or come about

**unique** (yoo NEEK) *adj.* being the only one of its kind

**A. Code Name** Use the code to figure out each vocabulary word. Each letter is represented by a number or symbol. This exercise will help you learn how to spell and recognize the vocabulary words.

| % | 5 | • | * | 2 | # | ! | 7 | ^ | & | 9 | ¶ | £ | $ | 3 | ¥ | + | = | ? | ÷ | 4 | ¢ | 6 | § | « | ç |
|---|---|---|---|---|---|---|---|---|---|---|---|---|---|---|---|---|---|---|---|---|---|---|---|---|---|
| a | b | c | d | e | f | g | h | i | j | k | l | m | n | o | p | q | r | s | t | u | v | w | x | y | z |

1. 4 $ ^ + 4 2      _____

2. 2 # # 2 • ÷      _____

3. • 3 $ ? 2 + 4 2 $ • 2      _____

4. % ¶ ÷ 2 =      _____

5. * 2 ÷ % ^ ¶      _____

6. % $ % ¶ « ç 2      _____

7. % # # 2 • ÷      _____

8. 3 • • 4 =      _____

9. • 7 % = % • ÷ 2 = ^ ? ÷ ^ •      _____

10. % ? ¥ 2 • ÷      _____

**B. True/False** For each of the following, mark T or F to indicate whether the italicized vocabulary word has been used correctly in the sentence. If you have marked F, correct the sentence by using the word properly.

1. _____ We saw the same *unique* hat on every boy in the park.

2. _____ Please, tell me every *detail* of your date with George.

3. _____ The *effect* of the car crash was carelessness.

4. _____ If they do not get here in time, feel free to *occur* without them.

5. _____ The *consequence* of not studying, was a poor grade.

6. _____ Joe will *analyze* the plot of the story in a written report.

7. _____ To *alter* the plot, the writer did not change anything.

8. _____ Bravery is a *characteristic* of many heroes.

9. _____ The *affect* of eating too much ice cream is a stomach ache.

10. _____ A common *aspect* of fairy tales is magic.

_____

_____

_____

_____

_____

_____

_____

_____

_____

Use this page to write down academic words you come across in other subjects, such as social studies or science. When you are reading your textbooks, you may find words that you need to learn. Following the example, write down the word, the part of speech, and an explanation of the word. You may want to write an example sentence to help you remember the word.

**dissolve** *verb* to make something solid become part of a liquid by putting it in a liquid and mixing it

The sugar *dissolved* in the hot tea.

_____

_____

_____

_____

_____

_____

_____

_____

_____

_____

_____

_____

_____

_____

_____

_____

Use these flash cards to study words you want to remember. The words on this page come from Unit 1. Cut along the dotted lines on pages V25 through V32 to create your own flash cards or use index cards. Write the word on the front of the card. On the back, write the word's part of speech and definition. Then, write a sentence that shows the meaning of the word.

| | | |
|---|---|---|
| ignored | resumed | strategy |
| compelled | improvising | reassuring |
| formidable | epidemic | intersection |

*verb*

paid no attention to

I ignored his rude comment and went on talking.

---

*verb*

forced

Honesty compelled him to tell the truth.

---

*adjective*

impressive

The titles on the long summer reading list were formidable.

---

*verb*

began again, continued

The hikers resumed hiking after stopping for lunch.

---

*verb*

making up or inventing on the spur of the moment

The cooking contest called for improvising with on-hand ingredients.

---

*noun*

outbreak of a contagious disease

The flu epidemic caused school to close.

---

*noun*

set of plans used to gain success or achieve an aim

The general presented his strategy for the attack.

---

*adjective*

having the effect of restoring confidence

The sound of applause was reassuring to the nervous performer.

---

*noun*

the place where two or more roads cross

Their house was at the intersection of Maple Street and Route 45.

Use these flash cards to study words you want to remember. Cut along the dotted lines on pages V25 through V32 to create your own flash cards or use index cards. Write the word on the front of the card. On the back, write the word's part of speech and definition. Then, write a sentence that shows the meaning of the word.

Use a fold-a-list to study the definitions of words. The words on this page come from Unit 1. Write the definition for each word on the lines. Fold the paper along the dotted line to check your definition. Create your own fold-a-lists on pages V35 through V38.

slackening     _____

_____

vital     _____

_____

tumultuously     _____

_____

resilient     _____

_____

vowed     _____

_____

diplomats     _____

_____

summoned     _____

_____

intersection     _____

_____

ignored     _____

_____

resumed     _____

_____

Fold In ←

Write the word that matches the definition on each line.
Fold the paper along the dotted line to check your work.

easing; becoming
less active _____

extremely important or
necessary _____

noisily and violently _____

spring back into shape _____

promised solemnly _____

government representa-
tives who work with
other nations _____

called together _____

place where two or more
roads cross _____

paid no attention to _____

Fold In ←

began again, continued _____

Write the words you want to study on this side of the page. Write the definitions on the back. Then, test yourself. Fold the paper along the dotted line to check your definition.

Word: _____

_____

Word: _____

_____

Word: _____

_____

Word: _____

_____

Word: _____

_____

Word: _____

_____

Word: _____

_____

Word: _____

_____

Word: _____

_____

Word: _____

_____

Fold In ←

Write the word that matches the definition on each line.
Fold the paper along the dotted line to check your work.

Definition: _____

Definition: _____

Definition: _____

Definition: _____

Definition: _____

Definition: _____

Definition: _____

Definition: _____

Definition: _____

Definition: _____

Fold In ←

The list on these pages presents words that cause problems for many people. Some of these words are spelled according to set rules, but others follow no specific rules. As you review this list, check to see how many of the words give you trouble in your own writing. Then, add your own commonly misspelled words on the lines that follow.

| | | | |
|---|---|---|---|
| abbreviate | auxiliary | census | deficient |
| absence | awkward | certain | definitely |
| absolutely | bandage | changeable | delinquent |
| abundance | banquet | characteristic | dependent |
| accelerate | bargain | chauffeur | descendant |
| accidentally | barrel | chief | description |
| accumulate | battery | clothes | desert |
| accurate | beautiful | coincidence | desirable |
| ache | beggar | colonel | dessert |
| achievement | beginning | column | deteriorate |
| acquaintance | behavior | commercial | dining |
| adequate | believe | commission | disappointed |
| admittance | benefit | commitment | disastrous |
| advertisement | bicycle | committee | discipline |
| aerial | biscuit | competitor | dissatisfied |
| affect | bookkeeper | concede | distinguish |
| aggravate | bought | condemn | effect |
| aggressive | boulevard | congratulate | eighth |
| agreeable | brief | connoisseur | eligible |
| aisle | brilliant | conscience | embarrass |
| all right | bruise | conscientious | enthusiastic |
| allowance | bulletin | conscious | entrepreneur |
| aluminum | buoyant | contemporary | envelope |
| amateur | bureau | continuous | environment |
| analysis | bury | controversy | equipped |
| analyze | buses | convenience | equivalent |
| ancient | business | coolly | especially |
| anecdote | cafeteria | cooperate | exaggerate |
| anniversary | calendar | cordially | exceed |
| anonymous | campaign | correspondence | excellent |
| answer | canceled | counterfeit | exercise |
| anticipate | candidate | courageous | exhibition |
| anxiety | capacity | courteous | existence |
| apologize | capital | courtesy | experience |
| appall | capitol | criticism | explanation |
| appearance | captain | criticize | extension |
| appreciate | career | curiosity | extraordinary |
| appropriate | carriage | curious | familiar |
| architecture | cashier | cylinder | fascinating |
| argument | catastrophe | deceive | February |
| associate | category | decision | fiery |
| athletic | ceiling | deductible | financial |
| attendance | cemetery | defendant | fluorescent |

| | | |
|---|---|---|
| foreign | minuscule | proceed |
| fourth | miscellaneous | prominent |
| fragile | mischievous | pronunciation |
| gauge | misspell | psychology |
| generally | mortgage | publicly |
| genius | naturally | pursue |
| genuine | necessary | questionnaire |
| government | neighbor | realize |
| grammar | neutral | really |
| grievance | nickel | recede |
| guarantee | niece | receipt |
| guard | ninety | receive |
| guidance | noticeable | recognize |
| handkerchief | nuisance | recommend |
| harass | obstacle | reference |
| height | occasion | referred |
| humorous | occasionally | rehearse |
| hygiene | occur | relevant |
| ignorant | occurred | reminiscence |
| immediately | occurrence | renowned |
| immigrant | omitted | repetition |
| independence | opinion | restaurant |
| independent | opportunity | rhythm |
| indispensable | optimistic | ridiculous |
| individual | outrageous | sandwich |
| inflammable | pamphlet | satellite |
| intelligence | parallel | schedule |
| interfere | paralyze | scissors |
| irrelevant | parentheses | secretary |
| irritable | particularly | siege |
| jewelry | patience | solely |
| judgment | permanent | sponsor |
| knowledge | permissible | subtle |
| lawyer | perseverance | subtlety |
| legible | persistent | superintendent |
| legislature | personally | supersede |
| leisure | perspiration | surveillance |
| liable | persuade | susceptible |
| library | phenomenal | tariff |
| license | phenomenon | temperamental |
| lieutenant | physician | theater |
| lightning | pleasant | threshold |
| likable | pneumonia | truly |
| liquefy | possess | unmanageable |
| literature | possession | unwieldy |
| loneliness | possibility | usage |
| magnificent | prairie | usually |
| maintenance | precede | valuable |
| marriage | preferable | various |
| mathematics | prejudice | vegetable |
| maximum | preparation | voluntary |
| meanness | previous | weight |
| mediocre | primitive | weird |
| mileage | privilege | whale |
| millionaire | probably | wield |
| minimum | procedure | yield |

When you are reading, you will find many unfamiliar words. Here are some tools that you can use to help you read unfamiliar words.

## Phonics

Phonics is the science or study of sound. When you learn to read, you learn to associate certain sounds with certain letters or letter combinations. You know most of the sounds that letters can represent in English. When letters are combined, however, it is not always so easy to know what sound is represented. In English, there are some rules and patterns that will help you determine how to pronounce a word. This chart shows you some of the vowel digraphs, which are combinations like *ea* and *oa*. Two vowels together are called vowel digraphs. Usually, vowel digraphs represent the long sound of the first vowel.

| Vowel Diagraphs | Examples of Unusual Sounds | Exceptions |
| --- | --- | --- |
| *ee* and *ea* | steep, each, treat, sea | head, sweat, dread |
| *ai* and *ay* | plain, paid, may, betray | plaid |
| *oa, ow,* and *oe* | soak, slow, doe | now, shoe |
| *ie* and *igh* | lie, night, delight | friend, eight |

As you read, sometimes the only way to know how to pronounce a word with an ea spelling is to see if the word makes sense in the sentence. Look at this example:

The water pipes were made of *lead*.

First, try out the long sound "ee." Ask yourself if it sounds right. It does not. Then, try the short sound "e." You will find that the short sound is correct in that sentence.

Now try this example.

Where you *lead*, I will follow.

## Word Patterns

Recognizing different vowel-consonant patterns will help you read longer words. In the following sections, the **V** stands for "vowel" and the **C** stands for "consonant."

## Single-syllable Words

**CV – go:** In two letter words with a consonant followed by a vowel, the vowel is usually long. For example, the word *go* is pronounced with a long *o* sound.

In a single syllable word, a vowel followed only by a single consonant is usually short.

**CVC – got:** If you add a consonant to the word *go*, such as the *t* in *got*, the vowel sound is a short *o*. Say the words *go* and *got* aloud and notice the difference in pronunciation.

## Multi-syllable words

In words of more than one syllable, notice the letters that follow a vowel.

**VCCV – robber:** A single vowel followed by two consonants is usually short.

**VCV — begin:** A single vowel followed by a single consonant is usually long.

**VCe — beside:** An extension of the VCV pattern is vowel-consonant-silent *e*. In these words, the vowel is long and the *e* is not pronounced.

When you see a word with the VCV pattern, try the long vowel sound first. If the word does not make sense, try the short sound. Pronounce the words *model, camel,* and *closet*. First, try the long vowel sound. That does not sound correct, so try the short vowel sound. The short vowel sound is correct in those words.

Remember that patterns help you get started on figuring out a word. You will sometimes need to try a different sound or find the word in a dictionary.

As you read and find unfamiliar words, look the pronunciations up in a dictionary. Write the words in this chart in the correct column to help you notice patterns and remember pronunciations.

| Syllables | Example | New words | Vowel |
|-----------|---------|-----------|-------|
| CV | go | | long |
| CVC | got | | short |
| VCC | robber | | short |
| V/CV | begin<br>open | | long<br>long |
| VC/V | closet | | short |

**Mnemonics** are devices, or methods, that help you remember things. The basic strategy is to link something you do not know with something that you *do* know. Here are some common mnemonic devices:

**Visualizing** Create a picture in your head that will help you remember the meaning of a vocabulary word. For example, the first four letters of the word *significance* spell *sign*. Picture a sign with the word *meaning* written on it to remember that significance means "meaning" or "importance."

**Spelling** The way a word is spelled can help you remember its meaning. For example, you might remember that *clarify* means to "make clear" if you notice that both *clarify* and *clear* start with the letters *cl*.

To help you remember how to spell certain words, look for a familiar word within the difficult word. For example:

*Believe* has a *lie* in it.

*Separate* is *a rat* of a word to spell.

Your *principal* is your *pal*.

**Rhyming** Here is a popular rhyme that helps people figure out how to spell *ei* and *ie* words.

***i*** before ***e*** — except after ***c*** *or when sounding like* ***a*** *as in neighbor and weigh.*

List words here that you need help remembering. Work with a group to create mnemonic devices to help you remember each word.

_____     _____

_____     _____

_____     _____

_____     _____

List words here that you need help remembering. Work with a group to create mnemonic devices to help you remember each word.

_____     _____

_____     _____

_____     _____

_____     _____

_____     _____

_____     _____

_____     _____

_____     _____

_____     _____

_____     _____

_____     _____

_____     _____

_____     _____

_____     _____

Use these sentence starters to help you express yourself clearly in different classroom situations.

## Expressing an Opinion

I think that _____

I believe that _____

In my opinion, _____

## Agreeing

I agree with _____ that _____

I see what you mean.

That's an interesting idea.

My idea is similar to _____'s idea.

My idea builds upon _____'s idea.

## Disagreeing

I don't completely agree with you because _____

My opinion is different than yours.

I got a different answer than you.

I see it a different way.

## Reporting a Group's Ideas

We agreed that _____

We decided that _____

We had a different approach.

We had a similar idea.

## Predicting

I predict that _____

I imagine that _____

Based on _____ I predict that _____

## Paraphrasing

So you are saying that _____

In other words, you think _____

What I hear you saying is _____

## Offering a Suggestion

Maybe we could _____

What if we _____

Here's something we might try.

## Asking for Clarification

I have a question about that.

Could you explain that another way?

Can you give me another example of that?

## Asking for a Response

What do you think?

Do you agree?

What answer did you get?

Cut out each bookmark to use as -a handy word list when you are reading. On the lines, jot down words you want to learn and remember. You can also use the bookmark as a placeholder in your book.

| TITLE | | TITLE | | TITLE | |
|---|---|---|---|---|---|
| **Word** | **Page #** | **Word** | **Page #** | **Word** | **Page #** |
| _____ | | _____ | | _____ | |
| _____ | | _____ | | _____ | |
| _____ | | _____ | | _____ | |
| _____ | | _____ | | _____ | |
| _____ | | _____ | | _____ | |
| _____ | | _____ | | _____ | |
| _____ | | _____ | | _____ | |
| _____ | | _____ | | _____ | |
| _____ | | _____ | | _____ | |
| _____ | | _____ | | _____ | |
| _____ | | _____ | | _____ | |
| _____ | | _____ | | _____ | |
| _____ | | _____ | | _____ | |
| _____ | | _____ | | _____ | |

Cut out each bookmark to use as -a handy word list when you are reading. On the lines, jot down words you want to learn and remember. You can also use the bookmark as a placeholder in your book.

| TITLE | | TITLE | | TITLE | |
|---|---|---|---|---|---|
| **Word** | **Page #** | **Word** | **Page #** | **Word** | **Page #** |
| _____ | | _____ | | _____ | |
| _____ | | _____ | | _____ | |
| _____ | | _____ | | _____ | |
| _____ | | _____ | | _____ | |
| _____ | | _____ | | _____ | |
| _____ | | _____ | | _____ | |
| _____ | | _____ | | _____ | |
| _____ | | _____ | | _____ | |
| _____ | | _____ | | _____ | |
| _____ | | _____ | | _____ | |
| _____ | | _____ | | _____ | |
| _____ | | _____ | | _____ | |
| _____ | | _____ | | _____ | |

Use these cards to record words you want to remember. Write the word, the title of the story or article in which it appears, its part of speech, and its definition. Then, use the word in an original sentence that shows its meaning

Word: _____ Page _____

Selection: _____

Part of Speech: _____

Definition: _____

_____

My Sentence _____

_____

Word: _____ Page _____

Selection: _____

Part of Speech: _____

Definition: _____

_____

My Sentence _____

_____

Word: _____ Page _____

Selection: _____

Part of Speech: _____

Definition: _____

_____

My Sentence _____

_____

Use these cards to record words you want to remember. Write the word, the title of the story or article in which it appears, its part of speech, and its definition. Then, use the word in an original sentence that shows its meaning

Word: _____ Page _____

Selection: _____

Part of Speech: _____

Definition: _____

_____

My Sentence _____

_____

---

Word: _____ Page _____

Selection: _____

Part of Speech: _____

Definition: _____

_____

My Sentence _____

_____

---

Word: _____ Page _____

Selection: _____

Part of Speech: _____

Definition: _____

_____

My Sentence _____

_____

## Using the Personal Thesaurus

The Personal Thesaurus provides students with the opportunity to make connections between words academic words, familiar words, and even slang words. Students can use the Personal Thesaurus to help them understand the importance of using words in the proper context and also avoid overusing words in their writing.

Use the following routine to foster frequent use of the Personal Thesaurus.

1. After students have read a selection or done some writing, have them turn to the Personal Thesaurus.

2. Encourage students to add new entries. Help them to understand the connection between their personal language, which might include familiar words and even slang, and the academic language of their reading and writing.

3. Call on volunteers to read a few entries aloud. Point out that writers have many choices of words when they write. Help students see that audience often determines word choice.

N

nice

admirable

friendly

agreeable

pleasant

cool

phat

A

B

C

D

E

F

G

H

I

J

K

L

M

N

O

P

Q

R

S

T

U

V

W

X

Y

Z

*(Acknowledgments continued from page ii)*

**Code Entertainment**
"The Monsters are Due on Maple Street" by Rod Serling from *The Monsters Are Due On Maple Street*. Copyright © 1960 by Rod Serlin; Copyright © 1988 by Carolyn Serling, Jodi Serling, and Anne Serling. Used by permission. CAUTION: Professionals and amateurs are hereby warned that "The Monsters are Due on Maple Street," being fully protected under the copyright laws of the United States of America, the British Commonwealth countries, including Canada, and the other countries of the Copyright Union, is subject to royalty. All rights, including professional, amateur, motion picture, recitation, lecturing, public reading, radio, television and cable broadcasting, and the rights of translation into foreign languages, are strictly reserved. All inquiries should be addressed to Code Entertainment.

**Demand Media, Inc.**
"How to Download Ringtones for a Cell Phone" from *www.ehow.com*. Copyright © 1999–2007 eHow, Inc. Article used with the permission of eHow, Inc., www.ehow.com.

**Dial Books for Young Readers, a division of Penguin Young Readers Group**
"The Three Century Woman" copyright © 1999 by Richard Peck, from *Past Present, Perfect Tense* by Richard Peck. Used by permission of Dial Books for Young Readers, a division of Penguin Young Readers Group, a member of Penguin Group (USA) Inc., 345 Hudson Street, New York, NY 10014. All rights reserved.

**June Hall Literary Agency c/o PFD**
"One" from *When I Dance* by James Berry (Copyright © James Berry 1990) is reproduced by permission of PFD (www.pfd.co.uk) on behalf of James Berry.

**Harcourt Education Limited**
"Tenochtitlan: Inside the Aztec Capital" from *The Aztecs: Worlds Of The Past* by Jacqueline Dineen. Used by permission of Harcourt Education.

**HarperCollins Publishers, Inc.**
"Sarah Cynthia Sylvia Stout Would Not Take the Garbage Out" from *Where the Sidewalk Ends* by Shel Silverstein. Copyright © 2004 by Evil Eye Music, Inc. Used with permission from the Estate of Shel Silverstein and HarperCollins Children's Books. From *An American Childhood*. Copyright © 1987 by Annie Dillard. Used by permission of HarperCollins Publishers.

**Harvard University Press**
"I'm Nobody (#288)" by Emily Dickinson. Used by permission of the publishers and the Trustees of Amherst College from *The Poems Of Emily Dickinson*, Thomas H. Johnson, ed., Cambridge, Mass.: The Belknap Press of Harvard University Press, Copyright © 1951, 1955, 1979, 1983 by the President and Fellows of Harvard College.

**Edward D. Hoch**
"Zoo" by Edward D. Hoch, copyright © 1958 by King Size Publications, Inc.; © renewed 1991 by Edward D. Hoch. Used by permission of the author.

**Henry Holt and Company, Inc.**
Excerpt from "My Dear Cousin Tovah" from *Letters From Rifka* by Karen Hesse. Copyright © 1992 by Karen Hesse. Used by permission of Henry Holt and Company, LLC. All rights reserved.

**Information Please®**
"Fall of the Hindenburg" *www.infoplease.com*. Information Please® Database, Copyright © Pearson Education, Inc. All rights reserved. Used by permission.

**Alfred A. Knopf Children's Books**
"The People Could Fly" from *The People Could Fly: American Black Folktales* by Virginia Hamilton, copyright © 1985 by Virginia Hamilton, illustrations copyright © 1985 by Leo and Diane Dillon. Used by permission of Alfred A. Knopf, an imprint of Random House Children's Books, a division of Random House, Inc.

**Barbara S. Kouts Literary Agency**
"The Bear Boy" by Joseph Bruchac from *Flying with the Eagle, Racing the Great Bear*. Copyright © 1993 by Joseph Bruchac. Used with permission.

**Little, Brown and Company, Inc.**
"The Real Story of a Cowboy's Life" (The Grandest Enterprise Under God 1865–1874) from *The West: An Illustrated History* by Geoffrey Ward. Little Brown and Company. Copyright © 1996 by The West Book Project, Inc. Used by permission.

**Naomi Long Madgett**
"Life" by Naomi Long Madgett from *One and the Many*, copyright © 1956; *Remembrances of Spring: Collected Early Poems*, copyright © 1993. Used by permission of the author.

**Edna St. Vincent Millay Society**
"The Courage That My Mother Had" by Edna St. Vincent Millay, from *Collected Poems*, HarperCollins. Copyright © 1954, 1982 by Norma Millay Ellis. All rights reserved. Used by permission of Elizabeth Barnett, literary executor.

# PHOTO AND ART CREDITS